To Rohan

Roop!

MORE HUMAN

DESIGNING A WORLD WHERE PEOPLE COME FIRST

STEVE HILTON

WITH SCOTT BADE AND JASON BADE

1 3 5 7 9 10 8 6 4 2

WH Allen, an imprint of Ebury Publishing,
20 Vauxhall Bridge Road,
London SW1V 2SA

WH Allen is part of the Penguin Random House
group of companies whose addresses can be found at
global.penguinrandomhouse.com

Penguin
Random House
UK

First published by WH Allen in 2015
This edition first published by WH Allen in 2016

www.eburypublishing.co.uk

A CIP catalogue record for this book is
available from the British Library

ISBN 9780753556634

Typeset in India by Thomson Digital Pvt Ltd, Noida, Delhi
Printed and bound in Great Britain by Clays Ltd, St Ives PLC

Penguin Random House is committed to a sustainable future
for our business, our readers and our planet. This book is made
from Forest Stewardship Council® certified paper.

MIX
Paper from
responsible sources
FSC® C018179

STEVE HILTON is cofounder and CEO of Crowdpac, a Silicon Valley political tech start-up, and a visiting professor at Stanford University. He was formerly senior adviser to Prime Minister David Cameron and played a leading role in the modernisation of the Conservative Party and in the implementation of its government reform programme. Steve is a graduate of New College, Oxford University, where he studied philosophy, politics and economics. He now lives in California with his wife and young family.

SCOTT BADE works on the communications team of Michael Bloomberg and Bloomberg Philanthropies. He previously researched international security at Stanford University's Freeman Spogli Institute of International Studies. Scott graduated from Stanford University and lives in New York.

JASON BADE lectures on social problem-solving at Stanford Law School and is active in the impact investing space. He often advises start-ups and social entrepreneurs on strategy and human-centred design. Jason graduated from Stanford University and lives in California.

CONTENTS

FOREWORD TO THE UK PAPERBACK EDITION

Since I wrote *More Human*, some big changes have taken place in politics. Against most people's expectations, the Conservative Party won the 2015 election with an overall majority. Even less predictably, Jeremy Corbyn was elected leader of the Labour Party. In America, as I write, Bernie Sanders and Donald Trump are giving 'establishment' candidates a run for their money in the presidential election. David Cameron has completed his negotiation with the EU, and now ... the country will vote to leave or stay.

This book, too, has undergone some changes. I produced a version for the US – and I prefer it to the original. So when the time came to publish a paperback version for the UK, I wanted to use the American edition as the basis – adapted, of course, for a British audience, and to take account of recent political developments on both sides of the Atlantic. I have also reflected on and taken account of some of the reaction to *More Human*.

The book was not (and is not) meant to be an instrum of partisan cheerleading, so I have been heartened t many commentators note that key themes in *More* could apply equally to, or be adopted by, both left and right. Some suggested I should have run for Labour leader. I took it as a compliment!

Clearly the Labour leadership campaign went in a very different direction. I disagree with Jeremy Corbyn on many issues, but while his answers may be wrong (and some are very wrong indeed – downright dangerous, even), many of the questions he's asking are absolutely right, relevant and timely. Over the past year or so, I have found myself repeatedly enraged by the way that the 'insular ruling elite' I wrote about in this book's first edition arrogantly, patronisingly, contemptuously dismiss him. The truth is that Corbyn, like all of the populists of the moment – the SNP, UKIP, or even Donald Trump and Bernie Sanders in America – embodies a reaction to the policy failures of the political establishment. The discontent they channel is real and cannot be ignored by the ruling elite. I salute those who throw bricks at the establishment for pointing out its many flaws, even if they aren't necessarily the ones we should call for the repairs. While the changes espoused by the would-be revolutionaries are often untenable or unwise, we do need to address the problems that make people pine for such extremes.

Democracy is still the best political system, but as long as it is controlled by vested interests, it will lack legitimacy; that means fixing politics so it is more representative, more inclusive, and more responsive to citizens. I have included a new chapter on Politics in this edition of the book.

Capitalism is still the best economic system, but as long ·s so much of it is rigged, it will be irretrievably stained; ιt means fixing it by making the rules governing markets ·r for workers, consumers, entrepreneurs and society – ιdermining it by destroying the competition that is its lifeblood. Again, this topic is now covered in a chapter of its own, separate from the first edition's chapter on 'Business'.

Of course governing requires more than rhetoric. It requires grit, compromise and maturity. It requires adapting the best-made plans to events, and doing all you can to move enormously complicated systems in the right direction. Believe me, I tried – and discovered (and was insanely frustrated by) how hard change can be. Real change will only happen with leaders whose strategies encompass policy implementation as well as policy creation; who learn about problems with their heart, but solve them with their head; who deeply understand the lives of those they're working to serve. It's hard work.

But too often this reality is used by the elite and the insiders to dismiss the possibility of big, radical change. Revolutionary change is not 'serious', they say. Calm down and leave it to us 'grown-ups'. Well, the people are getting restless. The 'grown-ups' don't seem to be making much progress. Maybe they're not so 'serious' after all.

Since the publication of the first edition of *More Human*, I have become even more convinced that the central problem facing our societies is a concentration of political and economic power in the hands of a tiny number. This revised edition shows how that power can be placed back where it belongs – in the hands of the people.

California, February 2016

INTRODUCTION

On 9 June 2014, Jennifer Devereaux boarded a JetBlue flight from New York to Boston. She was travelling with her two young daughters. Everything seemed normal: the passengers found their seats, the announcements were made, the plane left the gate and moved towards the runway for take-off. But then it all started to go wrong. The captain announced that there had been a delay and the aircraft would have to wait on the tarmac for around forty-five minutes. Jennifer's three-year-old daughter announced that she needed to use the bathroom. Because they were just waiting around on the tarmac, Jennifer thought it would be fine to get up and take her daughter to the toilet – they were sitting just a few rows away.

Big mistake. As soon as she started getting up, a JetBlue cabin crew member zoomed up and yelled, with that special kind of rudeness we all know and love: 'Ma'am, you're going to have to sit down.'

'But I'm just taking my little girl to the restroom.'

'You need to sit down right now. The captain has the seatbelt sign switched on.'

'Please, can you let us go? She's a three-year-old and she can't wait.'

'Ma'am, I'm ordering you to sit down and fasten your seatbelts. You need to comply with my instruction.'

That was just the start.

After another half-hour or so, the poor little girl couldn't hold it any longer and wet herself in her seat. Jennifer, upset and wanting to do anything to reduce her daughter's discomfort, called a crew member and asked whether she could have something to mop up the mess – a cloth, some napkins, anything. The flight attendant walked off – and didn't come back. After a few minutes of waiting, Jennifer couldn't bear it any longer. She remembered she had a sweater in the overhead bin and thought she could use that to dry her daughter's seat a little. So she stood up to open the bin and – you guessed it – a crew member raced down the aisle and screamed at her to sit down. Jennifer explained that because no one from JetBlue had brought her anything, she was just trying to get her sweater so she could mop things up and surely, as they weren't even moving, it would be okay to—

'It doesn't matter what it is – the seatbelt sign is on, and you have to sit down right now!'

In disbelief – remember the plane was just sitting on the tarmac – Jennifer kept going, reaching for her sweater.

'That's enough, ma'am. Sit down now!'

Defeated, Jennifer did as she was told. You can imagine how she felt. And worse, how her poor little girl felt.

Then the captain's voice came over the intercom.

'Ladies and gentlemen, I'm afraid that we have a noncompliant passenger on board and are going to have to return to the gate to remove them from the aircraft.'

That 'noncompliant' passenger was Jennifer, trying to look after her three-year-old daughter who needed to use the bathroom.

Rude, aggressive, lacking in compassion – even though, thanks to the last-minute intervention of an off-duty pilot seated nearby, the flight crew finally relented and allowed Jennifer and her daughters to remain on board, JetBlue's behaviour towards that family was inhuman. Talking about it after the event, Jennifer said, 'Why can't we just treat each other with kindness and decency, like human beings?'[1]

It's a good question and one this book will try to answer. You could look at that story and say, 'Well, that's just the way some of these airline employees behave. You see that kind of thing all over the place with officious bureaucratic-minded people. That's just life.'

But it's not just life. Being inhuman is not the natural order of things. People don't instinctively behave that way: they're made to by the circumstances they're in and the structure of the world around them. And being inhuman is not just about bad behaviour – it's actually a big part of our deepest problems. Economic problems: our efforts to end poverty, to deal with rising inequality, to make sure everyone has the chance to get a decent, well-paid job. Social problems: how our children grow up and are educated, how we organise the places we live and the healthcare we receive. Political problems too: the way we're governed and the way we make policy. We are designing and building a world that is inhuman. Government, business, the lives we lead, the food we eat, the way our children are raised, the way we relate to the natural world around us … it's all become too big and distant and impersonal. Inhuman.

In governments the world over, political leaders who mean well (and who are, if anything, underappreciated for the good they do) preside, frustrated and impotent, over vast bureaucratic systems that routinely disappoint and leave citizens enraged that they can't control what affects their lives. The schools we send our children to, the hospitals that care for us when we're sick, the very food we eat – we've allowed these intimate things, that matter so much, to be provided by anonymous, distant, industrialised machines. Business, such an awesome vehicle for human ingenuity and interaction, has become dominated by a detached and unaccountable global elite who think that the solution to the social and environmental problems *they cause* is to fly to Davos and pontificate on 'panels' and in 'plenaries'. Technology, with its incredible power to liberate and educate, has become unhealthily fetishised as an end in itself, while those who dare to question its remorseless rise are dismissed as mad – or, worse still, old-fashioned. Nature? Who cares, let's conquer another planet.

We're told: things are getting better. Growth is up! Big Government is on your side, along with Big Business and Big Energy and Big Food and Big Tech and Big Media, all giving us Big Savings! Big Value! But the problem is, we're not Big. We are quite small, actually. We tend to be happiest when we can relate to each other in a human way. We do best when things are organised on a human scale.

But size is not all that matters. Big is not always bad, and small is not always beautiful. Just look at a company like Airbnb, the website that allows people to rent out spare rooms, flats or entire homes. It has enabled previously unimaginable new personal connections, showing that scale and technology don't have to be inhuman. There's an even more significant point about technology. The information revolution is giving us untold power: people talk warily about Big Data, but the truth is that big data is flowing into our own hands, giving us the chance to make decisions and choices as never before.

For all these reasons – the problems and the opportunities – it's time for a real shake-up. We need to make the world more human.

This aim of this book is to kick-start the debate. I don't have all the answers, but at least let's ask the right questions. In the summer of 2015 Hillary Clinton, in a revealing conversation with a Black Lives Matter activist, said, 'Look, I don't believe you change hearts. I believe you change laws, you change allocation of resources, you change the way systems operate.'² She's half right. Of course, in the end, in order to make a difference in people's lives, you do need to change laws, budgets, systems. But the starting point – especially when the changes needed are really big – *is* to change hearts, and that's my primary aim in this book. *More Human* offers an argument, not a prescription. It is not a comprehensive survey of every problem out there; I've focused on areas where I have the greatest knowledge and experience and, frankly, on the things I care about most. I know there are important things left out.

Chapter 1 looks at politics. We all know our system is broken, beset by cynicism and corruption; we can see the rage at the political machine. But is there something constructive we can do with that rage? My answer is yes. I believe we can bring about the kind of revolution people are yearning for, but without yelling at each other – instead, getting involved, working together, crafting the radical reforms we need, as a community of people rather than a collection of positions. Politics is the starting point for government, and that's the subject of Chapter 2. We need to change priorities so government focuses more on real people than abstract numbers. We need to change the way policy is made so those who make it understand the lives of those who experience it. I'll look at how innovations in the way we design products have the potential to transform how we design government programmes too. But we must also tackle the structure of government, a structure that too often impedes progress; the inefficiencies and needless centralisations of federal, state, and even local power that accentuate the worst of government while suppressing its best.

In Chapter 3 I take aim at our schools, where industrialised processes for cramming knowledge into children's heads are churning out young people equipped for the last century, not the current one – and making them miserable in the process. Similarly, in Chapter 4 I argue that the care has been ripped out of healthcare by bureaucracy and an obsession with 'efficiency' that undermines one of our most human instincts: looking after other people when they're not well. But we should also look after ourselves, an aim made more difficult by the vast culinary-industrial complex: our taxpayer-subsidised factory food system, which I'll investigate in Chapter 5.

Corporate bureaucracy is a common theme in this book, and I address it directly in Chapters 6 and 7, looking at the hotly contested arguments over capitalism and the role of business in society. In Chapters 8 and 9 I take on the topics of poverty and inequality and show how a more human way of looking at them – with a particular focus on families – could move us further forwards than the somewhat sterile debates we've seen so far.

Children are humans too: that's Chapter 10. One of the most profound failings of the modern world is that it undervalues the needs of children. This may seem strange in an age when family life is celebrated, parenting advice is everywhere, and the imperatives of 'child protection' trump all other concerns. But as I will argue, we're getting it completely wrong. We are blasé about the impact of technology on children's lives and at the same time are undermining one of the most natural, human, and, above all, developmentally important aspects of children's lives: play. Finally, Chapters 11 and 12 examine the world around us: the spaces we design for ourselves and the way we relate to nature.

Throughout we'll meet people who, in their own way, are making the world more human – extraordinary people you may not have heard of yet. Nadine Burke Harris is a San Francisco paediatrician in the vanguard of reshaping how we see the effect of adverse childhood experiences on children's life chances. Jamie Heywood is an engineer who has used his brother's tragic death to change the way we see medicine. Paul Willis has made pig farming ethical on a large scale, and Jason Pittman has a vision of the classroom of the twenty-first century. We'll engage with some of the world's brightest minds who are helping lead the way to a more human future, like E.O. Wilson, perhaps our greatest living thinker on ecology, and Sebastian Thrun, the Silicon Valley technologist who is reshaping skills training for the digital age. I'll also introduce some of the people I've been lucky enough to work with, both in California – such as Sarah Stein Greenberg, who taught me 'design thinking' at Stanford – and in the UK – like Rohan Silva, my closest friend and former colleague in government, now creating the world's most innovative creative work spaces; or Louise Casey, an amazing civil servant who is leading the programme charged with turning around the lives of Britain's most troubled families.

This book – the analysis and the ideas – is the product of my experiences in government, politics and business, most of them in the UK. For two years, I worked at Number 10 Downing Street as Senior Adviser to Prime Minister David

Cameron and had the incredible privilege of being in a position to help implement policies and reforms that could tackle many of the problems addressed in this book – and you will find some of the lessons reflected in these pages. Prior to that I was part of the team that led the modernisation of the Conservative Party's political strategy and policy programme. And before that, with my firm Good Business, I spent years working on social and environmental issues from a business perspective. In 2012 I moved to the San Francisco Bay Area with my wife, Rachel, and our two children. I was fortunate enough to take up a teaching post at Stanford University and went on to found a political technology start-up, Crowdpac.

When I served in government I was called a 'blue-skies' thinker, the government's 'ultimate radical'. Another way of putting it: I was the annoying, crazy person. So is this book, as some will suspect, basically just a list of all the 'crazy' things I wanted to do in government but they wouldn't let me? Well, yes, partly. But a much bigger part of *More Human* is based on the thinking I've done since leaving government and reflecting on what I got wrong as well as what went right. In particular, the book conveys what I've learned as part of the incredible, entrepreneurial community at Stanford, especially its renowned Institute of Design, or 'd.school'. At the d.school, students are taught to solve problems by starting with people – what they need, how they think, how they feel. Learning to teach there has been a transformational experience and has profoundly affected my point of view on almost everything. In Chapter 2 I look at how we might apply the d.school approach in government, but its principles of human-centred design are present in every chapter.

My experiences as a government veteran turned Silicon Valley CEO have profoundly changed how I view policy challenges. Unquestionably government can learn a lot from the tech sector, and harnessing some of California's entrepreneurial spirit could go a long way towards improving the sclerotic institutions that dominate our lives.

I also aim to do something else: provide the view of an outsider to politics. That may seem odd – some would say I was the ultimate insider. But I never felt that way. Although I am a close friend and supporter of Prime Minister David Cameron, there are plenty of positions I take in this book that would fit more comfortably in the Labour or Green Parties. Although I am a fan of markets and decentralisation, as you will quickly learn in this book I am also a strong believer in well-organised and well-funded state intervention to tackle social problems. I'm as anti-establishment as the best of them (or worst, depending on your point of view), yet I'm pro-immigration – not just because I'm the son of Hungarian refugees and a Brit now working in America but because I believe it's vital for both Britain and America's future success. I strongly support marriage equality and generous parental leave for mothers and fathers; in fact, I believe in marriage equality so much, I even think straight people should get married if they're going to have children. Yes, I'm afraid this book will likely goad right and left in equal measure. And that's okay. (Not least because my political tech start-up, Crowdpac, is non-partisan.)

To be honest, goading the two old parties is precisely what I want to do. We live in a political system that is almost completely broken, ossified into a structure that most people simply can't identify with. I hope this book can challenge voters and politicians alike to think about solutions that cut across ideology and the narrow dogmas of party politics. As shown by the introduction of the world's first national living wage law by my (Conservative) former colleagues, you don't have to be on the political left to be on the side of workers. But equally, you don't have to be on the political right to recognise that unleashing (reasonably regulated) markets is often the best solution to a given problem, even social goods like education and healthcare. Indeed, whole sectors can benefit from a judicious blend of government and market-based solutions that might appeal to and repel extreme bases in equal measure.

Although Britain sometimes seems broken, it is still making great strides. I hope I can help point the way in a few places. That starts with government. It's time for us all to envision the country we want for ourselves, not the country politicians (and their donors) tell us we should have. The wise men – and they are mostly men, still – of the political and governing establishment may scratch their heads in bewilderment at the rise of candidates they consider to be 'not serious' – but the public, I'm afraid, no longer trust the serious people to steward their interests. In a way, that's unfair. In my experience most politicians are good and sincere public servants. But the systems that have been built up over decades frustrate their efforts at accomplishing anything, let alone actually changing the systems. We all know the famous *Little Britain* sketch, 'Computer says no.' That's certainly how government feels to the proverbial 'little guy'. But, alarmingly, it's all too often how it feels to the people in charge too.

That's why changing the underlying systems – and not just the policies – really is so important, a priority I return to time and again in different contexts in this book. I believe it is eminently possible. Across the world we may soon see the birth of a new kind of politics that eschews left and right for engagement and transparency. We seek government that is effective and responsive, society that is orderly and fair. Those are values – intrinsically human ones, I might add – that no political movement can claim as its own.

***

There's another important point to bear in mind that makes the idea at the heart of this book more relevant and urgent than ever. In the last few decades great advances in science have given us new insights into who we are as humans: how we think, feel, and behave – and why. Neuroscience, social psychology, behavioural economics – work in these fields means we can now base our judgements about how to organise things much more soundly on what we scientifically know. These human insights don't just tell us more about humanity; they also tell us that making things more human is itself natural.

For example, evolutionary biology shows that in the course of human history we have become ever more empathetic. Scientific and economic progress has in part been accompanied by an expanded consciousness of the experiences of fellow human beings. We have in some ways become more human, even as the world we have built for ourselves pushes in the other direction. The expansion of our capacity to communicate and collaborate with each other has enhanced our capacity to understand each other's realities. As we've got to know one another better, we've extended basic protections and rights to ever-wider swathes of humanity.[3]

Although our capacity for empathy has evolved, it has always been one of our defining traits as humans. And there are other human values that define us and for which we should strive. Not everything can be quantified by data or captured on a spreadsheet. There are certain things that we simply accept make life worth living: purpose, happiness, beauty, compassion, laughter, love, joy. These are the things that dignify our lives and that every individual deserves the chance to experience. Another key part of our humanity lies in our differences. Fulfilment in life will come through different things for different people – whether it's faith, literature, work, friendship, music, children ... even baking a perfect loaf of bread. The burden of society – specifically of government – is to provide the greatest chance for us to find what life means and then live it to the fullest.

Society has another burden, though: to protect us from and help us to overcome our inherent flaws, the troubling aspects of our nature. For all the good of humanity, there are plenty of impulses that are harmful, traits like avarice, malice and intolerance. These also are human, and although we shouldn't forget that, we should do all we can to help people avoid the worst of their demons, especially when their weaknesses hurt others. There is evil and terrible cruelty in our world. We see it in the crazed, Islam-derived brutality of ISIS, but while we confront and defeat it militarily, ideologically, politically, financially, diplomatically – as we must surely resolve to do – we must remember that there will be no final victory in this, the defining war of our age, unless we triumph at the individual, human level too.

But we are both individual and social creatures. We work better, as I will argue throughout this book, in communities, families, social networks, and on small-scale levels. So how, then, if human nature is naturally inclined to be human, have so many of the institutions that shape our lives become so big, distant, and removed from the human scale?

Think of it in historical terms. (Spoiler alert: for those readers familiar with the speeches of David Cameron, especially 'the early, funny ones' as Woody Allen might have described them, this is an argument you will recognise.) Before the Industrial Revolution, politics, government and business were almost entirely local – because they had to be. Rulers simply did not have the information and reach to make decisions about individual people's lives or run centralised bureaucracies. Local governors or feudal lords were delegated almost all sovereign power, answering only nominally to the far-off capital. Bureaucracies existed, but even the most sophisticated ones in China and the Ottoman Empire relied heavily on provincial officials. Corporations were limited to the most complex of businesses – like banks, even then often in quasi-official roles. Companies like the East India Company or the Rothschild banking empire delegated wide autonomy to local officials; superiors at the centre had only the most limited strategic control. This period we could call the pre-bureaucratic age.

As with many things, war, commerce and technology changed the dynamic. With larger armies and more sophisticated warfare, the conflicts of the French Revolution and Napoleonic eras saw full-scale mobilisations that could only be managed through hierarchical and complex bureaucracies. At the same time, Napoleon applied these principles to the civilian part of his growing empire and created the first modern law code, the Code Napoléon, and an administrative state to implement it.[4] Meanwhile economic trends led to similar developments in America. The invention of the cotton gin in 1793 spurred a revolution in the American cotton industry, but it required scale to really be revolutionary, especially in the form of railroads to connect distant farms and merchants. Unlike maritime trading companies, the railroad companies upon which the American cotton industry relied needed centralised management to ensure safety and efficiency (sharing track and sharing the seas are two very different matters). Bureaucracy was the only way to accomplish the logistical feat of connecting entire continents with one system.

Just like the cotton producers, railroad companies also had to consolidate, as building rail infrastructure was, by definition, large scale and expensive. Only big firms could manage the undertaking, and as the demand for capital correspondingly increased, a new, centralised banking system sprang up to finance it all. Bureaucracy was a cycle that built itself, feeding back into its own further expansion and centralisation. The new interconnected systems that enabled military and industrial growth soon spread to other aspects of life. Centralised governments were now able to build bureaucracies to run things on behalf of citizens, and government evolved into an accretion of massive hierarchies. Over the course of the twentieth century this model grew into the form of government that we have today. Along with its counterpart in the business world, it was – and is – the bureaucratic age.[5]

Bureaucratic modernisation brought a whole range of benefits, from universal schooling to a professional civil service, from healthcare to the rule of law. In Britain it built a national infrastructure and enabled a global empire. These same centralising mechanisms that enabled growth in the public sector eventually conquered the rest of the economy. With efficient transport and technology, unprecedented quantities of raw materials flowed to factories that, powered by steam engines, could now produce and distribute manufactured goods. Firms adopted the administrative apparatus of the bureaucratic railways, and the modern corporation was born. As commercial empires emerged, a cult of management science soon dominated, whereby businesses – and, eventually, government departments – were run by those at the top applying principles of 'engineering' to the workers below. It was all about mass production, mass management, mass distribution – and as the Second World War mobilised the American and British economies on national scales, the large corporation became a fait accompli. Coupled with automation and other improvements in technology, the process continued unabated; vast conglomerates were commonplace by the 1960s. The age of the independent local business wasn't over, but it was dealt a huge blow.

The inexorable growth of big business throughout the last century and a half has brought great benefits; in many respects someone on an average income in the UK, America or Europe today has a higher standard of living than even the very richest did a century or so ago. But the mostly national corporations of the mid-twentieth century that had at least some sense of connection to and responsibility for their local communities have given way to rootless global entities – private-sector bureaucracies – many of which have lost all sense of community, of perspective. The never-ending trajectory of mergers, consolidation and growth has a cost – and not just a financial one (repeated studies have shown that corporate mergers generally destroy value for the acquiring firms' shareholders).[6] We are no longer driven by a human economy; we don't know where our products come from or how they are created, and too many of our corporate bosses have no conception of their workers' or customers' experiences. We live in an age when the effects of our decisions seem less and less important because we don't really know what they are. We 'love a bargain' but don't see the appalling conditions endured by the people who produce a product that can be sold so cheaply. We troop to the supermarket but don't see the small businesses and farmers whose livelihoods are wrecked by 'everyday low prices'. The human consequences of our choices are felt by people separated from us by time, space and class.

In government, too, we continue to live with a system that is a relic of the past. It did work once, but we're no longer in the age of either sail or steamship, so why are we still governed as if we were? Empire is no longer relevant, and many of the services that government provides – education, health, social services, welfare – are well established and no longer require centralised bureaucratic systems to run them. Simply put, the raisons d'être of centralised government no longer justify it. But its costs remain.

You can see it in the way that twentieth-century factory-style approaches – standardisation, automation, mechanisation – still infect intrinsically human areas like education, healthcare, food and housing. We used to think factories equalled progress. They were sanitary, standardised and quality controlled. They took urchins off the street while providing the middle and working classes with once-only-dreamt-of luxuries. Having tens of thousands of cows or chickens on a single farm seemed like the modern thing to do. But that vision is now out of date.

It's not just the arc of history, bureaucratic momentum or mass standardisation that has led us to this point; we need to apply a critical eye to our unrelenting quest for progress and how some of our leaders – in government, politics, business and society – define it for us. Where I live now, in Silicon Valley, the goal is to be bigger, faster, cheaper. Does that equate to better? Much of the time it does. But too often the 'progress' we are offered is not an improvement; it's just more 'efficient' and, worse, more efficient for the producer, not the user. Astronauts used to consume Tang, a powdered orange drink, because it is compact and nutritious (a requirement on space missions). But should we substitute it for actual orange juice? Or oranges? Just because something is more 'efficient' doesn't mean it's better.

The misguided quest for efficiency has led to negative side effects that are only now being understood. As technology critic Evgeny Morozov points out in his book *To Save Everything, Click Here*, efficiency can undermine much of what makes us human: 'Imperfection, ambiguity, opacity, disorder, and the opportunity to err, to sin, to do the wrong thing: all of these are constitutive of human freedom, and any concerted attempt to root them out will root out that freedom as well.'[7] I would add that a world programmed to perfection is no longer a human world: without problems to solve and imperfection to inspire us, we would become complacent. We would not only lose our ability to innovate and be creative but, worse, our world would become sterile. If we never get lost, we will never go to unexpected new places. If we never have to repair things, we will cease to tinker and make anew. Without the spontaneous discoveries – and mistakes – that so enrich us, humanity stagnates. Mother Nature itself is often 'inefficient', providing us with two kidneys, for example, where one is enough. Efficiency is not always bad, but we need the cultural confidence to say no, to reject efficiency for human priorities that matter more.

As you will see, this book calls for dramatic changes in how we do things. Some might ask whether that is really necessary. They could point to the UK's economic growth, political stability and social safety net; the falling crime; the strength of our culture; and the growing vibrancy of our cities and say, 'Things are pretty good. Sure, they can always be improved, but take it easy … we just need a touch on the tiller, not a change of course.'

Really? Have you noticed that it tends to be the wealthiest and most powerful who say things like that? Life is certainly good for them. But look around: life isn't great for most people, and in many ways it is getting worse. With years of stagnating wages, people don't feel as though they're getting ahead.[8] They're underpaid and overworked (Chapter 8). They aren't gaining the skills they need (Chapter 9). They're unhealthy because nutritious food is not only more expensive than heavily processed, toxic junk (Chapter 5) but often inaccessible. And their children – without the in-built advantages of their richer peers – are falling behind (Chapter 9).

But the inhumanity of much of modern life – in schools, in hospitals, in urban planning – is no concern for the elites because they (we) don't have to experience it. Our children go to private schools, we supplement our NHS care with private insurance, and we eat our organic food from Waitrose or the farmers' market. When life gets rough, we go on exotic holidays or to our tastefully appointed vacation homes. When things get busy, we employ nannies, housekeepers and delivery people to buy ourselves more time.

For most people, though, the current system simply isn't working. Incremental change isn't working. This is true in America, where I now live; and it's true in the UK. But there is hope: small signs that things can be different; examples of the kind of change we need. I have seen them and learned from them over the last few years I've spent in California, and some of those signs of hope are profiled in this book. That is, of course, not to say that everything on the West Coast of the USA is perfect. America has its problems, just the same as – in many cases far worse than – the UK. In both countries, when most people haven't seen a rise in living standards for over a decade and many have seen a fall, when daily life is often such a hassle, when people's quality of life is below what they see in other countries, when there is a massive underclass persistently poor in every way for decade after decade, I think this calls for a sense of urgency. It's a crisis, and it demands a big shake-up, not steady-as-she-goes. But our debates feel small, stunted, fiddling around the edges – and this fuels the dissatisfaction with politics and the political system, increasingly expressed in support for fringe parties and politics.

***

For all these reasons I think we need a revolution, not evolution, and I want to show you in this book that it's possible. That we can heal Britain's malaise by putting power back in people's hands, taking back control over the things that matter to us from the anonymous, distant bureaucrats in government and business. We can move to something better: a post-bureaucratic age, an age when things work on a comprehensible and controllable scale. An age that is more human.

Apart from any specific changes, however small, that might happen as a result of the people, stories and ideas that follow, I also hope that they collectively help you to see the world a little differently. A little more humanly. And who knows where that might lead?

The modern world is a fantastic place full of excitement and ingenuity. But as we continue to invent and innovate and move forward, we should remember what makes us human: people, relationships, spontaneity, emotions. As we create and spread wealth and opportunity, build a world of technological wonder, remake our institutions, and push the boundaries of knowledge, we should try to do so in line with these essential human truths.

CHAPTER 1

POLITICS

People love to complain about government – and yes, there's plenty to complain about. (There is also much we can do to make government work better, as we'll see in the next chapter.) However, before we even get to government, we have politics. Politics underpins government. If we want to make government more human, we need to start with politics.

You might think that spending a lifetime in democratic politics would be a positive attribute for a political candidate. Yet 'career politician' is now one of the worst insults imaginable. In just the last year, outsiders like UKIP's Nigel Farage, Labour's Jeremy Corbyn, and the SNP's Nicola Sturgeon all had their moments exactly because they were perceived to be outside the political mainstream. Politicians have never been popular, and each new generation brings a new kind of backlash, but despite the Conservative victory in 2015, it seems that in many parts of the country the mood has turned violently against the existing political system.

This is a shame. Politics might seem like a weird blood sport, fascinating only to insiders, but it's much more than that. A healthy political system means that solutions to problems are debated, citizens' voices are heard, and society maintains a stake in how it is governed. More than that, it is a necessary conduit for the vast majority of the change proposed in this book. And that is how it should be. In a democracy, our political system is the only institution that truly represents us: our wishes, our rights, our aspirations.

That's why instead of just railing against our broken political system, we should try to fix it. I agree with those who say that Britain's problems demand a revolution, not evolution. But I also believe we can harness the political system to achieve it, that we can have a revolution without yelling at each other, a revolution based on real reform. That needs politics – more human politics.

It starts with engaging more people in the political process. It's not just Britain; in most democracies trust in politics is falling – and one of the main reasons is people's belief that their participation doesn't matter. Democracy is in crisis: in Britain (and America, and Europe) it no longer seems that 'we the people' are being served by it, but rather the interests of the wealthiest. It seems today that political legitimacy stems not from votes, but money: the more of it you have, the more government pays attention to your concerns.

We have, in some ways, regressed. Corruption used to be the norm in most countries, democratic or otherwise. Power was inherited and bought, political appointments traded for favours in a system where the elites literally owned the state. But although it is no longer so explicit, the ascent of big money and its lobbyists means that while there is no explicit quid pro quo, it is hard to mistake what donors intend when they make political contributions. Or what businesses want when they take politicians to dinner, the opera, the Brits or Wimbledon. We may not have aristocratic courts and inherited offices, but our democracies are increasingly captured by a ruling class that seeks to perpetuate its privileges. Our democratic system has, in the apt word used by political scientist Francis Fukuyama, 'decayed'.[1] America, where the rich and powerful literally buy the outcomes they want from the political system, is no longer in any proper sense of the word a democracy; it is a *donocracy*. The EU is no better: spend time in Brussels and you will find in the European Parliament and Commission a vast, stinking cesspit of corporate corruption gussied up in the garb of idealistic internationalism.

The fewer people in control, the fewer people who need to be influenced and swayed. At least in America, economic, cultural and political power is dispersed. In the UK, centralisation is a gift to the vested interests. When the corporate bosses, the MPs, the journalists – and the authors of books like this – all live near each other, go to the same dinner parties as each other, even choose the same holiday destinations as each other, an insular ruling elite precipitates. They flit and float between Westminster, Whitehall, the City; between government, corporate boards and shadowy advisory firms. Regardless of who's in office, the same people are in power. It is a democracy in name only, operating on behalf of a tiny elite, no matter the electoral outcome. I recognise it because I was part of it. Although there is no conspiracy – and I know from personal experience that almost all politicians and officials have good intentions – the assumptions, structures and rules that govern daily life are not subject to anything as unpredictable as the will of the people. No wonder voters feel that others' voices are being heard more than their own. It's because it's true.[2]

Politics is supposed to be a platform for people power, not plutocrat power. And despite the desire for the former, we still seem to stuck in the latter. In the 1950s and '60s, politics was relatively simple. It was based largely on class, with workers voting Labour and the middle class and wealthy voting Conservative. Accordingly, around 90 per cent of votes went to one of these two parties. But by 2015, the combined figured had dropped to just over two-thirds.[3] Clearly voters are searching for new options. But our political system is structurally deficient: our political views are more nuanced than the simplified two-party model the ossified electoral system forces onto us. Many of the ideas and proposals I will propose in this book would be at home in parties across the political spectrum; others wouldn't be welcome anywhere. In a true democracy this is fine. Hardly anyone is a 'dyed-in-the-wool' anything, anyway. And in today's age of nearly unlimited information, we can form a much more complex worldview. Yet in public life you have nowhere to go if you take Conservative views on taxes, Green views on the environment, and Labour views on social justice. Unless you want a protest vote, outside of Scotland your vote will invariably go to one of two parties. Our politics falsely project binary simplicity, and that's a massive turn-off for many voters.

And frankly, when the Westminster elite who run the system across the major parties all sound basically the same, your vote really goes towards upholding the same system. Our views are not 'politician'; they're human. We need our politics to reflect this.

This is especially urgent because the results of the 2015 General Election indicate that politics is moving beyond the simple labels of party, even if our politicians aren't. The Conservatives might have won a parliamentary majority, but the British electorate is clearly no longer as tribal as it used to be. It votes Tory and Labour still, but also Green, UKIP and SNP. New and unorthodox challenges to the two biggest parties are regrettable for them, but not for the vitality of our democracy, which is only strengthened when we diversify political options.

There is a new kind of politics that goes beyond traditional party lines, a politics that eschews left and right for engagement and transparency. Tony Blair wrote in his memoir that he believes the new axis of politics is 'open vs. closed' and that we will concern ourselves less with ideological purity than with which politicians and their methods are most effective.[4] He is exactly right: increasingly we seek government and society that works, that is fair, and that is responsive. Those are values that can't be claimed by any political movement as their own.

Independents' day

At the local level, the picture is in even greater flux. One of the most exciting political developments of recent years has taken place in the least likely of places: the gentle country town of Frome, in Somerset. In 2010, fed up with partisan councillors, a group of civic-minded citizens got together and decided to run things on their own, resolving to stay independent of any of the national parties. By organising in a loose electoral alliance, Independents for Frome (in essence a party without a manifesto), they ensured that they would have the flexibility they needed to make council decisions on their merits, without the influence of a national party line.

'This group of seventeen people has within it a range of views,' says Patrick Macfayden, one of the co-founders of the movement who has added intellectual fire power to the experiment by giving it a name ('flatpack democracy') and a manifesto (*Flatpack Democracy* – picked up by then Communities Secretary Eric Pickles when he visited the town). 'If there'd been a majority – even of one – for one of the main parties, I'd be worried. Because, as we're now seeing at Westminster, they'd go out and say, 'Sod the lot of you, we're going to do what we want.' You know – twelve seats more than everyone else and they're bringing back fox hunting. We couldn't do that, because we have such a wide range of people.' Instead, the council can take each issue as it comes, addressing it without the baggage that comes with a wider political agenda.

The movement has spread to other towns because voters are tired of politicians turning local issues into partisan issues. 'Our basic mantra is that there is no place for mainstream party politics at this level,' says Mike Dudley-Jones, who was elected in a similar but separate effort in the Cheshire village of Alderley. There, voters deposed the entire Conservative-led parish council – and even sent a new representative to the Cheshire East council. Like the residents of Frome, they recognised that to see real change, they would have to take drastic action. As Macfayden, from Frome, says, 'It has to be total revolution or nothing: that was our stance.'[5]

Of course at the national level, it would take a revolution just to elect independent candidates *within* the party system. The rigidity of the two-party system is not only enshrined in all parts of our politics, it stultifies it. While (unlike in America) money plays a far lesser role, party organisation (for which money is very much needed) determines all. Just imagine the challenges an independent-minded candidate wishing to run in the UK would face. To have any shot at a victory, they would need a campaign with an organisation – one which today, generally, can only be provided through a political party. So they would have to be selected as a candidate for one of the major parties. But instead of letting the voters decide, that process is controlled centrally by a constituency party run, of course, by party insiders. So anyone with independent-minded views – and disinclined towards strict party loyalty for the sake of it – would be immediately disqualified. Even if an independent candidate *did* get on the ballot, it would be next to impossible for voters to realise there might be a candidate who genuinely matches their views outside the Labour/ Conservative binary. We need to help independents get on the ballot – and get noticed once they are there.

I'd like every political candidate to challenge the central party narrative, to advocate for politically risky positions. But what I'd like even more is to see candidates be able to run for political office – whether that's for the local council, Parliament or, increasingly, mayor, without the financial and logistical support of one of the main parties. You shouldn't have to be a multi-millionaire for that to be possible.

That's why I've decided to bring my political technology start-up, Crowdpac, to the UK.

Crowdpac: giving politics back to people

Crowdpac is designed to give people a practical way to improve how politics works within the system we have. We want to give politics back to people – in America, in Britain and around the world – and give an effective political voice to more than just the rich and powerful. So we're building simple tools that make it easier for people to engage effectively in the political system: voting, funding campaigns, running for office. In all these crucial areas we want to boost participation, involve more voters in the selection process, spur higher turnout at elections. We want to encourage more small donors so we dilute the influence of money, vested interests and party machines – all serving to reduce the time candidates need to spend fund-raising. We want to infuse politics with new blood, so we want to help more independent – and independent-minded – people to run for office. We want to give voters more options than the stale two-party duopoly. And for us at Crowdpac, all this starts with the thing that so much else depends on: good, objective information about politics and elections.

Just as in America, our aim will be to democratise politics – crowdfunding political campaigns and giving people simple, objective information about the candidates on their ballot. But we must also demystify the process of running for office. With Crowdpac UK, we will help real people, not just Westminster-connected elites, contest political office.

Separation of powers

One of the reasons political reform is so crucial is that our system is so needlessly political. The executives who run our government – secretaries of state and ministers – are not technical experts or even policy wonks. They are politicians. And while many are well suited to the roles they occupy, limiting the selection pool to members of the ruling party who happen to be in Parliament is hardly the right way to get the best people.

Mark Carney, the Governor of the Bank of England, is not a politician. He's not even British. But the Chancellor and Prime Minister hired him because they decided that he was the best person in the world for the job. Yet the same can't be said for the positions of foreign secretary or chancellor, whatever you may think of the job that the present incumbents are doing. While those positions, being the most prestigious, tend to be filled by competent people, the same isn't always true for the lesser ministerial roles. Filling a Cabinet, much less an entire Government, is an inherently political task.

Campaign promises must be upheld, key party constituencies must be appeased, personality conflicts must be avoided. It was even worse during the Coalition with the extremely tricky politics of keeping a whole additional party happy.

If we want government to actually function effectively, the UK would benefit from some serious constitutional reform: namely a separation of powers. A small step was taken towards this in 2009. With the establishment of the Supreme Court, the highest court in the land is no longer also part of Parliament. But in the same way that judicial powers have now been separated from the legislature, executive powers should, to a significant extent, be separate too.

Why shouldn't the most important management posts in the country be filled by the best available people, rather than just the best available politicians in the ruling party? Shouldn't we want people in government who are focused on doing a good job, rather than getting promoted in the next reshuffle?

Such a reform would also serve to make Parliament a better legislative body. Instead of splitting their time between executive and legislative roles, MPs would be able to focus exclusively on writing and debating laws and applying scrutiny to government departments. Without the obvious conflict of interest of both running and holding the departments to account, oversight would be much improved. MPs would be able to return to the true purpose of their role: representing their constituents in Parliament and being effective legislators. If British politics moved to a separation of powers of this kind, it would not only improve the quality of representation and legislation; I think we'd be able to attract higher quality people to become MPs in the first place – especially if we embolden independent candidates as I suggest above.

The EU

Of course, any tangible reform, any restructuring of British politics, any redistribution of power in British governance will be meaningless if one larger reform doesn't take place: to the UK's relationship with the European Union.

The European Union was born on lofty ideals. And for many years, it served a valuable purpose. As an expression of the liberal values of democracy and freedom, it was a beacon to the subjugated peoples of Europe – including those in Hungary, from where my parents fled. But today, the EU is not a beacon of democracy and freedom but the opposite: indeed the EU has become the institutional manifestation of almost everything I argue against in this book.

A democracy is based on the notion that the people – or their directly elected representatives – are able to decide issues for themselves. And yet membership of the EU brings with it constraints on everything from employment law to family policy, all determined through distant, centralised processes we hardly understand, let alone control. To a degree that most British citizens would find astonishing, ministers in the elected government of the day are prevented from doing the things they want to do by EU rules. You may say: well, that's government for you – it always involves compromise. Indeed it does, but at least in a democracy the compromises are clear and transparent and can be argued over and influenced by the people who are affected by them. No such possibility exists in the grotesquely unaccountable EU. As I say to my American friends who have little detailed grasp of how the EU works: 'All you need to know is that the EU has three presidents, none of whom are elected.'

And then look at the EU's assault on freedom – which matters to me just as much as democracy. In many ways I am a classical liberal. I am pro-market, pro-enterprise, pro-trade, pro-immigration, pro putting power in people's hands.

The EU, of course, does the opposite. It is anti-market, stifling innovation and competition with its statism, corporatism and bureaucracy. It is anti-enterprise, acting in the interests of the big businesses that have corruptly captured the levers of power in Brussels through their shameless lobbying and insider deal-making. The European Union is anti-trade, locking developing countries out of world markets with its evil Common Agricultural Policy that feather-beds French farmers while keeping African farmers trapped in poverty – and despair. The EU is anti-immigration, with its shambolic internal rules leading to Britain turning away inventors and entrepreneurs from around the world. And I don't think even the EU's most fervent supporters would ever claim that it 'puts power in people's hands'. The whole point of the EU is to take power *out* of people's hands in pursuit of a greater good. The trouble is, it's not good enough.

For decades, we in Britain have enjoyed complaining about 'Brussels bureaucracy'. Don't worry, I'm not going to have a rant about 'straight bananas' and their ilk. Rather, I want to draw attention to a defect of the EU that has drawn less scrutiny in this country. Yes, it's bad enough when EU bureaucrats make the rules; but it's far worse that they are influenced by a corporate lobbying operation second only to America's. What chance is there for popular participation in the political process in such a corrupt, opaque system? Membership of the EU is enabling a gradual corporate takeover of our country.

These were issues that a reformed EU might address. I could certainly live with an imperfect EU that nevertheless showed some degree of openness to a fundamental, structural reorientation towards the dispersal rather than the accretion of power. But it is perfectly obvious to everyone, including David Cameron, that no such reorientation will ever be countenanced. The arrogant and dismissive treatment of Britain's relatively modest demands in the 2015/2016 negotiations shows that the EU is just not interested in anything other than superficial change. You might as well hope for Vladimir Putin to embrace liberal democracy. Of course, the EU is perfectly entitled to such a disposition. But it's as well to be clear about it.

And from that clarity should come an informed decision to leave. To regain control over our country's destiny, so that a democratically elected government in Britain is free to carry out its mandate, whether that's left, right or centre. For me it would mean economic and employment policy that makes Britain the best place in the world to start and grow a business; family policy that makes Britain the best place in the world to bring up children; competition policy that finally allows us to prioritise the small, the local, the 'inefficient', the beautiful, the human.

Others would have a different agenda. But don't you see, if we win the votes, we should be allowed to make it happen. That's what it's all about. That's why I think we should leave.

People ask: what about the economy, and access to Europe's Single Market? Would we end up like Norway? Or Switzerland? No. We're bigger than that; better than that. Our independent relationship with the EU would be more like that of our peers, like the US. America is not a member of the EU but the last time I checked, General Motors had no problem selling cars there. Or Heinz, selling ketchup. Or Starbucks, coffee.

Why should we fear independence? That makes no sense. Britain produced the Industrial Revolution, the locomotive, the light switch, the World Wide Web. That's to say nothing of our cherished political and social legacies, from the world's first free parliament and government based on Enlightenment ideals to the first insurance scheme, to the first stock exchange to the first national health service. All on our own. All without membership of the European Union. Come on, people, are you really telling me we can't thrive and rise as a democratic, free country again?

The UK has one of the oldest and most respected democracies in the world, and we should take confidence from that fact. But if it is to maintain the confidence of the people it represents, it is in need of serious reform. Improving the way our political system works – in particular, attacking the concentration of power and elite influence – is essential. As Harvard law professor and democratic reform activist Lawrence Lessig puts it, 'It's not that mine is the most important issue – it's not. Yours is the most important issue. But mine is the *first* issue – the issue we have to solve before we get to fix the issues you care about.'[6] This is the starting point: if we want to make our government more human, and our world more human, we first have to mend our broken political system and make politics more human too.

CHAPTER 2

GOVERNMENT

I once wrote a book called *Good Business – Your World Needs You*, which was based on a simple argument: business runs the world. The world needs changing. Let's use business to change the world.

Looking back, with the benefit of my experience since then, working with some of the world's biggest companies to try to solve social and environmental problems and then working in politics and government to do the same, I can see that I was – how shall I put this? – wrong.

Business does not run the world. In the end, government sets the rules by which business operates, and rightly so. Government is – at least notionally – accountable to people in a way that businesses are not. Businesses clearly make a huge contribution to society, both positive and negative, and they should try to improve it. But if we really want to change the world – if we want to make it more human – then we must use the mechanism designed for that purpose: government. As we saw in Chapter 1, we need to change the way we choose our governments by fixing our broken political system and getting more people involved. But we also have to change government itself: the priorities of those within it, the way policy is made and implemented, and the way the whole thing is structured.

More human priorities for government

Sir John Cowperthwaite was the financial secretary of Hong Kong in the 1960s and the man widely credited with creating the conditions for its phenomenal economic success. When asked what advice he would give to a poor country trying to get richer, he said, 'They should abolish the Office of National Statistics.' Cowperthwaite believed that the collection of economic data simply encouraged governments and bureaucrats to needlessly and destructively interfere in the economy, so he refused. This infuriated his masters in London. When they sent a delegation to persuade him to change his approach, Cowperthwaite literally sent them straight back on the next plane.[1] I love that story for its wonderfully British rebelliousness. But that rather eccentric episode from the 1960s also highlights the big problem with government today: its prioritisation of numbers over people. Of course it sounds obvious, trite even, to argue that government should 'put people first'. And yet it doesn't happen. Look at any government's priorities: the focus of federal, state, or even local government bureaucrats, the things that drive big decisions – it's actually about numbers, about economics.

The political world's focus on economics was most famously captured by Bill Clinton's 1992 election campaign strategist James Carville when he scrawled 'The economy, stupid' on the office walls of Clinton's headquarters. In government, money reigns supreme, and I don't just mean lobbying and political donations. The most prestigious posts are the economic ones: in Britain, it's the Chancellor of the Exchequer. All the top civil servants want to work at the Treasury; moving to work anywhere else in government is seen as a demotion. The official calendar is dominated by economic announcements – job statistics, quarterly growth numbers, inflation, interest rates, what's happening in the stock market. In government it really *is* the economy, stupid.

You can understand why. Economic growth – more money – pays for the human things that really matter. For an individual or family, the more money you have, the better life tends to be. Money doesn't buy happiness, but it can certainly eliminate many of the things that make us unhappy. Money provides security and opportunity. It is often those who have never experienced what it's like to have little or no money who say it doesn't matter. Try telling that to the mother of three who's working two jobs to feed her children and still can't afford to buy nappies.

So I don't have any problem with the idea that the government should concern itself with how to improve society's economic circumstances. Political leaders could have many worse aims, after all, than making their people more prosperous. Prosperity generally has brought us longer, healthier lives, with better education, more art and leisure, greater civic and political participation – all good things. Economic growth has been a decent enough proxy for these important human outcomes.

My argument is different: it is not about challenging the value of economic growth but about the *way* our government goes about it. We've made a narrowly defined representation of the economy – economic indicators – the priority while forgetting that 'the economy' represents something deeper: our actual lives as they are lived. Basing everything on numbers pushes government policy towards mechanical, bureaucratic systems rather than more organic approaches that put people first. Take a so-called economic issue like jobs. It's just as much – if not more – a social, human issue. Of course you can fiddle around with interest rates and taxes, and that will have some effect on unemployment rates. But the effects are far less certain or predictable than economic policymakers let on. The wiser and more self-aware of them know that there is very little they can do to 'improve the economy' or 'create jobs' in a general sense. If you want to see more jobs created and more people able to take them, the things that really work are specific, human things.

Help people get the skills they need. Help them gain the confidence and support to become entrepreneurs. Help make sure children are brought up in a way that gives them the character and the capacity to learn, to train, to hold down a job. None of the social policies required to bring about these ends are captured in the job numbers or the growth statistics. But they are critical to achieving the economic results we seek. On the surface, economic issues are human issues at their heart. Social policy *is* economic policy, just more effective.

We know from the latest developments in neuroscience and evidence from long-term research that the conditions in which a child grows up, especially in the first few years of life, have a crucial impact on the rest of their lives: whether they will work or be on welfare, a contributor to society or a cost. But government doesn't prioritise spending on the causes of social problems; it wastes money on the symptoms. This flaw is systemic. It's not because politicians and public officials are stupid or useless or malevolent; quite the opposite: they are mostly highly intelligent, dedicated and public spirited. The problem is a system that forces every decision into a framework that is literally inhuman. It's one of the reasons citizens feel that so little of any real substance seems to change, regardless of what party or politician is in power.

To design a more human world, we must change the priorities of government. We have to start from the notion that certain things *must* be in place for people to lead a decent life, that government's overarching priority should be to lay the infrastructure, in its broadest sense, that will allow that to come about. Of course, there's physical infrastructure – roads and railways, energy grids, and utilities. But we need human infrastructure as well – education and health services, early childhood education, mental health, relationship and family support.

Infrastructure's problem, though, is that it tends to need expensive upfront expenditure before the benefits flow. As a society, we already make a certain commitment to this idea. We subsidise our children's education, for instance, because we think of it not as a cost but as an investment that will enable productive lives later on.

This isn't new. In Britain the Victorians thought like this 150 years ago. As economist Diane Coyle points out, so-called Victorian values aren't just prudish or conservative; they 'also speak of hard work, self-improvement, and above all self-sacrifice for the future'.[2] The Victorians had the forethought to build tangible investments in their communities like railways, canals, sewers, town halls, libraries, concert halls and modern hospitals. Meanwhile, they strengthened society through the police, trade unions, mutual insurers, learned societies and the nursing profession. This 'sense of stewardship', as Coyle described it in the context of the Victorians, is what can fundamentally define success or failure for a society.

Today we have shirked our duties as stewards. We have chosen the tyranny of a narrow short-term economic calculus over Britain's long-term future.

One way to think about it, as Oxford economist Dieter Helm suggests, is to distinguish between spending money on assets and spending money on liabilities.[3] Infrastructure is an asset. Yes, it costs money initially, but we can predict (and later record) its 'dividends', such as the economic activity a new fibre-optic network produces or the money an early childhood intervention saves later on. That money goes in the 'plus' side of the ledger and, in any sensible accounting system (like the one used by businesses), can be offset against the spending. Eventually it will pay for itself. But in government, infrastructure spending isn't treated any differently. Tackling unemployment by building a high-speed broadband network that would help in the creation of new jobs is counted as no different from handing out the same amount of money in welfare payments. Tackling crime through parenting programmes that could prevent offending in the first place is counted in the same ledger as keeping criminals in jail. Long-term human needs come second to the short-term imperative of the numbers; sensible, long-term policies are rejected because their dividends come down the road. The numbers rule, in a totally irrational way, and we end up with budget-based priorities instead of priorities-based budgets. So the real priority for reform should aim to create a whole new system of national accounts.

I wanted to tackle this – frankly quite geeky – question of government accounting systems and their impact on policy priorities so early in the book because it's a good example of something we will see over and over in later chapters. To really change things, we need to understand the underlying causes of problems, and more often than not they are structural and systemic. It's easy to say (and people have been saying for many years): 'Why don't we have amazing modern infrastructure like the Chinese do?' or 'Why don't we have fantastic services for families and children like Nordic countries do?' The reason we have such short-term thinking in government – whoever is in power – is not that politicians, or civil servants, or even voters are choosing the wrong priorities. The reason is systemic. The system of our national accounts forces the wrong priorities. Our politicians once understood the need to build for the future; instead, the system of government accounting has defeated them. If we want government to have more human priorities, we will need to change that system.

A more human way to design and implement policy

In 2000, Tony Blair floated a new idea to clean up antisocial behaviour on British streets. He proposed that offenders be made to pay an on-the-spot fine of £100; if they didn't have the money, they'd be taken to a cashpoint to withdraw it. The policy was never implemented. One of the main reasons was because it turned out that the 'yobs' targeted by this policy did not usually have £100 in cash 'on the spot', or a bank account to withdraw it from; often they did not even have £100 to their names.[4]

Why did Blair make incorrect assumptions about those committing street crime? Come to think of it, how did anyone in any government anywhere conceive that stupid new tax, that waste-of-money antipoverty programme, that white-elephant urban-regeneration plan, and so on? It's easy to blame 'useless politicians', jumped-up aides', and 'incompetent bureaucrats'. But that's simplistic; we need to go deeper. One reason for the failure of so many government programmes over the years – and the dissatisfaction so many people feel with the public services they receive – is the fact that the people the programmes or services are designed to help are too often an afterthought. The lives of average people – especially the poor or those interacting with social services – are simply unknown to policymakers. Blair and his advisers' daily reality was so far removed from that of the people who made trouble on the streets that no matter how right the theory, the policy could never work in practice.

Don't think that politicians don't care about people or the effects of their policies – they do, most of them, sincerely and deeply. It's just that by the time politicians are in their government offices, trying to find slots in their overfilled schedules to actually think about policy and its implementation, they're unable to do so on a human scale, in a human way.

It's not just the design of policies; it's the delivery too. Consider the New Enterprise Allowance (NEA), another well-intentioned idea, this time from the government I worked for. It was aimed at helping people get off unemployment benefits – and was in fact a policy I helped create and fought hard to introduce. The idea was that some unemployed people might want to start their own businesses, so if we could get each of them a loan and some advice from a mentor, they'd be on their way. The NEA loan would be administered through Jobcentre Plus offices, which were already in most communities. When the programme was launched, the initial uptake was disappointing and the Treasury officials in charge of its funding wanted to cancel the whole thing. Rohan Silva (my closest friend and former colleague in government who you will meet a lot in these pages) was curious about why the programme, loosely based on a similar one that had been extremely successful in the 1980s, wasn't working. On a hunch that perhaps it wasn't being pitched in the right way, he asked the officials running the policy what the staff at Jobcentre Plus offices were trained to say to potential candidates and what their reasons would be for granting or turning down a loan if the conversation got that far.

The officials had no idea. They never gave it a moment's thought. They just assumed that because the opportunity was available, anyone who wanted it would sign up. A low level of sign-ups must have meant the policy was defective. The government was about to cancel a potentially effective programme without any sense of how it was being implemented where it really mattered: the human point of contact between people.

The d.school at Stanford

In 2012 I came to Stanford University, where I taught a number of courses, including some at its Institute of Design, or d.school. This required me to reflect on how we did things in government – what we did well, what we did badly, and what we could have done differently. That reflection has been profound. I now realise why so many policies fail, why so much money is wasted, why so many promises fall short, why this happened in our administration – and in every government. It has to do with a mindset, an attitude, an approach in which policymaking is much more about theory than practice, where the people making the policy and the people implementing it make no real effort to understand, in detail, the lives of the people who the policy is for. I have no hesitation in saying to my students that the single biggest improvement we could bring to policymaking in government is to put people at the centre of the process. That may sound platitudinous. But I mean it in a very precise way, based on what I learned at

Stanford about the process of human-centred design – or, as it is known at the d.school, *design thinking.*

Formally established in 2004 as the Hasso Plattner Institute for Design at Stanford, the d.school is the academic home of design thinking. In the late 1980s the software usability engineer Donald Norman put forward his vision of user-centred design, and by the late 1990s and early 2000s designers at the Silicon Valley design firm IDEO (the company responsible for Apple's first mouse), started to realise that they could apply user- (or human-) centred design (by now also called design thinking) not just to objects, products and software but also much more broadly. In the 2000s design thinking was being applied to entire business models, not to mention consumer experiences. By the time the d.school was founded it was clear that because innovators in almost any discipline are creating new things – whether business ideas, healthcare interventions, education policies or consumer services – and that the act of creating is an act of design, graduate students from any university programme would benefit from a design-thinking education. Stanford's d.school was established to give them that opportunity. It's now run by Sarah Stein Greenberg, my brilliant co-teacher and the person who more than anyone else has helped me understand what design thinking is all about and how it could help improve policy-making and implementation.

At the d.school students are guided through a process that, though inevitably messier in practice, can be explained in a handful of straightforward steps:

1. Empathise with the user
2. Define the problem
3. Generate ideas

4. Prototype solutions
5. Test the prototypes
... keep testing, adapting, and improving.

Empathy is not a word you hear very much in government. But to understand a problem and imagine a solution requires an understanding of the people affected. This is an act of empathy, and human-centred designers put themselves in the shoes of those they are designing for. Empathy requires close, highly detailed observation of people in the context in which they'll be using the product or service in question. This borrows from the anthropological practice of ethnography, which assumes that observations and open-ended interviews reveal more about a person's beliefs, needs, emotions and desires than opinion surveys and market research ever could. In the design-thinking process taught at the d.school this means talking to 'users' before doing anything else, which really means listening to users. Politicians, of course, will say they listen to their constituents all the time, either directly or through polls and focus groups. But this is different. The kind of empathy work required for design thinking is about deeply understanding the life of the person you're designing for, forcing yourself to be open-minded rather than selling your own ideas.

The first stage of the designers' process includes observing users in their day-to-day routines and immersing themselves in the user's environment for days, even weeks on end. The acclaimed urban theorist and writer Jane Jacobs captures precisely this sentiment in her 1961 masterpiece, *The Death and Life of Great American Cities*. She writes that the only corrective to ineffective, top-down city planning – generally by 'visionary', egotistical architects and politicians – is to base policy on 'true descriptions of reality drawn not from how it ought to be, but from how it is'.[5]

These true descriptions of reality are the basis for step two: defining the problem. This might seem straightforward, but it's surprising how frequently policymakers solve the wrong problem – a superficial one, a symptom rather than a cause – or a problem perceived in one way by the outside world but totally differently by those actually experiencing it. A great example comes from a student project that began at the d.school as part of a course called Entrepreneurial Design for Extreme Affordability. In 'Extreme', as the course is popularly known, teams of Stanford graduate students come together for over six months to work on different problems facing the world's poor. Each group, which deliberately mixes up students from any field – law, medicine, business, history, computer science – is paired with an international NGO to solve a specific problem in an extremely affordable way.

One team was tasked with developing a lower-cost baby incubator to be piloted in rural Nepal (nearly 1 million children die each year globally from complications due to premature birth[6]). The team of four first met in January 2007 when the course began. They spent two and a half months researching incubators as well as infant mortality and the medical requirements of premature babies. It is customary with Extreme for one or two of the students on each team to visit their partners on the ground. For the incubator team Linus Liang, a computer-science student, travelled 7,000 miles to Nepal along with two other student groups working on similar health-related problems.

'We were very ambitious – we landed, got to the hotel, and went to the hospital that day,' Linus recalls. 'We did exactly what design thinking instructs – lots of interviews, observations, etcetera. We talked to at least twenty doctors and then went to the neonatal intensive care unit and observed all the different doctors and nurses, the amount of noise – everything.'

Linus discovered one odd thing. There were incubators everywhere, but they sat empty. 'There's this hospital with nothing, no resources – there's mould growing on the walls,' Linus recalls, but 'they had all these donated incubators. Some [of the instruction labels] were in Japanese, some were in German – there were all these different languages. And all of them were pretty damn good. So Linus asked the next question: given that Nepal had all these incubators, why did it have such a high infant mortality problem? It turned out that many of the country's premature births happened in rural villages, far away from the hospital and the life-saving incubators. The babies were dead on arrival.

It was clear that the d.school team needed to go deeper to understand the problem. So they got on a bus and went to a village outside Kathmandu. 'It was kind of horrible what they had out there. There was no infrastructure.' In the village they visited it became quickly apparent that the team's initial idea – a cheaper incubator for hospitals – wasn't going to get them anywhere. There was no running water, no local hospitals – just shacks with barely trained 'doctors' who did their best to serve the villagers' medical needs. The incubators they used were simple wooden boxes with light bulbs in them, most of which were burnt out anyway, some for as long as four years. They told Linus that they had no money to buy new bulbs, but in any case there was nowhere to buy them, nor electricity to power them.

'You slowly learn all the constraints. And then we started designing for that when we came back,' Linus explains. 'That's when we really understood the need.' Back at Stanford the team used its findings to develop a new point of view.

They were no longer looking to design a cheaper, simpler incubator for local hospitals: 'We wanted to design for the mothers who have no actual healthcare system, no water, no electricity, no transport, no money.' The team redefined the problem they were trying to solve, drawing on the empathy they had gained. And it was at this point that they could start to generate ideas for what a solution might look like.[7]

This might sound familiar – who hasn't sat through a 'brainstorming' session to come up with something clever or creative? But this step in the design-thinking process, like the others, is usually given short shrift by politicians and policymakers, many of whom already have solutions in mind that they're trying to advance, based often on ideology rather than empathy with the people they're trying to help. One of my favourite teaching moments at the d.school is our demonstration of a bad brainstorm versus a good brainstorm. Take it from me – most of the ones you see in government are bad. The cardinal rule for getting good results? Defer judgement. Whether you're alone or with a group of colleagues, the best way to kill potentially good ideas is to point out their flaws at the moment you're trying to come up with them. That's not to say that there's no such thing as a bad idea. Of course there is. But the time for evaluating ideas is not when you're trying to generate them.

For me, the part of the design-thinking process that offers the greatest contrast with how things are done in government is the final stage: prototyping and testing an idea. The key is to embrace experimentation, testing a concept with cheap and rough prototypes before investing more in its development. This is a world away from how government does things. Yes, there are pilot programmes – but these typically cost many millions of dollars and are launched with great fanfare. The incentive is to prove that they work, not to find out whether they do. Prototype testing is not piloting. For example, rather than building a website – still a costly exercise – you could literally sketch it out on pieces of paper, put it in front of people and get feedback on how they would use it, simply by asking them to point at boxes they would 'click' on and why. The methodology of rapid and low-cost prototyping and testing taught at the d.school is now the basic modus operandi for every tech firm in Silicon Valley, from the biggest names to the smallest start-ups.

And that's exactly what the d.school team working on the incubator problem did next. Using the insights gained from Nepal, they shifted their focus from the hospital and the clinician to the village and the mother. The team reframed the problem from 'building a cheaper incubator' to 'keeping premature babies warm'. The result was a wrap like a sleeping bag, warmed by a special heated insert, all costing about 1 per cent of the price of an incubator. When the course was finished, the team set themselves up as a company (called Embrace) and moved to India, determined to bring their concept to a stage at which it could actually be deployed. They continued testing new versions, each time gaining fresh insight from the mothers whom they watched using the prototypes. Small tweaks came from observation: a plastic window over the chest, allowing doctors to see at a glance if the baby was breathing, or a simple OK/Not OK indicator in place of the previous numerical temperature gauge that the mothers didn't trust (digital displays tend to malfunction so often that there's an automatic suspicion of them). From its humble origins as a student project, Embrace has now expanded its operations across Asia, Latin America and Africa and has gone on to save 50,000 lives – and counting.[8]

Designing policy for who we are, not for who we ought to be

It's amazing what you can discover when you listen to people. But a more human approach to policymaking doesn't just mean paying attention to details on the ground; it's about understanding behaviour too. Over the last thirty years psychologists, neuroscientists and economists have systematically catalogued ways in which we consistently fail to live up to traditional expectations of how humans 'ought' to behave. This means that we now have a rigorous body of work, rather than just our hunches, that we can use to enhance the effectiveness of public policy.

For example, economics assumes that we value money objectively – that a dollar gained causes as much pleasure as the pain from a dollar that's lost. But in the late 1970s psychologists discovered that we tend to be much more averse to a loss than we are keen to have the equivalent gain. This work was so disruptive to traditional economics that its discovery by Daniel Kahneman and Amos Tversky earned the Nobel Prize in 2002.[9] An interesting application of the principle was an experiment in a Chicago school district. For many years school administrators around the world have tried to incentivise better teacher performance through bonuses awarded at the end of the year if certain targets are met. In Chicago Heights a group of University of Chicago academics tried an approach based on this behavioural concept of loss aversion. They gave the teachers their bonus at the beginning of the year and told them that at the end of the year, all or parts of it would be taken away if they didn't meet specified goals. Two control groups were also established: one in which teachers were given no performance incentive and one involving a traditional end-of-year bonus. The results were spectacular: the performance of the students taught by teachers in the two control groups was about the same, suggesting that the traditional performance bonus doesn't really make much difference. But in the group where the teachers were given an upfront bonus with a threat that it would be lost, the students' results improved two to three times more than in the traditional bonus group.[10]

More human policy design would also recognise that we often neglect to do things that are in our own best interest – and that we even say we want to do – like put money in our pensions, exercise, and remember to go to doctors' appointments. But government policy has been designed and implemented for decades based on the assumption that people will behave with perfect foresight and self-control. Consider government's approach to fighting poverty: programmes of the Left traditionally consist of giving money, jobs, food and other 'free stuff' – as critics like to call it – to alleviate material deprivation, while programmes of the Right traditionally try to improve economic incentives so that poor people can 'lift themselves up by the bootstraps'. Both approaches, as social policy commentator David Brooks has pointed out, errantly 'treat individuals as if they were abstractions ... shaped by economic structures alone, and not by character and behaviour'.[11] The simple truth is that our actions don't always match our intentions. Human things like forgetfulness get in the way.

People also tend to do what they think other people are doing. One of my favourite examples comes from an experiment that psychologist Robert Cialdini carried out in Arizona's Petrified Forest National Park. He posted signs drawing attention to the high incidence of looting pieces of ancient wood. They backfired: letting people know that theft was frequent – normal even – actually increased theft.[12]

Traditional efforts by governments to change people's behaviour so often make this classic mistake – highlighting the negative behaviour they want to *dis*courage rather than promoting as a social norm the positive behaviour they want to *en*courage.

Awash with data

We need a more human approach at least in part as an antidote to policymakers' increasing over-reliance on data. I'm not against using data as a policymaking tool; it can help us understand the extent of a problem's existence, scope and distribution as well as its trend over time. Data can help us see whether existing policies are having the desired effect or if concepts that worked well in one place are effective in others. Perhaps data's most crucial function is helping us understand what has *generally* worked or failed before. But when it comes to the design of specific programmes or the way public services are actually delivered, it's dangerous to make assumptions based on data, as if all people and situations were the same. Here's David Brooks again, on efforts to combat teenage pregnancy: 'A pregnancy ... isn't just a piece of data in a set. It came about after a unique blend of longings and experiences. Maybe a young woman just wanted to feel like an adult; maybe she had some desire for arduous love, maybe she was just absent-minded, or loved danger, or couldn't resist her boyfriend, or saw no possible upside for her future anyway. In each case the ingredients will be different. Only careful case-by-case storytelling can uncover and respect the delirious iconoclasm of how life is actually lived.'[13]

At the height of the crack-cocaine epidemic in the 1990s, New York City police commissioner Bill Bratton instituted a programme called CompStat in an effort to radically realign the department around a clear principle of accountability for crime reduction. Police officials were required to attend weekly meetings at which they discussed the key data of the week, with statistical trends analysed across departments and over time. Although it was largely credited with reducing the specific measured crimes (muggings, murders, etc.), the programme precluded tactics that might have been more effective in the long term but were less amenable to measurement, such as trust-building in communities. Events like the 2014 riots and over-militarised police response in Ferguson, Missouri, and the brutal chokehold arrest and subsequent death of Eric Garner, an unarmed petty criminal in New York, are partly the result of such a targets-driven culture. Bratton, who advocates CompStat around the world, himself acknowledges that too much attention has been placed on 'the numbers of stops, summonses and arrests' and not enough on 'collaborative problem-solving with the community'.[14]

This data obsession and the results it evokes is one reason why so many people in America (and in Britain) are losing trust in the police. In Ferguson, the public – in this case the African-American minority – has been egregiously abused by the city government through its police and court system. A US Department of Justice (DOJ) report found that 'Ferguson law enforcement practices disproportionately harm Ferguson's African-American residents'. Though it found 'substantial evidence that this harm stems in part from intentional discrimination in violation of the Constitution',[15] the DOJ report was instructive for laying bare the insidious effects of a targets-based policing culture. The NYPD might have made errors with CompStat, but those errors were at least made with the intent to reduce crime and make

New York a safer city. In Ferguson the police prioritised 'productivity' – read: writing citations – and residents were seen 'less as constituents to be protected than as potential offenders and sources of revenue'. Meanwhile a court system punished constituents who couldn't pay, trapping them in a vicious circle of fines, debt and ultimately prison that laid waste to their lives.

Justice may have been carried out to the letter of the law in Ferguson, but it was hardly according to its spirit. In Ferguson, targets undermined the effectiveness of the very services they are supposed to help improve. Take this example of a Ferguson man who fell foul of Ferguson police:

In the summer of 2012, a 32-year-old African-American man sat in his car cooling off after playing basketball in a Ferguson public park. An officer pulled up behind the man's car, blocking him in, and demanded the man's Social Security number and identification. Without any cause, the officer accused the man of being a paedophile, referring to the presence of children in the park, and ordered the man out of his car for a pat-down, although the officer had no reason to believe the man was armed. The officer also asked to search the man's car. The man objected, citing his constitutional rights. In response, the officer arrested the man, reportedly at gunpoint, charging him with eight violations of Ferguson's municipal code. One charge, Making a False Declaration, was for initially providing the short form of his first name (e.g., 'Mike' instead of 'Michael'), and an address which, although legitimate, was different from the one on his driver's licence. Another charge was for not wearing a seat belt, even though he was seated in a parked car. The officer also charged the man both with having an expired operator's licence and with having no operator's licence in his possession. The man told us that, because of these charges, he lost his job as a contractor with the federal government that he had held for years.[16]

Did racism cause the criminal justice system to abuse targets? Or did a targets culture lead to racist abuse? Probably both. Certainly there was truly horrific racism and corruption in Ferguson, and it is a fact that the African-American population disproportionately bore the abuse of the criminal justice system. But the Ferguson scandal was also the consequence of how the system operated. Ferguson's police force was judged not by how safe the streets were but by how many tickets its officers could write, and the courts were judged not by how just their proceedings were but by how many fines they could levy. Racism may have led Ferguson's system to target African-Americans, the town's most vulnerable and least powerful demographic, but any system set up to privilege citations and the revenue they produce over due process is destined to result in corrupt and unfair results. Targets disguised those injustices as the results of legitimate law enforcement.

So while the scandal was intimately linked with racism, it wasn't inextricably so. Any unhealthy obsession with data will have a deleterious effect on police–community relations. Indeed, such a scenario in the UK is eroding public trust in the police. When the issuing of a fixed penalty notice was defined for statistical purposes as a 'cleared-up crime', it's no surprise that police forces went on a rampage of aggressively hassling basically law-abiding people for the most minor (often traffic-related) offences. It's much easier to do that than clear up an actual crime, involving actual criminals – and if they're both counted the same way in the crime figures, who wouldn't take the easier option? Jim Bueermann, president of the US-based Police Foundation and a former police chief, admits, 'If you ask a traffic officer how many tickets he wrote today, their emphasis is on writing tickets to meet a number, as opposed to a desired outcome, which is safer streets.'[17]

Over-reliance on targets, on data, is certainly not the only factor contributing to mistrust in the police; indeed, data is a valuable tool in understanding the policing needs of a community. Nonetheless, Ferguson offers a cautionary tale. Though with its racial tinge, it was an American phenomenon, it wasn't uniquely so. If we continue to move towards policing by data, it's not so hard to imagine such a drastic breakdown of order happening here in Britain (or anywhere else for that matter).

When the police see citizens as data points, their actions become beholden to statistics, not good police work. So let's not confuse measurable actions like stops, citations, fines and arrests with the true goals of safer streets and citizens. Instead, police should continue to heed the words of Sir Robert Peel, the British statesman who started London's Metropolitan Police, the world's first modern police force: 'The police are the public and the public are the police.'[18] What a presciently more human thought.

'Go out into the real world'

In the end numbers are just not that helpful in actually designing or implementing policy in government and in public services like the police. For example, knowing whether a family is above or below the poverty line tells us nothing about *why* that's the case. And if we don't know why a family is in poverty, we can't know how to design programmes to help that family out. No statistics or set of data can substitute for the intimate, nuanced knowledge that a policymaker should internalise by going out and experiencing the complexity of the world where the policy will have its effect.

In government in the UK we tried to move things forward. In 2008, while we were still in opposition, Rohan ordered ten copies of *Nudge* by Dick Thaler and Cass Sunstein, a book that sets out the case, in theory and with practical examples, for using behavioural economics to improve people's ability to make decisions. The book promotes a sort of 'libertarian paternalism': steer people in the desired direction without outright compulsion. David Cameron picked up a copy from the pile on Rohan's desk and shortly thereafter started referring to it eagerly. Within weeks of becoming prime minister Cameron gave the go-ahead to set up a 'nudge' unit of our own. Under the direction of social psychologist and Cabinet Office veteran David Halpern, the Behavioural Insights Team worked with government departments to help improve policy design, now replicated in the US federal government in the shape of the White House Social and Behavioral Sciences Team. Nudges aren't just cute tricks to tack on to existing policies. One of the most successful – and oft-quoted – nudges instituted by the Cameron government was to require large companies to auto-enroll employees in their pension plans, increasing pension savings dramatically.[19]

Design thinking, too, has started to make inroads in government. After Rohan's experience of the New Enterprise Allowance brought home to him how detached officials were from the actual people government policies were trying to help, he decided something had to be done to bring the users of government programmes into the way programmes were designed. 'I was so frustrated by the officials' answers to these basic questions about the way this policy was presented to the people who might benefit from it,' he recounts. 'What is the script? What posters are up? What materials do people get if they're interested? Just imagine the individual lives that could have been changed, the amazing businesses started, the jobs created, if there had just been this small change, if there had just been a moment's thought given to the actual human interaction. Why is there such a dislocation between policymakers and reality? And this is just a small policy in the overall scheme of things. Think about all the policies right across government and how much more effective they could be.'[20]

Rohan initiated a process to bring design thinking into the heart of government. He met with experts at the Royal College of Art, Jeremy Myerson and Anthony Dunne, as well as Tom Hulme from the UK office of design firm IDEO. From that came the idea to run a design-thinking course for top civil servants. 'I wanted to devise a systemic response to this systemic problem,' Rohan says. So in November 2012 he convened a group of a couple of hundred of the UK's top civil servants at Number 10 Downing Street for a design-thinking workshop. The venue, the State Dining Room, emphasised the importance of the enterprise: 'I chose that room very specifically because it's the grandest room at Number 10,' Rohan recalls. 'Civil servants are a pretty cautious bunch, and Whitehall is not a particularly amenable place to new ideas, so I wanted them to understand that this was serious.' Professors from the Royal College of Art's new Service Design programme, who led the day-long crash course, made good use of the space, covering it in Post-its (the global medium of design thinking, I've discovered since teaching at the d.school). Cabinet Office minister Francis Maude kicked it off; Cabinet secretary Jeremy Heywood and head of the Civil Service Bob Kerslake weighed in to make closing remarks. 'The day was bookended by the people in charge,' Rohan explains. 'I did everything I could to frame this as legitimate and mainstream.'[21]

There are now signs that design thinking is entering the bloodstream of the Civil Service. The recently established

Open Policy Making Team was a product of that day's events. It works with departments across the Civil Service to bring more of a human-centred mindset, and an approach involving rapid prototyping and testing of ideas, to their policy efforts; now it's helping to make design thinking part of the core training programme for all Whitehall Civil Servants. The Ministry of Justice (MinJ) and the Government Digital Service have been particularly enthusiastic. MinJ has embraced an 'agile' design approach to both their digital and offline interactions with those who use its services. Of course all this – the jargon, the Post-it notes, the brainstorming – is easy to mock, or portray as the latest management fad. In fact it's much more than that. It's a fundamental reorientation of policymaking, from a focus on bureaucratic needs and priorities to the real lives of the real people government is supposed to serve.

But let's not get carried away. Although there have been steps forward – for example, Prime Minister David Cameron commissioned intensive 'mystery shopping' research so he could learn how policies were actually being implemented in the real world; Megan Smith, the US chief technology officer, brought together teams of engineers and health experts at a day-long 'hackathon' to design a better Ebola suit[22] – the vast majority of government policymaking and implementation is still mired in a bureaucratic mindset. The number of politicians, policymakers, and other public officials who have even heard of human-centred design or behavioural economics, let alone experienced it, is minuscule. And although OPM has been somewhat successful, some of those trying to infuse design into government have run into trouble. When Karen Courington, a former congressional aide who took part in a class I taught at the d.school, tried to infuse the US Congress with a bit of design-thinking spirit, she met fierce resistance. After asking the Senate clerk whether she could set up a non-partisan room with whiteboards where staffers could meet and brainstorm policy ideas – perhaps with a few Post-its! – he told her, 'No, there'll never be a whiteboard in the Capitol as long as I'm here.' [23]

So although having specialist units, like the UK's Open Policy Making Team or nudge units, is a promising start, we won't see transformational results until the principles of design thinking are integrated into the everyday habits of every government employee at every level. That means government officials regularly spending time with their 'users' – that is, citizens and frontline workers. Of course, elected officials and civil servants are busy, but perhaps instead of spending half their time in meetings being briefed on policy problems, they could go out and experience them. Before designing a new parenting programme while in government, I went along to parenting classes and talked to the parents about their experiences. Before implementing one of our government's biggest and most ambitious domestic policy initiatives – National Citizen Service, a kind of universal, non-military personal development and community service programme for teenagers – we spent years prototyping and testing the model. Both programmes were better for it.

A more human way of organising government

But there's still a problem: scale. Too often the people making decisions are too far from the people affected by them. How can policymakers (most of whom are holed up in London or other administrative centres) possibly achieve such a nuanced awareness of people in communities around the country? Even regular visits and 'immersions' are no substitute for the local knowledge embedded in those who live, work and play; who struggle, strive and cope in their own towns and neighbourhoods. Not to mention the fact that capturing such a rich understanding of each region and town, and then tailoring policy and programmes accordingly, would be impossible to deliver from central government. Unless government were closer to home – closer to people …

Saint-Céneri-le-Gérei (population 140) is a fairly unremarkable village in French Normandy. But for nineteen years, between 1995 and 2014, it was remarkable for its mayor: Ken Tatham, an Englishman from Leeds. Tatham's path to the mayor's office started when he decided to forgo university in Britain, instead travelling around Europe. In Spain, he met the Frenchwoman who would become his wife. Her father had a second home in Saint-Céneri-le-Gérei, where they married. They lived in Paris for a while but ultimately returned in 1969 to raise a family in the village which, he says, is 'one of the most beautiful in France'. Tatham's wife was a village councillor and he was constantly telling her: 'You should do this and that' – and she got a little annoyed and said: 'Why don't you get involved yourself?' Tatham, who by then was a dual citizen, was eligible to run for office. So in 1995 he ran for the council, won, and became mayor. At first people were a bit sceptical. 'A lot of the villagers didn't take too kindly to having an Englishman as mayor,' he recalls, 'especially as the English had demolished the village castle at the end of the Hundred Years' War,' but 'they forgot that very swiftly … it used to come back as more of a joke in the end.' Tatham found that local government in France was quite different from local government in England. In France, mayors form a central part of civic life: 'If somebody has a problem, it becomes yours,' he says. 'You're like a social assistant in a way. Your door is always open to people and their problems no matter what they are.'[24]

There are nearly 37,000 mayors in France, one for every commune, village, town and city. Unlike local government in the UK, French mayors have real, autonomous power.[25] But the French get more than powerful, accountable public figures in their mayors: they also get a personal representative in government. Tatham was intimately involved in the lives of his citizens. 'If anything goes wrong or if there's any sort of problem they come and see me.'[26] He remembers getting a call one Christmas Eve. 'We were eating the Christmas meal and suddenly the telephone rang. Somebody told us that an enormous wall to the castle had fallen on the main road,' which in the village was fairly narrow. As it was Christmas, the normal road and municipal workers weren't around, 'so we all trundled off there,' Tatham recalls, 'and picked up the stones to make a small passage for at least one car to get by.' Even though this fell outside his 'official' duties, Tatham happily helped out. Life might sometimes be difficult for *Monsieur le maire*, but the advantage of the French system is that if something goes wrong, there's someone down the road who, if not directly responsible, is at least there to help. Residents have a human connection with the state: 'They know someone's listening,' Tatham says.

Big government disasters

We've seen how government tends to be focused on the wrong priorities – numbers rather than people – and we've seen how government tends to go about things the wrong way, failing to put people at the centre of the policymaking process. These are deep and important flaws. But there's something deeper still. A flaw that can't be corrected by a change of focus or a new approach. A flaw that is structural.

The biggest problem with government today is that the people making the decisions are too far from the people affected by them. Government is too big, too distant. The UK has one of the most centralised governments in the world: to an absurd and counterproductive degree, things are run from the centre. Britons have no Ken Tatham at the local level (or any level for that matter). While in France the average size of the population in the lowest tier of executive government is 1,500,[27] in the UK it is 150,000.[28] As a result, our connection with the state is inhuman: bossy letters; demands for payment of taxes; maddening bureaucracy if you want to do the simplest thing. Who can name their councillor? Or the leader of their council? Or their MP? Or pretty much anyone in government apart from the famous faces at the very top?

As a result, accountability is fuzzy – lying with endless obscure bits of government and bureaucracies with multiple overlapping responsibilities that are not clearly defined, least of all to the people who matter most: citizens. Decisions about – and crucially, funding for – local services are determined in London as ministers and officials in central government, rather than local leaders, dictate city, town, village, even neighbourhood-level policies.

Here is a comically bizarre example of the British state's staggering centralisation. Tony Blair's government had the perfectly reasonable aim of wanting people in hospital to eat better food. So they hired television celebrity Loyd Grossman, former presenter of the BBC's *MasterChef*, to advise on menus. Among other things, Grossman asked the Secretary of State for Health to require that henceforth, all macaroni cheese served in the National Health Service should be 'four-cheese macaroni cheese'. I am prepared to believe that four-cheese macaroni cheese is better than the single-cheese variety; but I am not prepared to accept that the number of cheeses in every pasta dish in every hospital in the country should be decided by a minister in London.

When decisions are made by those out of touch with the reality on the ground, the outcomes are worse: policy aims are not met, money is wasted, and people feel increasingly disconnected from, frustrated with, and unable to have a say in, their government. (Just one in five British voters thinks government acts in their best interests.)[29] Big, centralised government – a relic of the bureaucratic age – is one of the main reasons for the growing distrust of and dissatisfaction with politics. Ministers pretend they can solve every problem and never do; on the occasions when things go right, it's often just luck. Bloodless bureaucrats puff up ministerial egos with unrealistic assurances of impact and effectiveness that typically turn to dust – but only after a reshuffle has moved the minister on and the same civil servants can agree with the new boss how ridiculous it all was in the first place. Systems designed in the pre-telephone age, never mind the pre-Internet age, creak and crumble with the strain of keeping up with the expectations of citizens who want to be in control, not controlled from on high. The whole centralised farce, played out year after year, parliament after parliament, government after government: Labour, Conservative, coalition – people see little difference whoever is notionally in charge because little underneath, in the structure of government, actually changes.

But there is one thing that has changed: our ability to do something about it. Thanks to the information revolution, technology and innovation, we really can take power out of the hands of centralised, bureaucratic government and place it where it belongs – in the hands of the people. If we are going to see any transformational improvement in the way we live, in our economy, in our society, then power must be dispersed.

***

The hubris of big, bureaucratic government has grown to the point at which its self-inflicted catastrophes are now clearly undermining support for government itself. It used to be said that centralised government is more efficient. Occasionally, yes. There are obviously certain public policy objectives that are best handled at the national level. Localising our foreign policy doesn't make much sense. But many problems that beset government arise precisely because they are handled at the wrong scale. This is most obviously the case when it comes to the contracting out of enormous parts of the state to external organisations, often in the private sector. But the problem is not the contracting out: it's the size of the contracts.

In *The End of Big*, Nicco Mele identifies 'nerd disease', in which technical experts make things needlessly complicated in order to justify their own maintenance services. He describes consulting for a business that had an online staff in one building and another team in a warehouse across the street shipping orders. The company wanted to integrate the computer systems for the two sides of the business, and the technical staff were advising the CEO to spend $1 million on a contract with an external supplier. Instead, Mele suggested something different: simply have someone walk between the buildings twice a day with the orders.[30]

As expensive as nerd disease is when things go according to plan, it is even worse when they go wrong. The ramifications tend to be massive. Instead of a small local failure, it's national and affects everyone in the system, often all at once. And because bureaucrats and contractors are reluctant to inform superiors of problems (to protect themselves politically), they often only become apparent when it's too late. Consequently, big government contracts end up mired in waste, failure, fraud and abuse.[31]

In Britain, we had a potent example with the NHS National Programme for IT. Tony Blair wanted to reform the NHS, and among his perfectly admirable goals was to make it more patient focused, with best practice spread around the system. Blair decided in 2002 to build a single electronic network that would store patients' records centrally and make them accessible to doctors and hospitals across the NHS. Conceptually, that's an important idea. As we will see, electronic patient records are a crucial step in delivering a more human approach to healthcare. But the attempt to implement this idea through a big national contract? Problems soon arose.

It all started with nerd disease. The Department of Health was ill-equipped for such an ambitious project, so it hired a number of consultants, one of whom, Richard Granger, formerly of Deloitte, took over completely. The first mistake was to nationalise the project; the NHS would manage it centrally. This would be overseen by Granger through a new agency called Connecting for Health (CFH). But building the project became too difficult. Over five years, the project's cost estimates ballooned from an initial £2.3 billion contract to £6.2 billion to £12.4 billion.[32] In a 2006 interview with the *Financial Times*, Lord Warner, the health minister in charge of the project, admitted that the costs could reach as high as £20 billion.[33] Meanwhile, despite delays, the withdrawal of major contractor Accenture from the project and significant technical problems when the system was delivered, Granger, the politicians, and other bureaucrats involved maintained their support for CFH. Political scientists Anthony King and Ivor Crewe observe in *The Blunders of Our Governments* that Granger 'was keen not only on succeeding but on being seen to succeed'. Contractors didn't want to incur penalties, and politicians didn't want to lose the political capital they had invested in the scheme.[34]

By 2007 Granger was out, but it would take another four years before CFH was put out of its misery. Even after the project was shut down the costs kept mounting, and the latest estimate of its lifetime costs was £9.8 billion, after years of wasted effort and multiple failures.[35] What a terrible waste of money. Regardless of Granger's competence, the true problem was the sheer scale of the project. The Blair government expected the NHS to build one of the most ambitious IT systems anywhere, without trials or pilot projects, without significant feedback from doctors and healthcare workers, and with little technical capacity.[36] While the project succumbed to a combination of all of these difficulties, the scale of the failure can be singularly attributed to needless centralisation. After all, the bigger the project, the harder the fall.

The trouble with bureaucracy running amok in this way is that it has the unfortunate tendency to keep running amok. During the twentieth century, as we turned to the state to organise vast new areas of activity – education, health, welfare – we tolerated bureaucracy in order to achieve scale and efficiency. But once the ball started rolling, bureaucracy begot more bureaucracy; government grew larger and more distant. To this day governments follow the same basic formula, choosing distance and centralisation for the sake of assumed – but rarely demonstrated – efficiency, all at the expense of accountability.

A powerful mayor in every town

To democratise the levers of power (and restore faith in politics and government), we need a total transformation of our political system into one that operates on a human scale. Margaret Thatcher's government is perhaps the sole example in recent British political life of such a radical structural shift. Believing that state control of industry was holding the country's economy back, she privatised (among others) British Gas, Jaguar, British Telecom, British Aerospace, British Steel, British Airways and BP, and deregulated many other industries, including finance and energy. She wanted to 'give power back to the people', she said. Whether you support or oppose her agenda, she clearly effected a major transformation in the role of the state. But while she may have decentralised economic power through policies like the promotion of home and share ownership, she was not exactly radical when it came to dispersing political power. Indeed, the Conservative governments of the 1980s and 1990s have been accused of exactly the opposite: of centralising power by taking policy discretion and funding away from local councils and giving central government increased control over local budgets, rules and development. So while Thatcher demonstrated that radical change is possible, she also symbolised the work that still needs to be done.

We need to make government and public services more accountable, more transparent and more effective by applying the techniques and innovations that have transformed many consumer markets in recent years, with higher and higher levels of user control and service quality. Government needs to be small, nimble and above all more local. Some policy areas – monetary policy, the armed forces, foreign affairs – are by necessity a national endeavour. But the vast majority – welfare, education, healthcare, social services, planning, conservation, policing, economic development – can and should be delivered locally. We need to devolve to the human scale.

The most human possible scale is that of individual people and their families. Alan Milburn, the former Labour Health

Secretary, remembers at nine years old coming home one day to his council flat and finding the door painted yellow; in the morning it had been red. 'The colour wasn't chosen by my mum. Nor by my granddad. It was chosen by the council – but they didn't live in that house, and we did.'[37] This story shows that the best possible decentralisation is directly to people themselves, so they can make as many of the decisions that affect their lives as possible. That is typically how the richest and most powerful members of society live, and we should want those same freedoms for everybody.

Where individual control is not possible, where collective provision and decision-making are required, we need government. And the first step towards a less centralised, more human structure for government starts right where we began this section: with mayors. A directly elected local leader is recognisable, accountable and responsive. Whoever put faith in a committee? Mayoral government is more human. It is also more pragmatic; often non-partisan, mayors are doers. They might nominally identify with one party but their typical concerns are fixing street lights, not bloviating about political controversies. They focus on getting things done because they literally have to live with the results. Making the buses punctual, the parks clean and the city centre thrive might not inspire intellectual debate in newspaper opinion pages but they're the stuff of everyday life: they are what matter to most people.

Of course, it's not enough simply to have a mayor. Mayors must have real power. Somewhat ironically (given that in our over-centralised country pretty much everything is decided in London), while London does have a mayor, he or she has comparatively little power to wield or budget to deploy. It's better than nothing, and it's encouraging to see more power being devolved to Manchester (with a mayor for the metropolitan region and more control over health, social care and business taxes), but most cities and towns in the UK don't have directly elected executive mayors. You might say that some of England's largest cities had the chance to move to a mayoral system of local government, and they said no in referendums held in 2012.[38] Of course people said no. They were not offered the kind of strong mayors seen in other developed countries, an institution with real power to drive change and manage policy effectively at the local level.

America's system is a great example. Mayor Michael Bloomberg of New York implemented a radical school reform programme, made aggressive fiscal reforms to balance the budget, and took bold steps for public health like banning smoking in public areas and trans fats in restaurants. He was a prodigious policy innovator – whether in developing new ideas for tackling poverty, greening the city, or encouraging volunteerism and philanthropy. While Bloomberg certainly had policy misses, he was able to use his influence as a single accountable figure to take the courageous but unpopular decisions an anonymous council would never make, such as confronting teachers' unions or challenging religious bigotry.[39]

It's not just in America. Mayor Bertrand Delanoë of Paris saw the success of Lyon's bike-sharing programme and started Paris Vélib', now the second largest such system in the world. And it goes beyond big cities, too. In France 80 per cent of mayors are responsible for fewer than 1,000 residents each,[40] but they still have local policy discretion.

Even in Britain, this is not a new or foreign idea. It's the more recent centralisation that's out of place. Strong civic leaders appear throughout the histories of Britain's greatest cities. Joseph Chamberlain, a nineteenth-century mayor of Birmingham, perhaps represents the pinnacle of British localism. He provided the big, simple things local people needed – like clean water, natural gas and education (he campaigned for universal schooling). But he also knew that it took more than that to truly nourish a community, and actively sought to provide access to art through museums, and learning through the foundation of the University of Birmingham. In Victorian Liverpool, Sir Archibald Salvidge, chairman of the local Conservative Party, was known as the 'King of Liverpool'. He used his influence to build the Mersey Tunnel, connecting the city with Birkenhead, in the hope of revitalising its port. Salvidge worked to find the funding for the project, which became a symbol of the feats cities could accomplish on their own. Liverpool under Salvidge (like Birmingham under Chamberlain) benefited from investing in public assets, public transport, and electric and gas companies. Salvidge knew that these investments paid for themselves, and the Liverpool Corporation, buttressed by the strong local government led by Salvidge and others, was able to pay for a revitalisation of the city, including comprehensive public housing for 140,000 people (15 percent of the population) and a transport system that connected the city to the suburbs.[41]

Decentralising power is not just about the principle of control or the practice of pragmatism. It is also the best way to generate and test new ideas. In the United States, experimentalism is seen as a critical part of localism. Governors at state level and mayors at municipal level pioneer fresh approaches and policies that get adopted elsewhere in America and sometimes the world over. Former San Francisco Mayor Gavin Newsom is a great example. In 2004, he used his local executive power to preside over the first gay marriage in America. It prompted years of public debate, referenda and legal wrangling – but the result is one of the biggest social changes in history, with the legalisation of gay marriage sweeping across the United States and the world. That incredible, liberating revolution began in earnest with the conviction of an assertive mayor. President Obama's healthcare plan was based on the reforms of Mitt Romney, Massachusetts' former governor. The mayor of Providence, Rhode Island, Angel Taveras, won the Mayor's Challenge (a prize established by Mike Bloomberg to encourage local civic innovation) for his initiative Providence Talks, which helps poor children, who hear millions fewer words during childhood than their more affluent peers – hampering cognitive development – to close the 'word gap'. Providence Talks is a groundbreaking early-childhood intervention programme in which parents wear devices that record how many words they say on a daily basis and receive regular advice on how better to talk to their children. The idea is to establish a model that other places can follow. In America, in areas as diverse as civil rights, education, the legalisation of medical and recreational marijuana, environmental protection, assisted suicide, food safety, even the regulation of drones ... change often starts at the bottom and trickles upwards. It's even true in Japan, where the most recent advance in gay rights has come from a district in central Tokyo, Shibuya Ward, which announced in February 2015 that it would give same-sex couples the same legal rights as married heterosexual couples – a major step forward in a country that while tolerant of homosexuality, grants gay couples relatively few rights.[42]

Can anyone in the UK name a single modern-day policy or innovation that began at the local level? For all the problems of US government and politics, America has at least one thing right: for the best results, policy innovation cannot happen in a vacuum, and it cannot all come from the top. This role of local jurisdictions as 'laboratories of democracy', articulated by Supreme Court Justice Louis Brandeis and based on the Tenth Amendment of the US Constitution, might be an American creation but its applicability is universal. We should bring it to the UK.

MVG: minimum viable government

Strong mayors are just the beginning. In Silicon Valley there is an overused cliché about when to launch your start-up that nevertheless contains an element of wisdom: *minimum viable product*, or 'MVP'. It means you should get your business idea out in front of real customers as quickly as possible. If you wait until your product is perfect before you launch it, you're too late. Hence, MVP: the smallest, simplest version of your idea that might possibly work. When it comes to public policy our rule should be MVG – minimum viable government. To avoid the pitfalls of big, bureaucratic, inhuman government, we should always aim to decentralise power. Ideally, this would be directly to people themselves so they can make as many of the decisions that affect their lives as possible. Power – and budgets – should be devolved to the level that is just large enough to be practical.

This would vary for different areas of policy: it is of course impractical, indeed impossible, to decentralise everything. The key to dispersing power effectively is the rather wonkish term, subsidiarity, which means devolving power to the lowest possible level. It is supposed to be the operating principle of the EU – a claim that is rightly met with hollow laughter in most quarters. But it makes sense in theory and is a good guide for Minimum Viable Government. For example, when it comes to the regulation of ozone-depleting chemicals, arms control, or (as we'll see later) meaningful animal-welfare rules, MVG is the international level. For policy areas like immigration, or product safety standards, it's the national level. For urban transport and economic development, it's the city (or metropolitan region). And throughout any decentralised system, there will need to be some kind of fair redistribution of resources. But in a wide range of policy areas – especially social policy – we can decentralise power much further than anything we've seen in recent political history.

To determine how far to decentralise, there is a clue in evolutionary biology. British anthropologist Robin Dunbar found that based on the size of our neocortex, humans can only have around 150 meaningful relationships at once, and that villages and hunter-gatherer societies worked best at a median population of this size.[43] This has been extrapolated by others to include work settings and other groups. In Sweden, for example, the heads of the tax authority are using the idea of 'Dunbar's Number' to restructure the organisation, reasoning that if you can't know more than 150 people, you can't work well with more than that number either.[44] W.L. Gore & Associates, the innovative materials company, builds a new office each time an existing one is about to exceed 150 people.[45] I'm not proposing that we carve up the world into governing units of 150 people. But I mention Dunbar's number because it shows how low we can go if we really want to understand 'human scale'.

When it comes to government, the closest viable unit to this scale – the level at which people can realistically know and interact with their leaders and decision-makers on a direct human basis – is the neighbourhood. This might not comprise as few as 150 people, but it's certainly not as many as 150,000 (the average number living in the lowest tier of executive government in the UK today).[46] The neighbourhood is a vivid expression of the concept of Minimum Viable Government, and more policy could be run at that level than you might think. Parks – obviously. Schools? Certainly – especially if we make our school system more human, along the lines set out in the next chapter. How about social services? Or welfare? Some aspects of these services, unlikely as it may sound, are actually ideal candidates for devolution to the neighbourhood level. They are intensely personal, human services, absolutely demanding the kind of empathetic approach described earlier in this chapter. Neighbourhood governance goes with the grain of human history, traditions and behaviour. It's our neighbourhoods and our villages that we identify as our communities. And in the future, technology could help make neighbourhood governance more realistic, with services like Nextdoor – a kind of Facebook for your neighbourhood – offering new and convenient ways to bring people together in a community at the local level.

Localism will face inevitable challenges. People talk about the dangers of a 'postcode lottery' – as if everything was uniform (and uniformly good) under centralisation. There's a postcode lottery *now*. At least with proper decentralisation (of power and budgets) local people would be in control: instead of a postcode lottery, postcode power. Others point to local government scandals like the sex-abuse case in Rotherham and say: 'See – look what happens when power becomes entrenched and unaccountable in a local one-party state.' Yes, but that's like saying we should condemn cars because there are car accidents; it's actually an argument for dispersing power more, not less.

It seems that everyone in government is in favour of devolution as far as their level, but no further. (If you're at the top, that's not very far.) But radical localism is an essential step towards a more human system of government. If more power is devolved, those in control will be members of the community, not far-off rulers. No more faceless committees: local politicians will actually know their constituents (like Mayor Ken Tatham in Saint-Céneri-le-Gérei) and therefore, as the writer Nassim Taleb has argued, be less likely to be wasteful or corrupt. It's harder to betray your community's interests if you have to live with the consequences, right there among the residents. Instead of decisions being made in distant Whitehall or even the council chamber, which can often feel just as distant, decisions for communities will be made *by* communities *in* communities. Not only would this improve the quality of policymaking, make government more responsive, and help citizens feel better represented – it would be harder for special interests to game the system, for lobbyists to buy the outcomes they want, and for mistakes to have such devastating consequences.

Pedants might say: 'How are you going to implement all the ideas in your book – including the decentralisation of power – without a strong central government to push it all through? It's contradictory.' No, it isn't. It's just a question of sequencing. Of course it's true that it would require bold central government action to bring about the decentralisation that Britain needs. Just as it's true that many recommendations in this book would require strong central government leadership or enforcement, even after decentralisation of many political powers had taken place. The principle of Minimum Viable Government doesn't mean everything should be decentralised, but spurious arguments like these are often thrown up as distractions by those who basically think nothing should be decentralised. It's always easiest to stick to the status quo and conjure fears of the 'chaos' that radical change would bring. But only radical change is enough to deal with the deep problems our democracy now faces.

Positive deviants

Sometimes, however, the most human (and most radical) thing government can do is realise that people can solve their own problems and get out of the way when it's prudent to do so. One particular expression of this idea holds great potential: the power of positive deviance.

In 1990 Jerry and Monique Sternin, workers for the charity Save the Children, moved to Vietnam to set up a programme to fight child malnutrition in poor rural villages. While conducting surveys to understand the scope of the issue they grew curious about the handful of children who, despite coming from families as poor as all the others, were perfectly healthy – *the positive deviants*. What were these kids doing differently? If they could discover behaviours that enabled even the most materially deprived parents to raise healthy children, the implications would be tremendous. They found that *all* the parents of the positive deviants collected tiny shell pieces from crabs, snails and shrimp from rice paddy fields and added them to their children's diet along with the greens from sweet potato tops. *None* of the other families did. Both these ingredients, though free and available to anyone for the taking, were commonly considered to be inappropriate, if not dangerous, for children and so were generally excluded from their diets. In addition, in five of the six positive deviant homes, parents were abnormally hygienic. Another difference: parents would generally feed their kids twice a day (before and after work in the fields). Parents of the positive deviants, however, instructed caregivers to feed their children regularly throughout the day. Though total daily calories were no different, because of the small stomach size of children under three, those with multiple meals were absorbing up to twice the nutrition with the same amount of food.

These findings enabled aid workers to set up home-grown educational programmes that passed on the lessons to other parents. The beauty is that the solution required no more resources than the villagers *already* had. The answers to the problem were right there in the community with the people who lived there.[47] Imagine if we designed our domestic policy programmes with a 'positive deviance' approach. Imagine if policymakers went to the very populations they were trying to help to find not just problems but solutions as well. Near where I live, in Oakland, California, a project called the Family Independence Initiative (FII) is doing just that.

Part of the problem of poverty, according to FII's founder Mauricio Lim Miller, is that government defines poor people by their problems, neglecting – and even inhibiting – what they're already doing well. So at FII, staff are explicitly *forbidden* to advise families or give them ideas. For 'helpful' people (as social workers tend to be), this is a very difficult – sometimes impossible – impulse to control. But stepping back is essential, as it creates a vacuum that families fill with their *own* ideas. 'The best and most culturally relevant solutions are embedded in community,' Lim Miller explains, 'and people build and strengthen their social networks when they look to friends and neighbours who have successfully faced similar challenges.'[48] FII provides income support on the condition that its clients record and make steps toward achieving basic goals on issues like income, debt, health, education and relationships and that families meet once monthly to discuss their goals. Staff are allowed only to ask open-ended questions like: 'What do you think should be done?' and 'Do you know of anyone who successfully did what you want to do? Can you ask them for help?'[49]

According to Lim Miller, 'When we respect families to lead their own change and give them access to resources the way middle- and upper-class people access them, they begin to transform their lives.' It wasn't easy: families used to the traditional (literal) give and take of welfare programmes were looking for direction from FII staff. After they received none, they started to share goals, then ideas. Sometimes it was clear that families were on their way to making a mistake.

Jorge and Maria-Elena were a recent immigrant couple, refugees from El Salvador's civil war. After seven months of meetings, in which Jorge and Maria-Elena had mostly talked about their health and their children's education, they declared they were going to buy a home. A Spanish-speaking real estate broker had promised them they could buy a house in their neighbourhood, and friends would help them meet the down payment. It took all the self-control Lim Miller and his staff could muster to stop themselves from 'saving' the couple from what was – obviously to them – not going to be a rosy situation. But rather than intervene, Lim Miller told his staff to track them and simply accept that people had to make their own mistakes. The house was purchased, and the broker made his commission. But Jorge and Maria-Elena were now saddled with a mortgage that was 65 per cent of their income. Losing the house seemed all but inevitable. Lim Miller felt bad, and his staff were upset they had let this happen.

But that's when the couple surprised them. 'We had assumed the family was clueless,' Lim Miller recalls, 'but at some point they had recognised that they were in over their heads. They had included a refinance clause in their mortgage.'[50] With the help of their friends, they renovated it, increasing its value so they could refinance the house and bring their mortgage down to 40 per cent of their income. 'From that point on,' says Lim Miller, 'I promised myself that I would try to avoid underestimating people's ability to solve their own problems.' (The couple still own their home, by the way.)

What makes this story interesting is the ripple effect that an organic, human success story has on others in the community. Now Jorge and Maria-Elena's friends knew what to do – and not to do – to buy a house. Two months after the refinancing everyone started saving more because they wanted to buy a home too, just like their friends. Within eighteen months the four other families in their FII cohort had purchased homes, but without using the predatory broker. By helping families find other families who succeed in overcoming problems associated with poverty, Lim Miller is building a self-perpetuating platform from which the working poor don't just walk away with lessons learned but also inspiration.

The results are clear: household incomes of the initial twenty-five families increased by nearly a third after two years. Moreover, 40 per cent had bought new homes within three years.[51] A year after the programme's income support payments ceased, household income still increased (now 40 per cent higher than baseline).[52] After extending the programme to San Francisco, the numbers continued to impress: among families there, in two years household income increased by an average of 20 per cent, half of school-age children showed improvements at school, and three of five households reduced their debts. The initiative has since expanded to Hawaii and Boston, where within one year of its operations incomes increased 13 per cent.[53] 'When you come into a community that is vulnerable with professionals with power and preset ideas, it is overpowering to families and it can hold them back,' according to Lim Miller. 'But the focus on need undermines our ability to see their strengths – and their ability to see their own strengths.'[54]

Lim Miller found that when people – even if just at the neighbourhood level – are given a bit of responsibility over their lives, a bit of power, they wield it well. It's a lesson we need to apply throughout our system of government. We need to find ways to give power back to the people who can use it most effectively.

We've grown used to government that doesn't seem to respond to our needs. It seems to worry about the problems of someone else, somewhere else. When it does touch us, it seems endlessly bureaucratic. Government is not and should not be the solution for every problem. But where it is necessary, there is no reason for it to be so aloof and unresponsive. The imperative to shake it up is urgent. And our opportunity to initiate the kind of big change we need is right before us, with the commitment of all parties to the decentralisation of power following 2014's Scottish independence referendum. If we don't use this chance to dismantle our antiquated, sclerotic, bureaucratic-age state and put something more human in its place, we will pay a heavy price: the guarantee of still more years of government underperformance and political discontent.

Those who serve in the public sector have an awesome responsibility; most are genuinely public spirited and well intentioned. Let's unshackle them from the structures that inhibit them. Let's change the accounting structures so we design policy for the long term, solving problems at their root causes. Let's change the working structures so we design policy based on real people's needs. And let's decentralise power, bring it closer to people, and put it directly in people's hands when we can.

If we do all this, we will certainly make government more human. We might even make it more popular.

CHAPTER 3

SCHOOLS

South Korea's education record is the envy of reformers around the world, with its students consistently topping international league tables. Korean students do well in tests, because preparing for tests is all they do. The competitive culture of Korean schools, in which all the students in a given class are ranked against one another, and the culture of Korean families, which equates academic success with family honour, means that when a student falls behind in class rankings, families pull out all the stops to ensure success. They might hire tutors or nag them to study. Or they might just send them to a *hagwon*. Hagwons are, according to Korean journalist and academic Se-Woong Koo, 'soulless facilities, with room after room divided by thin walls, lit by long fluorescent bulbs, and stuffed with students memorising English vocabulary, Korean grammar rules, and maths formulas. Students typically stay after regular school hours until 10 p.m. or later.'[1] According to Koo, who taught at one of these schools for a time, Korean students might succeed in the tests, but they suffer elsewhere. Koo remembers how his students lost clumps of hair, hardly slept, and were even suicidal (like half of Korean teenagers).[2] Suicide is in fact the leading cause of death for South Koreans aged fifteen to twenty-four.[3]

By most measures Palo Alto, California, is a stunning success story. One of the wealthiest municipalities in America, it lies at the centre of Silicon Valley, is adjacent to Stanford University, and has some of the nation's best schools and recreation. But Palo Alto residents have another activity: volunteers patrol the railroad tracks. They aren't crossing guards, nor are they trying to stymie some crime epidemic. They're trying to prevent the community's children from killing themselves.

'When it comes to tangible measures of success, I think a town's teen suicide rate is the better indicator than the number of kids with top grades or SAT scores.'[4] Julie Lythcott-Haims is a Palo Alto parent with a unique perspective on American youth: for many years she was the dean of freshmen at Stanford. And although Palo Alto's children are among the brightest in the country, they kill themselves at an alarming rate.[5] 'Here in Silicon Valley success seems to be admission to Stanford, a start-up by the time you're a late teen or in your twenties, maybe a Tesla in your driveway,' says Lythcott-Haims, who has now written a best-selling book on the subject.[6] 'We have these trappings of success that we inadvertently ask our children to aim for when in fact it's the narrowest possible definition. And then we measure their accomplishment towards those goals by things like standardised tests. A score that is in the 99th percentile nationally is only in the 75th percentile in Palo Alto, and yet Palo Alto is a community that expects excellence of its kids. So even those who on a national scale are achieving on the highest possible level are made to feel mediocre here because it's virtually impossible for a child to distinguish themselves. This culture breeds in our kids a sense of hopelessness – that they'll never somehow make it from the 75th percentile into the 80th, 90th, and so on.'

Palo Alto is obviously an extreme case, but it is not unique: all across America and in Britain too, the entire basis of the school system is driving our sons and daughters to conform to a single, outdated version of education 'success' – and it's ruining their lives. 'Colleges like Stanford seem to demand of a young person that they have a singular noteworthy achievement by age seventeen,' says Lythcott-Haims. 'It's become more and more of an arms race. Look at what we ask kids to do. And yet kids are chronologically the same as I was twenty years ago, and there's still only 168 hours in the week … Kids try to do what they think is necessary in order to be successful, to meet their parents' approval and their community's standards. But to do so, they are mortgaging their childhood.'[7]

This, it seems, is what it we are striving for. It is inhuman.

Khan Lab School

Jason Pittman didn't begin his professional life as a teacher. He started his own tech company, but when he found himself rushing home from work to get to his volunteer teaching gig, he realised it was time for a career switch. So he went to graduate school and soon afterwards took a position teaching fifth graders at a public elementary school in Alexandria, Virginia, a suburb of Washington, DC. 'I had such a wide variety of student need,' Pittman recalls. 'More than half our families lived below the poverty line. But we also had quite a few that were fairly well-to-do. We had first-generation immigrant families that were just getting started in the United States, and we had parents who were lobbyists on Capitol Hill.[8]

'I had a little girl from El Salvador … no English-language support at home. But she was reading out of a college geology textbook! She was so in love with understanding the Earth better. I had another who was ten years old. He had left Somalia and was in a refugee camp in Kenya. He came into my classroom not having spent a day in school in his life. According to the school district, I was supposed to be teaching him American history, fractions, reading comprehension … but none of it made any sense to him.' What frustrated Pittman was the curriculum's absurd rigidity. 'If I taught the fifth-grade lesson that was in the state's standardised curriculum, it was, no matter how hard I tried, the right lesson for absolutely nobody. I could make it an average lesson, but I could never really make it valuable to even one student in my class. There was such a wide variety.'

One day he tried something different. 'I pretty much threw up my hands and told the class: "I'm so sick of disappointing you every day – what would you like to do? What would be something fun we could just do together?" A couple of kids wanted to build a robot, so we got some NXC chips [NXC is a programming language used with Lego robotics] and put them on robotics parts. We had a couple of kids who were into gardening, so we got them in the garden. The girl from El Salvador who was into geology, she ended up lecturing the class on types of rocks and how they were formed. All of a sudden it was fantastic – my students were doing well by every way I could assess them, even on standardised tests, and I didn't even teach to the test!'

Pittman then started to run a programme aimed at preparing children for a science-orientated magnet school in the area. On a weekly basis he would teach science, maths and technology to all seven hundred students in his school, from pre-kindergarten to sixth grade. From the start Pittman diverged quickly from how science is typically taught. 'The traditional science-lesson format starts with the teacher giving a concept, then explaining how it all works. You give a bunch of step-by-steps to prove that what I told you at the beginning of the lesson is true, and then I ask you to write a conclusion verifying what I told you at the beginning. There's no science in that at all, obviously. So I dropped the cookbook-recipe science format. I just said, "Look, let's just rip out all the procedure pages from these lessons." I basically said, "Let's just play with this a while – let's tinker with it." And we used the question to actually get to the answer.'

Pittman's lab quickly became a sanctuary for bored students across the school. 'I left the lab open every day so they could come in and work on their projects,' he remembers. 'They could come down and work in the garden, work in the lab, and build their robot or their rocket or whatever it was they were excited about.' Once again, it worked. Pittman's low-income students were closing the gap with their better-off peers. He was so successful that he's since won multiple national teacher-of-the-year awards. First Lady Michelle Obama visited his 13,000-square-foot educational garden, and he was twice selected as an 'educator-at-sea' for *National Geographic,* joining oceanographic explorer Dr Robert Ballard (discoverer of the *Titanic*) on board his vessel E/V *Nautilus* to conduct lessons from maritime expeditions.

But then, out of the blue, Pittman's programme was cut from the school's budget. Eliminated entirely. 'It was so frustrating. I felt like I'd proven that we have a better way here, and we can actually serve kids and not serve tests.' But that's not what the school was interested in. His methods couldn't be tested or quantified or regulated, so when the budget tightened, it was his programme that was cut. Thankfully a group of local business owners and parents got together and started a charity specifically to raise money for his programme. It was an imperfect solution, though. Pittman went from teacher to perpetual fundraiser. 'Every year I had to be a part of the advocacy, making speeches at fundraisers, raising my own salary. And I was still getting the same pressure to help kids practise multiple-choice tests.'

So here was a teacher, recognised on a national level and achieving incredible results for low-income students, being forced to spend his free time raising the money to pay his own wages (which were, in any case, being systematically cut). He'd had enough. During an appearance on the public radio show *This American Life*, he described how he went to the Pentagon to receive a science-teaching award and then got back home to find another pay cut. 'My frustration sort of hit a peak,' he recalls. After talking to the host Ira Glass about what was going on, Pittman announced, on air, that he couldn't do it any more. 'As it turned out, making yourself available in front of two million people is not a bad way to find something else!'

A couple of months later the phone rang. It was Sal Khan, the hedge-fund analyst turned social entrepreneur who founded Khan Academy, one of the world's most popular online learning platforms. 'I had been using Khan Academy in my classroom, so I thought it might be a joke.' It wasn't. Khan wanted to start a school – a prototype for the school of the future, one that could literally help every school in the world teach children in a more human – and more effective – way. And Pittman would be just the right person to help it get going.

Khan Lab School is that prototype. Launched in September 2014 with a handful of children, it's a year-round, mixed-age, mixed-gender 'one-room-schoolhouse'. It is 'mastery-based' and free of grade levels and grade assessments, meaning that each child moves at a pace that's right for them. They aren't advanced just because the calendar says so. As Pittman explains, 'We were trying to get kids to practise a certain skill until they can demonstrate it at a proficient level.'

At Khan 'traditional' academic learning manifests itself in lessons by the teachers – sometimes one-on-one, sometimes in small- to medium-sized groups – as well as computer-based tutorials from Khan Academy and Udacity (whose founder we'll meet in Chapter 9) that mix videos and exercises students work through at their own pace. But this is combined with something much more radical. The students always seem to be building things. Like a giant ribcage made out of cardboard, paper, and papier mâché. They could have learned about a ribcage with a diagram or by passing around a plastic model, but these students learned by building one – big enough for them to stand inside. The project started out with students thinking about ways in which they were similar to one another. They used an online course from Udacity to learn about the human genome, discovering that our organs and internal systems are largely the same, which led them to zero in on the ribcage.

Pittman's philosophy as a teacher is that students should be 'makers' as well as learners. 'There's a basic human desire to create things,' he says. 'If we can let that sit in the driver's seat, it will be much easier to get kids investing in their own education.' One of the experiments at Khan Lab School was to devote the afternoon to creation time. 'There's a high level of engagement because you're building these projects with groups of friends.' Contributing to their own learning in this way also 'eliminates the "When will I ever use this?" question,' says Pittman. '"Well, you'll use it this afternoon in the giant ribcage project," I tell them.' It's not just a free-for-all, of course: 'We curate the content behind the afternoon projects in the morning. There's knowledge acquisition, direct instruction, and practice in the morning, and then you're putting those skills to work in the afternoon.' For instance, to build the giant ribcage, his students applied the geometry they had been learning during morning lessons.

Self-directed projects like this aren't just a better way to engage students from hour to hour; they teach a broader set of skills that are essential to being a better learner overall, regardless of the subject. Traditional content areas – maths, writing, reading, communication, art, music and physical activity – are all important at Khan. But there's much more: teaching the skills that enable children to acquire knowledge themselves and, perhaps even more importantly, developing in them the intrinsic desire and motivation to do so. For over a century there has been a pervasive belief in education that you have to make children learn content in blocks of time, or 'lessons', as we know them. Forty-five minutes of maths, then English for forty-five minutes, and so on. The Khan Lab School philosophy is to turn this on its head – to replace the traditional 'extrinsically motivated' approach with a sense of independence and responsibility in the students themselves, with the freedom to choose what they work on when, what projects they choose to do, where to set things up, and so on. As Jessica Lahey writes in her book *The Gift of Failure*, 'The quickest way to kill off your child's interest in a game, topic, or experiment is to impose your will on her learning.'[9]

Although some students at Khan were at first not used to having so much ownership over what happens next or to having so much attention paid to things like 'perseverance', 'cooperation', and 'entrepreneurialism' alongside maths and science, they bought into it pretty quickly. 'Students have so much responsibility in everything – from setting up the furniture, setting up lunch every day, cleaning up … scheduling their own lessons if they think they need instruction. They're organising around what the learning tool should be. And it's wonderful,' says Pittman with a smile.

He is spot on. I know this first-hand. One of those kids he's talking about? He's my son Ben.

Acton Academy

If you want to see a school that is rethinking education even more radically, you should go – as Rohan and I did in 2012 – to the Acton Academy in Austin, Texas. We were intrigued by this new school we had heard about and wanted to see what lessons it might hold for school reform in Britain.

Acton Academy, a school for five- to sixteen-year-olds, focuses on teaching character, not content. Started in 2009 by Jeff Sandefer, a Texas energy entrepreneur who later went on to found one of the top business schools in America, Acton uses the Socratic Method: its teachers are 'guides' who facilitate 'journeys' and 'quests' for the students, who work with each other to learn organically. Sandefer rejects the idea that students should be *taught* anything, reasoning that only a few teachers can be the best at teaching a particular subject anyway. In order to 'learn to know', Sandefer uses games, activities and technology to inspire children to seek out information for themselves, in the process holding themselves accountable for their own learning.

His curriculum also emphasises 'learning to do'. Students take part in activities that build skills and give them real-world experience. In one instance, rather than read a story book or hear a lesson on the American Revolution, students dressed up in eighteenth-century colonial costumes and simulated for three days the situation in the run-up to the War of Independence. By putting themselves in the place of the American revolutionaries, they didn't learn just history but also how to solve problems, negotiate, and empathise with others. Such character traits are central to the third part of the curriculum, 'learning to be'. Students take part in long 'hero's journeys' that have many steps on the way to an end goal, for instance finding 'the world's greatest treasure' stolen by an 'evil sphinx'. Each week the students have to overcome a new challenge to get closer to their goal. Along the way they act, perform role play, and practise public speaking, creative-thinking, problem-solving, decision-making, and time management. These tasks inculcate honesty, patience and gratitude.

Jeff Sandefer's ultimate vision is for a school with no teachers at all, where the students run the place entirely, the older ones taking responsibility for the younger ones, and all children collectively taking responsibility for the entire running of its community life. The level of responsibility and empowerment given to Acton students is far greater than in any university I have ever heard of, yet they are six, seven, eight years old and, as Rohan and I saw when we visited, thriving in this extraordinarily bold, innovative school regime. We looked on as a plan was being developed for the next school year: the ideas and themes that the students would be exposed to. They included Karl Popper on the scientific method and Nassim Taleb on 'antifragility'. Anyone who thinks that a more human, progressive, innovative style of education lacks intellectual rigour had better think again.[10]

Now there are fifteen Acton schools, with eight more in the pipeline. After his year helping to set up Khan Lab School, Jason Pittman moved on, but the experimentation keeps going, and Ben is still thriving. Chris Chiang, the academic director of Khan Lab School, is in fact incorporating many aspects of the Acton approach in those experiments. As journalist Jason Tanz writes in his profile of the Khan Lab School in *Wired*, 'The point here isn't just to build a better school but to refine a model that other educators can build on – to change education across the country and the world.'[11]

Factory schools

The terrible truth about our education system today is that it is more like South Korea's – children with hair falling out from stress and the highest youth suicide rate in the world – than the Khan Lab School, whose children negotiate with their parents to stay on at the end of the school day. We have dehumanised our children's education. Schools treat students like statistics, mandating lesson plans across regions – even countries – to hit specified test results. We obsess over how our children rank compared to their peers, both at home and abroad. If they aren't 'falling behind' the Chinese or the Singaporeans, they are falling behind each other or even themselves. The fact that Palo Alto – with its intense pressure, mental illness, stress and suicides – is considered the pinnacle of our public education system is a harbinger of a serious problem.[12]

The regimented, top-down approach not only turns children off learning by treating them all the same; it also discourages teachers, the very people best positioned to respond to each child's learning needs. Industrialised, mechanised, centralised, today's education system is outdated and ineffective. Our children are mass produced in schools that are literally designed to resemble factories. This is a disastrous way to prepare children for their lives. It takes the creativity and individuality out of learning, forcing children into a common style instead of letting them evolve intellectually into independent-minded people. We need to leave behind the nineteenth-century mindset. It's time for more human schools.

The enthusiastic reaction to the documentary *Most Likely to Succeed*, a damning indictment of our factory school system, shows that people are starting to understand how destructive it really is.

The culture of tests is a big part of the problem. Measuring students' success by their performance in an academic test is superficial. It ignores the deeper learning that will actually help them thrive. Education policymakers' obsession with test scores, particularly in maths, is in part motivated by their own desire – need – to 'prove' the success of their policies. It's also a way of evaluating teachers. But the price children pay is relentless drilling and the neglect of unquantifiable skills that are actually – and increasingly – more important. Worse, if you examine the tests forensically, they fail even on their own terms.

Consider PISA, the Organisation for Economic Co-operation and Development's (OECD) Programme for International Student Assessment. It's the yardstick everyone uses. This might make some kind of sense if it were an effective yardstick. But it isn't. Politicians trumpet PISA scores as if they were a key factor in economic success, yet Germany and the United States, two leading global economies, lag behind countries like Vietnam and Poland.[13] Many assume that the PISA rankings are based on rigorous, statistical analysis of educational data from around the world. They're not. The scores are based on a one-off test taken by a tiny sample of children in each country. And the test itself is hopelessly flawed. It is long – two hours – and many students simply

don't finish.[14] Not all students are assigned all the questions
or even all the sections, so sometimes they are given a reading
or maths score without having answered a single reading or
maths question.[15] Considering its international scope, the test
obviously faces cultural challenges, but it totally fails to address
them: questions in different languages create inconsistencies
across countries, and some countries, particularly in Asia,
teach directly to the PISA test, whereas other countries
treat it as simply something that is done casually once a year
alongside whatever they're doing anyway. Questions used in
some countries are thrown out in others. The test also fails to
take into account disparities within a country. Using PISA tests
to drive our education policy is the height of irresponsibility.
You might as well use some random opinion poll.

Perhaps its biggest flaw is the 'headline factor'. No matter
how nuanced PISA's reports may be, it is the league tables
that get all the attention and drive headlines – and thus put
pressure on policymakers. This is the GDP of the education
world, the metric that drives all yet includes just a fraction
of what matters. Yes, maths is important. But because of
PISA, we focus on maths excessively. To succeed in the
twenty-first century economy, children need to learn to be
creative and collaborative; drilling them for tests fosters no
skill except memorisation, no character trait but individual
ambition. Obsessing over maths will not nurture adaptable
and entrepreneurial children but rather 'worker bots' who
are readily replaceable by technology. The culture of tests is
a fitting symbol for schools as factories, complete with bells,
separate facilities, and batches of children. Yes, the basics of
literacy, numeracy, history and science – subjects taught and
tested in factory schools – are important, but we also need to
focus on developing the skills that will enable our children to
succeed in a globalised, knowledge-based, rapidly changing

world. Success is no longer just about learning facts; it's about more human skills like empathy, self-regulation, conscientiousness, teamwork, resilience, problem solving, innovation and critical thinking – skills that will give children a platform on which to build a successful, happy life.

These 'twenty-first-century skills' reinforce each other. Teamwork has been shown not just to improve output, communication and planning but also – through increased engagement with others' ideas – to lead to even more learning and skills enhancement than going it alone.[16] Self-discipline has been shown to be more important than IQ in predicting academic performance.[17] And global CEOs consider creativity to be the most important leadership trait.[18] Factory schools that shame failure kill the impulse toward entrepreneurship and risk taking that we should most want to encourage. It also threatens the strength of our democracy: 'In any complex society, differences of opinion are inevitable,' Tony Wagner and Ted Dintersmith write in the book *Most Likely to Succeed*. 'But consider how differently our country might approach these problems if most citizens were equipped with the ability to critically analyse, collaborate, communicate, and creatively solve problems.'[19]

Our current education system is designed to ignore these vital skills. Creativity is consigned to art class. We say we're teaching critical thinking, but we test it with box-ticking exercises that have 'correct' answers, regardless of how thoughtful they are. We tell ourselves that students are allowed to plot their own intellectual journey, but really that just means choosing between chemistry and physics. And although we stress individual achievement, we forget the power of collaboration for success; humanity's most celebrated individuals almost all rely on (sometimes lesser-known) partners to achieve greatness.[20]

As the social policy commentator Jenni Russell points out, we have a generation of children learning how to take tests – an obsession that crowds out any focus on character development – with disastrous results:

> *On my son's first day in a state school reception class, skinny, pale Madison tugged at her mother's arm to ask a question and was told to f*** off. At the end of the day, four-year-old Wayne was left crying in the classroom as his mother, a Caribbean woman with a mysterious job, a council flat and a brand new 4x4, set the pattern for his school life by failing to pick him up.*

> *The school had no interest in dealing with these children's emotional states so they never flourished, despite sitting through hundreds of literacy and numeracy hours. They fought, swore, cried, failed to read and fell further behind with every passing year. By the time they were 14, both were truanting most of the time. Madison ended up with a couple of GCSEs and Wayne, who had joined a gang, with none. A dozen years of public investment in these children's education had been so badly focused that it had created two truculent, ignorant, helpless people.*[21]

This is no surprise if we look at what is considered 'success' by the system today. Schools have no incentive to think about social and emotional learning, character or twenty-first-century skills unless they serve the very instrumental function of improving test scores. No student is graded on grit, no teacher evaluated on how entrepreneurial their students are. A study undertaken by psychologists collaborating across Oxford, Cambridge and Exeter Universities shows that in schools, mindfulness, a calming technique based in Buddhism, reduces mental health problems, improves well-being, and makes children better students.[22] But it has no place in a factory school, in a world of tests.

All this is central to our arguments about inequality. 'If you care about equity, schools are the only place where you can expose every child to the same chances,' says Barbara Chow, an American education policy expert. That children not exposed to social and emotional learning outside school might not get it at all disadvantages them doubly: standardised tests have been shown to inherently disfavour less fortunate students.[23] The system seems insidious to Chow, who suspects 'it produces what it is designed to produce: it's a sorting mechanism that perpetuates social order.'[24] Every once in a while someone else gets through, and it's used as evidence that the system isn't rigged.

End the testing madness

We need to stop judging students and teachers by test scores. That doesn't mean abandoning tests entirely; used diagnostically, tests can help teachers track their students' progress, identify problem areas, and plan relevant lessons. They can also shed a light on inequity; civil rights leaders are strong supporters of standardised tests because they provide a way to compare poor black students in East London with their wealthy white counterparts in Notting Hill. Test scores can identify and highlight injustice. But as soon as testing becomes a basis on which to sort students or, worse, judge them, we induce a damaging rat race.

Instead of treating testing as the default method for organising or evaluating learning, educators should have to justify every standardised test they administer. First, any standardised test whose purpose is to rank students, evaluate and compensate teachers, or admit students to a school or college shouldn't exist. Any test that does exist should only serve some valuable human function like individual student diagnostics or giving policymakers an idea of disparities between schools (in which case, results might be anonymised). Even then, educators should do everything in their power to find alternative ways of fulfilling those functions – standardised tests should *always* be a last resort.

Trusting teachers

Putting tests back in their place is just the first step. We must also turn our attention to the school system's most human element. My friend and former colleague Michael Gove, the former UK education secretary, talks often about how the most powerful factor influencing the quality of education is the human part: the teacher. We have amazing people who enter the education world to share their gifts, and yet we shackle them, limiting their ability to do what they know is right, particularly through testing. 'Exams are like limits for the teachers,' says Sergio Juárez Correa, a somewhat rebellious – and, as a result, extraordinarily successful – schoolteacher in Mexico. 'They test what you know, not what you can do, and I am more interested in what my students can do.'[25]

Correa teaches at the José Urbina López Primary School in Matamoros. A border city of half a million, it's a grim place, at the crossroads of an interminable drug war. The school is built next to a rubbish dump and has been nicknamed *un lugar de castigo* – 'a place of punishment'. Here children are lucky to survive childhood, let alone dream of careers and success.

As you'd expect, Juárez Correa's students were disengaged from the official curriculum, which bored even him, and their test scores were correspondingly low. He was desperate to try something different. According to writer Josh Davis, who profiled Correa and his students in the magazine *Wired*, he voraciously read educational materials online, trying to find something to stimulate both him and his students. It was on one of these searches that he discovered the work of Sugata Mitra, an educational theorist in Britain who experimented with giving computers to children in poor countries and letting them direct their own learning experiences through online material and lectures. Mitra's work, rooted in the methods of educational reformers like Maria Montessori and Jean Piaget, took hold of Juárez Correa, and he resolved to try it in his classroom. Perhaps, he thought, this was what would shake him and his students from their stupor?

On 21 August 2011, Juárez Correa walked into class on the first day of the school year. He told the children that they had potential and that 'from now on, we're going to use that potential to make you the best students in the world.' His approach would be completely radical: he didn't have computers, but he could pose open-ended questions and give his students as much autonomy as possible to work out the answers. For instance, instead of explaining fractions, he wrote on the whiteboard '1 = 1.00' and then wrote '1⁄2 = ?' and '1⁄4 = ?' His training would suggest explaining the concepts of fractions; instead, using Mitra's methods, he stayed silent and let his students stew it over. He brought various coins in to help them work it out; the students noticed that two half-peso pieces were the same as four quarter-peso pieces, prompting a debate on the nature of what one-half meant. One student, Paloma Noyola Bueno, quickly understood and helped convince the other students of how fractions worked, counting out the *centavos* for each side of the pile.

This streak of brilliance in Paloma, it would turn out, was not a fluke. One of the great tragedies in the world is the inequality of opportunity for the multitude of bright children who never get a chance in education. It's not just tragic for them personally but for all of us: society will never gain from the gifts they have to offer. Whether through class barriers, infant mortality or poverty, many don't get the opportunity even to go to school. The students in Juárez Correa's class had it better than most: they were at least there. And he was curious about Paloma: she excelled at relatively simple tasks like the basic fractions exercise and then others way beyond that. One day he raised the bar to a seemingly impossible height. He told the story of Carl Friedrich Gauss, an eighteenth-century mathematician, who, as a student, had famously answered an extremely difficult question in just a minute: Juárez Correa thought he'd try the same question, not expecting anyone – even Paloma – to solve it. So he asked the class: What is the sum of every number between 1 and 100? Within a couple of minutes Paloma raised her hand: 'The answer is 5,050. There are 50 pairs of 101.' It was so simple, so elegant, but so advanced for a child of Paloma's age. Juárez Correa, awed, asked Paloma, who had until then showed no real love for maths, why she hadn't engaged before. 'Because no one made it this interesting,' she told him.

When national testing rolled around in June, Juárez Correa was anything but enthusiastic, but it had to be done. It was a good sign at least that his students breezed through it. Although Correa didn't put much stock in the results, even he was excited when he learned a few months later how good they were: the previous year 45 per cent had failed maths, and 31 per cent had failed Spanish. Those numbers had now dropped to 7 per cent and 3.5 per cent respectively. But it was the highest-achieving students who proved a real shock. Three placed in the 99.99th percentile for Spanish, ten at the same level for maths. Paloma had the highest score in the school: 921. When the school's assistant principal showed Juárez Correa the results, imagine his surprise when he moved the cursor over the high score for the region: it was 921. Then he moved it to the high score for the country. Paloma was the top maths student in Mexico.

Without Juárez Correa's experimentation, his students would not have succeeded; instead of being feted in Mexico City and in articles read around the world, Paloma Noyola Bueno might still be languishing next to a dump. Juárez Correa is the kind of teacher we need everywhere. We need to draw our most creative thinkers and doers from the rest of society into teaching as if it were the latest tech start-up. We need our superstars to be teachers, our teachers to be superstars (even if fame is not the result).

One of the reasons our system relies so much on tests is that we don't trust teachers. To see how successful a different, more human approach can be, we can look to Finland, home of one of the most successful – and decentralised – education systems in the world. The Finnish school system is a perfect example of subsidiarity. In Finland, schools are 'small-scale democracies', according to Finnish education scholar Pasi Sahlberg, with the only centralised aspects relating to professional requirements for teacher training and standards regarding learning outcomes (not teaching methods or test results). Teachers and school-level principals are given tremendous leeway in developing their own curricula, with the understanding that they know their own students and local conditions best.

In many circumstances policymakers would be concerned at placing such trust in education providers at a local level. Finnish officials solved this dilemma by putting only the very best people there to begin with. Good people don't need bureaucratic guidance to do what's right; they do what's right because responsibility lies with them and because they're good – and Finland is a land of unequivocally great teachers. Year after year Finland attracts all its new primary-teacher students from among the best graduates. To teach in Finland is so competitive that only one in every ten applicants is accepted for preparation. All Finnish teachers must earn a master's level degree that includes theories of pedagogy and is research based. The expectation is that teachers learn not just to teach but to learn – and innovate and share what they find out – for the remainder of their careers. Teaching in Finland is a highly respected professional career, akin to being a medical doctor, lawyer or architect (one poll even ranked teaching ahead of these three as being a 'dream profession').[26]

It's not just that having good teachers enables policymakers to trust teachers without testing their students to death; not having the tests is what attracts and keeps the best teachers in the first place. It's a 'culture of mutual trust', explains Sahlberg.[27] 'Although the pursuit of transparency and accountability provides parents and politicians with more information, it also builds suspicion, low morale, and professional cynicism.'[28] By the time they enter upper-secondary school, Finnish students will have *no* experience of taking high-stakes tests, progress instead being judged differentially by their teachers against students' respective characteristics and abilities.

So what happens when you let highly trained and respected teachers on the loose with no standardised tests to hold them accountable? You get a fantastic education system. Though most Finnish educators think PISA exams measure only a narrow band of what's important (one of the reasons they prefer no standardised testing is that it allows more time to be spent on 'non-core' subjects like art and music), the country scores exceedingly well on them, often placing first or second among other countries in maths, science and reading since the early 2000s. Yet Finnish fifteen-year-olds spend less time on homework (about thirty minutes per day) and in class than peers anywhere else.[29] And teachers spend almost five hundred fewer hours in the classroom per year than their American counterparts.[30] They understand that if quality is high and circumstances right, *less* teaching can mean *more* learning, as most students can only absorb so much in a passive lecture format anyway. They have to be out exploring, investigating and arguing with their peers.

In many fields it's taken for granted that only the best can join. Teaching should be one of them. We need to elevate its position in our society. We should pay teachers more, hold them in high regard, and then hold them to the high standards they deserve. We need to trust them, treat them like professionals. As we'll see in the next chapter, doctors and nurses are distracted from caring for their patients when bureaucracy becomes too burdensome. The same is true for teachers, who are subject to a huge number of regulatory and reporting requirements. If we respect our teachers, then instead of being recalcitrant labour unions, our teachers' associations could be an arbiter of professional quality like their counterparts in medicine, law and engineering. As leading British educational reformer Sir Anthony Seldon puts it, 'If teachers are to have the status of [these] other professions, they need to have a serious professional body at their head.'[31]

We could also trust students more. Instead of complicated, top-down systems for measuring teacher effectiveness – which aren't that useful anyway – why don't we just ask the students what's going on? One study found that asking students how much they agree or disagree with specific statements such as 'In this class, we learn to correct our mistakes' or 'My teacher wants us to share our thoughts' can tell you quite a lot. These questions allow for nuance; they are intentionally vague, which not only makes them harder to game but also, more importantly, levels the playing field between subjects that are easily quantified (maths) and those that aren't (teamwork).[32]

A more human way of evaluating teachers is ever more vital as we see a new threat of standardisation and centralisation coming over the horizon. Media companies like Pearson, Disney, McGraw-Hill, and Houghton-Mifflin Harcourt, some of which already own school textbook publishers, are also pushing into the classroom, leveraging education technology as a new sales and marketing strategy to get as many eyeballs as possible on their products.[33] Instead of repudiating the old factory model of standardised tests and all the depressing bureaucracy that surrounds them, these so-called reformers want more. In a Pearson report ominously titled 'Preparing for a Renaissance in Assessment', authors Peter Hill and Michael Barber, in a shockingly blunt embrace of the worst aspects of the factory-schools model, argue against teacher autonomy and in favour of top-down testing to put them in their place: 'Without such a systematic, data-driven approach to instruction, teaching remains an imprecise and somewhat idiosyncratic process that is too dependent on the personal intuition and competence of individual teachers.'[34] This desire – mania, really – to produce endless data, fed by tests, is pure centralisation. Uber-centralisation, where teachers are the problem and tests are the answer, where testing is a 'solution' not to the pedagogic challenge of educating children but to the management challenge of running a school.

If we end standardised testing, empower teachers and close the factory schools, what should rise in their stead?

Can we really have an education system designed to meet the modern world's dynamism and interconnectivity? Rather than a lumpen, monolithic travesty designed for the needs of the 'average' child, is it possible, on a mass scale, to teach all our children in a way that puts each of them first, as humans?

Decentralising education

New York City's education system used to be characterised by huge high schools with a capacity of up to 3,000 each. They were disproportionately attended by poor and minority students, who had graduation rates as low as 40 per cent.[35] When Mayor Michael Bloomberg came into office he set out to close these 'dropout factories'. He closed many large failing high schools and replaced them with small specialised ones. Called Small Schools of Choice (SSCs), they follow a localised, competitive model: they were created independently by community organisations featuring year groups no larger than a hundred students, built around different themes, with personalised learning. These new small schools are holistic; given that most of the students are at risk of dropping out, they also offer community and social-service support. In these new small schools 71.6 per cent of students graduate, as opposed to 62.2 per cent in normal schools; among black male students, an especially vulnerable demographic, 42.3 per cent enrol in college, compared to 31 per cent at conventional schools.[36] All this at a lower cost per student, because fewer students now need an extra year to finish. New York is showing that moving to smaller, locally controlled schools – just like in Finland – can make a big difference.

These examples and others, like Khan Lab School, Acton Academy and many more, show us that there are now real alternatives to the century-old, one-size-fits-all school. These modern alternatives offer new and effective ways of educating our children, but the dominance of factory schools remains a structural barrier to a more human education system. Until, like Mayor Bloomberg, we actively close them down, the vision of educating most children in fresh, innovative and more human ways will remain just that.

Some in the UK point to academy schools as the answer to removing this structural barrier. Academies are independent schools within the local state system: they're not private or fee paying, but they can avoid the systems, rules and curricula forced on mainstream schools. They have a long heritage; similar to charter schools in the US, they were first introduced as grant-maintained schools by Education Secretary Kenneth Baker under Margaret Thatcher in 1988, and later championed by John Major. Labour at first opposed them (in 1998, Tony Blair's government abolished them), but later reintroduced them in 2000 under a different name – academies. Labour's academies were meant to replace failing schools, but when David Cameron came to power, Michael Gove, his education secretary, dramatically accelerated the programme, allowing all schools (not just struggling ones) to convert to academy status. There are some great charter schools, just as there are great academies. But there's a problem. The academy school movement – major advance though it is – still doesn't address the underlying structural issue: that there are simply not enough fresh, innovative and more human schools on offer.

Changing the structure of the system

To provide more human schools for every child, we need to go deeper – to the very structure of the system. 'Factory school' is not some pejorative term plucked out of thin air. Our education system today is rooted in the Industrial Revolution. Charles Dickens captured the essence of the industrialised-education mindset in the form of Thomas Gradgrind, the headmaster in his novel *Hard Times*. Gradgrind is determined to suppress his pupils' imaginations, and teaches them only facts, seeing children's transformation into machines as the ultimate educational virtue. William T. Harris, the US commissioner of education at the end of the nineteenth century, praised the direction schools were taking at the time. That a 'modern' school had the 'appearance of a machine' was the very quality that proved its worth. Machine schools, he found, fostered 'punctuality, silence, and conformity to order'.[37] Perhaps Harris is excused by the context of his times: obedient factory workers were needed in abundance, as those with 'semi-mechanical virtues' – his words – were both more productive and less accident prone. Though it's hard to say which came first, factory schools are perfectly intertwined with the government bureaucratisation and centralisation we discussed in the last chapter. Centralisation, after all, is an industrial factory's distinguishing feature. Mass manufacturing extended to the people who made the products: a standardised workforce required schools to work in concert, each producing the same type of student. A diverse school system would be complete anathema.

Since outputting uniform workers is no longer society's goal, we need to move on. The centralisation of our school system distorts and deforms, giving power to those in charge but conferring almost no advantage on those who should come first – our children. Schooling, by its nature, should be a local, intimate process. We're so used to the status quo that most of us never stop to acknowledge the fact that parents and teachers don't need the bureaucracy of the school system at all. In fact, you could argue that the whole regime of standardised tests exposes this reality. Parents and teachers don't need standardised tests to know which children are performing well and which need more attention. We accept tests as the best way to monitor our students' learning, when really they're the only tool distant administrators have at their disposal. We 'need' the tests, because *they* need the tests. But the deeper truth is, we don't actually need the administrators. In many ways, getting rid of them is even more important than getting rid of the tests.

Of course, we need a centralised education authority for a few specific things: the fair distribution of funding across regions and towns, an accreditation process to ensure that not just anyone can claim to run a proper school, some basic common standards to ensure that children are taught what they're supposed to be taught – history that celebrates Britain's achievements without ignoring its abuses, for instance, or science that doesn't teach creationism as scientific theory. But that's about it.

Real school choice

If we're to empower teachers and close the factory schools; if we're to have an education system designed to meet the modern world's dynamism and interconnectivity; if we're to teach all our children in a way that puts each of them first, as humans, then the first thing we need to do is dispense once and for all with the idea that the right way to run education is for government to provide 'a good local school' in every neighbourhood. The lazy philosophy of 'one school per neighbourhood' is exactly what has led to the outdated factory school model we need to get away from. Even if government authorities give 'autonomy' to a local school, even if the local school is run as an academy or independent of local authority control, the problem is that there is one local school – a monopoly. As in other areas of life, it's the fact of the monopoly that does the damage, that enables – indeed requires – standardisation and a factory approach.

Yes, you can point to individual examples – wonderful, creative, innovative state schools within the current local monopoly structure. Lucky you if you happen to live near one. But these are the exceptions. Why shouldn't every child, everywhere, have the right to an exceptional education? That will only happen if we end the local school monopoly. Progress comes from innovation, innovation comes from competition, and competition comes from choice.

Of course 'school choice' has been a political slogan for decades. But the kind of choice that proponents of this idea usually argue for is barely choice at all. It's the illusion of choice – between one dominant school in an area and one alternative, or maybe, in larger towns and cities, between the closest big school and four or five others within a reasonable distance. It's no surprise that critics of school choice have found a receptive audience for their argument that this 'isn't parents choosing schools, but schools choosing parents'. I agree.

To get to a more human education system, one that gives every child the chance to go to a school that is perfect for them – whether that's something like the extreme entrepreneurial innovation of Acton Academy or the more mainstream version in Finland, whether it's a traditional school or a progressive one, an academic curriculum or one focused on character – whatever it is, whatever is perfect for every child (knowing that no two children are the same), the only way to achieve this is something wildly, fantastically more radical than anything we've seen or talked about up until now. Not just the odd boutique school here and there, not just two or three, or four or five, or even eight or ten schools in every area. I mean twenty, thirty local state schools for parents to choose from, schools that are smaller (a reasonable aim for a human-scale school would be, perhaps, 150 to 300 students) and schools that offer whatever approaches they think might attract parents and children in that neighbourhood. Each child is unique, as is each teacher. In order to thrive they need to be able to find the school that fits them, that fits their uniqueness. This is what a more human education means.

We need a completely open, local marketplace for schools. Teachers, educational entrepreneurs and groups of parents must be permitted to set up schools, free of bureaucratic restrictions and hassle. Parents should have a free choice of where to send their children, and a voucher should follow that choice. Government's role in the school system would focus on fair funding and licensing, making sure that all children have equal access to a school and that only fit and proper individuals and organisations are permitted to establish and run them.

This is not some outlandish fantasy. The demand is there, the ideas are there, and it doesn't have to cost more. The assumption that a new school is more expensive is often just the result of old-fashioned thinking, or worse, the efforts of local bureaucracies to cling on to their monopolies. They define a school as exactly what it is today – a big factory – insisting on unnecessary and often byzantine requirements about building size, parking spaces, land use, traffic access ... you name it. This is how the vested interests in local (and central) government managed to block expansion in the number of Michael Gove's new 'free' schools, even though parents wanted them. The idea that we can't have a school in a converted office or high-street retail space, for example, has nothing to do with what would benefit our children, and everything to do with the established monopoly providers fearing they would be shown up by any competition. New schools with more human ways of educating children are there if we want them. There are many models, all with advantages and disadvantages – we shouldn't pick one from on high. But their popularity points the way to what our school system might one day become – a place where teachers and students are treated as people.

There's one more reform we need, one more vital step on the road to a more human education system. To make sure that the local schools marketplace is truly fair and egalitarian, we must not discriminate against different types of schools run along different lines. Government-owned schools, charter schools, non-profit social enterprises, for-profit schools … as long as they are all funded on a fair basis and are free rather than tuition-paying, true educational diversity means all of these being given an equal chance to offer children a great education in the state school system. It's particularly important that we should allow organisations that make a profit to run schools. The current discrimination against 'profit-making schools' is particularly random and bizarre, given that huge chunks of state school operations – the technology, the textbooks, the buildings, the testing (!)[38] – are provided by for-profit companies. I'm not quite clear why the idea of making profits is okay for all those activities but not for running schools. In fact, one of the most inspiring examples of social justice, emancipation of the poorest, and the transformative power of education that I've ever seen was a visit to a profit-making school. It happened to be in one of the world's worst slums, in Lagos, Nigeria.

James Tooley, a professor of education at Newcastle University, has helped establish and champion private for-profit schools in some of the poorest parts of the world. These schools are transformationally better than the failing state-run schools so depressingly propped up by corrupt local bureaucrats, the United Nations, international aid, and the whole panoply of sanctimonious, ignorant, hypocritical hand-wringers who argue that the evil 'profit motive' mustn't violate the noble innocence of education. (Oh, wait, apart from the private schools and private tutors used by the policymakers and pundits who peddle those views.)

When we were accompanying the prime minister on a 2011 visit to Africa, Rohan and I asked to see one of James Tooley's schools in one of the worst slums in Lagos. Whereas the UK-government-backed school, run by the state and financed via the Department for International Development (DfID), was a disaster, the Tooley-backed for-profit school was a sensation: eager children in pristine uniforms learning literacy, maths, science – with the help of a solar-powered computer. This is in the middle of a slum. Literally. To get there, Rohan and I had to pick our way through stinking, festering garbage, open sewers, ramshackle structures that could and would be washed away by the next rains. To arrive at that school, peep over the makeshift wall, and see rows and rows of eager pupils happily studying in the midst of utter chaos and squalor was completely astonishing, incomparably inspiring.

Let me repeat: this is a for-profit school. The parents – all of whom live in the slum, the poorest people in the world, part of that economic category lightly bandied around as 'living on less than a dollar a day' – these parents, who earn less money in a year than a liberal commentator who rails against 'profits in schools' would spend on a good lunch, choose the for-profit school over the free state-run alternative. Why? Because it's better. And surely that's all we should care about – the quality of the education, not the organisational form, right?

Some might say that the argument I've set out here is crazy: there's no way we can end the local school monopoly and create a completely open local schools marketplace. There's no way we can bring the kinds of educational approaches I've described in this chapter into the mainstream – they go way too far for most people. There's no way parents have either the time or the inclination to evaluate schools and choose between them in a local marketplace. In the innocuous but devastatingly destructive cliché, 'Parents just want a good local school.'

Think of the parents in Nigeria, who actively sought out James Tooley's school. They live in one of the world's poorest slums and fight every day for access to clean water, shelter and enough food to eat. Yet they take the initiative to find the best education for their children. If they, with everything stacked against them, can take an active role in education and choose a better local alternative, of course parents in Britain can too. Yes, there are some dysfunctional families who would struggle to do the best for their children in an open schools marketplace. But why should everyone else be denied the choice of a more human education just because of a problem few?

Critics of decentralisation and choice ask how parents can decide on schools without a metric, some standardised measure to compare one school with another, based on a test of some kind. But the premise of the question is intrinsically flawed: tests can tell you something but not the most important things: the human things. Parents and students know what a good school is without looking at statistics. They just need to visit the school. They get a feel for the principal, the teachers, the building, the environment, the culture. I wrote earlier about the importance of trusting teachers and students. If we trust students and their parents, we can empower them to fuel a revolution in education.

Critics might also point to Khan Lab School or Acton Academy and say they're elite because they are private and fee-paying. Yes, they are. But why shouldn't we make the best, most innovative education available to everyone? Universities, secondary schools, even teaching basic literacy were once elite activities until we decided they were for everyone. The same applies here: Why should the best in education be a luxury for the few? Making sure our children have an equitable start is one of the most important tasks of society, and schools are one of the most important institutions in a child's life. We should be troubled by the fact that different children in different places have vastly divergent and unequal experiences.

Radical school choice might seem extreme, but at its heart it is human. It simply involves trusting parents, teachers and students. We need to shake up a system that has failed so many of our children. Piecemeal reform has only made a small difference for a few. It's not enough: we need to fundamentally change our mindset towards learning, a mindset stuck for over 150 years. As long as education is centralised and run by government; as long as schools are factories, our children will suffer. They will continue to be treated like outputs, like commodities, like cogs in a machine. But children are not products. They are our future, and they deserve to be treated like individuals. It isn't about ideology; it's about the values of our society. Surely we want to live in a world that prizes creativity, rewards ingenuity and fosters brilliance? Our school system today is designed to crush these things. Let's create a system that encourages and inspires all of our children. Let's close the factory schools and make our schools more human.

CHAPTER 4

HEALTH

Jane Locke, a forty-six-year-old woman, was being treated for cancer at Stafford Hospital. Cancer didn't kill her, though. She died after contracting three superbugs, C. difficile, MRSA and a streptococcal infection, during her stay. 'They left her in sheets that had faeces on,' said her mother, June. Around the same time, John Moore-Robinson ruptured his spleen in a cycling crash. In their rush, doctors at Stafford Hospital failed to notice the severity of the twenty-year-old's condition, gave him painkillers and sent him home, where he died. Gillian Astbury, a sixty-six-year-old diabetic woman, died after Stafford NHS nurses failed to provide her with the routine insulin she needed to stay alive: they didn't notice her high blood sugar, so she lapsed into a coma from which she never emerged. Ellen Linstead's body was so infected with the C. difficile which killed her that she had to be buried in a sealed bag. Her daughter, Deb Hazeldine, complained that there was faeces on her mother's hands so often that she regularly would wash it off herself. Reports have suggested that in the years up to the scandal breaking, there were between 400 and 1,200 deaths that never should have happened in a hospital of Stafford's expected quality.[1] Elsewhere in the NHS, at Walsall Manor Hospital, eighty-six-year-old Frederick

Thomas died – but not of the hip replacement for which he was admitted (that operation was a success). In twelve days, not a single doctor or nurse noticed that he was both malnourished and dehydrated, an error that could have been corrected simply by hooking him up to a saline drip.

It's too easy to think of the disgusting treatment of those patients as isolated cases. It's much worse than that. They reflect reflect a deeper, structural problem.[2]

We are rightly proud of the idea of the NHS. What a wonderful thing that anyone can receive healthcare for free, based on their medical need and not their ability to pay. The guarantee of affordable healthcare is a hallmark of a decent society – and one which few countries are able to boast. But we tend to conflate two things that are not related at all: the idea of state-supported healthcare and the institution that provides it. It's a brilliant idea that anyone can get medical attention without worrying about cost. What's not brilliant is the behemoth institution that has emerged to deliver this promise. Having one centrally controlled organisation with over a million employees (the NHS is the fourth largest employer in the world after the US military, the Chinese army, and Walmart[3]) is perhaps the best way to take something that should have been the epitome of humanity (what could be more human than to care for others?) and send it down a path of industrialisation, mechanisation and dehumanisation.

Furthermore, by consolidating medical operations in large centralised hospitals, distant from local communities, we have created a clinical environment that actively fights intimacy and personalised care. 'Efficiencies of scale' have become enemies of effectiveness, allowing decisions to be made far from patients, and responsibility to be avoided. NHS hospitals have been described as 'conveyor belts' that 'churn' out their patients whom they treat like 'parcels'.[4] Patient volume is high; physicians and staff are overbooked and forced to multitask; distraction and fatigue are endemic. The scandals in Mid-Staffs and elsewhere are symptoms of a larger truth: that in our health system today, patients have become outputs; their health outcomes, products; our hospitals, factories. It's not the fault of those who work in the NHS. As in so many other areas, it's the structure that's to blame.

Factory hospitals

It's hard to care in a factory hospital. Go to a hospital today, and it can be an ordeal: navigating the large car park, walking what feels like miles through corridors, travelling in giant lifts before finally reaching a soulless waiting room where you have to sit endlessly to be called. Need a test? Walk through another mile of corridors to another soulless room. Then wait hours or days for the results. This only describes the experience of people who are outpatients. For those who are admitted, it gets worse. Patients eat factory food – how else to serve it in such an institution? – and stay in sterile, depressing rooms. But the worst part is that treatments are commodified: tests done without doctors ever entering the room, medicine performed on and around the patient but seldom with the patient.

According to Jocelyn Cornwell of the Point of Care programme, 'today's hospitals are vast, time is at a premium and in these busy medical factories care of the person can unfortunately get squeezed out'.[5] Joyce Robins, the patient advocate who described the NHS as a 'conveyor belt', elaborates further: 'Patients are sent into hospital and then rushed out before they are ready.'[6] Those at the top see this problem too: more often than not, hospital stays are a 'series of brief encounters', as Jeremy Hunt, the Health Secretary, put it – and the lack of continuity in care means that patients and their families don't know who's in charge to ask questions of or make requests to.[7] Sometimes, the medical staff don't even really know their patients. That 'failure to see the person in the patient', as a report by the King's Fund on point of care puts it, dehumanises the patient and can lead to serious problems. In the report, one woman describes the distress caused to her eighty-seven-year-old mother:

> . . . the ambulance crew were the only people in the entire seven weeks who formally introduced themselves and asked what she would like to be called. Thereafter, for the first six weeks of her admission, she was called Elizabeth, which is her first name, which she has never been called in her life, ever. She's only ever been called by her middle name. But the NHS IT system records your name. All her labels were wrong. In spite of the fact that on a daily basis all of us told the people caring for her that her name is Margaret, and that is what she likes to be called if they want to call her by her first name, all of them called her Elizabeth. And that became very significant when she became confused.[8]

In a bureaucracy, paperwork reigns supreme and, as at Mid-Staffs, patients can end up ignored, sometimes with horrific consequences. Our factory hospitals are designed for everyone but patients and their families. We can design physical spaces that are palliative and soothing – just having plants and using natural light over stark fluorescents would be a start. But I want to ask a more fundamental question. If everyone – from patients, to relatives, to doctors, to investigators, to patient advocates, to the Health Secretary – agrees[9] that our current system dehumanises patients and inhibits the kind of care we want to see, why do we persist with this way of doing things?

iPatient, or real patient?

The argument for the status quo is that our standardised, bureaucratised, factory hospitals, healthcare providers, and insurers are 'efficient': they bring together the expertise, technology and facilities needed for specialist procedures, operations and complex treatments. Efficiency, of course, is the argument for many things, especially the role of technology in healthcare. Used well, technology can be positively transformative in healthcare just as in other fields. But it can also hinder care by putting efficiency ahead of the patient. Stanford medical professor Dr Abraham Verghese is an evangelist for the physical examination for this very reason. 'I joke, but I only half-joke, that if you come to one of our hospitals missing a limb, no one will believe you till they get a CAT scan, MRI or orthopaedic consult.' Technological tests can be invaluable, but not when doctors rely on them too much or even forsake actually examining the patient. 'I've gotten into some trouble in Silicon Valley,' Verghese says, 'for saying that the patient in the bed has almost become an icon for the real patient who's in the computer. I've actually coined a term for that entity ... I call it the iPatient. The iPatient is getting wonderful care all across America. The real patient often wonders, where is everyone? When are they going to come by and explain things to me?'[10]

If technology replaces human contact when healing is what's called for, it makes healthcare less human. But interestingly, when it replaces the *bureaucracy* of healthcare, technology can make it more human. Used right, technological advances can create more space for doctors to interact with their patients. As technology gets cheaper and smaller, going to a big factory hospital will be less and less necessary; instead, local doctors will be able to use devices like GE's Vscan. Vscan is a handheld ultrasound machine that replaces the huge ones otherwise used. Doctors can thus administer ultrasounds personally, even in a patient's home, and get instant results. The patient need never go into the cold, dark testing room again.[11]

Telemedicine, once a pipe dream, is increasingly a reality that frees patients from the burden of cumbersome tests and lengthy hospital visits. In Estonia, digital monitoring is such that doctors often have no need to see their patients for routine tests. Like other European countries, Estonia faces a demographic pyramid, with the population of senior citizens expected to increase greatly. The key then to providing care to the ageing and elderly, according to President Toomas Ilves, is to prevent them from getting sick in the first place. That's why Estonia is looking into telemedicine to monitor people who are especially at risk, like the elderly.[12] President Ilves predicts that 'in the future, we'll be monitoring people constantly, certainly older people, so that before you get really sick you go see a doctor.'[13]

Estonia has already revolutionised health information through its Electronic Health Record (EHR). Started in 2008, the EHR does not centralise medical records but rather integrates them into a standard format readily available for both the patients and their doctors. Estonians, through their national ID system, have digital access to their records and those of their children and can control which doctors can see which parts of their records. And although the government can compile statistical data or track disease outbreaks, that data is anonymised and is never outside a patient's control.

Electronic medicine needn't just be a question of digitising records. Ali Parsa, the founder of a British health start-up called Babylon, sees his virtual health service as the solution to several problems that have long plagued the medical system. First is the simple fact that most people in the world have little or no access to healthcare – and technology can get it to them. But, like the Estonians, he also sees a future where medicine becomes preventive instead of reactive.[14]

Babylon doesn't pre-empt the traditional doctor yet – there is still a need for in-person procedures and examinations. Increasingly, though, much of medicine can be performed remotely. And that, Parsa, believes, is actually more human. His patients prefer to have a video conference on a phone or tablet rather than visiting the health centre or the hospital. 'Patients appreciate not leaving the comforts of their own home to spend, on average, three hours to get to a doctor's surgery. My mother, for instance – every time she gets her blood pressure taken at her doctor's [office], it's high, while every time she has it done at home, it's not. We all know it's because of the stress of getting to the surgery at her age and meeting the doctor too.' With telemedicine 'patients use the same medium to talk to their doctor that they use to talk to their friends and family. It's a much friendlier experience.' Increasingly, too, medicine can be brought to the patient. Parsa concedes that sometimes you need to go in for a test, but why bother if it's something that can be done at home? If a patient needs a run-of-the-mill blood test, Babylon sends a courier to deliver a simple prick-your-finger test that the patient can do at home and then send back by courier to get the results within the day.

It's not just with Babylon that we get a glimpse of what the future of medicine could be. Technology can be harnessed to put healthcare in the hands of the patient through medical apps and social networks. HealthTap, an American start-up, allows users to post questions to be answered by one of more than 60,000 doctors in its 'expert network'. For a monthly subscription, users can connect via video to a doctor, who can write prescriptions, within minutes – twenty-four hours a day, seven days a week. For those with chronic conditions, parents with young children or caregivers, such a service could be a lifesaver – or at least less of a hassle than multiple doctors' surgery trips a month.

Mango Health, a mobile app, ingeniously combines human behaviour and technology to help patients better manage their medications and other treatments. Jason Oberfest, the company's founder and CEO, used to work in gaming and realised that 'everything we've learned in behavioural design and user interface to keep people engaged in games could be applied to healthcare.'[15] Oberfest and his team designed Mango Health like a game: users enter their medications and other treatments – for instance, specific exercises or reminders to drink water – into the app, as well as when and how to do it. The app will then remind them when it is time to do a treatment or take a pill. But just as a game has incremental rewards, Mango Health gives patients points every time a reminder is complied with. By partnering with third parties, Mango can offer rewards at certain levels of point accumulation.

Mango Health is also an example of how an app can help other areas of medical management. It has a database of every medication approved by the US Food and Drug Administration, including negative interactions, so that if a patient enters a new medication that clashes with an existing one, the app will warn the patient of the conflict. It will also, if the patient allows it to, communicate with doctors, sending them real-time data about how their patients are complying with their treatment. The app prompts patients to record how they are feeling (with a few simple options like 'good' or 'so-so'), so instead of retrospectively asking a patient how they've been doing, doctors can actually know in real time, to correspond with the introduction of new treatments or failure to follow them.

Social networks are another way that technology is helping to make healthcare more human. Jamie Heywood's brother Stephen was diagnosed with ALS, or Lou Gehrig's Disease, in 2006. ALS is an orphan disease – one not prevalent enough to attract the attention of drug company research towards a cure. In addition to designing solutions to the daily physical obstacles Stephen faced, Jamie, an MIT engineer, set about developing a treatment for the disease itself, founding a research institute with Stephen's wife. Then he created PatientsLikeMe, a social network that connects patients suffering from the same diseases with each other and their doctors, creating 'feedback loops' whereby healthcare providers can quickly learn how patients respond to their treatments. 'The faster the feedback loop, the more responsive it is to humans.' So PatientsLikeMe harnesses human connectivity to increase responsiveness.[16]

PatientsLikeMe has designed its system 'to discover if interventions have impact in the real world' but goes a step further by actually empowering patients to make that determination. PatientsLikeMe aims to discover the overall efficacy of different approaches to treatment; it is designed to work globally. 'Great systems learn across boundaries,' Heywood says, and he is exactly right. If medicine is to get better, its practitioners and their results can't be walled off from one another. That's why PatientsLikeMe is so revolutionary: it is 'inherently democratic'. And it is intrinsically human. Patients log on and document their outcomes and experiences, giving doctors, drug companies and everyone concerned a real-time social network to understand their practices better while, for the first time, giving patients a role as true partners, able to learn from and bolster each other in bad times. 'Patients contribute research ideas, they are involved in the design of trials and experiments, and they keep doctors honest. They interact around the data themselves, so if there's something not quite right, they will dive right into that.' Ultimately Heywood hopes to reinvent the healthcare system: 'imagine a world where everyone else's experience can help improve your own.'

Healthcare that makes you sick

Factory medical systems deliver one type of healthcare, typically in the form of a procedure or pill of some sort. But in the face of some conditions or diseases, certain behaviours and exercises or nutritional and lifestyle adjustments might be more effective. The factory health system is not designed to prescribe something non-medical or innovative – or if it does, it's only after a battery of tests and exams to confirm that a more complicated procedure didn't work.

Obviously there are many conditions and diseases that are best treated by medical procedures or drugs. But health is not just a function of medicine. More than just optimising the effectiveness of a particular procedure, a more human healthcare system would optimise individual health and well-being. As Jamie Heywood saw, today's medical system is based on how well a particular action was executed – 'Was the hip successfully replaced? All right then, success!' – rather than its actual, ultimate effect on the patient: 'Can you walk without pain since the procedure we did last year, Mrs Smith?' As a result, the system needlessly precludes non-medical interventions, not to mention the path almost never taken – non-intervention – from its repertoire of solutions.

Having feedback systems in place based on ultimate health outcomes would also help us see where treatments – even administered with the best of intentions – make us worse. Nassim Taleb talks at length about the danger of this phenomenon, *iatrogenesis*, the harm caused by treatment, that results from our deeply rooted desire to intervene or, as he puts it, 'this need to do *something*'.[17] The problem with this approach is that interventions aren't costless. There is no drug in the world without an adverse side effect. There is no surgery without risk of greater injury. There are certainly many conditions for which we absolutely need the medical system. Steve Jobs famously tried to treat his pancreatic cancer with fasting and juice diets, later regretting his decision to forsake conventional treatment.[18] But without understanding the full long-term costs and benefits of any one regimen, including less invasive treatment or non-intervention altogether – knowledge that a rigorous feedback system would give us – we take tremendous risks prescribing otherwise healthy people with powerful treatments.

Our bodies are exceptionally complex, and attempts to oversimplify the interactions that happen within them in order to mechanise them courts unintended consequences. Doctors almost automatically prescribe proton pump inhibitors (e.g., Prilosec, Nexium, Prevacid) to people experiencing heartburn or stress (50 million in England in 2014 – a 6 per cent increase over 2013 alone)[19] – but more than six in ten prescriptions are inappropriate according to the *British Medical Journal*.[20] The drug works by reducing acid levels in the stomach. This certainly eliminates heartburn, but it increases the risk of infection (acid kills germs in the things we eat) as well as vitamin deficiency (acid is also necessary to break our food down) and even heart attack.[21] Considering that for many people simple changes in diet or behaviour, like eating an evening meal earlier, can eliminate acid reflux disease altogether, altering the chemistry of our bodies so casually for so many people seems haphazard at best.

Now, Nassim Taleb explains, pharmaceutical companies find themselves 'scraping the bottom of the barrel, looking for disease among healthier and healthier people, lobbying for reclassification of conditions'.[22] Perhaps restless leg syndrome (RLS) really is a medical condition, and for those it seriously afflicts, a treatment is a godsend. But did it require GlaxoSmithKline to run an aggressive marketing campaign promoting prescriptions of ropinirole, usually used to treat those with Parkinson's? They also lobbied doctors directly to 'educate' them about the disease.[23] Doctors in the journal PLoS Medicine accuse the company of 'disease mongering'.[24]

Restless leg syndrome isn't the only disorder with a 'modern cure'. In the decade leading up to 2013, prescriptions to treat ADHD have more than trebled in England to now over one million per year.[25] Even greater excess can be found in the United States, which spent an incredible $10.1 billion to treat the condition in 2014.[26] Dr Michael Anderson, a paediatrician near Atlanta, Georgia, and an outspoken critic of the overtreatment of ADHD, still finds himself prescribing pills to the low-income elementary-aged patients he treats who are having trouble in school. 'I don't have a whole lot of choice,' he says. 'We've decided as a society that it's too expensive to modify the kid's environment. So we have to modify the kid.'[27] Our factory health system puts the needs of the children's factory-school system over the needs of children themselves. We're taking children with very normal child behaviour – being energetic – and categorising them as ill and in need of treatment for the convenience of the adult world that serves them. It's a completely inhuman 'chemical strait-jacket', says Dr Nancy Rappaport, a child psychiatrist who works with low-income children.[28]

Such 'strait-jackets' aren't costless. One family with four of its children in Dr Anderson's care has a shelf lined up in the kitchen with all their medications: Adderall for the twelve- and nine-year-olds, Risperdal (an antipsychotic mood stabiliser) for the two eleven-year-olds, and – to top it all off – Clonidine, a sleep aid for all four of them to counteract the other drugs. When one of the children started to go through puberty, the Adderall he was on caused him to begin hearing voices and imagining people around him, a recognised side effect of the drug. Having become suicidal at one point, he even spent a week in a psychiatric hospital and was consequently switched to Risperdal.[29] This is surely madness, cruel madness.

Dehumanised, factory healthcare is not just limited to pharmaceuticals. Back pain is one of the most overtreated conditions there is. The best cure for chronic back pain is usually pretty basic: over-the-counter pain relievers, ice and heat, gentle exercise. Yet the trend of overtesting, overdiagnosis and overtreatment continues to grow. The US spends $86 billion a year on back pain – much of it on unnecessary MRI and CT scans, prescription pain narcotics, and injections or surgery. People with routine back pain are eight times more likely to have surgery when they've been referred to have an MRI scan.[30]

All this is the entirely predictable product of Big Health, the factory healthcare system we have built: big hospitals operated by a big bureaucracy working with big pharmaceutical companies. Patients – people – take a backseat to the imperatives of the system itself. None of this is to say that it is irretrievably broken, or cannot claim great results. We are healthier and longer lived as a species than we ever have been, and much of that is to do with our state-of-the-art abilities to cure disease and treat traumatic emergencies. Doctors are among the cleverest and most caring people anywhere: it takes a very special type of person to become one. But they're often caught up in a system that cares more about doing something – anything – than doing what they know to be best, which is often nothing at all. To do that is to imagine a system that looks at health as something that goes far beyond the repertoire available at the doctor's surgery, emergency room or operating room.

Slow medicine

The Slow Food movement, developed as a direct response to 'fast food' (see Chapter 5), has inspired doctors as well. Proponents of 'slow medicine' argue that in making medicine 'reductive' and 'mechanical', we forget that human bodies are complex organisms that can often heal themselves.

Dr Victoria Sweet, who was a doctor at Laguna Honda Hospital in San Francisco, America's last almshouse (which has since closed), is one of those proponents. Laguna Honda Hospital was unique. 'It looked like a medieval monastery,' Sweet recalls. 'It had cream-coloured walls and a red-tiled roof and a bell tower and turrets. The hospital was huge, on 62 acres of land in the middle of San Francisco and it had 1,178 patients. [There was] the chapel, which looked more like a small church with polished wooden pews and real stained glass, and then we went outside and [there was the] greenhouse, the aviary, and the barnyard.'[31]

Sweet was both a doctor and a historian of medicine. Her subject was the medieval abbess Hildegard of Bingen, who among her many talents as a composer, writer and polymath also wrote on medicine. Hildegard believed that the human body was like a plant and, accordingly, 'took a gardener's approach to the body. She did not focus down on the cellular level of the body; instead she stood back from her patient and looked around,' describes Sweet. 'She followed the patient's body; she did not lead.'[32] Hildegard believed in the body's *viriditas*, or vitality, and that, given the right conditions, it was perfectly able to heal itself.

Sweet didn't really understand this concept until she treated her patient Terry Becker, who was homeless and an addict. Becker, Sweet recalls, had woken up one day paralysed from the neck down. She was diagnosed with a very rare viral disease, but because it has no treatment and tends to get better with time, she was admitted to Laguna Honda. Medically, Terry's biggest problem was that by sitting in a wheelchair, she had acquired an enormous bedsore. Doctors had tried skin grafts three times, but the bedsore had become too large to operate on.

'When I saw that bedsore for the first time, I was absolutely shocked,' Sweet recalls. 'It went from the middle of Terry's back to her tailbone. It was so deep that I could see the bone at the base of Terry's spine. It was filled with all this decayed tissue from the failed grafts. It would have to heal on its own. I couldn't imagine how Terry would survive all the infections she would get.'[33]

Despairing over what to do, thinking that this bedsore was 'probably the end of Terry Becker', Sweet asked herself: What would Hildegard do? 'Maybe Hildegard would just remove what was in the way of Terry healing. So what was in the way? All the dead tissue was in the way and had to be moved. Anything that was uncomfortable, like wrinkled bed clothes or a hard mattress or any medication that she didn't absolutely need ... Then I thought, Hildegard would fortify

Terry's *viriditas* with the basics: good food, fresh air, deep sleep, sunlight. So that's what I did. And it was amazing to see how fast Hildegard's prescription began to work.'

At Laguna Honda, patients weren't treated mechanically but organically ... humanly. 'Medicine is personal, face to face. And when it's personal, it works,' Sweet says. In our rush to offer an immediate prescription, a mechanical 'fix', we often forget that time and care can be the most natural – and effective – treatments of all. This is what she calls 'the efficiency of inefficiency'. She is fond of a quote from Dr Francis Peabody, a noted professor at Harvard Medical School in the early twentieth century: 'The secret of the care of the patient is caring for the patient.'[34] Often what would otherwise be seen as inefficient is actually most efficient. When we put bureaucracy ahead of patients, 'in the interest of efficiency, we became less efficient', she says.[35]

A pie is in the oven, vintage tracks are playing, and half a dozen women are gathered around the kitchen counter at Pathstone Living, a nursing home in Minnesota tailored for those suffering from memory impairment. It's a typical afternoon there, with staff offering a wide range of activities for the senior citizens in their care. Staying busy, it turns out, can relieve the agitation that's common among those suffering from Alzheimer's or dementia. At another nursing home such agitation would be managed with antipsychotic medicines, which are approved to treat serious illness, like bipolar disease and schizophrenia: over 300,000 nursing-home residents are prescribed them annually in the United States. But antipsychotics increase the risk of death for those with dementia.[36]

Beatrice DeLeon experienced overmedication first-hand. An Alzheimer's patient, DeLeon was sent to a care facility not for her memory but because she had had multiple falls. Even though over-prescription of antipsychotics – a 'chemical restraint' – is banned by law, 'they just kept giving her more and more', says DeLeon's husband, Manuel. 'And I noticed when I used to go see her, she'd just kind of mumble, like she was lost.' Beatrice was administered two very strong drugs that effectively made her a mumbling pile of flesh, writes Ina Jaffe, the journalist who visited her. Doctors prescribe these drugs like sweets; a 2011 US government study found that 88 per cent of Medicare[37] claims for antipsychotics were for dementia or other conditions for which these drugs were not intended.[38]

Although enforcement against nursing homes that over-prescribe antipsychotics is weak,[39] Dr Tracy Tomac hopes Pathstone Living provides an alternative. Pathstone's new 'anti-antipsychotic' approach came after Tomac, a psychiatrist and medical consultant there, decided with a colleague to see whether they could reduce the drug's use. They tried it at one of the smaller nursing homes run by the same charity, Ecumen. By six months in, they were successful – everyone was off antipsychotics. So Ecumen decided to scale the approach to all of its nursing homes across the state, about a dozen in total. Their initial goal? Reduce their use by 20 per cent. After the first year? Down 97 per cent. Now at Pathstone, only 5 to 7 per cent of patients are prescribed antipsychotics at all. Shelley Matthes, who's in charge of quality assurance for Ecumen, says that the numbers were not the only thing that changed: 'They started interacting … people who hadn't been speaking were speaking. They came alive and awakened.'

The programme, which came to be known as 'Awakenings', derives much of its success from training staff simply to pay attention to people. Although individualised dementia care is not an original concept – the nursing staff borrowed from techniques demonstrated elsewhere – attending closely to patients in a human way eliminates the need to medicate them for the behavioural problems dementia can create. [40]

Death and dignity

If there's one aspect of healthcare most guilty of an inhuman approach, it's how we care for those at the ends of their lives.

Sheila Marsh was dying. Stricken with cancer, the seventy-seven-year-old had one wish: to say good-bye to her favourite horse, Bronwen, for whom she had cared for twenty-five years at the stables near her home in north-west England. So the staff at the Royal Albert Edward Infirmary in Wigan, where Sheila stayed, arranged for Bronwen and another of Sheila's horses to come and visit, wheeling her outside to greet and be nuzzled by them. Though unable to speak due to the ravages of her disease, she 'gently called to Bronwen and the horse bent down tenderly and kissed her on the cheek as they said their last goodbyes', according to Gail Taylor, one of the nurses. Sheila died soon afterwards, but her medical staff had helped end her life in quiet dignity, fulfilling her final wishes to bid farewell to the horses that had meant so much to her. [41]

That Sheila had such a dignified death in a hospital is extraordinary, really. Because death in much of the developed world is a horrendous experience. Most people, of course, want to die a quiet death at home surrounded by their loved ones. But instead, many die in a hospital, hooked up to ventilators and IV drips, surrounded by beeping monitors, lying in a sterile room, clinging to life but drained of soul.

We suffer tremendous indignity in the last years of our lives. Our bodies fail us, but doctors, obliged to preserve life at just about any cost, work to prop up our dying organs, our weakening limbs, our tenuous grip on reality. And we make things worse by letting people die exactly where they don't want to end their lives: while a majority say they would prefer to die at home,[42] only 21 per cent do; 53 per cent die in hospitals.[43] The sad part is that of those who die in hospitals, some 40 per cent have no medical reason for being there.[44]

It is deeply inhuman that most people's final moments are not as they'd like them to be. And factory hospitals are inappropriate places for the elderly, as geriatrician Dennis McCullough points out: 'Large "industrial-scale" environments like hospitals focus on disease and tend to lose sight of the complexity of an older person. Speed is at a premium and slower-moving, slower-responding elders don't fit well with the pressured environment of fast medical care.'[45] But hospitalising elders is also, from a public policy perspective, a bad idea for the rest of us. Caring for patients in their final six months of life costs the NHS about a fifth of its annual budget (or about £20 billion) with an expected rise to £25 billion by 2030.[46] Some 20 per cent of hospital beds were occupied by those who were dying and who often had no medical reason to be in hospital.[47] So if no one wants to die in hospital and it is so costly to the system for people to do so, why do they? And how can we give people a more dignified and more human end-of-life experience?

The problem is that we don't have nearly enough hospices, and the solution, clearly, is to invest in better hospice care and end-of-life community services. One report estimates that an investment of £500 million – just 2.5 per cent of the total the NHS spends annually on end-of-life care – in community services, hospice care and family-care capacity would allow up to 50 per cent of people to die at or close to home rather than in hospital.[48] And we can help people work out what they want. One of the great tragedies of end-of-life care is that even when patients have preferences, we don't ask them what they are. We certainly don't help patients work it out. So, erring on the side of the medical principle 'to do no harm', doctors continue to intervene to prolong life, even when we might not want them to. That's where living wills, also called 'advance directives', come in. Living wills help relatives and loved ones know what to do in case of medical dilemmas in which patients are incapacitated and can't make decisions for themselves. Most people don't have them – only 30 per cent in the United States[49] and fewer than 10 per cent in the UK[50] – but having an end-of-life discussion not only ensures patients' desires are carried out, it also lowers costs.

Communities like the town of La Crosse, Wisconsin, are leading the way. Bud Hammes is a medical ethicist at Gundersen Health System, a local hospital in La Crosse. He found that without living wills, most of his patients' families had no idea what to do when patients were in a coma or on life-support machines. Despite years of illness, no one had thought to have the conversation. Consequently 'the moral distress that these families were suffering was palpable. You could feel it in the room,' he says. Hammes resolved to help families solve the problem in advance and started a programme to train nurses to ask people if they wanted to fill out an advance directive. The idea caught on, and now it is the norm in La Crosse to have a living will; in fact, 96 per cent of those who die in the town have documentation for their end-of-life wishes, and it is normal for neighbours to gossip about who doesn't have one. And although this wasn't the goal, medical costs at Gundersen Health System have declined as patients make clear they don't want to be kept on dehumanising – and expensive – life support.[51] (One study found that for those patients with advanced cancer who had end-of-life conversations with their physicians, their overall cost of care was 35.7 per cent lower than for those who never discussed their preferences. And in case you think that lower costs mean lower quality of death, the study found just the opposite: it was those who incurred higher costs that tended to suffer more.)[52] By helping patients make their wishes known, Hammes has made death in La Crosse more dignified.

Hennepin Health: getting creative about healthcare

25 February 2013. It was a few minutes before 9 p.m. 'Ron' was getting ready for bed, and his phone started ringing. He was about to receive some very urgent news.

For four months Ron hadn't felt his usual self. At fifty-five, he was used to not feeling quite right, having spent his life working in hard, physical jobs. But even a hardened construction worker can only take so much. Finally Ron scheduled a visit at a local clinic, and after he'd described his symptoms, the doctor there decided they should do some lab work. Later, just as he was getting ready for bed, came that phone call: it was the doctor he had seen earlier that day. Ron's blood sugar was high, so high that he had to go to the emergency room right away. If he went to sleep, she told him, there would be a good chance he would never wake up.

Further testing revealed that Ron had a kind of type 1 diabetes that is particularly slow to manifest and progress, and his was acute: his blood sugar would oscillate between tremendous extremes in a single day (one day between 36 milligrams of blood glucose per decilitre of blood to 586; to put this in context, most people's levels don't exceed 180). Such extremes complicated Ron's life beyond just the physical consequences of his condition. He soon lost his job of almost ten years because the now-frequent trembling he experienced made him unsafe (his boss saw him shaking as he descended a ladder). He managed to find work elsewhere, but because his diabetes could incapacitate him without any prior warning, it was challenging for him to keep even the jobs for which he was qualified, as employers wanted advance commitment to a full day's work. Finally, after falling into a diabetic coma that summer, Ron used up the last of his unemployment benefits. By 15 September he was homeless.

It's easy to think of Ron's case as one of a health problem leading to a social problem. But it was just as much a social problem exacerbating a health problem – a vicious circle. Being homeless and diabetic is a deadly combination. Kim Evers, a diabetes expert who worked with Ron from his initial diagnosis, witnessed his health deteriorate further after he became homeless. Proper nutrition is paramount for managing diabetes, especially when it's as acute as Ron's. But whatever nutrition instructions Evers gave would be almost impossible for him to manage while he remained homeless: meals were irregular and, when available, often highly processed and sugar laden. Not having access to a refrigerator made storing insulin, which requires cold storage to prevent spoiling, almost impossible. Diabetics need somewhere to rest when tired, which happens easily and often, but shelters tend to close during the day. All in all, being homeless and diabetic can be a death sentence.

Thankfully Ron lives in Minneapolis, Minnesota, where he's part of an incredible healthcare experiment: Hennepin Health. Local leaders created it to serve people exactly like him.

With just over 1.1 million people, Hennepin County isn't huge, but with Minneapolis at its centre (and over one in five Minnesotans), any experiment in healthcare delivery there would be ambitious, especially as this one was aimed at some of the most complicated and expensive users of the healthcare system. The project got its start after the state legislature passed legislation to allow the county to test new ways of serving these new patients.[53] Launched in 2012, Hennepin Health is a four-way partnership between departments or affiliates of the Hennepin County government, bringing together traditional health providers with social services. This hybrid organisation receives a predetermined per-member-per-month payment from the state to cover the entire health costs of its beneficiaries. Such 'capitation payments' are actuarially determined for each person in the system, and any savings are kept as long as standard of care is maintained. This means that in Hennepin the four partners, who were accustomed to operating independently, would now jointly share one budget so both cost savings and overruns would be spread equally across them.

Thanks to this incentive structure, the four partner agencies coordinate on non-medical work as well as traditional health services. For example, although the county's main social services agency – one of the four – is funded separately from the capitation payments, it now makes sure its programmes are integrated with the medical services Hennepin Health provides because it receives a portion of any medical savings. The result is practical care aimed at the root causes of patients' poor health, regardless of how far outside the 'traditional' health sphere they fall.

Back to Ron, homeless and suffering from diabetes. In the eyes of his healthcare workers at Hennepin (like Kim Evers), finding Ron safe and stable public housing became a medical necessity. His homelessness was *their* business. So Evers 'prescribed' a team of social service workers trained in exactly this task to find Ron an affordable place to live. Now Ron has a place to rest when his blood sugar spikes or drops (sometimes causing blindness), to cook his own nutritious meals, and to refrigerate his insulin. He's still far from healthy; the road ahead is long and uncertain. But Ron now has a better shot at staying healthy than he ever would have. For him the best medicine wasn't in the refrigerator; it *was* the refrigerator.[54]

Hennepin provides instructive lessons. In every community, for every population type, no matter how well off, there are a variety of components that form the fabric that is a person's health – all of which must be tended to. This is precisely why traditional house calls – virtually killed off by modern medicine because they are 'inefficient' – are actually vital. Dr Sandeep Jauhar passionately advocates house calls for some patients, because they can help doctors understand the real impediments to a patient's recovery. 'One patient of mine had severe heart failure that rendered him too weak to come see me,' Jauhar writes. 'He lived only a mile from the hospital, so I went to visit him. In his kitchen sink was a mess of dirty dishes. I looked in the fridge; it was nearly empty. There were canned soups on the counter, all loaded with sodium, precisely what he should not have been consuming … It didn't matter which medications I ordered at the pharmacy; he had no way to get them.'[55]

Our health system and the providers within it should study the communities they serve to find ways to help enhance their members' health far beyond providing pharmaceuticals and medical procedures. Some of it is terrifically unoriginal: investing in parks and bike paths and sponsoring farmers' markets or school nutrition programmes. But why stop there? Imagine health providers partnering with cooking schools, investing in adult sports leagues, building gyms and community centres – all of which not only keep people active but, perhaps even more importantly, foster the social relationships that maintain health into old age.[56] And given the health benefits of stable families (for more, see Chapters 8 and 9), perhaps one day our health providers will see their role as including parenting and relationship support too.

That's what a more human healthcare system looks like – not just dishing out drugs and carrying out operations.

One non-profit organisation is already working with communities in America to do just this. Author and *National Geographic* explorer Dan Buettner set out in 2004 to document the lifestyles of people around the world who had lived past the age of one hundred. After he and the scientists he worked with interviewed hundreds of these centenarians, they identified five communities – Ikaria, Greece; Okinawa, Japan; Ogliastra Region, Sardinia; Loma Linda, California; and Nicoya Peninsula, Costa Rica – with an abnormally high number. Buettner designated them 'blue zones', and founded a non-profit organisation, the Blue Zone Project, to spread the lessons. The Blue Zone Project now works with towns in Iowa, California and Minnesota to identify and invest in projects that have been shown to increase longevity, like additional drinking fountains throughout town, colour-coded parking places that add two hundred steps to get to the store, community gardens, community walking clubs, and volunteer programmes for local business people to walk kids to and from school.[57]

Whether these ideas are exactly right is not the point; they represent the right type of thinking about the very human causes of and impediments to good health. We can no longer afford for our doctors, nurses and carers to be cogs in the machinery of industrialised medicine. They must be stewards of health.

A radical reboot for the NHS

So what should we do to fix things? We need to bring the NHS back to a human scale, so the people who work for the NHS can emphasise care. We know that doctors and nurses want to care, want to be more human – but in a factory-hospital system, bureaucracy gets in the way. Health secretary Jeremy Hunt had to actually sign a directive that the names of attending physicians be written over the beds of their patients because too many mistakes were being made. I'm not attacking Mr Hunt; he understood the problem and moved to fix it. But how dehumanised has the NHS become when doctors have to be forced to remember who their patients are?

The British healthcare system needs a transformative reboot to undo the cumbersome factory health apparatus that, although built in the name of efficiency, now serves as a barrier to better – and less expensive – care. Because the truth is, the very structure of our system – the very structure of the NHS – is designed to stop things like Jamie Heywood's PatientsLikeMe, Victoria Sweet's Laguna Honda or the amazing Hennepin Health system. The NHS is designed to perpetuate one particular rigid, centralised and frankly outdated approach to healthcare.

The essence of the reboot we need should be decentralisation. The former Labour Party health secretary in Tony Blair's government, Alan Milburn, once said that the NHS should be 'an idea, not an institution'. The central idea of the NHS – universally available healthcare that is free at the point of use – is a great idea, worth cherishing. But just because such a system is funded by government doesn't mean it has to be provided by government in the form of a massive bureaucratic institution. So in practical terms, making the NHS more human means implementing Alan Milburn's vision: a radical break-up of the NHS structure, the creation of a taxpayer-funded healthcare marketplace, and a radical dispersal of healthcare provision from centralised to community-based locations.

The centrepiece of this more human healthcare system would be the new marketplace for healthcare services, where many different providers – from small to large, traditional to innovative – compete for patients on a level playing field. Why? Because when patients choose, we're more likely to have innovation and a focus on quality care. We're more likely to have a system where the incentives are designed to put people first: to satisfy patients rather than bureaucrats at the NHS. And to bring the human touch back to medicine, we're more likely with this system to see care devolved to the smallest practical unit. It's true that there aren't enough – and there isn't enough demand for – specialist doctors to be spread around every community. But equally, there is no need to warehouse them in huge buildings – giant, Kafkaesque labyrinths that impose themselves on sick, frightened and vulnerable people.

If we can make hospitals more human, we can take the first step towards setting a tone that puts people first. By working not in large hospitals or medical centres but small local ones, doctors can establish a more personal relationship with their patients. For the vast majority of our health needs, a highly localised system is ideal – localised even to the point of your mobile device. We need a system built around people, their needs and what really works for them – not the medical establishment. An open healthcare marketplace would be a huge step in that direction.

Of course, completely free markets don't really work for healthcare. For markets to work properly, you need good information available to all participants. In truth, even in the age of googling your symptoms, patients will not have enough information to make really well-informed medical decisions. They certainly won't be able to anticipate the kind of care they'll need in the future, which makes it difficult to choose the best provider for themselves today. Even in the moment when care is needed, patients don't know whether they really need a treatment or not, relying on doctors. In these ways health is different from education. In health you will always need some sort of provisioning authority to determine the appropriate standard of care for any given diagnosis. And to a certain extent you will always need some sort of rationing of care across the system. These characteristics of healthcare make it difficult to introduce unconstrained supply-side choice in a true market. But just because a normal market doesn't work for healthcare provision doesn't mean we should write off the use of market features entirely. We can have a 'free at the point of use' system with a provisioning authority that determines the appropriate levels of care for any circumstance – all while letting a myriad of different organisations compete for the actual provision of care itself. This combination would not only drive innovation, but drive it in the direction of patient satisfaction and lowered costs – a huge departure from the NHS today.

Just as with schools, the only way to bring about the transformation we need is to understand that the problem is structural. We need to transform the structure so that smaller, more innovative, more human providers of healthcare can operate within the NHS guarantee: state providers, private providers, mutual organisations owned by their workers ... This is why it's so important to distinguish between the idea of the NHS and the institution of the NHS. The idea of the NHS is and always will be profoundly human. The institution? Not so much.

The medical advances of the last century – even just the last decade – are nothing short of astonishing. We're living longer and fuller lives than at any prior point in human history. The things doctors can now do to improve the quality of our lives can often seem miraculous. And with the application of data science and gene technology to medical problems, we can expect this progress to accelerate, perhaps exponentially. For a good part of the last century, there's no doubt that large-scale factory hospitals enabled health outcomes never before experienced. But we're in a new century now; science and technology have evolved to make this model out of date. With no more excuses to prop up the big, centralised health system, it's time we moved on – because a country that ignores the human side of healthcare really misses the point.

CHAPTER 5

FOOD

What has happened to us that we think it's all right to throw live chicks into a mincing machine just because they're male; that piglets' tails are chopped off and their front teeth broken to prevent 'stress-induced cannibalism', and chunks of their ears cut out for identification, all without painkillers; and that cows are milked to breaking point so they live out just a third of their natural lives? This is how you get your food. This is how I get my food. This is where pretty much all of us get our food, because what we typically eat today has been farmed in factories and manufactured in factories.

It's the 'farmed' part that's truly indefensible. The fake food concocted from artificial ingredients by vast industrial machines, food production that's just another branch of chemistry – well, it may be disgusting and make you unhealthy, but in the end it's a question of taste. (Although, as we'll see, it's not quite as simple as a question of consumer choice). The way we treat animals, though? That's a question of ethics. Farmer and poet Wendell Berry describes eating as 'farming by proxy'. In the case of eating factory-farmed animals, it's cruelty by proxy. If we don't care about the sickening things I've just described, we've lost one of the qualities that is essential to human beings: the capacity to be empathetic. More animal cruelty = less human.

Of course none of us is deliberately choosing to torture a pig when we buy a hot dog. But as we've seen in other contexts, people are often made to behave in inhuman ways by the systems and structures around them. When it comes to factory food and cruelty to animals, our shopping and eating habits make us complicit in horrific acts. But it's simplistic just to blame consumers. That allows the real culprits off the hook: the politicians, regulators and business executives of the culinary-industrial complex, whose grotesque practices are encouraged through subsidy and permitted through inadequate regulation. The resulting pervasiveness of factory food in our society makes it hard for even the most conscientious consumer to avoid propping up this rotten, inhuman system. It is a structural problem. That's why, if we're going to do anything about it, we need to go deeper than participating in campaigns to shop differently or supporting animal welfare charities. We need to dismantle and reconstruct the entire food industry.

Factory farms

Most summers when I was young we would visit my family in Hungary. My grandmother grew most of her fruit and vegetables in the garden, and there were chickens running around the place. On the other side of town, with the other side of the family, it was pigs: my family owned a small salami factory. My cousin and I would help out, and that included killing pigs. And I mean really killing them – by hand. Lots of blood. But I was pretty young then, and anyway, over there they were … you know, Communist. A bit backward. Actually, as I now know, the way we treated and killed pigs in our small local meat-processing business was much more humane than the horrors taking place in the big industrialised plants in the more 'advanced' UK where we lived.

For most of my life I – like most people, I suspect – never gave much thought to the origins of my food. I began to develop a greater understanding while working on these issues with some of our clients during my time running Good Business, the corporate responsibility firm I started with Giles Gibbons in 1997. But then, in 2013, at Rohan's suggestion, I read Jonathan Safran Foer's *Eating Animals*. I know there are other books like it, but that's the book I read, and it influenced me hugely, opening my eyes to the sickening world of filth, pollution and abuse that is responsible for the food we consume.

Factory farms are disgusting places. A quick YouTube search for one of the many undercover activist videos shot at chicken, egg, beef, milk, veal or pork factories will suppress even the most robust appetite. But the point is this: it took reading a book for me to understand the unconscionable origins of much of the food I ate and prepared for family and friends. Reading a food label in the supermarket would have been useless. When I buy a burger for my children at the zoo café or eat in a restaurant, there isn't a label, not even a company website I can check. The vast majority of fast-food places have neither a brand to protect nor an incentive to respond to animal-welfare concerns. I'd love to know how many of the 'conservationists' at the London Zoo, for example, who prattle on with tediously gushing self-righteousness about 'Asiatic lions' or 'Philippine seahorses' or whatever, have the first idea about the lives of the chickens, pigs and cows they serve up for lunch?

No one can be sure how their food has been produced, not the people at the zoo, not the shelf stacker at your supermarket, not the waiter in your restaurant. Of course, that's just how the Big Food industry likes it, going to aggressive lengths to stop activists from documenting what happens in factory farms. Keeping us in the dark makes the ethical issues abstract, not something that busy, practical people trying to live their lives can spend time or energy on. There's no individual animal for us to picture in our mind's eye, looking back at us, suffering.

Nonetheless, thanks to a few exceptionally brave campaigners, who pose undercover, sneak around at night, and often risk harsh penalties for photographing farm conditions (under what are known as 'ag-gag' laws), we do know the abuse that goes on. Do not be in any doubt: the meat we eat relies on systematic cruelty that is documented, widespread, and beyond the most sadistic thoughts you can imagine. It's not a question of whether animals are being tortured for our food; it's a question of whether we care enough to stop it.

For me, this is very personal. I love food. I love cooking. When we moved to California, Rachel and I decided to raise chickens with our sons, Ben and Sonny. It is one of the most pleasing things you can imagine – seeing your children run outside in the morning to let the chickens out of their coop, fascinated as they peck around, excited to collect the eggs. Of course, I see that this is the stuff of parody, that the first thing defenders of our inhuman, industrial food system will say is that objecting to it is all very well, but all very elitist. Big Food is cheap food, and most normal people can't keep chickens, can't afford your free-range, hand-reared, artisanal, grass-fed whatnots. Big Food and its lobbyists claim that intensive, 'efficient' production of food is the only way to feed the world's growing population affordably. This is false, as we shall see, but those who want to see food produced through more human, less barbaric means are often dismissed as being out of touch. You know: 'Let them eat seasonal, organic, locally sourced, fair-trade cake.'

This caricature of 'bad but cheap' versus 'good but expensive' misses the fundamental point: Why do you think factory food is cheap? It's not because it's inherently cheaper or more 'efficient' to farm animals and process them in a highly mechanised way. We've chosen to make it cheaper as a deliberate act of policy, through direct and indirect corporate subsidies, regulations and laws designed to protect Big Food and crush any challenge to it from those who want to do things differently. 'Most people have little idea just how much they are paying for food in hidden ways,' says Patrick Holden, founding director of the UK-based Sustainable Food Trust and one of the world's most thoughtful food activists. 'The failure to introduce true cost accounting into food and agricultural policy is the biggest single impediment to the wider uptake of more sustainable farming.'[1] Humane food appears to be more expensive because all its costs are included in the price. With factory food, we pay its costs in other ways.

There is a growing cost to our health. Our ability to treat infection is slowly coming under attack as a result of the excessive antibiotic use on factory farms. In the UK, nearly half of all antibiotics are used on farm animals, not humans (in the US it's 80 per cent).[2] This is considered necessary not only to keep animals from dying – because their quarters are so squalid, overcrowded and diseased – but also to promote quick growth. Thanks to a combination of aggressive breeding and antibiotics, chickens that would otherwise take fourteen weeks to mature require only six in a factory (according to poultry scientists in a 2013 article, if 'humans grew at a similar rate, a 6.6 lb newborn baby would weigh 660 lbs after two months').[3] In the last five years doctors have observed an alarming rise in urinary tract infections as well as sepsis, particularly from antibiotic-resistant strains of E. coli. This is part of a larger trend: already at least 2 million people annually in the United States acquire serious infections from bacteria that are resistant to the antibiotics designed to treat them; 23,000 people die.[4]

Factory farming isn't responsible for all resistance to antibiotics; we use them on ourselves and even our pets at levels far higher than we should. But the genes in an increasing number of resistant cases have been found to match bacteria found on 'conventionally' – that is, industrially – raised meat, specifically those given antibiotics.[5] In the words of Sir Liam Donaldson, formerly Chief Medical Officer for England: 'Every inappropriate or unnecessary use in animals or agriculture is potentially signing a death warrant for a future patient.'[6]

Antibiotics used to promote quick growth in livestock are now doing the same thing to people. According to studies by public health researchers, 'chronic mass exposure' to antibiotic 'residue' is now believed to contribute directly to our growth, increasing our propensity to gain weight above and beyond food's 'nutrition facts'.[7] The World Health Organisation and US Centers for Disease Control and Prevention have also sounded the alarm, yet the reaction from the factory food industry as well as most agricultural regulators has been slow to non-existent.[8]

Although antibiotic resistance threatens everyone, including vegetarians and free-range enthusiasts, those of us who eat factory meat – and even crops from nearby fields – are much likelier to get ill directly from it.[9] Just as urban slums do among humans, the high density of animal confinement increases the chance of disease. These breeding grounds give us contaminated food: in the United States 69 per cent of store-bought pork and beef and 92 per cent of poultry are contaminated with E. coli bacteria, more than 85 per cent of which is already resistant to antibiotics.[10] In the UK, in July 2014, the major supermarkets launched emergency investigations into the spread of Campylobacter bacteria – which in the UK sickens 280,000 people a year and kills 100 – to as much as two-thirds of all fresh chicken sold in Britain.[11]

It's not just about animal confinement. The problem with our factory system is that food – all of it, not just meat – is combined, mixed and redistributed so widely that a single sick cow or contaminated batch of vegetables can infect the food supply across the country almost overnight. In a Welsh chicken plant run by major poultry producer 2 Sisters (whose customers include most big supermarkets), an investigation discovered dead chickens routinely being picked off the floor and put back into production lines, a factory floor flooded with chicken guts and water from scalding tanks that had gone more than three days without being cleaned (meaning around 250,000 birds had passed through it) – all in the span of one month. While the company described the allegations as 'untrue, misleading and inaccurate', you can view the images yourself and come to your own conclusions.[12]

This industrialisation of food might look 'efficient', but it creates massive risks that make the whole system inherently vulnerable to devastating and costly outbreaks. This isn't to say that small-scale farmers aren't susceptible to animal infections, but at least in those cases meat can be more easily isolated and contained. With a national – international – system of collecting, mixing and spreading food, one 'rotten apple' can cause problems on a vast scale.

'This food, and this way of eating, is killing us'

Factory food goes way beyond meat. Michael Moss, a Pulitzer Prize-winning journalist at the *New York Times*, spent over four years researching and reporting on the science behind processed food, talking to hundreds of people in or formerly employed by the food industry as well as combing through thousands of internal documents. In his revealing book, *Salt Sugar Fat*, he explains how factory food is engineered to be addictive.

Moss tells the story of Howard Moskowitz, one of the food industry's go-to consultants for fine-tuning its products. A mathematician with a PhD in experimental psychology from Harvard, he got his start in the unlikeliest of places: the US Army, which had called on him to help solve the problem of getting soldiers on the battlefield to eat the food rationed to them. (After a while, soldiers would find their ready-to-eat meals boring and not finish them, creating waste and possible energy deficits.) What *would* soldiers eat ad infinitum? White bread. Though it would never get them excited, Moskowitz explains, 'they could eat lots and lots of it without feeling they'd had enough.'[13]

This is called 'sensory-specific satiety'. According to Moss, 'it is the tendency for big, distinct flavours to overwhelm the brain, which responds by depressing your desire to have more.' Eating bland food (like white bread) might fill you up, but you don't feel like stopping. This insight would launch Moskowitz's long career helping food companies make their products more addictive. For over three decades he's been a paid 'optimisation' consultant for Big Food companies like General Foods, Campbell Soup, Kraft and PepsiCo. 'I've optimised soups,' he says. 'I've optimised pizzas. I've optimised salad dressings and pickles.'

To achieve this, consumers are paid to sit for hours in focus groups, giving their input on every sensory detail you can imagine – taste, touch, the rather creepy-sounding 'mouth feel', packaging, smell and so forth. The data is then processed using a complex statistical method called conjoint analysis. Moss explains, 'It's not simply a matter of comparing Colour 23 with Colour 24. In the most complicated projects, Colour 23 must be combined with Syrup 11 and Packing 6, and on and on, in seemingly infinite combinations.' The goal: to find consumers' 'bliss point'.

How do you attain bliss? In case the title of Moss's book wasn't too much of a giveaway, it's with salt, sugar and fat. Not necessarily more of all of them – there's a 'Goldilocks' point for each – but certainly nowhere close to moderation. The simple truth is that salt is addictive. Sugar is addictive. Fat is addictive. Who cares if eating too much of them makes people unhealthy? Certainly not Big Food. If you're running a factory-food company, the whole point is to get people to eat more and more of your product.

Let's look at sugar in particular. It's everywhere, and in excess. A Müller strawberry yogurt Fruit Corner contains 22.8 grammes of sugar, about the same as a KitKat (23.8 grammes).[14] A typical 330 ml can of soft drink contains 35 grammes of sugar – that's nearly nine teaspoons. Disgusting if you actually imagine scooping each one in, but we don't, because they're easily dissolved (i.e. camouflaged) directly into the food.[15] You'll find added sugar in your sausages, breads – even the whole grain ones – ready meals, soups, burgers, crisps … the list goes on. Subway's Meatball Marinara 6-inch sub has 11 grammes of sugar (about three teaspoons).[16]

Sugar is hidden in just about every processed food, mainly because it is addictive. Twenty-four per cent of Heinz ketchup is pure sugar.[17]

Making consumers physically addicted to their products is a carefully calibrated science into which the Big Food companies put huge effort. According to Moss, five hundred chemists, psychologists and technicians were put to work at the Frito-Lay (maker of Walkers crisps and other snack foods) research centre in Dallas, measuring and optimising every variable they could. My favourite tool described by him is the company's $40,000 chewing simulator. They used it to answer questions like how brittle the perfect chip ought to be: 'People like a chip that snaps with about four pounds of pressure per square inch.' Consider Cheetos. With annual worldwide sales of over $4 billion, it's a big business.[18] Its most important feature, according to food scientist Steve Witherly, is 'vanishing caloric density' – the cheese puffs' ability to dissolve instantly on your tongue. 'If something melts down quickly, your brain thinks that there's no calories in it … you can just keep eating it forever.'[19]

As you might expect, this food, and this way of eating, is killing us. The rapid rise of heart disease and diabetes in Western society is directly linked to our diet. A report by the UK government's Chief Scientific Adviser Sir David King warned that costs associated with obesity and people being overweight will hit £49.9 billion per year by 2050.[20] That's over £1,200 on average a person will pay annually in extra taxes to subsidise the treatment of diet-related disease.[21]

The bottom line: factory food is toxic, and the only way to understand how it has become so pervasive is to understand the business of factory farming. Not just factory farms for animals but also the farms growing the crops on which this whole inhuman, industrialised monstrosity is built.

'No future in farming'

Matt Rothe always wanted to be a farmer. Raised on a large family farm in Colorado, perhaps the most exciting day in his childhood was the day his father showed him how to use the tractor ... and let him drive it. 'It's corn as far as you can see in any direction,' Matt explains. 'And despite the fact that you're only going three miles per hour, you're always making a little progress towards the end of the field, and there's such a sense of satisfaction when you get to that final row, and you turn around, and the whole thing is done.' By his senior year in college in 1994 Rothe had been doing a lot of thinking about his future. In April he called his father and told him what he'd decided: he wanted to 'come home and farm'. He thought his father would be thrilled; instead, his father told him: no, there's just no future in it. What he meant was: no future in farming the way they farmed. No future in a family farm. 'It was hard for both of us,' Rothe says. 'I can't imagine being a father and listening to my son and telling him he couldn't come back and run the business – the business that had been in the family for twelve generations.'

Rothe moved out to California and got a job running one of the best-known suppliers of humanely produced meat in the state.[22] After that he went to business school. Just as he was finishing his degree, he found out his dad had been diagnosed with pancreatic cancer – a year-long death sentence. Rothe started spending much more time at home, being with his father, helping him manage the farm's affairs, and getting a glimpse into what the business was really like. 'I started taking a look at all the spreadsheets,' he says, 'all of the profit-and-loss statements, the balance sheet.' It turned out the farm was close to bankruptcy. After his father passed away, Rothe and his mother had no choice but to sell. 'There was this feeling of helplessness, of seeing the farm disappear for good in our family. My dad was the twelfth documented generation of family farmers in our family. And there wasn't going to be another one.'

Several months before his father died the two had been sitting at the kitchen table, and Rothe's dad started to tell his son a story, the same story that, many years before, his own father had told him. It was the story of how the tractor ruined farming.

'It used to be that we had horses, and they did all of our work,' he began. 'The cycle of the day was that you'd get up in the morning, feed the horses, feed yourself, go out in the barn, saddle all the horses, get them all connected, and you'd go out and work in the field until noon. Then you'd come back, get the horses some water, a little food. You would eat. And you'd take the horses back out in the afternoon to work either until they couldn't work any more or you couldn't work any more. And at the end of the day you'd put the horses back in the stable. Everyone would go to sleep, and you'd get up the next morning and do it again. Then one day they invented the tractor. And this tractor was going to be the saviour for farming. This was going to make farming easier; it was going to make it more profitable. We were all going to get rich: 'Go buy a tractor!' Think about it … you went from a horse, which is one horsepower, to a tractor, which is scores of horsepower. It was a giant leap forwards in terms of technology on the farm.'

But tractors were expensive. Farmers didn't have a lot of money, so they took out loans to buy them. That wasn't really a problem – after all, the tractor was going to make them exponentially more productive – but then the tractors broke down a lot and needed lots of fuel, so they had to take out loans to run them, and then they realised that the tractor was so productive, they were no longer limited by hours in the day but by how many acres they had. Except that without enough acres, they couldn't actually pay off the tractor. So they took out more loans, bought more land, and farmed it like never before.

'Everybody is getting a tractor,' his dad continued. 'All the neighbours now have tractors. Everybody is more productive, everybody is buying more land, everybody is producing more food. And because there's more of it in the market, the prices are declining. The reality is that we're not really any better off financially because prices have come down as a result of our productivity. And we have all this debt that we have to service. At least with the horse we had the promise of only working a twelve-hour day because that's all the horse could work. Now we're working all day every day just to service this tractor.'

At that moment, sitting at the kitchen table, listening to his dad in his bathrobe talking about tractors, it all clicked for Rothe. 'My grandfather's story of the tractor is basically an allegory for every technology that's been developed since. That includes artificial pesticides, fertilisers, genetically modified organisms. It includes the specialisation of farming equipment and technology. It's all the same story.'[23] These technologies we've developed – which on the surface have led to highly 'efficient' farming of the same crop in huge fields (much easier for the tractor to plough through) – actually mask the decline of productive capacity in our soils. We produce more calories now than we ever have, but it's an illusion. In reality the underlying asset, the soil, is declining – and not just its fertility: overworked farms leave soil overexposed to wind and water erosion. As Rothe explains, there's no question that this is a far 'cheaper' way to produce food. But that's only because its costs are borne by future generations of consumers and farmers for whom one day this system of monocultures, fossil-fuel-based fertilisers, and soil depletion will collapse.

Consider: as soil health declines, farmers must compensate with more and more nitrogen fertiliser. But not all of it gets taken up by crops; rather, it ends up in the air (fuelling climate change as nitrous oxide), in our rivers and oceans (killing off entire marine ecosystems), and in our drinking water. And soil is relatively finite, taking five hundred years to produce just two centimetres.[24] There are also the pesticides we have to filter from our water, the flooding precipitated by eroded fields, the loss of habitats for critical species, let alone the species themselves ... the list goes on. In November 2014, the New Economics Foundation attempted to calculate the industrial agricultural system's environmental costs. Their upper estimate came to £7.2 billion a year for the UK alone.[25]

Farming never used to be a depletive act. It was the ultimate symbiotic relationship between man and nature. Though each crop would take something from the soil – how else would it grow? – it would give something back too. Legumes, like clover, would be planted during off-cycles to fix nitrogen in the soil, nitrogen that other crops like vegetables, fruits and grains need to grow well. This is why for generations farmers would rotate the crops they grew within their fields each season. Meanwhile grazing livestock would create fertiliser – for free – greatly reducing if not eliminating the need to buy artificial inputs as well as making waste management a far easier task. Nitrogen fixation, a natural process, converts nitrogen in the air into ammonium in the soil, which can then be picked up by all other plant types and converted to plant protein. Simplistically: no nitrogen, no crops, no food.

The availability of food is obviously a basic requirement for humans, and until the mid-nineteenth century, population growth in Europe was largely constrained by the amount of reactive nitrogen in the food supply. To keep up with demand, reactive nitrogen was mined directly from coal, saltpetre and guano. But then, at the start of the twentieth century, Fritz Haber, a German chemist, worked out how to convert natural gas into nitrogen fertiliser. It was considered nothing short of alchemy. Managing multiple crops on a farm, rotating them so that soil nutrients can be properly restored, isn't conducive to industrial techniques. But the availability of industrial fertiliser made possible the introduction of vast, tractor-able expanses of single crops like corn, wheat, soy and sugar that can be farmed in massive volumes. Now these are the basic ingredients of the factory food – junk food – that has come to dominate our diet.

As technology like fertilisers, engineered seeds and machinery made industrial farming possible, traditional family farms have been swallowed up into the giant factory farming corporations that dominate our food supply today. Industrialised feed production led to industrialised animal production, and the factory farm was born. As big companies tend to do, these giant agri-businesses – companies like Cargill, and Monsanto – have turned their market power into political power, successfully lobbying for the things that would make their life easier and the life of the ever-shrinking number of family farms harder.

When people say it's elitist to want a more human food system because factory food at least delivers cheap food for hard-pressed families, tell them about the subsidies. Factory food is 'cheap' because it's subsidised in multiple ways, whether you like it or not. British farmers received £3.2 billion of direct subsidy in 2012,[26] and the vast majority supported food production that was neither sustainable nor humane (96.5 per cent of farms in the UK aren't registered as organic, and about a quarter of all cropland is used to produce cereals for livestock feed).[27]

In many ways the subsidies that really matter are implicit, the indirect subsidies that are multiple orders of magnitude bigger. We pay the financial costs of the health and environmental damage that the Big Food companies cause – costs that they avoid. This means we first pay for factory food when we buy it, then we pay taxes and higher insurance premiums to counter its negative impact on our health and environment, and then again we pay through our taxes that subsidise the Big Food companies. Taxes are supposed to pay for things that are good for society but wouldn't happen otherwise. And yet here we are, subsidising commercial activity that harms the public. It's nuts.

We can change this. We can design a food system that's better for our health, better for the environment, better for animals. We can design a food system that is more human.

The Niman Ranch pork company

When I worked in the British government we tried to reduce the harm done by Big Food through voluntary agreements – what we called 'Responsibility Deals' – through which the companies would make their food less toxic. The idea was that this would actually be a quicker way to achieve concrete outcomes like reductions in salt, fat and sugar than going through a process of regulation. These efforts were ultimately superficial because they didn't address the deep structural forces at play. The key to making food more human on a mass scale lies in new business models that can produce better, healthier food systematically. The UK has many excellent small-scale examples of food produced in a more human way. But it's in America, where the worst forms of industrial farming were born (and persist), that entrepreneurs are now creating the building blocks of a new and more human food system.

In 2015, Chipotle, the US-based 1,700-branch chain (with locations now in Europe and Canada) serving custom-built tacos and burritos made from freshly prepared, recognisable ingredients, was hit by a series of food-related sickness outbreaks that called into question the chain's food safety practices and which are still under investigation at the time of this writing. Any flaws in Chipotle's food safety standards, however, do not detract from its leadership on animal welfare, where it still ranks among the best in the industry. Case in point: when one supplier failed animal welfare inspections, Chipotle temporarily stopped serving pork at over a third of its restaurants rather than continue buying and selling the inhumanely raised meat.[28] Chipotle's commitment to food that's produced in a more human way is a key part of its brand. They're proving that fast food can be made at scale using humane, sustainable meat. What's less well known is that much of Chipotle's ability to buy humane pork at the scale it does rests on the ingenuity of one man determined to prove it was possible.

A little over a decade ago Steve Ells, Chipotle's founder, read an article called 'The Lost Taste of Pork' in an obscure food magazine called *The Art of Eating*. There writer Edward Behr describes the 'best pork' he had ever eaten and details the old-fashioned practices of the farm it came from, run by a man named Paul Willis. After ordering some to try for himself, Ells was hooked. He was determined to make his burritos with meat from farms like Willis's.[29] But how could one small farm supply thousands of restaurants around the world?

A down-to-earth, fourth-generation farmer from Iowa, Willis has been raising pigs – all free-range – since the mid-1970s. 'I learned to do this when I grew up, and it was common,' he explains. 'I liked the idea of the animals being out on the pasture. Pigs were part of your crop rotation – we were growing corn, soybeans, oats and hay – and one of the things you had were pigs.' Over time Willis was able to grow the farm to more than a thousand pigs. Like many other pig farmers around the country, he had built a sustainable, profitable livelihood for himself, one that respected the land, the animals and the community.

Then at some point in the 1980s Willis started to notice confinement buildings popping up, buildings designed to house tens of thousands of livestock packed together as closely as possible. They started out small – individual buildings on farmers' land – but by the 1990s, when factory farms had infiltrated the pig industry, buyers no longer wanted to deal with small farms like his. 'They started to squeeze us out of the marketplace. They would bid us a lesser price or rate our meat poorer quality, since it yielded less.' (Pigs raised outdoors have bigger lungs and hearts because they use them running around and doing what pigs naturally do.) But Willis refused to change. 'Going in one of those buildings convinced me that I just never wanted to raise animals like that.' The sound, the crowded conditions, the concrete, the palpable misery – all have an overwhelming effect on anyone who sets foot in a modern factory farm. 'I think the thing that really knocks me over is the odour – the hydrogen sulfide and ammonia. You can't take enough showers to get rid of it, even if you're in there only a minute. I lived on a farm, grew up with farms – my grandparents, my parents and so forth. And this was a brand-new smell, something we had never experienced before.'

Willis makes sure his pigs 'can be pigs'. Recognising that they, like humans, require companionship, he never introduces one animal into a social group that's already established. He'll also make 'retreat areas' with straw bales to give timid animals a place to get away from their aggressive peers. (Contrast this with the 80 per cent of pregnant sows in factory farms, churning out piglets with little respite their entire lives, raised in steel-and-concrete pens that prohibit them from turning around, a practice defended on the grounds that it prevents the cruelly stressed pigs from injuring each other.)[30]

As farms consolidated around him (almost 600,000 small farmers went out of business between 1979 and 2004),[31] Willis looked for a way to keep farming the way he knew was right. His answer was also consolidation – but on farmers' terms, not industry's. He started reaching out to other local-farmer networks, finding people who raised pigs in a similar way and paying them a premium price. Little by little, welfare standards were established, and with fellow humane livestock pioneer Bill Niman as a partner, the Niman Ranch Pork Company was established. Today it comprises 500 farmers and can't increase supply fast enough.[32]

In addition to a price premium, the pork company members receive a guaranteed price floor, to protect against unexpected drops in the market, and are able to use their scale to economise on processing, distribution and marketing. Willis and Niman created a business model that would allow farmers to confidently stick to a more human approach even in the face of their industrialised, mechanised competitors. Now, thanks to Paul Willis, you can buy humane pork not just at high-end restaurants and grocery stores but also in the mass marketplace.

A different but equally promising challenge to the industrialised food system is being pioneered by Belcampo Meat Company, based in Oakland. Its business model focuses on just one ranch, owning some 20,000 acres in northern California as well as the entire supply chain needed to support it. For its 2,000 cattle and 13,000 other animals such as quail, sheep, goats, rabbits and chickens, that means one slaughterhouse and a handful of retail butcher shops (there are seven already in California). The farm, the processing, the retail – all in one business. According to founder Anya Fernald, bringing it all together isn't only more profitable; it also assures that standards are upheld. Raising the animals is really only half the battle, after all. You could be the most caring, humane rancher in the world but still have to use a third-party slaughterhouse which doesn't share your values. This leaves far too many questions unanswered. Fernald wants to know: 'How was it actually killed? How was the handling leading up to the kill? How long was it sitting on the truck?[33] She designed Belcampo to make sure there were no missing links in the supply chain.

The key for Belcampo is bringing everyone together, from the rancher and slaughterhouse cutter to the butcher and customer, such that where your food comes from is no longer some black box – in fact, every single piece of meat is completely traceable, as the system is so straightforward and transparent. It's human scaled. Fernald acknowledges that Belcampo can't sustainably grow beyond eight or nine stores, but this doesn't mean the model can't. She envisages a multiplicity of Belcampos, each with its own management team, butcher's shops, slaughterhouse and ranch. 'When businesses that are producing food get to a large scale, quality takes a nosedive and communication breaks down.' For a meat model that's focused on health and husbandry to work profitably, she insists, the supporting business structure must be large enough to turn a profit but not so large that it becomes out of touch.

Niman Ranch and Belcampo show us two different ways of raising humane, sustainable meat profitably and at a scale beyond just one-off family farms selling what they produce at the farmers' market each week. But to deliver non-factory food (not just meat but everything else) at a meaningful scale, we must also think about how it's sold.

Booths, a small supermarket chain in northern England, is showing that making a profit and bringing people good, healthy and humane food are not mutually exclusive. Its aim, says chairman Edwin Booth, is 'making really good food choices available to as many people as possible'. Sometimes that means local and organic, but sometimes that means food imported from around the world. It involves a responsibility to customers, but also to suppliers, which takes many forms. There is the labelling, now widespread in all supermarkets, that shows where cuts of meat or produce come from. But unlike the big supermarkets, Booths' butchers actually know the farmers and fishermen, and the company treats them well. Harry Wilson, who raises lamb in Cumbria, is a loyal supplier: 'I don't think consumers understand how tough it can be in farming, about the constant pressure on price,' he says, but Booths does, paying 'market price plus a premium: £4 an animal. It adds up.' And unlike factory-meat buyers who care for quantity over quality, Booths takes the opposite approach. 'We had a conversation last year with a buyer from Booths who said they'd prefer to take good [quality lamb] rather than volume. If we only have fifty-five that have reached the right weight [as opposed to their typical sixty a week] that's what they'll take … And when we go to our nearby store in Kendal they have a sign up saying which farmer produced the lamb on sale.' This is all part of the company's mission, says Booth. 'We have to be good corporate citizens. We have to care about our suppliers' employees. We have to care about the rural economy.' As the *Observer* food writer Jay Rayner notes: 'I can't for the life of me recall ever hearing anyone from the big supermarkets say anything like this.'[34]

Booths gets it. Farmers have one of the most stressful, underpaid, under-appreciated jobs in the world. We literally need them to survive, yet we squeeze their pay in the name of '50p off'. As a result of good corporate responsibility – and radical transparency – Booths has learned how to do things the right way.

In London, a start-up called The Food Assembly is using technology to challenge the industrial food system. It is an online food-retail platform that eliminates most of the extra cost of buying from local, sustainable producers by cutting out the physical store, saving on buildings and wastage. To do this, they organise weekly, two-hour 'assemblies' – pop-up markets – where producers and consumers come together to fulfil their orders. This is not unlike community-supported agriculture or fishery schemes, in which households subscribe to a particular farm to receive a basket of goods each week (you get to decide what you like and how much of it you want). The Food Assembly expands access to good food – real food, not fake, factory food – to people who might never otherwise see such items in the supermarket or get to the farmers' market. This expanded reach of even the smallest producers allows them to bring down costs in ways their size would otherwise preclude (not to mention the fact that because of the shortened supply chain, they get to keep more of each sale). What's really revolutionary about The Food Assembly is that it fundamentally changes the supermarket model to one of production on demand. Instead of baking, say, one hundred loaves of bread, selling out some days and wasting half on the others, the producers on The Food Assembly's platform know precisely how much they need to make (you place your order two days in advance). These savings make good food even more accessible.

Jamie and the food revolution

So yes, a more human approach to food is emerging. How can we encourage it? Some have argued that the key lies in consumer information and education – changing our food culture. Ending bad food starts with an appreciation of good food – not just how to eat it but knowing where it comes from and how to cook it. A good place to start? Our children. If you think food marketing to adults is deceptive, what the food industry does to children is far worse, with a combination of cartoon characters, prizes, online games and social pressure used to full effect (more on this in Chapter 7). But even if parents guard against the insidious influence of food media, schools can often let them down.

No one has done more to shine a spotlight on this over the years than the heroic Jamie Oliver. By turning millions of people on to food, by making it cool to cook, by running fantastic campaigns against bad food with programmes like *Jamie's School Dinners* and *Jamie's Food Revolution*, he is the single best thing that has happened to our food culture. And Jamie himself would be the first to acknowledge that he's building on the work of other great leaders, like Alice Waters, the visionary pioneer from Berkeley, California. Her Chez Panisse restaurant helped bring healthy, sustainable food to the height of global popularity (at least among elites and hipsters) that it now enjoys. Waters's mission is to take her food revolution mainstream. After she started a garden and teaching kitchen at a nearby middle school some twenty years ago, her Edible Schoolyard project has grown into a fully fledged educational resource centre. Its in-person seminars and online network provide curricula and practical resources for educators who not only see the vital connection between well-nourished children and their educational outcomes but also understand the need to teach students about the food they eat and where it comes from.

But as Jamie and Alice have found, the culinary-industrial complex doesn't want you to know about the food you eat and where it comes from.

Upset by a planned McDonald's restaurant near the Spanish Steps in Rome, Carlo Petrini, an Italian journalist from Piedmont, founded in 1986 an organisation called Slow Food. Since then, Slow Food has become a global movement, coming to represent much more than an opposition to fast food. Its motto, 'Good, clean and fair', captures precisely the opposite of what our food system has become. Its conference in Turin every two years brings together thousands of farmers, fishers, ranchers, food artisans – and, of course, eaters – from every corner of the earth to share each other's cultures and, most importantly, reveal the faces – the stories – behind what's being enjoyed. One of Slow Food's most compelling proposals is a 'narrative label' for foods, with details like animal breeds, types of feed, pasture type and location, and animal welfare all clearly spelled out.

Why focus on the narrative? What about all those certification schemes you see everywhere? Standards, kitemarks, different terms approved by governments and regulators – isn't that the way to inform consumers and thereby change behaviour? The problem is, these bureaucratic schemes are just another black box that consumers don't really understand and can't see into; they're not human, just like PISA scores in education.

With a few exceptions (like the Soil Association's 'organic' mark), they can be easily gamed, obscuring the truth so that a carefully crafted facade can be more easily believed.

In America, there's a TV ad (for Geico, an insurance company, as it happens) about a chicken travelling across the country. Wherever it goes – along train tracks, into a diner – it sends selfies back to the farmers who raised it. As the camera pans out from the farmers sitting on their veranda, we see hundreds of chickens roaming freely across the countryside to the narrator's message: 'If you're a free-range chicken, you roam free. It's what you do.'[35] This is what you might imagine when you see 'free range' on meat you buy in the supermarket. It's what you're supposed to imagine. It's what the words 'free range' literally mean: freedom. Rolling outdoor pastures, animals able to behave naturally, roaming about, eating grass, little bugs, whatever they want.

Well, roaming free may be what you do if you're a chicken in an insurance ad, but it's highly unlikely to be what you do if you're an actual free-range chicken in the real world. It is perfectly permissible, within the relevant EU labelling rules, for 'free-range' chickens to spend most of their lives cramped inside huge indoor barns. What about 'cage-free'? Sounds good, no? Although cage-free chickens are literally not housed in cages, farmers can get away with providing them bedded space that is half the size of a piece of A4 paper, and still be completely within the rules.[36] And within both free-range and cage-free labelling schemes, it is perfectly acceptable to treat animals with antibiotics and to carry out cruel and disgusting practices like throwing live chicks into mincing machines.[37]

The truly depressing fact is that this is what passes for good in our current system. Most of these 'humane' free-range and cage-free products are slightly better than the vast majority of meat and dairy products with no animal welfare claims at all. But nothing is worse than the use of humane-sounding terms that have no specific standards associated with them at all, terms like '100% natural', 'farm fresh', 'high animal welfare', 'corn fed' or 'no added hormones'. (These last two are particularly egregious, as you will often see them on the menus of smart restaurants trying to give themselves an aura of quality. All chickens are 'corn fed', and it is illegal to inject any poultry with hormones; saying so doesn't tell you anything about whether or not they were raised in horrific conditions.) The use of these terms amounts to deliberate lying by the culinary-industrial complex to cover up factory farming's grotesque cruelty to animals. It is a scandal.

Information is a vital part of making markets work properly, but in the food market today the information that's supposed to efficiently connect buyers and sellers is not information at all. Despite all the controls and specifications that govern food labelling and advertising, consumers are misled and lied to on a daily basis. Why is it acceptable for my milk carton to feature images of cows strolling around on grassy hills when they're actually confined inside and fed unhealthy diets of corn and soy, not the grass their digestive systems were designed to eat? Why is it acceptable for chickens to be called 'free range' when they're captive indoors for half their lives? Why don't I have a right to know what kinds of antibiotics were pumped into the bacon I'm about to serve my family at breakfast? What about the TV ad for pasta sauce that suggests it was cooked in some home-style kitchen? How can the Big Food company responsible give that impression when it was actually made in some giant grey industrial vat with a whole slew of chemicals that wouldn't be out of place in a science lab?

As we are misled on animal welfare, so too are we misled about our food's nutritional value. The latest marketing gimmick from Big Food is to trumpet the vitamins their food contains. But this is a con. In order to cut costs and increase shelf life, natural nutrients are removed during processing. Then, to be able to tout their products' nutritional benefits, factory food companies add artificial nutrients to replace what their own machines have stripped bare. The result is a total deception; food brands advertise the vitamins they've added, signalling to the consumer that no matter how much salt, fat or sugar is present, it has nutritional value and is 'healthy'. Even commercial 'whole wheat' is often just white flour to which bran and germ are added back in.[38] Meanwhile we lose the benefits of nutrients that work better in their natural forms. In addition, although the advertised vitamins and nutrients might be good for us, they don't help with diet-related diseases like heart disease and obesity. Processed 'health' food is healthy in all the wrong ways. Westerners are really not at risk from vitamin deficiency (compared to the 2 billion in poor countries who are), and yet we eat this 'healthy' processed food that actually makes us obese and diabetic.[39] One UK survey found that many cereal bars had more sugar than sugary cereals.[40]

It's not just that loosely regulated claims, certification schemes, packaging and advertising misrepresent what's gone into the food we buy. In many cases it really is outright lying. One study in Leicester found that over 40 per cent of meat products collected from butchers, retailers, wholesalers, manufacturers, fast-food outlets and caterers contained other species of meat than those that appeared on the labels. In 17 per cent of samples meat of the undeclared species was the primary ingredient.[41] In the UK, some 7 per cent of cod and haddock is mislabelled; in Ireland, it's a quarter.[42]

Meanwhile, 30 per cent of fish in Spain and 32 per cent in Italy is mislabelled.[43] For some specific fish it's far worse: 82 per cent of smoked fish in Ireland and up to 80 per cent of bluefin tuna in Paris is mislabelled.[44] Fish in the United States are so regularly mislabelled that the government actually has a task force devoted to fighting 'seafood fraud'.[45] Whereas 74 per cent of sushi bars were found to mislabel their seafood, 94 per cent of random samples of red snapper taken from retailers across the United States were found not actually to be red snapper.[46]

Carlo Petrini's idea of narrative labelling takes us towards a more human – and more effective – answer: just let people see what's going on. In 1906 journalist Upton Sinclair published *The Jungle*, which exposed the dreadful conditions in the American meatpacking industry. The public uproar that ensued led to one of the most significant consumer protection laws ever passed: the Pure Food and Drug Act. I think it's time for another uproar.

There's a simple rule we should introduce that would start to address Big Food's lying and misrepresentation. Any food product must have a reasonable proportion of its packaging and any promotional materials, such as TV ads, devoted to showing the precise conditions it was made in. A pack of frozen chicken nuggets would have a photo of the actual farm the chicken came from. A TV ad for hot dogs … a video of the pig pen. That 'homemade' pasta sauce? Let's see a picture of the factory, steel vats and all, not some fake pastiche Italian country kitchen constructed in a studio. Look, I'm not saying all of the packaging and promotion of food products should be truthful, just a reasonable amount – say, 20 per cent. That still leaves 80 per cent for lies and deception. To make sure it's all real and above board, there should be a requirement that every part of every facility of every factory farm and every food factory be live-streamed on the Internet so people can see exactly what's going on and track their food if they want to. In a world of cameras in every smartphone, the cost for producers would be negligible – and radical transparency of this kind would be more effective than any number of regulations and certifications. Who could object to it?

Well, people who get cross about 'the nanny state', I guess. Hmm. 'It's curious that we're open to social engineering when it's being done by corporations,' says the food writer and activist Michael Pollan. 'You're socially engineered every time you walk through the cereal aisle in the supermarket. The healthy stuff is down at your feet and the stuff with the most sugar and chocolate is at your eye level – or your child's eye level. That doesn't seem to bother us. But as soon as it's done by elected officials on our behalf, it's anathema.'[47] Kelly Brownell, a professor of psychology and public health at Yale University, argues, 'As a culture, we've become upset by the tobacco companies advertising to children, but we sit idly by while the food companies do the very same thing. And we could make a claim that the toll taken on the public health by a poor diet rivals that taken by tobacco.'[48] Perhaps the best advice is in fact Michael Pollan's: never eat food that has been advertised.

Beating Big Food

But in the end, changing our food culture, consumer pressure, more transparency … it's not enough. We've had consumer pressure for years and the problem is getting worse, not better. Still today, only 3.5 per cent of UK farmland is organic.

In any case it's not fair to put the burden for change on consumers when the Big Food producers have all their structural advantages: the subsidies, the lax regulation. To say that people should care more, that they really should shop differently, misses the point. They already care. But it's such an effort to shop differently. Hardly anyone has the time or inclination to investigate their poultry producer or get up early on Sunday morning for the local farmers' market. People are busy trying to earn a living, raise children, take care of their families. Food may be of great concern to some – as a hobby, as a way of life. But for those whose interests lie elsewhere, for whom grocery shopping happens online between paying the bills and replying to e-mails, for whom dinner is squeezed between two part-time shifts – why should good food be an out-of-reach privilege? How civilised can a society really call itself if humane, healthy, wholesome food is a luxury for those with the time and money to look for it? We need to make food that is produced in a more human way the norm. That will take much more aggressive action than fiddling around with labels or even TV ads, welcome as that would be.

Option one: we must account for the true cost of our factory food and adjust our tax, subsidy and regulatory regimes accordingly. Just as we have applied the 'polluter pays' principle to companies that damage the environment, we should require food companies to pay for their negative impact on the environment and public health. We already do this for ships responsible for oil spills off the coast. Extending a similar 'price correcting' penalty mechanism to food would finally set the true costs of factory food straight. These penalties would apply at several levels. For, say, soil erosion from vast, homogenous fields of corn, it would be applied to the whole operation or farm. But many of these penalties could be more precise. For example, we should introduce a Nitrogen Tax to discourage the use of depletive artificial fertilisers and encourage positive alternatives like crop rotation. This would make it feasible to introduce an outright ban on the most dangerous synthetic pesticides, since a more natural system of land husbandry would require less of their use. We also need to challenge the relentless march of genetic modification in our agriculture. This is not progress, as some assert, but a reckless interference with nature's finely balanced ecosystems, and it's time to call a halt.

True-cost accounting also means looking at harm that happens off the farm. For example, we know that added sugar in processed food creates extra health costs. Just as we apply taxes to cigarettes and alcohol, we could (and should) do the same to sugar. But a Sugar Tax should not just apply to sodas and artificially sweetened beverages (as advocated by Mike Bloomberg and Jamie Oliver); it should apply across the board, to sugary candies, cereals, and even that Subway Meatball Marinara sandwich. This was the recommendation the Dietary Guidelines Advisory Committee made to the US federal government last year.[49] In such a system, industrial agriculture would be free to exist, but it would have to pay for the costs of the harm it inflicts. Any profits, then, would come from the *real* value it offers consumers and producers, not from the exploitation of animals, farmers, taxpayers, or the environment.

We can't just focus on the bad, though. We have to support the good. So we should redirect taxpayer subsidies to farmers and producers who are doing the right thing. By 'redirect' I mean, of course, take them away from Big Food.

Now, if government tried to end the factory-food companies' subsidies and make them pay the true costs of their operations, here's what would happen. The bosses of the big food corporations would take to the airwaves and say the price of food would go up. Politicians, terrified of doing anything that raises 'the cost of living', would back off. But the 'cost of living' as measured by food prices doesn't include the cost of *dying* – the cost of us dying of heart disease and diabetes, of local habitats dying around us, of animals dying in disgusting circumstances that spread disease. None of that – nor other associated costs – is included in the price of factory food, in the cost-of-living figures. That's why nothing gets done.

If we redirect the subsidies while holding Big Food corporations financially responsible for the pollution (of all kinds) they get away with, the price of bad food will go up, but the price of good food – more human food – will go down. If we stopped subsidising industrial food – instead letting a fair, competitive and properly priced and regulated market take its place – and chose to lower the costs of fresh fruits and vegetables and humanely raised meat, we would save money for the taxpayer *and* lead happier, healthier, longer lives. (By the way, there is no excuse for good food to be expensive: Britain leads the EU in food waste,[50] throwing away about a third of its food and drink a year – the vast majority of which being avoidable.)[51]

It has to be said, though, that there is little chance of seeing the kind of political leadership we need in order to impose these measures. So here's option two: beat Big Food at its own game. There is an exciting approach being pioneered by the prominent London-based investor Jeremy Coller. He asserts that factory farms pose an increasing threat to companies' – and their investors' – financial returns, that they create risks for the industry as a whole, but that the markets ignore these risks.[52] So Coller and his foundation argue that the directors of any company in the food industry should assess and report these risks so their share prices accurately reflect the financial implications of the factory model. This would have the indirect effect of incentivising a more human, more sustainable model. But as an investor himself, Coller takes a more active stance and promotes the same to his peers. Coller Capital insists that all its own investments take animal welfare into account. This not only allows Coller to avoid companies that refuse to improve their abusive business model but also to campaign directly for change in the practices of companies they're already invested in.

A moral imperative

I think we should go much further, though. I believe that animal cruelty is an absolute moral outrage: there really is no incremental improvement, no optimal compromise to be had. So I think it's reasonable to take an absolutist policy position, as we do in defence of other moral principles. We don't tolerate a moderate view on rape or torture, nor should we. Over time our progress as a civilised species has been defined by what is added to this list of 'moral universalisms'. One of the most profound was on the subject of slavery, which used to be ubiquitous. Now, of course, it is accepted that slavery is morally wrong. Our norms, along with our economy (as profoundly tied to slavery as it was) adjusted, and we adapted. I think it's time we consider factory farms the same way.

In the introduction to this book I spoke of the empathy evolution: we have increasingly expanded our moral consciousness to include others less like us. Our ability to empathise is fundamental, its expression recognised in infants as young as one day old.[53] Every time we extend empathy, society moves forward. The philosopher Jeremy Bentham argued that if slavery is tyranny and people shouldn't be treated differently by race, why should animals be mistreated simply because they have a different number of legs or the inability to converse? In his mind difference created a slippery slope that allowed the cruel and tyrannical domination of one group over another. Who – or what – made up that 'other' group was immaterial: 'The question,' he wrote, 'is not, *Can they reason?* or *Can they talk?* but *Can they suffer?*'[54]

As proud as we are of our history, we also reflect with shame on atrocities committed by our great-grandfathers – and gratitude that we've come as far as we have in our moral evolution. When our great-grandchildren look back on today, they'll shake their heads at our gross abuse of animals. So the right policy response to factory farms is clear. We shouldn't just 'not subsidise' them. We shouldn't just regulate them better or make them more transparent. We should ban them.

To decide how a ban would be applied, we should look to existing definitions, like the practices itemised in the Business Benchmark on Farm Animal Welfare: close confinement, non-therapeutic use of antibiotics and other growth-promoting drugs, routine mutilation (like tail docking and breaking beaks), partially conscious slaughter, and long-distance transport.[55] Compassion in World Farming argues that animals ought to be free from thirst and hunger, discomfort, pain and disease, fear and distress and should be able to behave in a natural way.[56] Their goal is to eliminate factory farming by 2050.[57] And, of course, in our open, interconnected global economy, it must happen around the world, not just in one country. But slavery was banned around the world, eventually. Starting with Britain.

When he saw the subtitle of this book ('Designing a World Where People Come First'), my then seven-year-old son Ben said, 'for the next version, Dad, I think you should change it to make animals come first, and that's fair to everyone because humans are animals too.' Banning factory farms won't just be better for animals; it will make us better humans. In *Eating Animals* Jonathan Safran Foer notes, 'Factory Farm – This is a term sure to fall out of use in the next generation or so, either because there will be no more factory farms, or because there will be no more family farms to compare them to.'[58] It's up to us.

CHAPTER 6

CAPITALISM

'Out of the blue one day, we were told to build a thirty-foot stage.'

So begins the most powerful political ad of the 2012 US presidential election. To foreboding music and a montage of black-and-white photographs, Mike Earnest tells his story, and that of his colleagues, at a paper plant in Marion, Indiana. Building a stage was an unusual task for mill workers, but they did it, quickly and without question. A few hours later they were summoned back to the warehouse where earlier they had set up the stage, and a group of people walked out onto it – the plant management. The stage was for them. Assembled in front of the management, the workers were then told that all of them, all three shifts, were fired. Even though the factory was profitable, it wasn't profitable enough; the plant would have to close. And just like that, after years – for some, decades – of employment, they no longer had a job. 'Turns out that when we built that stage, it was like building my own coffin.'[1]

Who was allegedly behind this inhuman treatment of the loyal workers in that plant? The company that bought it and then sold it, Bain Capital, who the ad tells us made $100 million by firing all those workers. And who was behind

Bain Capital? The 2012 Republican presidential nominee, Mitt Romney. Critics of the ad, including Democratic rising star and now senator Cory Booker of New Jersey, protested that it unfairly distorted Romney's business career and was profoundly anti-capitalist. But to no avail.

Mitt Romney assumed that his exemplary – stellar – track record in business would help propel him to the most powerful job on Earth. At a time of economic difficulty, surely the American people would choose an experienced business leader, who had turned around company after company, to turn around America's stagnating economy? It didn't work out that way. In fact, the opposite was the case. It was precisely Mitt Romney's business background that was used by the Obama campaign to destroy him. Week after week Romney was pummelled with ads attacking him for being ... a capitalist. 'The Stage' was simply the most effective of many such spots. More recently the front-runner for the 2016 Democratic presidential nomination, Hillary Clinton, said in a speech in 2014: 'Don't let anybody tell you that, you know, it's corporations and businesses that create jobs.'[2]

It's not just the Occupy protesters, it seems. Anti-capitalist sentiment has gone mainstream – even in America, one of the most pro-business countries in the world. In the UK the BBC's business editor is regularly asked whether he is pro- or anti-business. Imagine the sports editor being asked whether he or she was pro- or anti-sport. Media and entertainment companies – businesses themselves, let's remember – serve up a relentless diet of hostile portrayals. Opinion polls show large majorities of people agreeing that business can't be trusted, is bad for society, and so on. These days, being anti-business, to question the capitalist system, is fashionable.

In many ways it's understandable. But it's also dangerous. Our progress as a society and our well-being as individuals depend on capitalism and on businesses being successful. In this chapter we'll get to the heart of what's gone wrong and show how we can change things for the better, how we can help build a more human economy. But first we need to remind ourselves of some basic truths that often get lost in the shouting matches of day-to-day debate.

'A script of hope'

Consider why capitalism exists in the first place. It's for the simple reason that individuals, acting together through a private organisation and backed with outside investment, by pooling resources, skills and labour, can produce more than the sum of their parts – not just 'profits' for 'capitalists' but also the goods and services we use every day and the innovations that have added years to our lives. Without capitalism, government could not provide social safety nets, pensions, free education and healthcare. Of course, that means businesses have to make profits; if they didn't, they would not attract investment, they would go out of business, people would lose their jobs, and governments wouldn't get their tax revenue. Nor would we get the goods and services and innovation that make our lives better. This positive circle is the mechanism that has helped billions of humans escape poverty and provided them with a quality of life that was unimaginable decades ago. When you boil it all down, the mechanism is really quite simple: it's just producing, selling and buying goods and services. It's also, as former British chief rabbi Jonathan Sacks observes, really quite human:

In the market economy throughout all of history, differences between cultures and nations have led to one of two possible consequences. When different nations meet, they either make war or they trade. The difference is that from war at the very least one side loses, and in the long run, both sides lose. From trade, both sides gain. When we value difference the way the market values difference … we turn the narrative of tragedy, of war, into a script of hope.[3]

The vast majority of companies profit from providing something people want, without doing harm to others. Making a profit and not polluting, or making a profit and paying a living wage – these are not mutually exclusive. It's self-defeating for anyone who cares about society or the environment to be 'anti-capitalist' or 'anti-profit'. It's all about how: How is capitalism carried out? How are profits made? That's what we should focus on, not a generalised condemnation of the whole enterprise.

And that word, enterprise, is important too. Trace any business back to its origins, and you will generally find an entrepreneur: an individual or group of individuals who had an idea, a dream, a mission, to make that better cart, to build that better car, to design that better cargo ship, and now, in the twenty-first century, to send that better rocket out into space – and back. The very notion of enterprise, the calling of the entrepreneur, is profoundly human. To believe in something, to believe you can do better than what's out there at the moment, to believe you can persuade other people to buy it from you, to believe it's worth taking a risk with your life, your reputation, your money or other people's money in order to start a business, that is a uniquely human thing to do. This is what we should remember. In our system of capitalism businesses – real businesses – are human. They're about bringing people together in a structured way to benefit each other and society.

Hewlett-Packard co-founder David Packard put it well in a speech to employees in 1960. This quote appears in my earlier book *Good Business*, and I'd like to include it here too:

> *Why are we here? I think many people assume, wrongly, that a company exists simply to make money. While this is an important result of a company's existence, we have to go deeper and find the real reasons for our being. As we investigate this, we inevitably come to the conclusion that a group of people get together and exist as an institution that we call a company so they are able to accomplish something collectively that they could not accomplish separately – they make a contribution to society, a phrase which sounds trite but is fundamental.*[4]

That social contribution of capitalism is achieved through trade. Trade is unique to us as a species and is essential for human progress. We've farmed for around ten thousand years, but we've traded for a hundred thousand.[5] Trade was inextricably linked to and financed the energy and communication revolutions that were instrumental in connecting disparate cultures from across the globe. Trade isn't just human; it gave rise to the society we know today. Science writer Matt Ridley explains that 'through exchange and specialisation, we've created the ability to do things we don't even understand.'[6] No individual knows how to do everything; we are a symbiotic community in which individuals need to work with others who have different talents. In place of destruction, peaceful economic cooperation ensures progress.

Trade rests on a simple premise, however, an implicit promise that if what you do is worthwhile, others will recognise you for it. This basic principle has throughout history empowered people to do great things with their knowledge and skills, to improve some little part of the world, putting food on the table, a roof over heads, and earning a sense of accomplishment, of contribution. Cumulatively these capitalist basics add up to human progress and a better society.

Yet there is a deep sense of hostility toward capitalism today – the kind that has given rise to populists like Jeremy Corbyn, who score points with cheering audiences by attacking capitalism. But it has also prompted more establishment – and generally pro-business – politicians like Barack Obama and Hillary Clinton to make anti-business pronouncements, knowing they would be well received.

You could say: Who cares if there is such strong anti-business sentiment today? Why does it matter if business, trade, capitalism are becoming more unpopular? It matters because rhetoric and attitudes have a real effect: if politicians see the public turn against capitalism, they are far more likely to enact policies and regulations that channel public anger and attack business. And that is self-defeating. If we undermine the climate for business overall, instead of addressing specific justifiable grievances, that will lead to less innovation, fewer jobs, fewer goods and services that make our lives better, and less money for government to spend on social problems and all the things we say we want from it. There's another real-world problem caused by anti-capitalist sentiment: if people get the idea that business is basically bad, they won't want to go into it. The whole positive circle of business, trade and capitalism depends on entrepreneurs feeling supported as they dream and plan and build. We shouldn't be putting them off; we should be encouraging them.

Business gone awry

What all this requires is a much more forensic approach than anything we've seen up until now. Although it is self-defeating to be simplistically 'anti-capitalism', it's equally wrong for its supporters to airily dismiss the public's concerns. The truth is, the Occupy movement made some very good points. And even though most people wouldn't dream of actually joining an Occupy protest, they share many of its sentiments, especially about that great demon of our times: Big Business. Yes, when it comes to Big Business, people are really angry.

We are angry with big businesses for paying obscenely high salaries to their bosses and exceedingly low ones to their workers. We are angry that the leaders of the businesses that caused the economic crisis are doing better than before. We're angry – we're driven mad by – terrible, inhuman, unresponsive, bureaucratic service; the stupid rules and fine print; the relentless sales tricks; the systems designed to suit the company rather than the customer; the infuriating phone menus; the impossibility of speaking to a human being; the inability of a human being, if we ever do get hold of one, to actually understand what we want, to empathise, to take responsibility, to help. We are angry about the homogenisation of our communities by chain stores. We're angry about pollution of the air, land, sea – and minds – caused by irresponsible manufacturing and marketing practices. And we are angry that these problems never seem to improve; in fact, they just seem to get worse. Business is big and getting bigger. Executive pay is high and getting higher. Homogenised high streets are bland and getting blander. Social and environmental problems are grave and getting graver. Customer service is worse and getting … well, you get the point.

On issues that are blatant, corporate culture seems hopelessly tone deaf. Take executive pay. In the UK, median household income has fallen more than 10 per cent since 2008,[7] yet in 2014 alone, the median pay of FTSE 100 chiefs was up 50 per cent.[8] In 2000, according to Incomes Data Services, a research group, FTSE 100 chief executives paid themselves 47 times more than their median full-time employee. Last year, it was 120 times more.[9] In 2015, median full-time pay across the UK was £27,600.[10] For the FTSE 100 executives? £4.28 million.[11]

This isn't just bad for employees; it's bad for business. Between 2001 and 2013, the value of FTSE 100 companies increased 31 per cent; profits, 47 per cent. Director pay? 315 per cent![12] Executives are taking an increasingly larger proportion of the pie, even after driving their firms into the ground. Apple paid Tim Cook over $100 million in 2014.[13] Does anyone seriously believe that Tim Cook, who strikes me as being an incredibly decent, modest man, highly devoted to his company, would leave or work less hard unless he continues to get paid $100 million a year? At least his company is performing well under his leadership. Martin Sullivan was paid $47 million when he departed from AIG (despite a share decline in excess of 50 per cent on his watch and a $182 billion bailout from the US government).[14]

So how does it happen? By design. Professors at the University of Cambridge examined the effect of compensation consultants on compensation. After looking at 1,000 companies from 2006 to 2012, they concluded: 'Overall, our study finds strong empirical evidence for the hiring of compensation consultants as a justification device for higher executive pay.'[15]

Because the most egregious examples of personal and corporate greed – and other vivid illustrations of capitalism going awry – tend to occur in large companies, many hold a powerful impulse that big business is bad and small business is good. I understand that impulse. It's emotional, and I sometimes feel it too. But it's simplistic and doesn't take you very far: some big businesses do bad things, but small businesses do too. Many big businesses do good things, and we should want them to continue. For example, size can enable innovation to be incubated and deployed in a way that benefits real people in the real world on a scale that's not possible in a small business. General Electric, Samsung and Honda exemplify this in industry; Google, Apple and Amazon in technology. It goes wrong when companies use their size or market position to get away with practices that hurt consumers, employees, suppliers, the marketplace, or society at large. The problem is not capitalism itself; it's not even big business. It's something else, and to discover what that is, we need to look at some specific examples.

Banks

Banks are the dominant example of what's wrong with capitalism and what needs to be fixed. When large banks – having long ago lost touch with any sense of human scale – screw up, they cause systemic problems. One of the people who understand this best is Nassim Taleb. As an insider, he has been highly critical of 'too big to fail' financial institutions. Nature, Taleb argues, never made anything larger than an elephant or whale for a reason: size breeds complexity, which in turns brings risk. As he argues in *The Black Swan*, much of that risk is hidden and is not always where we think it will be. When large institutions – like banks – get too big, the risk of a catastrophic failure multiplies:

Financial Institutions have been merging into a smaller number of very large banks. Almost all banks are interrelated. So the financial ecology is swelling into gigantic, incestuous, bureaucratic banks – when one fails, they all fall. The increased concentration among banks seems to have the effect of making financial crisis less likely, but when they happen they are more global in scale and hit us very hard. We have moved from a diversified ecology of small banks, with varied lending policies, to a more homogeneous framework of firms that all resemble one another. True, we now have fewer failures, but when they occur … I shiver at the thought.[16]

He said this in 2007. If only he'd known just how soon he would be proved right. Think about the big banks. Their lesson from the 2008 crisis: if they are enormous and unwieldy enough to be 'too big to fail', governments will have no choice but to rescue them. When Lehman Brothers was allowed to fail, the results proved that the contagion was too great; any more comparable failures would be catastrophic for the economy. Eric Holder, former US attorney general, has admitted government's impotence: 'I am concerned that the size of some of these institutions becomes so large that it does become difficult for us to prosecute them when we are hit with indications that if you do prosecute, if you do bring a criminal charge, it will have a negative impact on the national economy, perhaps even the world economy.'[17]

The banks' concentration of economic power equates to political power. Big banks get in the door of government and have disproportionate say once they do. What do they want? Rules that benefit them. They want to know they'll be fine, regardless of any mistakes they make. Their brand of capitalism is lobbying – and it works. In December 2014 Republicans slipped into a $1.1 trillion Budget Bill a measure that allows traditional banks, whose deposits are federally insured, to invest in a wider array of financial derivatives – the same type of risky investments that contributed to the 2008 financial crisis (and had been banned since the Dodd-Frank financial reform legislation was passed in 2010).[18] As bad as the measure is, how it got in the bill is even worse. Inserted by Kansas Republican congressman Kevin Yoder, who personally receives more money from the financial industry than any other in campaign contributions,[19] it was actually written by Citigroup in 2013 as part of legislation proposed then. A *New York Times* analysis concluded that seventy lines of the eighty-five-line section can be traced directly to the bank.[20] The move was so blatant that one satirical headline in the *New Yorker* read, 'Citigroup to Move Headquarters to US Capitol Building.'[21] According to the *Washington Post*, Jamie Dimon, CEO of JPMorgan Chase, actually called individual lawmakers personally to urge their support.[22] Rather than take entrepreneurial risks like a real businessman, Dimon holds government to ransom to protect his company from risk through special favours.

To use the academic term, Dimon, JPMorgan Chase and the other big banks engage in 'rent seeking' behaviour. Rent seeking is a technical way of saying that instead of profiting through the proper use of markets, the 'rentier' unfairly uses its power – or the industry's – to gain profits that exceed the benefits they are providing to society; that is, they make money by grabbing more of the pie rather than making it larger. Banks are unquestionably beneficial and necessary for all the good things about capitalism to exist – after all, they literally provide the capital – but by making themselves individually indispensable, they've given themselves the ultimate taxpayer-backed guarantee, off which they then profit.

Legislating the banking sector is difficult, perhaps, because banks and lawmakers are so intertwined. So many US House members want to be on the Financial Services Committee, which regulates the American banking industry, that four rows of seats have been added since 1980 to accommodate the demand. But members aren't joining out of their zeal for preventing another banking crisis or their passion for economic policy; instead, it's about personal, political finance. The 'cash committee', as it is known on Capitol Hill, guarantees fund-raising success, a necessity for any member of Congress but especially for new members who need to consolidate their position in their districts: remember that members of the House of Representatives face election every two years. The *New York Times* reported that Congressman Andy Barr, a freshman Republican, raised almost as much money in the first two quarters of 2013 from the financial industry as former House Speaker John Boehner. The committee chair, Republican congressman Jeb Hensarling, is one of the leading recipients of campaign money from the financial industry. What does it say when the man in charge of regulating big banks receives such a significant proportion of his campaign cash from them?[23] Neither Barr nor Hensarling are necessarily corrupt in the personal sense – although as the case of former Virginia Governor Bob McDonnell showed, there's plenty of that too – but it's hard to believe that money doesn't buy some kind of influence. Is it a surprise that regulations aimed at constraining special interests end up benefiting them?

Of course, it's also easier for banks to obtain the political outcomes they want when so many bankers serve in government and so many politicians and regulators work in banks. The revolving door whirs away at the heart of the incestuous relationship between them. In the UK, Sir Hector

Sants joined Barclays seven months after his departure as head of the Financial Services Authority.[24] Sir Jeremy Heywood, the country's top civil servant, spent years as a managing director at Morgan Stanley.[25] James Crosby, former chief executive of Halifax Bank and then HBOS, went on to be deputy of the Financial Services Authority – until he resigned over reports that he had fired a senior HBOS manager for warning of the bank's failure.[26] He rightly handed in his knighthood, but the fact remains that a former bank chief executive was hired to regulate the very institutions whose failure he had allowed to happen.

It's no different in the US: current US treasury secretary Jack Lew was once COO at Citigroup.[27] In 2008 Larry Summers, treasury secretary under President Clinton, received $2.7 million from banks, including JP Morgan Chase, Citigroup, Goldman Sachs, Lehman Brothers and Merrill Lynch, as well as over $5 million to advise hedge fund D. E. Shaw, before President Obama appointed him chairman of his Council of Economic Advisors later that year.[28] Before he held the same post under President Clinton, Robert Rubin was an executive at Goldman Sachs; afterwards he became chairman of Citigroup. Even Federal Reserve Chairman Alan Greenspan became an adviser to Deutsche Bank in 2007 after leaving office.[29]

It all stinks. The systemic corruption is truly shocking. While they're in the banks, they know they can one day end up supervising them in government. While they're in government, they know they can one day end up in senior positions in the banks. Who doesn't think for one second that these men – yes, they are mostly men – put the interests of the banks and the untouchable 'financial services industry' before the interests of the people? What is so laughable is that these same grand figures of the Establishment look down their snooty noses at the kleptocracy of Putin's Russia or the rampant corruption in places like China, and seem to think they're better than all that. They're worse. At least in Russia the corrupt elites aren't hypocrites too.

Supermarkets

If you want to see a business that hurts consumers, employees, suppliers, the marketplace and society at large, look no further than the supermarkets. They've driven small farmers and other suppliers out of business; they've turned our commercial centres into 'clone towns'. But this is part of the implicit deal we made with them: they got to open in our communities, set up out-of-town stores, drive independent shops out of business. In exchange we got 'convenience' and 'value': twenty-four-hour shopping under permanent bright lights; 'more choices'; 'lower prices'. Come on, look how cheap milk is these days! (Here's why, by the way: milk, a staple item, is used by the major supermarkets as a loss leader to get customers into stores.[30] In 2014, price wars saw Tesco drop its price for four pints from £1.39 to £1 – a price quickly matched by Sainsbury's and the Co-op, and the same that Asda had been at for a year. With the exception of Asda, which has now dropped its prices even further, these stores now charge only 25p more for four pints than two pints.[31] Consumers might benefit in the short term, but in the long term, their good fortune at the checkout is destroying a fundamental industry, putting immense pressure on dairy farmers whose products are sometimes sold for less than the price of water, and often at a loss.)

I know the argument in favour of big supermarkets. They say: consumers are choosing us, and that's why we're big.

We're big because we're popular. But are they? Do consumers really have much choice?

Tesco has a land bank that buys up vast amounts of prime real estate. As of late 2014, Tesco owned 4.65 million square metres of land in 310 sites in England, Scotland and Wales, the majority of which are undeveloped.[32] Tesco might one day hope to build on some of this land, but of course any property controlled by Tesco can't be used by a rival. While the gullible Competition and Markets Authority (CMA) (whose executives and associates might one day – who knows? – find themselves working for or advising Tesco, given the revolving door between regulator and regulated) found that supermarkets weren't holding land to 'impede the entry by rival grocery retailers into local markets' as a deliberate act of strategy, even though they concluded that at 90 sites which 'grocery retailers had prevented from being used for grocery retailing', this practice of 'land banking' acted 'as a barrier to entry in a highly-concentrated local market'.[33] According to a study of the Land Registry by the *Guardian* and aerial photography firm Getmapping, much of Tesco's banked up property is close to its existing superstores, and Tesco has not allowed rival grocery retailers to develop on its land (despite offers) even though it has no current plans to do so itself.[34]When Tesco and other supermarkets buy land, they place it under what is called a 'restrictive covenant', a legal provision that restricts future landowners in a particular way, in this case by prohibiting the future development of supermarkets on it.[35]

Over the years, the various competition authorities have looked into all this, and each time the message to the big retailers has been basically the same: 'Nothing to worry about here, it's all got up by the press, bit of a storm in a teacup really ... now be a good chap and fix this little thing over here or that thing over there and I'm sure it will all blow over.' None of these verdicts has done anything to change the structure of the market, the fact that four firms control nearly all (73 per cent) of the supermarket options available to consumers.[36]

So you can't point to consumer choice as evidence that people want this kind of thing. It's not people choosing Tesco; it's people having no choice but Tesco. The implicit justification for land banking and other unfair practices is that they give us cheap prices, so why should we care? Even putting aside the social and environmental costs that they expect others to pay – for example, the taxpayer in the form of wage subsidies to enable their low-paid workers to survive – you could just about go along with this argument if people were making a conscious choice between Tesco and, say, an independent local retailer with a different set of products, prices and ethical values. But there often is no choice.

Because of land banking and loss-leading prices, these stores don't face real competition; if they do have a competitor, it might even be owned by the same parent company. In fact, Tesco wanted regulatory permission to increase its local monopolies, arguing that the definition of how far away a competing store could be should be a thirty-minute drive, as opposed to a ten- to fifteen-minute one.[37]

But the real joke about our Faustian pact on low prices is that they have not even gone down for consumers. Despite allowing the big four supermarkets such dominant market power and despite some short-term falls, the price of food in Britain has risen faster than inflation and faster than in other countries. Between 2006 and 2015, for example, food prices rose 37.8 per cent in Britain compared to only 23.5 per cent in Germany and 13.3 per cent in France.[38] The Big Four might say they don't fix prices, but if they have so much power and market share that they can attempt hugely expensive strategies like buying up land or selling milk at a loss, or even alleged illegal ones like deliberately delayed payments to suppliers (ill-treatment of suppliers prompted an investigation in 2015 by the Groceries Code Adjudicator; the report was due to be issued in early 2016, after this book went to press), then our rules are surely broken.[39]

The concentration of economic and political power in the hands of this small number of big companies shows that regulatory regimes have failed to achieve the kind of real business and real competition we should want to see. Politicians, of course, instead of challenging these destructive, inhuman leviathans, give knighthoods to their bosses and put them on panels to advise them on 'business'. By what stretch of the imagination are these businesses? Why can't we just be honest about it and admit that when it comes to food retailing, Britain is not a proper market economy with real, competitive businesses but a stitched-up economy that manipulates prices, punishes farmers and other suppliers, and disfigures our civic and cultural heritage with Communist-style, top-down national uniformity? We're so used to this now, so numbed into accepting this as the way it has to be, that it's my accurate description of it that sounds extreme.

Bank and supermarket consolidation are part of a larger trend. In the US, health insurance and pharmaceutical mergers seemed to be announced weekly. A proposed merger between brewers Anheuser-Busch InBev NV and SABMiller PLC, already the product of prior megamergers, would command almost 30 per cent of the global beer market. In the appliance sector there are two-thirds fewer manufacturers than there were in 1996. The four largest

American grocers have increased their market share by half from 1997. According to analysis by USC researchers, most publicly traded companies are now in more concentrated industries than they were in 1996.[40] And yet, according to the *Wall Street Journal*, these mergers are going by with little contestation from antitrust authorities.[41]

In so many industries the concentration of economic – and thus political – power in the hands of a small number of big corporations is incontrovertible. Regulatory regimes have failed to achieve the kind of real capitalist competition we should want to see. Politicians, of course, instead of challenging these destructive, inhuman leviathans, laud their bosses and put them on panels to advise them on 'business'. By what stretch of the imagination are these businesses? In truth, when it comes to many of the most important industries that affect our daily lives, the United States is not actually a proper capitalist economy with real businesses competing in open markets but rather a corrupt, cosy cartel. But it's not the idea of capitalism that's at fault; it's the structure we've allowed it to assume.

Lobbying

Rather than fairly competing in the marketplace like real businesses, big businesses in all industries – not just the uncompetitive ones – consistently seek to capture the levers of power to serve their commercial ends. No practice exemplifies this better than lobbying, an industry itself these days, especially in places where regulatory power is concentrated, like Brussels, London and Washington, DC. There, politicians and aides go through a revolving door of public- and private-sector positions. Today, some 50 per cent of senators and 42 per cent of congressmen become lobbyists after they retire – up from just 3 per cent in 1974.[42] And now staffers don't even have to retire before becoming lobbyists; many top political advisers to senior congressional Democrats and Republicans run their campaigning organisations while working for clients at lobbying firms.[43] As government has grown, the possibilities for lobbying have grown too. New agencies and more rulemaking make for more – and easier – targets.[44] The impact is impressive: Senator Elizabeth Warren points out that while each round of federal budget cuts hit programmes for the working poor and middle-income earners, subsidies and tax breaks for businesses that make billions in profit remain funded at full level.[45]

But it's instructive to look beyond just the federal government. In Chapter 2 we saw the great promise of decentralised power and how the American states, as 'laboratories of democracy', show the best aspects of decentralised power. They are indeed a great model – unless they've been captured by corporate lobbying as well.

The American Legislative Exchange Council (ALEC) is the country's premier forum for legislators, think tanks, and corporations to meet to discuss issues. Unsurprisingly for a group run by corporate interests, ALEC pushes for bills that suit corporations. But delegates at ALEC meetings do more than just talk; they actually write legislation in committee. At these meetings legislators, whose trips to ALEC meetings are often paid for through a corporate 'scholarship fund', are joined by policy analysts and representatives from ALEC's corporate members, who pay between $3,000 and $25,000 to participate. Together they write bills that can be adapted across multiple states, often as a back door to legislative outcomes that are difficult to achieve at the federal level or as attempts to undermine federal rules outright. The

CAPITALISM • 179

committee then votes on a proposed bill. If a majority of
both the legislators and corporate representatives on the
committee approve it, it becomes 'model legislation' and is
posted on ALEC's website for legislators across the country
to use in their own states.[46] Indeed, broad applicability is
the aim; they feature 'insert state here' placeholders, so all
legislators have to do is remember where they live.[47] One
set of identical ALEC-backed energy bills was introduced
in Oregon, New Mexico, and New Hampshire; the bills,
which benefited companies like ExxonMobil and Koch
Industries, were, naturally, written at ALEC meetings in
which representatives of those companies participated.[48]
Remember the ag-gag laws Big Food uses to silence critics of
its abusive practices? ALEC's Animal & Ecological Terrorism
in America Act was the model for many of them.[49] In total,
more than 1,000 ALEC bills are introduced a year, with over
200 passed into law.[50]

I'm no constitutional expert, but I doubt that corporations
paying to write 'model legislation' that is implemented across
the nation was what the framers had in mind for American
democracy.

Some would argue that businesses writing legislation is
not quite as bad as it sounds: at least they understand the
issues, and so the legislation is less likely to have the errors
and unintended consequences that often arise from a
bureaucrat's lack of specific knowledge. That is undoubtedly
true: the model legislation written by these companies will,
I'm sure, accurately address the relevant issues. But accuracy
isn't really the point. The point is accountability: How can
people have confidence in their democracy when companies
can literally purchase the right to draft legislation? What
has this got to do with capitalism? With real business? With
enterprise? With markets?

You may be thinking: well, yes, that's America for you. We don't have that kind of corruption in Britain. Not so fast. Even in countries without massive spending on political campaigns, like the UK, you see the same effects. It's just more subtle. More British. First, remember that while the scale is totally different from the US, election campaigns and political parties do need to be paid for – to the tune of many millions a year. On the Left, the money comes from trade unions, which is its own form of corruption. On the Right, it typically comes from wealthy individuals; more precisely, Britain's economy being what it is, wealthy individuals in the financial services sector. This means that politicians end up spending their time in the company of a very narrow fragment of society. Nothing so blatant as the legislation-writing shamelessness of Citigroup in the US – but there's an influence none the less.

Second (and not so much in the spotlight because the focus inevitably falls on politicians) is the lobbying that targets the civil servants who in the UK system actually write the rules and regulations that make such a difference to commercial outcomes for companies. Undisclosed hospitality, gifts, the implicit promise of future seats on boards and consultancy contracts … all this is part of the very British form of corruption that goes on, most of the time completely hidden from view. Why do you think defence procurement is such an astonishingly expensive mess, with the armed forces stuck with equipment they don't want? Why do you think there is so much waste and inefficiency in the NHS? Why do you think so many low-quality, unwanted commercial and residential buildings pop up all over the place? Not least because the arms manufacturers and the pharmaceutical and medical supply companies and the property developers have got their teeth into the people in government who advise on and award the contracts. And it's repeated throughout the system: every sector, every industry. National government, local government. All of it corrupt as hell.

Big business has another advantage in the public sphere, one that is more subtle but just as powerful. When policy decisions affecting industries are made, big businesses, regardless of whether they or their representatives are physically present, are often the loudest voices in the room. This is because they have a powerful arm lock on politicians who are terrified of being branded 'anti-business'. They are culturally cowed into writing rules that benefit the dominant existing players and work to keep smaller, innovative challengers out.

Small businesses are having an increasingly difficult time, and it's no wonder: their competitors have used their power unfairly to bully, cajole, manipulate and muscle their way into maintaining market share. Take, for instance, the local pub: there were almost 70,000 pubs in 1980, but since then some 21,000 have closed,[51] with over 7,000 shuttered since the financial crisis.[52] Now, some 30 pubs close each week.[53] Ivy House, a South London pub, was the first of 300 to earn the newly established 'asset of community value' status, a policy that Rohan and I developed to try to level the playing field and which allows community groups to buy pubs rather than allow them to be acquired by developers to be torn down. But this kind of tactical response, however worthy, is not the answer.

Capitalism should not crush small businesses; it should enable start-ups to thrive and grow. Politicians who unquestioningly back big business make a terrible error. They confuse big business with all business, and they confuse stitched-up oligopolies with competitive markets. The correct posture on capitalism, the one that fairly benefits business and society alike, is to be pro-market, pro-competition, pro-enterprise. That does not equate to doing the bidding of our biggest companies.

Business or bureaucracy?

Big market power is bad for the economy, distorts our political system and is bad for society. We get energy companies whose profits between 2009 and 2013 increased from £8 per customer to £48, and are on track to earn £120 per household annually.[54]

But what is it that lies behind the key players in capitalism becoming so distant from and dismissive of human concerns? We could just blame the people in charge, writing it off to the fact that they're simply the 'greedy capitalists' of caricature. That is simple-minded. It's not the people, any more than it was in our opening story involving JetBlue. It's a *structural* problem with our economy, and it needs a structural solution. What we are experiencing today is a landscape of capitalism dominated by institutions that have become large, sclerotic, and driven by their own organisational interests rather than those of the people they touch – capitalism that is far removed from human scale.

The banks, the supermarkets, the other inhuman institutions that behave in these ways: they have nothing of the entrepreneur, the risk-taker, the real capitalist about them. They don't want to win by creating better products; they want to win by getting the government to rig the market so they won't be challenged. They are not real capitalist businesses at all; they are private-sector bureaucracies. Real capitalist businesses are different. They do not depend on regulatory capture for their commercial success. Real businesses want to do great things – for themselves, obviously, but also for their employees, their customers, their suppliers, their communities and the wider world. Great entrepreneurs don't rely on loopholes to make profits. Of course they want to win, but they want to win by having the best products and services – not the best lobbyists and lawyers.

Over the past few decades, as globalisation has gathered pace and business has become more bureaucratic and less human, successive campaigns – be they Nader's Raiders, the young activists inspired by Ralph Nader's consumer advocacy in the 1960s and '70s; the anti-globalisers of the 1980s and 1990s; or more recently the 'Occupiers' – have fought for social and environmental justice, stood up for the 'little guy' against the big corporations, raised awareness, and gained a great deal of public support. But nothing has really changed, for a simple reason. The 'anti-capitalist' movement, in all its various forms, with all its valid points, has been aiming at the wrong target.

They've been aiming at the symptoms, not the cause. The cause of the discontent that people feel with business today is not capitalism itself but the concentration of economic power in fewer and fewer hands. It's the transformation of businesses into bureaucracies, practically part of the government, writing their own laws, writing their own rules. And it's not just the activists and the campaigners who have got it wrong. Policymakers got it wrong too. The policy and regulatory response to the social and environmental problems caused by capitalism-as-bureaucracy has been yet more bureaucracy – more rules, more regulations. But as we've seen, the business bureaucracies that cause the problems in the first place know exactly how to get around rules, avoid regulations and go their own way.

As the real target comes into view, so too does the solution. It's not to pass still more fiddly regulations attempting to deal with this or that manifestation of what's gone wrong with capitalism. We've tried that, and it doesn't work. The real solution is one that we can find deep within ourselves, in a very human instinct.

Fair competition

Just as to trade is human, to compete is human too. If you watch two children at play, boys or girls, somehow or another they find a way to make whatever game they are playing into a competition. Sure, they have fun. But half the fun is that they are aiming for some sort of purpose, a victory, however small. Competition is built into us, even at an early age. And it has helped build the world we live in today.

But it has to be fair. It's not just competition that's hardwired. It's fair competition. Behavioural experiments have shown that to a surprisingly high threshold, we innately care more about fairness than rewards.[55] But you don't need a social scientist to tell you this. Just think about how we feel about cheating in our everyday lives. We love fair competition (Olympic underdogs!), but nothing grates on us more than cheaters (Olympic dopers!). When a number of beloved Major League Baseball players in the United States were discovered to be using steroids, the outcry led all the way to congressional investigations. This disgust at unfairness is strong and instinctive.

Trade and fair competition – so brilliantly blended by free markets – are naturally and distinctly human, both by themselves and together. And they represent the correct response to the very evident problems with the way capitalism is working today.

Capitalism, left to its own devices, quickly becomes concentrated and ossified – into bureaucracies that are neither fair nor competitive. So when 'pro-business' politicians say they want to leave business alone, what they're really saying is that they want to maintain the unfair, often uncompetitive status quo. They want a free market only after it has been structured to unfairly privilege their donors. Those on the Left also want to privilege *their* special interests (often labour unions) and broader ideological aims. But like those 'pro-business' politicians, they also ignore the underlying structure of capitalism, preferring to tinker all over the place to create the ideal economy they envision. They want a fair economy, but not a market one. This doesn't work either.

So what we need now – the practical, positive, constructive response to 'anti-capitalist' sentiment – is a massive shake-up in our economic structures, to make them more fair *and* more competitive. In a 2015 paper examining the world's billionaires, economists Sutirtha Bagchi of Villanova University and Jan Svejnar of Columbia University found that only when billionaires amassed their fortunes through political connections did the ensuing wealth inequality drag on economic growth. When billionaires earn their wealth through entrepreneurship, there's no negative effect.[56] Government has a role to play to ensure that the structure of capitalism – fair competition – is in proper working order, making and enforcing the rules that facilitate a healthy, fair, competitive market economy. What we have now is not real capitalism with fair competition; it is not a market economy. It is an economy of bureaucracies, by bureaucracies, for bureaucracies. Except they have the nerve to call themselves businesses.

Competition regulation needs to become much more aggressive. Fines should mean something and not just be part of the 'cost of doing business'. Scholars John Connor and Robert Lande found that collusion is too often a 'rational business strategy' and that participating in a cartel 'is a crime that, on average, pays'.[57] Regulation of capitalism is necessary, but that doesn't necessarily mean more rules; it means fewer, better rules, rules about the structure of markets more than the behaviour of individual companies – and better enforcement of those structural rules.

For guidance, we might look back to the reformers of the last Gilded Age. America may have been the place where laissez-faire capitalism first truly flourished, but it was also where leaders recognised the harms that a completely unfettered free market could have. Andrew Carnegie, John D. Rockefeller, J. P. Morgan, Leland Stanford – all were brilliant and innovative businessmen who truly helped to build the modern American economy and left lasting philanthropic legacies like Stanford University.[58] But they were guilty of enormous excess in their business careers, creating monopolies that limited the flow of American wealth to a small elite, to the detriment not just of their competitors but of the broader American economy that correspondingly lost out. Reacting to this excess, leaders like Senator John Sherman and President Theodore Roosevelt launched reform efforts. 'If we will not endure a king as a political power, we should not endure a king over the production, transportation and sale' of the fruits of America's economy, declared Sherman. He would go on to sponsor the Sherman Antitrust Act in 1890. His work laid the groundwork for Roosevelt's 'Square Deal', which provides a useful example of how government can help guide the free market to a fair balance. He recognised that the status quo was untenable, and he led the fight against predatory big businesses, the 'trusts', as they were called. With his mantra that every man deserved a 'square deal', he became known for taking on big corporate power. Among the many accomplishments of his so-called trust-busting, he broke up dozens of monopolies, including the railroad giants and the largest oil firm in the country, Rockefeller's Standard Oil.

Despite this storied history, America's – and Britain's and Europe's – competition authorities have lost sight of the proud heritage that precedes them. They follow the mandates set for them by politicians, mandates that are lacklustre at best and far from their original intent. 'Economic and political power can't be separated because dominant corporations gain political influence over how markets are maintained and enforced, which enlarges their economic power further,' writes economist and former Secretary of Labor Robert Reich. 'One of the original goals of antitrust law was to prevent this.'[59] So whereas current laws might stop a business from literally becoming a monopoly, they don't prevent the harmful practices of dominant players and certainly don't meet the standard Sherman or Roosevelt would have intended for them.

The definition of a competitive market should be radically strengthened. The crucial question should be: What are the 'barriers to entry?' – how easily can a new firm establish itself and compete in the marketplace? The rate of new-company creation has steadily declined since the 1970s, and although there are many reasons for that, uncompetitive barriers are certainly a part of the story.[60] This doesn't necessarily mean regulating the size of incumbents, although that's often a crucial component, but preventing them from using their power – be it size, political connections, ownership of assets and infrastructure, partnerships and contracts, and even cash – to unfairly stack the deck in their favour and keep new competitors out.

This is what the competition authorities should enforce. At the same time, the interpretation of the harm done by anti-competitive practices should be broadened. Today the competition rules are focused on one thing: 'customer welfare', expressed as 'price, quality, range and service'

(PQRS). In other words, as long as authorities think service is good enough, quality is high enough, and price is low enough – regardless of the harm that's done to achieve those things – then all is well. This obviously neglects harms done to society like putting small firms, whether competitors or suppliers, out of business or driving wages and working conditions down by unfairly using the advantages of scale and incumbency. We need to change that.

There's one more step we should take: a simpler and even more radical way of thinking about this. If the good things about capitalism come from real, entrepreneurial businesses, and the bad things come from those that are basically just private-sector bureaucracies, we need to boost the former and constrain the latter. How do we distinguish?

By returning to the concept of 'too big to fail'. Imagine that Tesco goes bust. In towns where it has used unfair practices to drive out competition, where will people shop? What will become of its properties? As Nassim Taleb points out, 'should [a megastore, in this case Tesco] go bust (and the statistical elephant in the room is that it eventually will), we would end up with a massive war zone'. Beyond losing access to a grocery store, high streets up and down the country would have giant holes that could take years from which to recover. 'It is completely wrong,' Taleb continues, 'to use the calculus of benefits without including the probability of failure,'[61] particularly when those costs are borne by consumers, communities and taxpayers. Whether a company, in the event that it failed, would need to be bailed out by the government is a good proxy for whether it is a real, entrepreneurial business or a private-sector bureaucracy. Taleb has an ingenious proposal for discouraging such bureaucracies: 'My suggestion to deter "too big to fail" and to prevent employers taking advantage of the public is as follows. A company that is classified as potentially bailable out should it fail should not be able to pay anyone more than a corresponding civil servant ... Such limitation would force companies to stay small enough that they would not be considered for a bailout in the event of their failure.'[62]

We should broaden the mandate of the competition authorities to require them to assess whether in their view a particular company, if it failed, would require support from the government. If the answer is yes, it is a bureaucracy, and should be treated as such. These companies would be subject to the same pay and compensation rules as their public-sector counterparts ... including for their senior management. This would have a powerful incentive effect. While almost all such companies would be big, it's obvious that not all big companies would fall into this category – not by a long way. Take Apple, the world's biggest corporation by value. If it went bust tomorrow, there would be no need for government to bail it out. There would be plenty of viable alternatives for consumers, employees, suppliers, shareholders. But if Tesco were to fail, or HSBC, you can bet there's a taxpayer subsidy or bailout on its way. That may well be right and necessary. But then let's not pretend that these corporations are real businesses. They're not: they're basically part of the public sector, so it follows that they should be treated like the rest of it.

We need competition not just for our economy to succeed but also for our society to flourish. Capitalism is the most efficient and effective way we have for distributing resources, spurring innovation, and spreading prosperity. When businesses are fair with their customers, their employees, their suppliers, their communities and themselves, capitalism is truly a beautiful and successful system. But uncompetitive capitalism, despite the short-term gains possible with it, ultimately collapses upon itself like a deck of cards. Monopoly can only last so long before it stagnates or overreaches. That's why we should privilege the sanctity of proper markets.

Real capitalism: challenging incumbents

Today the sector I know best, technology, provides the most apt examples of what that looks like in the twenty-first century. Technology companies have been criticised for concentrating gains in the hands of a small number of people; indeed, many accuse the largest tech giants of being outright anti-competitive. But this debate is fraught with misunderstanding. Because technology companies have the ability to create wealth in a timeframe and on a scale implausible in almost any other industry, their gains seem inherently suspect. Surely, many argue, when so much wealth goes to so few so quickly, something is going wrong. But this misunderstands the sector. Here size, scale, or even market share, on their face, do not automatically translate to structural dominance. The costs of building and scaling a software company are low and falling. Just as a giant company can rise rapidly, another can easily replace it. That's why the technology sector is a good example of a competitive market, and the kind of competitive pressure the leaders of tech companies feel is exactly the kind of pressure we should want to see applied to all companies in every sector of the economy.

I'm the first to criticise the often absurd, arrogant and frankly quite creepy techno-salvationism of many in Silicon Valley, successfully satirised by the TV show of the same name. But by looking at entrepreneurialism there, we can get a sense of what markets with high levels of entrepreneurialism, innovation and, above all, competition might look like elsewhere in the capitalist world.

Take Red Dress Boutique. Its founder, Diana Harbour, was bored with her 'secure but soul-sucking' office job, but she loved fashion. As an aspiring designer, she decided to build a boutique, curating fashionable but affordable outfits. So she started on eBay, selling outfits from her basement. Realising she needed to expand, she and her husband Josh dug into their savings and opened a shop in Athens, Georgia. After some initial success they moved online in 2010, at which point the business skyrocketed: $63,000 in sales in 2010 transformed to $7 million in 2013 and then to over $12 million in 2014, with a net profit of $2 million. Diana had something of value to offer the world, and the Internet enabled her to share it.[63]

Another Internet marketplace, Etsy, unleashes the wares of small designers using a platform that helps them compete with big retailers and global brands. By giving consumers the chance to buy unique items directly from artisans who make them – and to communicate with them as well – Etsy doesn't just support those whose local markets would be too small to survive; it also forges a human connection between maker and consumer. And it helps bring to market items that might never have been economical to manufacture on any scale or to stock in a store.

A more human economy is one in which people control both their own labour and their own assets. Technology is helping here, linking us in the emerging 'sharing economy'. By enabling people to provide services directly to others without substantial corporate infrastructure or intermediation, the sharing economy builds community in ways that typical corporate-consumer relationships do not. The essence of the sharing economy is that customers receive services not from professionals but from people like themselves. By definition, it's more human.

Airbnb epitomises the sharing economy. It's now a big company that competes with hotels (its latest valuation surpasses Hyatt),[64] but more importantly it is a platform for the actual sharing of assets. Airbnb is transforming the way people travel. It gives everyday people extra income by renting out spare rooms, and they get to meet others. Airbnb hosts are completely autonomous; they set their own policies, their own prices, their own schedules. Guests get to connect with real people offering rooms, apartments and houses. Rather than staying in a sterile hotel room, travellers are connected with a real Londoner, Chicagoan or Hong Konger. Often Airbnb guests socialise with their hosts and even develop friendships over repeated or reciprocal visits. It's a great example of the argument that in business 'big' is not necessarily bad; 'big' can be human – as long as it is a real business competing fairly in a real market.

Competition is always snapping at the heels of tech companies – even the biggest. Just as Amazon emerged to challenge the traditional retail industry, in an exhilarating turn of the circle we're now seeing more human competitors challenging Amazon. Postmates is a firm that would have been physically impossible to run, let alone conceive, without the latest technology. Postmates resembles Amazon in many ways: it sells a multitude of products in its online store, is based on mobile technology, and delivers products directly to consumers using a network of couriers, not unlike those seen in ride-sharing or meal-delivery services. But there's one big caveat.

'Everything that we're doing is anti-Amazon,' says Bastian Lehmann, the start-up's co-founder. Instead of sourcing and sorting products itself, Postmates sells the products of a network of local bricks-and-mortar retailers. Why bother with the logistics of a warehouse operation when there are stores already fulfilling that function? Instacart, another shopping delivery start-up, takes the same philosophy, delivering from both chain stores and local independent shops. 'We want to use the city as our warehouse instead of building a warehouse outside the city,' says Lehmann of Postmates. 'We want to be part of a city versus saying: "Here's a way that you can save $2 on an item, but nobody in your city earns a dime, but now you have a cheap DVD player – congratulations!"'[65] As innovative as Amazon is, it's already being disrupted. That is real, competitive capitalism, not bureaucracy. The fact that Amazon's challengers are trying to travel a more human road simply offers more evidence of business's power for good. Competition doesn't just force companies to offer better prices or better products; it can force them to think about how best to serve the whole human community.

Here's another example of the great, dynamic, positive circle that real, competitive capitalism represents. One of the challenges for participants in the sharing economy is the lack of predictability and stability. Working for a large corporation might often seem like soulless drudgery, but at least it's mostly stable: regular hours and a pension. Of course, even the grandest of corporations can go belly-up overnight, and there is nothing to prevent you from being laid off without much notice. But workers in the sharing economy experience hourly volatility, often not knowing how much money they'll make in a given day, let alone week or month.

Now entrepreneurs – once again, with technology – are tackling those challenges. Peers, a San Francisco-based organisation with 250,000 members, offers products and services to support so-called 'gig workers'. Take its Keep Driving programme. For $20 a month it gives drivers for car-sharing services like Lyft access to a temporary car in the event that their own is damaged or stolen. For drivers like

San Franciscan Michael Bendorf, whose hybrid Volkswagen was rear-ended in a four-car collision, this service prevented him from losing the $5,000 to $7,000 per month he normally would have earned during the time his car was being repaired. Peers is also filling other gaps that often pop up in the sharing economy, like insurance (many car and property insurers will cancel your policy if you lend or charge to share your car or home). Peers now offers a $1 million liability policy, in one-month increments (with no minimum), for those who make their space available to travellers via Airbnb, HomeAway, FlipKey or even Craigslist. 'What we're trying to do here is recognise the needs of a new class of worker,' says Shelby Clark, the company's executive director. 'There are hundreds of thousands of people across the country earning money in new ways. While they love the flexibility and that they can start earning right away, at the same time they're encountering new challenges, like making sure they have stable income.'[66]

One of the advantages that established firms have traditionally had over start-ups and 'gig workers' is that their scale has enabled bulk-buying discounts on things like administration, workspace and insurance. But the Internet is increasingly making this a moot point. Whereas firms like Etsy enable makers to sell their wares online, new payment services like Square allow small shop and restaurant owners to use nothing more than an iPad and a small plastic card reader to process card payments in person. Gone are the days when small entrepreneurs had to choose between 'cash only' or big, bulky and expensive IBM cash registers.

With dreary predictability, however, obviously beneficial products and services like these are being confronted by bureaucratic government resistance. With its breakthrough battery technology, Tesla is doing more than almost anyone to make electric cars economical on a large scale. But Tesla's innovations aren't limited to technology – and therein lies the problem. Rather than sell through dealer middlemen, Tesla sells its vehicles directly to the public through its own stores, where customers can explore one or two model vehicles and an example of the battery packs, then use touch-screen terminals to customise their order. This, however, disrupts the entire way dealerships operate. Across America Tesla has had to contend with lawsuits and legislative battles just for the right to sell its cars.[67] In some states it is only allowed to have 'galleries', where visitors can see cars but employees are prohibited from discussing prices or how to buy a car. And even those limitations aren't enough in some other states. In October 2014, for example, Michigan – home of Ford, GM and Chrysler – passed a law that bans even galleries.[68] It's a perfect example of government bureaucrats siding with private-sector bureaucrats, using outdated protectionist regulations to keep challengers out.

The Internet, argues leading Silicon Valley entrepreneur and investor Peter Thiel, makes it easy for customers to switch to the best products in a heartbeat. Although this ease is what enables the really great businesses to balloon in size overnight, it's what also makes even the most successful, established tech firms so inherently 'disruptable'. The companies I've highlighted aren't necessarily 'good' companies in the sense of their overall social impact, but they're proof of what insurgents can do when barriers are low. Unlike old industries in which control of one bit of infrastructure, like oil wells or pipelines or steel mills or railroads, enabled firms to lock challengers out and charge consumers whatever price they wanted, with the Internet, tiny start-ups can topple giants. Facebook was born in a dorm room and upended the seemingly formidable MySpace.

Google became more popular than Microsoft, but Microsoft had put IBM in its place before that. Look at the success of Instagram, WhatsApp, Snapchat, Slack, and Stripe. From nowhere risk-takers who had a vision built these companies, and they were rewarded because the market posed minimal barriers to entry. Facebook's acquisition of the first two (and attempt to buy the third) not only demonstrates the value these entrepreneurs created but also how susceptible it is to competitive pressure, despite its dominance and market size. And such acquisitions only encourage more innovation.

Capitalism is a force for good, but its distortion into private-sector bureaucracy, with uncompetitive markets dominated by entrenched corporations, is a fundamental malaise. There's nothing wrong with dominant companies, and there's nothing wrong with dominant companies that continue to dominate. But they must do so on their merits and not by entrenching their advantages through political power. The central answer is conceptually simple but will require immensely strong leadership to implement: take on the wealthy, powerful, endemically corrupt business elites and make them compete in the marketplace on fair terms. That's what capitalism ought to be, closer to what's happening in the technology sector today. Only that kind of deep structural reform will succeed in making capitalism more human.

CHAPTER 7

BUSINESS

In Savar, Bangladesh, next to the Genda Government Primary School, there's a river full of toxins from nearby textile factories. The 'suffocating' odour in the air makes students and teachers feel dizzy, vomit and lose focus. Debilitating headaches for students and teachers aren't uncommon; occasionally students faint. Ironically, the children of Savar are entirely dependent on these factories, which make the clothes we buy in the West. The income their parents earn allows them to go to school. But those factories are also the worst fixture in their lives.

They do protest about the pollution. But the industrial interests always win out. According to the school's headmaster, Mohammed Abdul Ali, 'We've never seen the owners take our appeals seriously … everything is going on as usual. They have a good relationship with the politicians. That is why they don't care.' Every now and again a reforming minister or regulator comes to power and attempts to do something but is inevitably stifled. For a short period Munir Chowdhury, an environmental official, held textile factories accountable, conducting raids and imposing fines. He didn't last; he was transferred to another department. More often than not, ministers are part of the problem. 'These people who are setting up industries and factories here are much more powerful than me,' says

Mohammed Abdul Kader, the mayor of Savar. 'When a government minister calls me and tells me to give permission to someone to set up a factory in Savar, I can't refuse.'[1]

I argued in the previous chapter that business is the most powerful force for progress the world has ever seen. One way or another, we all depend on trade, capitalism and the profit motive for the big positive changes we want to see in the world, from creating opportunity and tackling inequality, to providing the products and services that help make our lives richer and more pleasurable, to the innovations that help fight poverty, hunger and disease. There is no government in the world, no part of the public sector anywhere that does not rely on successful, profitable businesses for its very existence. To combine businesses with markets is evidence of our ability to create institutions that, broadly speaking, deliver human progress and make the world a better – and more human – place.

But too often business fails us. In the last chapter we saw how the structure of modern capitalism has helped create massive, often global corporations that manipulate laws, purchase political power, and use their economic might and incumbent advantages to suppress competition. These businesses objectively make a mockery of capitalism. There are plenty of others, however, that fail on a different count. They may operate in competitive markets; they might not lobby or litigate their way to the top; but they nonetheless do harm, not through their dominance or anti-competitive practices but simply by the way they behave.

Supply chain

In our globalised economy, to save themselves – and us, as consumers – money, many companies base their supply chains in places like Savar, where the rule of law is weak and the potential for corruption high. Too often they take advantage of holes and blind spots in the system that allow them to pass on all of the costs of their operations to exceedingly vulnerable populations.

Take the ubiquitous pair of denim jeans. Their blue colour might be their most inhuman feature. In countries like China, India and Bangladesh, wastewater that is used to dye and process textiles is routinely dumped untreated, saturating rivers and streams with carcinogens like chromium, lead, cadmium, arsenic and mercury. This not only poisons the factory workers and their families who live nearby; it kills off fields and local fish supplies as well. In the Pearl River Delta in China's Guangdong province the water literally runs blue from the synthetic pigments used to process 200 million pairs of jeans dyed there every year.[2] According to Green Cross Switzerland, 9 trillion gallons of water are used annually in textile production around the world. Most of it is dumped untreated.[3]

Sometimes our quest for low prices even kills: in 2013 garment makers in the Rana Plaza building in Dhaka, Bangladesh, were ordered back to work the day after cracks appeared in its structure. It collapsed soon after, killing 1,129 people.[4]

Over the past decade the Internet has done a great deal to help concerned consumers choose alternative, ethically produced goods. 'We sell online and through our store directly and skip middlemen,' explains Mark Spera, co-founder of BeGood Clothing, a San Francisco start-up. 'That's how we've been able to offer a disruptively low $15 price point on our T-shirts.'[5] The entire clothing line is made in Los Angeles and San Francisco in good conditions, by workers paid fair wages. And all from materials that are organically harvested and processed sustainably, without the use of harsh chemicals. The Internet has also allowed BeGood to be maximally transparent about how suppliers are treated. At their store and online each item carries an explanation of the materials and processes involved as well as the people and places along its supply chain. More information means better, more conscious choices.

The problem is that the jeans produced in Guangdong or the shirts made at Rana Plaza are cheap; the shirts sold at BeGood in San Francisco are, although relatively inexpensive, still not competitive with what's sold to the average Western consumer. But sweatshop textiles are only cheap because the businesses that produce them choose not to treat people decently. Taxpayers, not the businesses, then foot the bill for the harm they cause – assuming local officials or international governments do anything at all. So rather than perpetuating the fiction that social and environmental responsibility is an indulgence for the rich, we should be asking why we continue to subsidise companies that offload the true costs of their operations onto taxpayers.

Even supply chains that don't explicitly pollute incur costs we don't see. I live in California, where an epochal drought has led to severe water restrictions, replete with parched lawns, untilled acres and unflushed toilets. And yet while we worry about leaving the tap running, many of the products we use and consume require far more water to produce and to bring to us than we ever could consume through our taps. The almond has famously gotten a bad rap (each one needs about a gallon of water to grow), but other foods are just as bad: two ounces of rice take 15.1 gallons; a strawberry takes a quart. Animal products are even worse: four glasses of milk require 143 gallons of water, whereas just 1.75 ounces of beef require 86 gallons.[6] Meanwhile the average American uses thirty-five pounds of cotton per year, equal to 3,500 gallons, and a one-way cross-country flight uses as much water as 1,700 toilet flushes.[7] But again, because these processes are obscured, we don't understand them.

Workplace

Although the Internet might help concerned shoppers find BeGood's T-shirts (or indeed, save water), it can also do just as much to obscure abuse and harm. We make a fuss about corporations like Walmart because we can identify their employees – we see them in the aisles and at the registers. But online retailers like Amazon, however innovative and cost saving for consumers, can hide how they treat their people behind the clean facade the Internet allows them to put up. Amazon's workers are out of sight and, as a result, easily out of mind. Undercover investigations have revealed employees toiling in warehouses for low wages in slave-like conditions. One investigative report describes life for a temporary worker in his fifties at an Amazon warehouse in Allentown, Pennsylvania:

> [He] ... worked ten hours a day as a picker, taking items from bins and delivering them to the shelves. He would walk thirteen to fifteen miles daily. He was told he had to pick 1,200 items in a ten-hour shift, or one item every thirty seconds. He had to get down on his hands and knees 250 to 300 times a day to do this. He got written up for not working fast enough, and when he was fired only three of the one hundred temporary workers hired with him had survived.[8]

At an Amazon facility in Swansea, employees work fifty-plus-hour weeks at minimum wage. They'll be fired if they take more than three sick days in a three-month period (or get sick twice and show up late by a minute twice, or get sick once and are late four times, and so on). According to one undercover journalist who visited in 2013, strict fifteen-minute breaks start wherever the worker happens to be in the warehouse at the time, which could be a long walk away from a place to sit down. And that's after passing through airport-like security to be patted down (to prevent theft).[9] At the Pennsylvania warehouse employees are actually tagged with their own personal sat-navs so managers can govern their movements 'scientifically'. If employees don't go to the toilet nearest them, they are asked why.[10] Treating people like this is humiliating and undignified.

It's not just warehouse workers. A recent report in the *New York Times* highlighted the intense pressure on Amazon's white-collar employees, those working on software, product development and marketing. Employees faced 'annual cullings', often based on anonymous feedback from colleagues, who were all competing against each other; they openly wept in the office under the pressure; facing a boss described as an 'insatiable taskmaster', some employees worked for days without sleeping. Perhaps most troubling were the reports of employees in deep personal distress, facing family crises or even cancer diagnoses, who were given little to no flexibility and faced serious repercussions for their corresponding shortcomings.[11] This lack of compassion, this treatment of employees as mere cogs in a well-oiled machine, is certainly not outside an employer's legal rights. But it's not human. Yes, Amazon workers might be marginally more productive, but at what cost? Surely there is a better way to run a business.

In fairness, although Amazon did not dispute the accuracy of the allegations, Jeff Bezos, the company's visionary founder and CEO, has said these reports don't depict what he believes he's building. 'The article doesn't describe the Amazon I know or the caring Amazonians I work with every day,' he wrote, acknowledging that he would leave such a company himself if he thought the article painted a full and complete picture. Indeed, he said that any employee facing circumstances as described by the *Times* should immediately escalate the issue to Amazon's human resources department.[12]

In response to the earlier warehouse exposé, Amazon said, 'We're working hard to make sure that we are better tomorrow than we are today.' No doubt they are.[13] But warehouse employees, many paid just a few dollars above minimum wage, are still often required to sign heavily restrictive non-compete contracts, thereby limiting their ability to change jobs, even if they're just working seasonally. When one warehouse in Coffeeville, Kansas, was shut down, laid-off employees were admonished in their severance agreement to 'fully comply' with the non-competition agreement as they struggled to find new jobs.[14]

At Amazon, as at many big companies, it's the subordination of human values that allows harm to take place. Bureaucratic, tech-enabled systems eliminate basic humanity and the personal connection, kindness and empathy natural to nearly all of us. I don't know him, so I can't be sure, but I sincerely doubt that Bezos would, if he found himself in one of his warehouses with an employee betrayed by the personal GPS as having gone to the 'wrong' toilet, actually ask that employee why. The system, the process, the bureaucracy – these are things that distance people from each other.[15]

A culture of fair pay

Amazon is not alone. Companies everywhere proclaim that 'people are our greatest resource', yet too many treat their employees as nothing more than units of production, paying them as little as they can get away with, putting them on zero-hours contracts, imposing incredibly stingy – and counterproductive – sick, holiday and leave policies. But others choose to do things differently.

As we'll see in the following chapter, Costco pays its employees well above the living wage, and it is one of the most successful companies in the world – in a cut-throat, slim-margins industry. For them, paying a decent wage increases productivity, makes recruiting easier and lowers employee turnover. Whole Foods publishes the pay of every employee, from top to bottom. This might seem extreme, but it engenders social solidarity. When top executives make hundreds of times more than those at the bottom (they don't at Whole Foods), it's demoralising. J. P. Morgan purportedly said that he would never lend money to a company whose best employees were paid more than twenty times anyone else because it would be unstable. (In 2015 Jamie Dimon, JPMorgan Chase's CEO, made 221.7 times his average employee's salary.)[16]

This is not some immutable law of business. Ethan Berman was the founder and CEO of RiskMetrics, a financial services company that was, ironically, spun out of JPMorgan Chase in 1998. He insisted in a letter to his board that he be paid *less*. He wrote, 'Last year I was disappointed in the way I was compensated and I have therefore taken to writing this note in the hope that it does not happen again in 2005.' He continues, 'As I told the committee before last year's meeting, there is no amount of stock options, restricted stock or any other stock-based compensation that would make me feel more of an owner, or increase my commitment to the company,' he advised. 'Instead, I ask the committee in looking at the list to broaden its definition of "leaders" beyond employees with significant managerial or financial responsibilities to those who display time and time again the values that we as a company believe in and therefore "lead" others by example not by mandate. That, as much as any other attribute, will create value in the long run.'[17]

Berman was right: In 2008 RiskMetrics went public at a valuation of just over $1 billion. In 2010 it was acquired by MSCI for $1.55 billion – a 48 per cent increase in just twenty-four months.[18]

Time sovereignty

Treating people as human beings in the workplace means more than just paying them fairly, though. Businesses are in control of a broad range of conditions for their workers, including how much of their time they demand. Work is just one part of people's lives, and although employees have obligations to their employers, employers should respect employees' obligations to their friends, parents, children, or relatives and afford them as much flexibility as possible. Often totally unnecessarily from a business point of view, workplace culture too often enforces working days of twelve hours or more as norms. When new employees think the only way to be promoted is to work excessive hours, then the cycle simply continues. As one psychologist put it, 'long hours has become a proxy for good performance.'[19]

Sir Richard Branson, founder of the Virgin Group, is one boss who decided enough was enough. After an encouraging note from his daughter and reading that the 'take as much holiday as you want' policy at Netflix increased morale, creativity and productivity, he decided to do the same for salaried employees across Virgin. He wrote, 'It is left to the employee alone to decide if and when he or she feels like taking a few hours, a day, a week or a month off, the assumption being that they are only going to do it when they feel a hundred per cent comfortable that they and their team are up to date on every project and that their absence will not in any way damage the business – or, for that matter, their careers!'[20] Of course, this model has its pitfalls: social pressure may lead employees to take *less* vacation. But it should be admired for its innovative spirit. Time-off policies are critical to get right because they can have enormous impacts on family life. Becoming a parent should be a joyous milestone, not an occasion to lose a chance at a career or be laid off, as it is for many who work. Mothers in particular face brutal challenges upon having children, with workplace policies and cultures that make it difficult if not impossible to resume their careers. Couples should be able to get pregnant whenever it is right for *them*, and there should be comprehensive job protection for mothers who are. Until such formal protections are in place – and corporate culture to match – I'm afraid Princeton political scientist, think tank executive and former US State Department official Anne-Marie Slaughter is right: 'Women still can't have it all.'[21]

It isn't just about maternity or paternity leave, though. It's also about allowing parents to take care of their children, and sons and daughters to take care of their ageing parents. Many businesses impose negative consequences on workers who have to take time off due to a family emergency. Again, though this is a problem that affects all types of workers, it is felt acutely by low-wage earners. As with holiday time, whereas 90 per cent of high-wage workers have the flexibility to take paid time off or move their schedule around during a family crisis, fewer than half of low-paid workers have these same benefits.[22]

This is inherently inhuman. Family is central to human nature and the most important institution in society: being a parent is one of the most human acts possible, giving birth to a child even more so. But by becoming mothers, women end up bearing a steep cost for this indispensable duty. They suffer the indignity of losing out on career advancement, of being forced to choose between meaningful work and spending time with their children, and of every choice they make being wrapped in terrible guilt thanks to the failure of business culture to adapt to a world of gender equality.

Helping parents be better workers *and* better mothers and fathers at the same time is central to treating employees like people and making business more human. Better family leave policy especially matters to low-wage employees. Predictable hours, workplace flexibility, paid leave, days off – these are all part of the same theme: respecting workers by treating them well, treating them in a way that is more human.

Discretion and autonomy

You see the trend toward inhuman treatment of workers in other ways too, and again, technology can exacerbate but also help. Bosses are often incentivised by systems created by management consultants or software programmes bought in order to help improve 'efficiency'. The result: employees are inhibited from exercising their abilities to the fullest and not trusted to use their judgement, work autonomously, or make decisions outside specific frameworks.

Much of this comes from the drive to quantify performance. You can understand the impulse that led to Amazon forcing its warehouse employees to track themselves with countdown-beeping GPS devices, but how can that justifiable impulse be channelled into a more human approach?

Consider the annual performance review. Studies have shown that they are demotivating and serve little purpose, as bosses score most of their employees in the middle to avoid awkwardness.[23] The more human alternative is also the one that, more simply, improves performance: frequent, informal meetings. Most employees want to learn and improve anyway. Telling workers what's wrong or what could be improved ahead of time gives everyone a chance to take action: 'The boss's job is to fill in the gaps and accomplish results,' UCLA business professor Sam Culbert argues. 'It's not to give report cards.'[24]

Generally workers at every level want to take action to excel at their jobs. But for that they need sovereignty over how to go about doing them. It's easy to see how managers' impulse for 'quality control' leads to structures that drastically curtail discretion, but by treating workers like robots, they send a tacit message that they simply aren't smart, observant or creative enough to know how to accomplish the task at hand. This is inhuman. And it causes them to be inhuman towards others.

Some businesses are choosing to behave differently. MetroBank in the UK was founded only six years ago, in 2010, and determined to break the mould of its competitors (which universally rank badly for customer service). Its staff are incentivised with bonuses based not only on profit but also on customer service results. Branches are open 361 days a year, from 8 a.m. to 8 p.m. on weekdays, and calls must be answered by the third ring, twenty-four hours a day, seven days a week. Most impressively, customer-facing employees are to say 'yes' to customer requests as much as possible. They can say 'no', but only after seeking a second opinion from a colleague first.[25]

Zappos, the online retailer (now owned by Amazon), has built a brand on customer – and employee – happiness. In 2010 it even ran an advertising campaign featuring real-life recordings of calls its employees had with customers. The fact that employees are encouraged (and trusted – there are no phone scripts) to go out of their way to make customers happy is part of its business model and one of the reasons customers come back. In 2011 a Zappos employee sent a large bouquet of flowers to a woman she had spoken to on the phone after she was having trouble finding shoes that were comfortable enough for her sensitive feet that had been damaged by medical treatments.[26] Another time a customer service agent went in person to another store to buy a pair of shoes that were out of stock and deliver them to a customer who happened to be staying near the company's headquarters in Las Vegas … for free.[27]

In his influential business book, *The Outsiders*, investor William Thorndike Jr. profiles eight CEOs whom he found, over the course of almost a decade's worth of research, to be exceptionally successful. Though he didn't originally set out to write a book, his interest was piqued after discovering that many of his subjects managed their companies in the same way.[28] For example, 'there are two basic types of resources that any CEO needs to allocate,' Thorndike writes, 'financial and human.'[29] In addition to being frugal and humble, the best CEOs, he found, were expert at managing both. When it came to allocating capital, they were obsessive and hands-on. But when it came to managing people, Thorndike found that the best CEOs were master delegators, 'running highly decentralised organisations and pushing operating decisions down to the lowest, most local levels in their organisations'.[30]

At the time CEO William Anders took the helm of defence contractor General Dynamics in 1990, the military-industrial complex, propped up for decades by the Cold War, was collapsing around him. General Dynamics was no better placed: straddled with $600 million of debt and negative cash flow, it was not clear the firm would survive.

Coming from the military, most defence executives had brought with them the same highly centralised, bureaucratic style of management they were used to. Things would be different under Anders, though. After he sold off many of the company's units to focus on a few specific markets, Anders (and later his successors, James Mellor and Nicholas Chabraja) made it General Dynamic's top priority to spend capital efficiently and radically decentralise, with responsibility pushed as far down as possible into the organisation. Management from then on was to involve itself minimally in each division, holding subordinate managers 'severely accountable' (in the words of Chabraja) but left alone if they were performing well. 'By the end of Chabraja's tenure,' according to Thorndike, 'the company would have more employees than when Anders arrived but only a quarter as many people at corporate headquarters.'[31] Today General Dynamics is thriving: with over $2.5 billion in profits, the company is now worth over four times what it was when Anders took over. 'There is a fundamental humility to decentralisation,' Thorndike observes, 'an admission that headquarters does not have all the answers and that much of the real value is created by local managers in the field.'[32]

More human businesses give discretion to their employees. It's not a free-for-all, of course, but companies with even a somewhat decentralised culture are organisations filled with empowered problem solvers who understand their limits, know when to ask others for help (or refer upwards when need be), and use the creativity each of us have to make the little part of the company they're responsible for better. At Johnson & Johnson decentralisation is not only key to its business strategy but also how it supports employees. 'It gives you a tremendous opportunity to develop people,' according to William Weldon, the company's CEO. 'You give them a lot of opportunity to work in different areas, to work in smaller companies, to make mistakes and to ultimately move to larger companies.' Centralisation, however, is a tremendous risk: 'If one person makes one mistake, it can cripple the whole organisation.'[33]

Marketing

Regardless of their structure, there are certain behaviours that should be beyond the pale for every business, and one of the most widespread abuses today is targeted marketing to children. Children are exactly that – children – and it is simply not human for businesses to treat them as consumers. In 2006, the UK imposed one of the world's most stringent restrictions on advertising junk food to children. But even though it bans advertising junk food to children via television and print, British children are still exposed to junk food advertising. The rule is triggered only when a minimum threshold proportion of viewers are children, so as a result junk food adverts regularly air during family programmes like *The X Factor* and *Britain's Got Talent*, which, in absolute terms, rank among the top shows watched by children.[34]

Why does this matter? Because advertising junk food to kids works. According to the Institute of Medicine, food advertising directly affects food choices and purchase requests, in turn shaping diet and health,[35] particularly where children are concerned.[36] Moreover, food marketed with cartoon characters, such as Dora the Explorer, Scooby Doo, and Shrek, tastes better to children. In one study 85 per cent of children chose graham crackers (similar to digestives in the UK) with cartoon-decorated labels over the plainly wrapped alternatives; 55 per cent of them said the (identical) crackers from the cartoon package tasted better. For gummy candies, the bias was the same.[37] And even when fast food ads feature healthy food (to get around the restrictions), it still has a deleterious effect: the only effect for children exposed to such ads is that they want more fast food; the 'healthy' foods depicted do nothing to promote a healthier diet.[38]

It's not just on TV. Advertising is in even more places today, pervading mobile apps and games, social media and online banners. A 2012 study found that advertisements support 87 per cent of the most popular children's websites.[39] At least these ads are identifiable. The boundary between marketing and content, especially for children, is increasingly blurred. Food manufacturers now create websites with videos, original content and games, and 81 per cent of websites for foods that had been marketed on children's TV networks have games designed for children.[40] Product placement in TV shows and even in video games blurs the lines further. One study calculated that children view ten times as many Coke brand appearances through such embedded advertising than they do through traditional commercials.[41] So-called 'adver-games', which combine adverts with addicting games, attract children's attention. And age restrictions prove nearly impossible to enforce on social media, in which food advertisers have been found to regularly engage with children despite evidence of their ages.[42]

On top of the actual direct harm they do, these inhuman practices also give rise to the worst kind of corporate cynicism and spin. All the big offenders happily participate in studies and conferences about responsible marketing. I remember when running Good Business, I would be completely dumbfounded by some of the things clients of ours would say. Coca-Cola flat-out denied they ever marketed to children, despite their massive sponsorship of sports like soccer or their annual TV ad featuring 'Santa Claus coming to town'. Ho-ho-ho, Atlanta. McDonald's used to say, hilariously, 'We don't market to children. We market to families, and families have children in them.' Well, that's all right then.

But companies can choose to use their brand and product marketing for good. The makers of the popular children's television show *Sesame Street* signed a deal in 2013 with the Produce Marketing Association, who promote fruits and vegetables, to license its characters for free.[43] After becoming aware of company research showing that only 4 per cent of women consider themselves beautiful, Unilever launched the Dove Campaign for Real Beauty in 2005 and has been running it ever since. Its 2006 'Evolution' video, which shows in time lapse how makeup and digital editing can transform an average woman to looking like a supermodel, has over 18 million views on YouTube. It not only was shown to have a tangible – albeit short-term – effect on the self-esteem of girls who viewed the ad[44] but also sparked a global outcry calling for unmanipulated images in ads and media spreads; Jezebel, an online feminist news site founded the following year, launched with an offer of $10,000 for the best example of a magazine cover photo being retouched.[45] Dove's choice to sell products that not only avoid distortive views of female beauty but actually challenge stereotypes stands in stark contrast to the rest of the industry, which unfortunately has failed to catch up.

Although young children aren't necessarily buying the clothing and beauty products, the effects of advertisements promoting them have serious consequences. According to Common Sense Media, a San Francisco-based non-profit, 'Almost as soon as preschoolers complete the developmental task of mastering a concept of their bodies, they begin to express concerns about their bodies.'[46] Nearly a third of five- and six-year-olds think their ideal body size is thinner than what they perceive to be their own.[47] Remember: this is not kindergartners with a healthy awareness of their own obesity risks; this is mental illness in the form of body dysmorphia. According to research conducted by the Girl Scouts, 48 per cent of girls aged thirteen to seventeen 'wish they were as skinny as fashion magazine models'.[48]

Sustainability

No one should underestimate the value – and difficulty! – of delivering the business basics: as any entrepreneur or CEO will tell you, it's really hard to make a good product, provide a good service, and earn a profit on it. But when companies like Dove use their incredible power to simultaneously mix profit with positive social impact, we see the truly amazing potential of business. And one of the most encouraging business trends over the past several decades is business leaders' realisation that companies can take serious steps to minimise their negative environmental impact and still be profitable.

Ray Anderson founded his US-based carpet business, which would become Interface, Inc., in 1973 after seeing modular carpet for the first time in England. With each tile easily installed and removed, it was the perfect flooring to accommodate the rise of cubicles (and proliferation of wires and cords) across corporate America. Plus, damaged tiles could be easily removed and replaced, drastically cutting the cost of maintenance. 'I fell in love with the idea,' he said in an interview before he died. 'It just made so much sense.'[49] Customers agreed: within a decade the company had gone public. Over the next ten years Anderson would expand his empire to Europe and the Middle East, later extending to Asia as well and, over time, acquiring more than fifty other companies. Today Interface has grown to become one of the world's largest carpet manufacturers, with over $1 billion dollars in annual revenue.[50]

Carpets, however, are made primarily from petroleum; their manufacture requires an enormous amount of it – not to mention water and energy – and it produces a huge amount of unrecyclable waste. By the early 1990s people were starting to take notice. 'We'd begun to hear this question from customers that we'd never heard before – in so many words – "What's your company doing for the environment?"' Anderson recalls, 'We had no answers … It was very embarrassing. It was awkward for our sales people. It was awkward for our manufacturing people. For our research people.' So in 1994 the company assembled a task force to look into sustainability. Right before they launched their initiative the team asked Anderson – a prolific speechmaker – to say some words. Though he supported the task force's goals, he didn't really have anything to say – that is, until someone gave him a copy of environmentalist Paul Hawken's book *The Ecology of Commerce.*

'I had never given a thought to what we had taken from the earth or were doing to the earth to make our products – except to always be sure that there's enough of that stuff running through the pipeline to keep our factories running. It was a spear in the chest experience,'

Anderson said. 'I read it and wept. It laid out so clearly the problems of the industrial system. The system of which my company, my creation – this third child of mine – was an integral part.'

Now on a personal mission, Anderson pushed Interface researchers to look into every aspect of the enterprise that could be made more sustainable. They switched to renewable energy, eliminated as much waste as possible from their manufacturing plants, and made concerted efforts to 'close the loop' on their products so that they could be fully recycled at the end of their useful lives and turned into new products once again. Anderson's vision – what became known as Mission Zero – was for Interface to have no negative environmental impact by 2020. Ray Anderson died of cancer in 2011. He didn't live long enough to see Mission Zero accomplished. But company executives say that in the seventeen years leading up to his death, their environmental initiatives have reduced greenhouse gas emissions by 24 per cent, fossil fuel consumption by 60 per cent, landfill waste by 82 per cent, and water use by 82 per cent – all while avoiding over $450 million in costs.[51]

Around the same time as Anderson had his epiphany, Bill Whiting, the marketing director (and, later, CEO) of B&Q, had a similar experience. When a journalist asked him at a press conference how much tropical hardwood, much of which comes from precious rainforest, B&Q stocked, he confessed he didn't know. 'Well, if you don't know, you don't care,' the journalist replied. Stung, and now determined to know the answer, he hired a scientist, Dr Alan Knight, to come and work for B&Q as an environmental specialist. Knight dived right in, investigating the social and environmental problems associated with the timber B&Q sourced. He discovered that much of the company's timber was harvested using clear-cutting techniques, whereby entire forests are practically mowed down, devastating both natural ecosystems and local communities. So in 1991 B&Q announced that within five years it would only source timber from 'well-managed forests' – that is, forests where such destructive processes were not allowed.

But in 1991 there was little expertise on how to 'manage forests well', especially to meet the business needs of a large multinational firm with a complex supply chain like B&Q's. So Knight oversaw a forest laboratory in Papua New Guinea, where destructive logging techniques were commonplace. He and his team were interested in developing techniques to train local communities to manage their own forest resources in an environmentally responsible way (e.g., using portable sawmills allowed them to harvest only high-value timber, minimising damage and ensuring future yields). The project also developed systems for independent verification of well-managed forests so that timber buyers other than B&Q knew where their product came from and how it was harvested.

With this expertise B&Q was able to help create the Forest Stewardship Council in 1992, an independent NGO to set standards for forest management and oversee sustainable timber certification at a global level. As a result, countless forests – and the communities they support – have thrived. And B&Q – hardly a niche, 'ethical' brand on the fringes of the marketplace – was able not only to meet its target but also to apply the techniques it had learned to other products throughout its supply chain, setting the company off on an ongoing quest to better steward the people and nature it touched.[52]

Technology's promise

Although, as we have seen, technology can have a baleful impact on the human side of business, it can also work the other way, especially by improving information. The Internet enables consumers to discriminate on the basis of more than just quality and price: they can increasingly take human and environmental impact into account too. As companies like BeGood raise the bar about how much information is provided about consumer products, social impact becomes a consumer feature just like any other. This has been a winning strategy for firms like Patagonia, the environmentally sensitive – and enormously successful – maker of outdoor clothing. It has used its websites to show where and how its products are made, recently announcing the completion of a seven-year process to make sure all the down feathers used in jackets and sweaters are 100 per cent traceable and cruelty-free. One section of its website, the Footprint Chronicles, traces the journey of some of its products around a global map, showing images, videos and descriptions of each step along the way.

Or browse the website of Everlane, a much younger clothing maker. On the top of its homepage are links to its main sections: 'Men's', 'Women's', then 'Factories'. When you click on the page, up pops a map pinpointing each part of its supply chain, from leather shops to distribution centres to mills and factories. Each of them has a dedicated page showing basic data, like the number of employees, the date it was established, even current time and weather. Further down is a description of which products are made there, how Everlane found this particular factory, details on the materials it sources, and information about the factory's owner. If you scroll down, you can look at high-resolution images taken by Everlane's staff. Back on the individual product pages, which all link to their relevant factory-profile pages, Everlane takes transparency a step further, breaking down where every penny of the purchase price goes – from materials and labour to transport and profit.

PCH breaks down the supply chain even further. Founded by the Irish entrepreneur Liam Casey, PCH is one of the world's largest technology hardware manufacturing companies; it also makes most of its products in China. But that doesn't mean consumers can't see exactly how their products are made. PCH customers can go to the company's website, click on a product and see where it is made. But more than that, they can see the individual workers who worked on it; they can literally see their names and the times they clocked in and out of the factory. 'You see photos of production workers all the time. We actually name the workers,' says Casey. Rather than keep them anonymous, Casey feels it's important that his workers, wherever they are in the world, are credited for their contribution. 'It's natural,' he says, to highlight them. 'When you spend nineteen years building a company and these people work with you, they're a part of that story, so it's only right that you share the success with them and that they understand all the products they're working on and where they go.'

'Transparency is about a lot more than worker relations. It's also about engaging with consumers ... You can track a product right through all the workers involved in a product, the factories. Shipping time.' Casey believes that educating the consumer so completely allows them not just to buy a better product but also to make a purchasing decision that has wider benefits. 'If you give consumers the choice – here's information that shows a well-managed supply chain vs. one that's a black box – if you can share that information, they will make a decision that is a better decision.'[53]

It's not the Internet alone that's having a huge effect on businesses' social and environmental impact. Ubiquitous mobile technology can enable a hyper-transparent supply chain we could never have imagined twenty years ago. In previous decades 'corporate responsibility' meant the occasional, unannounced inspection, with the results being filed away or scanned into big PDFs hidden on investor-relations websites. But now, with mobile technology nearly everywhere, we can fundamentally change how we evaluate a company's working conditions, not to mention its overall impact on vulnerable communities.

'The current tool is an audit and certificate,' says David Bonbright, head of Covox, an innovative human-rights monitoring firm. 'It doesn't tell you how to solve any problems that might arise, just that there are problems.' So Covox takes a more human, twenty-first-century approach based on the fact that nearly every worker in the developing world – even the poorest – has a mobile phone. Workers are asked directly about their own conditions, questions like: 'Does your employer treat you fairly?' 'Are working conditions healthy and safe?' and 'Does the company respect your community's rights and behave like a good neighbour?' Every day a question like this is posed to a different representative sample of workers via text message to their mobiles; this way everyone's voice is heard. The results are immediately reported, collated and delivered. Now, rather than a twelve- to twenty-four-month lag in discovering that something is wrong on the ground, issues can be discovered and diagnosed continuously. And with basic (anonymised) user data such as gender and age, Covox can gain even further insight into particular issues and how they're affecting workers and their community. It's more than mere compliance, Bonbright explains. 'It's about capturing the voice of marginalised people who are part of the supply chain.'[54]

Tools like Covox aren't in the hands of every consumer yet. But they could be. And even if consumers are unable or unwilling to pressure for change, companies' embrace of such technology can improve local communities' ability to hold their own legal and regulatory bodies accountable. Indeed, it may be the key – or at least play a significant role – in building and sustaining legitimate local governance in some of the most corrupt and oppressive corners of the world. This is where technology proves itself, when wielded correctly, as an enabler of good business – and good government – empowering society to make sure corporations put people first.

Embracing competition

Most technology companies seek patents so they can jealously guard their tech from their competitors. Tesla, the electric car company based in California, has instead done the opposite, opening up all of its proprietary technology to the public in the spirit of moving the electric car industry forward. Originally, writes Tesla founder and CEO Elon Musk, 'We felt compelled to create patents out of concern that the big car companies would copy our technology and then use their massive manufacturing, sales and marketing power to overwhelm Tesla. We couldn't have been more wrong. The unfortunate reality is the opposite: electric car programmes (or programmes for any vehicle that doesn't burn hydrocarbons) at the major manufacturers are small to non-existent.' Musk's goal is a future of environmentally sustainable cars; he hopes to profit, of course, through Tesla, but he also realises that Tesla doesn't have the capacity to rapidly supply the world with electric cars. If the world is to wean itself from fossil fuels, he reasons, Tesla can't be the only electric car.

Musk's philosophy is admirably civic minded, but it also reveals the frustration many entrepreneurs feel about the way our legal system seems to serve entrenched interests (as we saw in the previous chapter) rather than true innovators. 'Too often these days [patents] serve merely to stifle progress, entrench the positions of giant corporations and enrich those in the legal profession, rather than the actual inventors,' he goes on to say in his letter announcing Tesla's decision to make public its technology. 'After Zip2 [his first company], when I realised that receiving a patent really just meant that you bought a lottery ticket to a lawsuit, I avoided them whenever possible.'[55] Innovation is really hard, but when companies approach it in the right way, collaborative competition rather than zealous rivalry can help move society forward.

Sometimes, though, large corporations aren't well placed to push innovation forward. Although they might be good at producing certain core goods and services efficiently and effectively, they just aren't the best at new thinking. Businesses that find themselves in this situation can react in one of two ways: they can either invest in erecting barriers to entry so that new, more innovative competitors can't get off the ground (see Chapter 6), or they can work with new entrants and form mutually beneficial relationships that produce more value for society than what either can offer on their own.

Executives at Santander UK, the British division of the global banking giant, decided several years ago that they weren't in the best position to lend to small businesses. So it now works with Funding Circle, a peer-to-peer financing platform, to direct customers there when it makes sense. 'SMEs [small- and medium-sized enterprises] need access to multiple sources of finance, and Santander's partnership with Funding Circle is a good example of how traditional and alternative finance can work together to help the nation's SMEs prosper,' Santander's CEO Ana Botín said when the partnership was announced in June 2014.[56] It's also a good way for Santander to stay relevant – and survive – in the new banking economy. Since then, other banks have struck similar deals, either with Funding Circle or its competitors.[57]

Santander has also set up its own venture fund to find and invest in promising start-ups in the banking sector, start-ups that may very well cause disruption to it. Santander is not alone. Investing in accelerators, incubators and venture funds is a growing trend among some large companies – from SAP to Walmart, Deutsche Telekom to Nike – who might otherwise try to lobby government to regulate and close down insurgents. Of course, many of these companies still do engage in the type of anti-market, anti-competitive behaviour we saw in the last chapter (Comcast has a venture investment division too), but that doesn't diminish the promise of more corporate engagement with innovators.

Mission

My favourite businesses, though, are not just those that provide value to the marketplace without doing harm but those whose profits are intrinsically linked to solving social or environmental problems. In the past five years thirty-one US states have passed benefit corporation legislation, allowing for-profit companies to legally pursue social and environmental impact in addition to profit.[58] The proliferation of 'B-corps', including the now publicly traded Etsy, shows that multiple bottom lines are not mutually exclusive.

Consider Revolution Foods: started in 2006 by two mothers who met in business school, the company has figured out how to inexpensively make and distribute wholesome, additive-free lunches to children eligible for government-subsidised meals at their schools. To make food kids will actually eat, chefs visit schools to conduct taste tests – co-founder Kristin Groos Richmond describes their meals as 'kid-designed' – and regional specialties, like jambalaya in Louisiana, are included on the menu.[59] The company feeds hundreds of thousands of students in a thousand schools in twenty-six cities, delivering over a million meals a week and generating close to $100 million in revenue. Most importantly, 80 per cent of their meals go to underserved communities. It's a business model that embodies the intersection of good public policy, human-centred design and real entrepreneurial spirit.[60]

Here's another wonderful, mission-driven company: despite high rates of pay and high levels of unemployed workers across the United States, there is a dire shortage of qualified software engineers. Meanwhile, millions in Africa can't find work. So Andela, a start-up human resources firm, finds and trains top recruits in Africa to then work remotely for top tech companies, far more affordably than recruiting engineers at home. Each candidate is trained for at least 1,000 hours.[61] And rather than charging them for tuition, Andela pays them – at a combined cost of about $10,000 per fellow, as they're called, for four months of training. Fellows then make a four-year commitment to the tech firms for which they'll work, which include Microsoft and Udacity (which we'll hear some more about in Chapter 9), and they can continue taking professional development courses throughout their tenure. Andela's founder, Jeremy Johnson, was inspired to start the company after a trip to Nairobi several years ago: 'I just became kind of blown away by the incredible under-utilised human capital that I saw everywhere,' he says.[62] The company has already had more than 15,000 applicants. Though they've only been able to accept less than 1 per cent of them, Johnson's goal is to train 100,000 developers across Africa over the next decade. 'Our hope and expectation is that the Andela fellows, as they go through the programme and graduate, play a key role in the continued growth of the continent.'[63]

Businesses are not governments. They can neither lock us up nor take our property. But they are tremendous organisations that accomplish tremendous things. Human progress owes an immeasurable debt to the ingenuity of the entrepreneurs, inventors and innovators who have used the vehicle of business to benefit us all. Business isn't without its faults, though. In this chapter we have seen examples of the good and the bad, and it's obvious that if we want to make business more human, we need to encourage the former and discourage the latter. Some of that, as we saw in the previous chapter (and the one before that, Food) can be achieved by reforming the structure of certain industries – to make them fully competitive or to eliminate subsidies that harm society. Other aspects of inhuman business that cause concern can and should be tackled by government through specific legislation and regulation – for example, to mandate more human family leave policies in the workplace.

But it can't all be done by government. In the end the many millions of businesses that exist in the world – most of them small – are run by people. We need those people to make more human choices about how they and their businesses behave. Just because new techniques, increased public consciousness or smart technology make running a *good* business more and more feasible – and at a profit too – does not mean it's inevitable. Businesses must *choose* to be good. And we must encourage them. Just as government should set the rules for fair markets, we should also demand it as investors, consumers and suppliers, and – wherever possible – from within, as managers and employees. If demanding is too aggressive, then we at least need to be more curious. In our daily lives, we should all be asking, 'Where does this come from?' 'How were the people who made it treated?' 'What are the effects on the environment?' Of course, for us to have these conversations, we need to know more. That's why moving towards a norm of openness, transparency and accountability – through a combination of technology, regulation and public pressure – is such a big part of the answer, a way to make all businesses more human businesses.

CHAPTER 8

POVERTY

This is how we deal with poverty today: there is a boy – let's call him Chris – from a poor family in East London. Like so many others in similar circumstances – in London, in America, in rich countries everywhere – Chris has all sorts of problems: mental health issues, acting out in school, getting into trouble with the police. Chris also has many well-meaning people from government trying to help him: social workers, probation officers, counsellors. One day the adults responsible for different aspects of his life planned a conference to discuss his situation. There were going to be eleven professionals present. Chris's mother went to see David Robinson, founder of Community Links, a remarkable organisation that for over twenty-five years has been fighting poverty in some of Britain's poorest neighbourhoods. She asked him to come too. 'Why?' he asked. There were, after all, already going to be nearly a dozen people there. She pleaded, 'I need someone on my side.'

How heartbreaking. She saw the social workers, the court officers – all of them – as her son's enemies. As David Robinson says, the well-meaning but ineffectual government assistance was so overwhelming that the mother practically needed an assistant to keep up.[1] They were all working on her son's problems piecemeal, with a different caseworker (or more) for each of his problems, pursuing the priorities and processes set by their part of the bureaucracy.

Yes, this is how we deal with poverty today – in a way that is inhuman. Chris and his mother's personal experience illustrate a broader disease. Today's vast, complex welfare system is clearly not working: how do we spend £120 billion a year fighting poverty and still have so many poor people?[2] With generation after generation in poverty, we're obviously not dealing with its root causes. But the truly remarkable thing, given how much money we spend on it, is that we're not even dealing properly with its symptoms.

The symptoms of poverty

Every year HSBC, the international bank based in London, recently under fire for its sterling work helping the super-rich – including its own senior executives – avoid taxes, holds its annual general meeting where shareholders gather to discuss financial results, hear executives speak, and make decisions about the company's governance. These meetings tend to be pretty boring, almost entirely predictable. But in 2003 the meeting was quite different. Sir John Bond, the company's chairman, had just finished his address. There was a celebratory mood in the air; much of the assembly had centred around HSBC's planned acquisition of Household International, an American loan company, and William Aldinger, its head, had been persuaded to join HSBC's management. As is customary, Sir John opened the floor to questions.

Up stood perhaps the last person he would have expected to see. The proud owner of just enough donated shares to earn him a spot at the meeting, the man standing to ask Sir

John a question was the man who cleaned his office every night. He said:

> *Sir John Bond, distinguished ladies and gentlemen, my name is Abdul Durrant, I work in the same office as the board members, the only difference is I don't operate computers. My function is to operate a mop and bucket. Yes, I am one of the invisible night cleaners. You may be wondering what the hell is a night cleaner doing here: we're supposed to be invisible. Well, I am here on behalf of all the contract staff at HSBC and the families of East London. We receive £5 per hour – a whole £5 per hour![3] – no pension, and a measly sick-pay scheme. In our struggles our children go to school without adequate lunch. We are unable to provide necessary books for their education. School outings in particular they miss out on. In the end, many of our children prefer a life of crime to being a cleaner … Sir John, we have met before. Will you consider your previous decision not to review the cleaning contract with OCS, so that I and my colleagues receive a living wage?[4]*

The working poor

Abdul's story touched everyone in the room, particularly Sir John. It wasn't just that the story was moving, or that people were impressed by Abdul's eloquence despite the fact that he was so completely out of place. His story was especially poignant because the board had just discussed the pay package for Mr Aldinger, who was now joining HSBC's management. His salary? £23 million (in excess of $35 million at the time) over the next three years. It was a contrast too stark for even the most avowed capitalists in the room. Abdul had made his point.

His situation was not – is not – unusual. He is among the 1.4 million or so British workers – about one in twenty – who earn the legal minimum wage.[5] Another 1.3 million earn within just 50p of it.[6] Worse, many of them really are just as good as invisible. Not only are they hidden from sight because of their night-shift hours but also because of the subcontracted process through which they're employed. 'They're one step or two steps removed from the original employer so it's very difficult to build up a picture of how many are working, in what conditions,' explains Matthew Bolton of campaign group London Citizens. 'Whoever you go to at whatever state of this subcontracting chain, they don't want to tell you.'[7]

These are the working poor. And for them life is terrible. Their struggles are not just about money but also dignity. Financial poverty leads to deprivations and challenges that are inconceivable for the rest of us. According to behavioural economist Sendhil Mullainathan, 'There's money poverty, there's time poverty, and there's bandwidth poverty … One of the things the poor lack most is bandwidth. The very struggle of making ends meet leaves them with less of this vital resource' – a resource essential to performing simple tasks and getting through life.[8] The poor are worse parents, they forget to take medications, they make bad decisions. But it is not about lack of love or skills; it's simply the inability to cope with so many things at once.[9] The rich can buy bandwidth in ways the poor cannot – they hire housekeepers, gardeners, assistants, accountants and nannies. They can go 'away for the weekend'; they take vacations. They can afford to take their time when making financial decisions. They can buy a shorter commute by choosing to live near where they work.

When poor people are constantly worrying about money, they neglect other areas of their lives. Scarcity of money affects scarcity of time, which in turn affects scarcity of mental bandwidth. All of these things feed on themselves, leading to worse and worse decision-making. And although most of us might take a break when life feels overwhelming, the poor cannot. 'Poor people can't say, "I'll take a vacation from being poor,"' Mullainathan explains.[10]

Unsurprisingly given the psychological stress of poverty, 'there's a strong association between poverty and low mental health,' says Princeton psychologist Johannes Haushofer.[11] This has broader health implications. When the poor neglect daily tasks, they also neglect to take care of themselves. 'I estimate 12 million Americans living in poverty suffer from at least one neglected parasitic or tropical disease,' says Dr Peter Hotez.[12]

We should remember that the working poor are not some 'underclass', bent on cheating the system. Or even teenagers earning a little extra cash in summertime.[13] In 2011/2012, for the first time ever, over half of the 13 million people in poverty in Britain were from working families; 1.42 million of them had part-time work but wanted full-time work. They're not poor for want of trying.[14] Low pay is often bandied about in political debates as a talking point. But just think about it for a minute. Think about it on an individual, human level.

Imagine if it were you. Imagine you got up every day, worked to the point where you were so exhausted you couldn't move, worked so hard you felt permanently, achingly guilty that you weren't spending enough time with your children and were missing moments with them that would literally never come again; imagine you worked like that, but your wages were so low that you still didn't have enough to live on. You'd then have a choice: you might take on an additional job, spend even less time at home, burden your body even more. Or you could take the physically easier but emotionally more difficult choice of giving up even more of your humanity: on top of all the other indignities you could go to the government, give up your independence and ask for a welfare payment – a handout, even though you were working as hard as you possibly could. Imagine how that would make you feel. This is a scandal.

We ended slavery because it was inhuman and wrong. As we saw in Chapter 5, it is time to end animal cruelty, because it's inhuman and wrong. And now I want to show you how we can end the moral scourge represented by the very notion of the 'working poor'. I'm not arguing this on the basis of 'efficiency' or 'growth' or any other financial or economic objective. I'm arguing this because I think it's morally unacceptable that anyone who works should not be able to live off what they earn.

The policy intervention most obviously aimed at helping to end poverty pay is the government-established 'minimum wage', based on the principle that no one should work without fair compensation. The idea got its start in 1896 when Australians, having just seen the abolition of slavery, resolved to treat all workers with dignity. They believed it was morally necessary to recognise workers as human beings, rather than costs of production, which is what many, as slaves, had literally been considered just a short time before. 'It would demean us all,' argued Alfred Deakin in 1896, an Australian legislator and later prime minister, 'if those who made our food and clothing or tended to our comforts and well-being were treated as inferior beings.'[15] By 1907 Australia's minimum wage had become a symbol of pride – and a beacon for reformers worldwide.

Britain owes the roots of its minimum wage to Sir Winston Churchill, a champion of free markets, who backed the country's first minimum-wage legislation in 1909. Arguing for it in Parliament, Churchill put it as well as anyone: 'It is a serious national evil that any class of His Majesty's subjects should receive less than a living wage in return for their utmost exertions.'[16] He would go on in that same year to create wage councils, which protected and set wages in the 'sweated' industries, a reform that would last over eighty years until the Major government of the 1990s.[17] John Major and the Conservatives (including me, as a junior researcher at the time) made the conventional right-of-centre argument against the minimum wage: that it would distort markets, leading to higher unemployment.[18] With the Trade Union Reform and Employment Rights Bill of 1993, Major abolished the wage councils; the only minimum wage at that point in the UK was in the agricultural sector. When Tony Blair and Labour took power in 1997, part of their manifesto was to restore a wage floor, but instead of doing it industry by industry, they resolved to create a National Minimum Wage. In July 1997, Blair created the Low Pay Commission, an independent body that began setting a minimum wage in 1998.[19]

The actual introduction of the minimum wage comprehensively defeated the arguments of those who had opposed it: it seemed to have no negative impact on employment or the economy more generally, and today at least the idea has cross-party support.[20] But at £6.70 per hour, it isn't enough. Despite a minimum wage, taking full-time and part-time workers together, 5.28 million people in the UK – 22 per cent of employees – live on wages that are considered below what is reasonable to live on. Over a fifth of British employees don't earn enough from their wages to afford the basic necessities of life, from rent to food to utilities to clothing.[21] Even more depressing is that those with low pay find it hard to advance to even slightly higher positions: almost a quarter of minimum-wage workers have remained at that rate for the past five years.[22]

Earning your own living is essential to human dignity, and psychologists have shown that autonomy and independence are vital for well-being. Yet just under 2 million people are working full-time while being paid by their employers at a level they can't live on.[23] These workers are robbed of their essential human dignity. While it's impossible to know exactly how many work full-time or part-time, some 2.3 million in-work British families qualified for Working Tax Credits in 2013;[24] they worked, but, instead of being independent, they were forced to rely on welfare handouts from the government. How can the minimum wage be an antidote to poverty when it doesn't provide enough to live on?

None of us should feel comfortable living in such a society. That many should have to work multiple jobs – tough, physical and sometimes demeaning jobs – in order to make ends meet is surely unacceptable. Of course, there's a distinction between part-time and full-time: if you work twenty hours a week, you shouldn't expect to make the same as someone who works forty hours. But if you work full-time, you should be paid enough to live on. End of story. There will, of course, always be people on benefits out of necessity, like the elderly or disabled, but society, quite rightly, does not expect them to work for a living. Everyone else should. There should be no such thing as the working poor.

A 'living wage' is the amount that's enough to live on if you work full-time (defined as 37.5 hours per week),[25] based on the costs of food, housing, energy, transport, basic leisure and so on. While there are various definitions, the most prominent one in Britain is calculated by the Living Wage Foundation, which in 2015 assessed the level as £9.15 per hour in London and £7.85 in the rest of the UK.[26]

In Australia – way back in 1907 – the minimum wage was a living wage – that's how it was defined.[27] It's what Churchill meant too when he equated a minimum wage with a living wage. But today the minimum wage is obviously not enough to live on. If it were, we wouldn't need to top it up with welfare payments. Wouldn't it be better – more human – if we dealt with this by paying a living wage in the first place?

The HSBC annual general meeting in 2003, with Abdul Durrant's remarkable speech to Sir John Bond, was a turning point for the living wage. A grass-roots community-organising group called London Citizens, based in the East End, had been running a living-wage campaign since the previous year (they had helped buy Abdul the shares which permitted him to speak). London Citizens' campaign now started to bear fruit: HSBC, and soon many others, would adopt a living wage for all staff on their properties – security guards, cleaners, caterers – everyone. Neil Jameson, who helped start London Citizens and was the driving force behind the campaign, convinced many politicians and employers to see not only the moral imperative of paying their workers a living wage but the good business sense it makes. To date, over 2,000 employers have been accredited by the Living Wage Foundation, including Barclays, Chelsea Football Club, Goldman Sachs, Lloyds of London, KPMG, and Nestlé, helping around 60,000 people.[28]

But there are still so many – over 2 million working families in the UK – who make barely enough to survive: 85 per cent of all bar and restaurant employees make below the living wage; 70 per cent of retail employees; 40 per cent of carers.[29] Carers!

After many years of campaigns and advocacy by a wide range of individuals and organisations (including by me in the first edition of this book), Conservative Chancellor of the Exchequer George Osborne introduced Britain's first National Living Wage in his 2015 budget. It's not perfect: it will take until 2020 to come fully into effect and ought to be higher to take into account proposed cuts in the welfare budget, but it does make Britain the only country in the world to uphold the value of work by mandating a living wage.

Yet the debate is hardly settled. There are strong camps in every party – particularly my own – that still don't support the living wage. While some are opposed on ideological grounds, much of the rationale centres around the cost to employers.

Do the right thing – it pays

There is an assumption that requiring employers to pay a living wage will cost jobs on a massive scale. As the original opponents of a minimum wage argued, higher wages mean higher costs for employers. But we don't need to speculate about this. We can look at some of the companies that have implemented a living wage. Like Costco.

Costco isn't just big in the United States; it's the second largest retailer in the world.[30] Its business model is simple: huge warehouses, cheap products, stacked high. And yet Costco pays its workers way over the living wage. Repeat: way over the living wage. In the United States employees earn, on average, $20.89 per hour, not including overtime. And 88 per cent of employees have employer-sponsored health insurance – a big deal in the United States where there is no free NHS.[31] For Costco a living wage is good business. Writing to Congress in support of a higher minimum wage, CEO Craig Jelinek wrote, 'We know it's a lot more profitable in the long term to minimise employee turnover and maximise employee productivity, commitment and loyalty.' Consider that 70 per cent of Costco's warehouse managers got their start on the floor, stacking boxes and collecting carts. Turnover is 5 per cent for those who have been there over a year. It's easy to understand where the loyalty comes from: management has increased wages every three years. During the 2009 downturn, when retail shops were laying employees off and cutting pay and benefits, founder and then CEO Jim Sinegal decided to do exactly the opposite: he gave workers a raise of $1.50 an hour. According to CFO Richard Galanti, 'The first thing out of Jim's mouth was, "This economy is bad. We should be figuring out how to give them more, not less."'

How much do these 'generous' policies cost? Admittedly, lower profits in the short term. But in the long term this ethos has paid off. Last year Costco made over $2 billion in profits.[32] Its share price has more than doubled since its pre-recession peak. And it's not as if Costco is passing on these costs to customers. It has a general policy to mark items up at no more than 15 per cent. For Costco, paying employees well makes financial sense. Of course, every company is different. But Costco demonstrates a fundamental principle: a living wage is not necessarily bad for business or jobs, even in a sector with as slim margins as grocery and discount retailing.

Think about the money a company makes as a surplus: it can choose to distribute that in various ways. Simplistically, a company can choose to invest its profits in new technology or innovative processes, it can give that money to its customers in the form of lower prices or higher value products for the same prices, it can give the money to its shareholders, or it can give the money to its workers in the form of higher pay and benefits. Obviously most well-run companies do a combination of these things. But what is the balance? At Costco it's tilted more towards workers. But elsewhere across the economy, instead of sharing more of their surplus with workers, companies have been choosing to give it to shareholders. Could that be because senior executives' pay and compensation are now so closely tied to their company's short-term share price? Whatever the motivation, the end result is that over the last ten years companies on the S&P 500 have spent almost 90 per cent of their profits on shareholder dividends and stock buybacks.[33]

The most frustrating part is that, as Costco has found, treating your workers fairly and paying them a living wage can actually help your business and, in the long term, boost share price. It is a lazy assumption, contradicted by the evidence, that putting shareholders first is the best way to succeed. It's especially ironic given the example set by one of America's great heroes of capitalism, Henry Ford. Ford doubled the daily wages of his employees amid a deep recession in 1914, declaring, 'If an employer does not share prosperity with those who make him prosperous, then pretty soon there will be no prosperity to share. That is why we think it good business always to raise wages and never to lower them. We like to have plenty of customers.'[34] He's not alone. Jack Welch, the former chief of General Electric, recently said that maximising shareholder value 'is the dumbest idea in the world'.[35] Paul Polman, CEO of Unilever, has called it a 'cult'.[36]

Better-paid employees work harder, are more open to changing job roles to suit their company's needs, and call in sick far less – one UK business that adopted the living wage reported a drop in absenteeism by as much as 25 per cent.[37] Living wage employers see higher morale (among all employees, not just the low-paid ones), an improved reputation and lower staff turnover.[38]

One objection you hear to the idea of a universal living wage is that although it may be possible for large or even medium-sized businesses, it would be devastating for small businesses. And that matters a lot when so many of the working poor are in the retail and hospitality sectors, where small firms dominate. It turns out that here, too, there's no iron rule – it's a question of choice. If you build higher wages into your business plan, you can make it work. The Living Wage Foundation has certified not just big corporations but small and medium-sized businesses too. Faucet Inn, a small chain of pubs in southern England, is a good example. According to Richard Stringer, the Group's operations director: 'Committing to the living wage is a real opportunity to give more to your staff to ensure that everybody who works for [us] has a balance of work and home life and family life.'[39]

Still, no matter how much evidence you provide or how many case studies you cite, people will ask, 'How can we afford it?' If we really want to make this happen, we need to make it easier for businesses. We need a 'business-friendly living wage'. Here's how it can be done.

The debate over low pay and the working poor captures only half the argument. It's not just about wages; it's also about taxes – business taxes. Think about what an inadequate minimum wage actually is. It allows a company to pay workers less than they need to live on because the government will make up the difference through welfare. A minimum wage that's too low for people to live on is a subsidy to business. In policy circles the fashionable vehicle for these subsidies is the concept of the 'tax credit' paid to low-wage workers, called the Working Tax Credit (WTC) in the UK and the Earned Income Tax Credit (EITC) in the US. These give unemployed people incentives to get into work, even if it's low paid. It has partly achieved that aim and done some good in lifting people from poverty,[40] but research shows that although wage subsidies like this increase employment, they also depress wages by allowing employers to pay less: one American study found that for every dollar spent on the EITC, only 28 cents were a net benefit to the recipient; 72 cents were captured by the employer in the form of lower wages paid.[41]

In the end it's still welfare, with the government topping up low pay – a subsidy to the employer and an insult to the worker. It's especially shocking that free marketers and conservatives seem to support these subsidies to businesses, presumably because they are branded 'tax credits'. What a triumph of spin. The really mad part is that at the same time as receiving wage subsidies *from* the government, companies are paying corporate and payroll taxes *to* the government. This is an insane merry-go-round of money: a company pays low wages to its workers; it pays tax to the government; the government then takes the tax and gives it back to the workers.

Economically, low pay is an unfair subsidy to big business. Politically it contributes to the need for a vast bureaucracy to slush money around the system. Socially it perpetuates cycles of welfare and a loss of human independence and dignity. Morally it dishonours the work of millions of people on whose labour society depends.

Here's a simple way to end it: let's introduce a true National Living Wage – in other words a minimum that's even higher than the one currently set – and cut employers' taxes by the same amount they're paying in higher wages. It would vary from place to place, ideally set by local authorities at a level that every full-time worker in the area could live on, without government or other handouts. The crucial element of this change would be the compensating reduction in business taxes – aiming for a revenue-neutral impact on employers.

Consider: in the UK, the Working Tax Credit (WTC) is funded by both employee and employer contributions to National Insurance. While a significant proportion of National Insurance contributions go to pensions and the NHS, they also go to topping up underpaid workers. Between 2012 and

2013, 2,295,000 families received a total of £7.1 billion in WTC benefits, an average of £3,094 per family.[42] According to the Living Wage Foundation and Resolution Foundation, a living wage of the sort I propose would increase tax and National Insurance receipts by £2.8 billion. At the same time, many underpaid workers would no longer need as much or even any government welfare to 'top up' their insufficient income. With the accompanying reduction in welfare bureaucracy, it's estimated that the government would save £1.4 billion. Altogether, a living wage would actually have a net positive fiscal impact of £4.2 billion per year.[43] Why don't we take that £4.2 billion and use it to help make the living wage affordable for business? The Resolution Foundation estimates that it would cost business £6.5 billion.[44] If we used that £4.2 billion to reduce companies' National Insurance contributions – perhaps starting with small or medium-sized firms who could least afford a living wage – those refunds would bring the overall cost to business down by almost two-thirds, to £2.3 billion. It's not perfect, but it's a start.

The causes of poverty

A business-friendly living wage would, by definition, end in-work poverty. But that isn't nearly enough; we need to tackle the causes of poverty too. In far too many cases poverty is generational, handed down like some perverse inheritance within a family. To end poverty we must break that cycle. Although economic policies can help fight the symptoms of poverty, it is social policy that will help us fight the causes. That has to start with children – like Sasha.

Sasha lives in the Bayview, one of San Francisco's poorest communities. Violence is rampant not only in her neighbourhood (she knew three people who were murdered) but also in her home: when her father drinks, he's physically abusive. He's in prison, but although he's not there to abuse her, his absence causes other problems. Sasha's mother had to work evenings to make ends meet, but because she couldn't find a babysitter for Sasha, she lost her job and, with it, the income to pay the rent. Now, after a bout of homelessness, they live in subsidised housing. Meanwhile Sasha – ashamed of herself and her family – is almost always tense with her mother, who is depressed but, because she is uninsured, is unable to get effective mental health treatment. Sasha has a hard time focusing in class, so she misbehaves: she is jumpy and often overreacts to provocation. She was recently suspended for kicking another girl. Her action wasn't justified, but she thought she was being threatened. After a life in her shoes, it was the only way she really knew how to respond. Sasha is eleven years old.[45]

She is also a patient of Dr Nadine Burke Harris, a local paediatrician. Her medical training took her to some of America's best universities: Stanford, Harvard, Berkeley. Yet when she chose where to locate her medical practice, she came to one of the country's most difficult neighbourhoods.[46] Soon after setting up her paediatric clinic in the Bayview, Burke Harris grew uneasy. She knew, as we all instinctively do, that being poor is not good for anyone's health. It's difficult to eat right; sleep is often disrupted; getting exercise is hard. But even these basic realities couldn't explain the common health problems she was seeing across her patients – conditions like asthma, learning disabilities, behavioural issues – far in excess of what was normal for children at their age. She began to wonder whether these conditions were somehow connected to the children's challenging circumstances. What if her patients' health problems were actually symptoms of something deeper, something more structural in their lives?

Toxic stress

In 1985 Dr Vincent Felitti was running an obesity clinic in San Diego, California. And he was stumped. Around half the patients who were participating in the programme, designed for those who were massively overweight, were dropping out, even when they were losing weight. He wanted to know why. He brought a couple of hundred of them into his clinic and asked them a standard set of questions – 'How much did you weigh when you started first grade?' 'How much did you weigh when you started high school?' 'How old were you when you married?' For a while nothing unusual surfaced. Then he made a mistake.

'I misspoke,' he remembers. 'Instead of asking, "How old were you when you were first sexually active?" I asked: "How much did you *weigh* when you were first sexually active?" The patient, a woman, answered: "Forty pounds."' Not quite understanding her, he asked the same question again. Her first sexual experience, it turned out, was with her father when she was four years old. Felitti was dumbfounded. 'I remembered thinking: "This is only the second incest case I've had in twenty-three years of practice."' So he continued the line of questioning with others. 'About ten days later, I ran into the same thing. It was very disturbing. Every other person was providing information about childhood sexual abuse. I thought: "This can't be true. Someone would have told me in medical school."'

Still not convinced he wasn't somehow biasing his patients, he asked other doctors at the clinic to ask the same thing. Sure enough, of the 286 people interviewed, most of them had been the victims of sexual abuse. For some, eating was a coping mechanism, a 'drug' that made them feel better, soothing depression, anger, fear. For others, being overweight provided a form of protection: in the case of one man, it had prevented other kids from beating him up in the school yard. For one woman, being fat made her an undesirable rape victim (when she was seven, her father told her the only reason he wasn't abusing her sister was that she was fat).

Despite many doctors' scepticism, Felitti found allies in Dr David Williamson and Dr Robert Anda, epidemiologists at the US Centers for Disease Control and Prevention. After years researching childhood trauma, determining which questions they would ask, and setting up the questionnaires, they began a trial in 1995. By 1997 they had asked over 17,000 patients passing through a San Diego clinic about ten types of childhood trauma, including sexual, verbal and physical abuse, family dysfunction, and emotional and physical neglect. They then were able to draw correlations between childhood circumstances and health conditions.[47]

The home environment, they discovered, played a crucial role in the health of the people they interviewed, particularly the children. Of the ten specific adverse childhood experiences (ACEs, as they dubbed them) they asked about, some two-thirds of the study participants had had at least one.[48] The doctors created a simple scoring system: one point for the presence of each type of ACE in a child's life. For example, if your parents had divorced during your childhood, you had a score of 1. If you were abused and had divorced parents, you had a score of 2. And so on. As traumatic experiences added up – as the ACE score increased – the worse the health outcomes. In the 1998 article where they published their results, they wrote that compared to someone with no ACEs, someone with an ACE score of 4 was 3.9 times more likely to have emphysema or chronic bronchitis, 2.4 times more likely to have hepatitis or jaundice, and 1.6 times more likely to have had skeletal fractures. They also found a significant relationship between ACE scores and risk factors for heart disease, liver disease and cancer. Those with an ACE score of 4 or higher were 2.2 times likelier to smoke, 1.6 times likelier to be obese, 4.6 times likelier to have been depressed in the past year, and over 12.2 times likelier to have ever attempted suicide.[49]

Nadine Burke Harris's own experiences in her Bayview clinic – and her hunch that something deeper was going on with her patients than just the symptoms of poverty – led her to Felitti and Anda's research. She realised she was witnessing ACEs taking place ... in real time. Her patients' problems had little to do with health per se; they had everything to do with their family environments. Sasha's domestic problems – the alcoholic father who physically abused her and her mother, the violence and murder all around her – these were not just unfortunate coincidences alongside her health problems. They were their cause. And the connection? A phenomenon called toxic stress.

Not all stress is bad. Positive stress is a mild response to a challenge or exciting event, like an exam, a big sporting occasion or a public performance. Although it might not feel great in the short term, experiencing positive stress as a child can help build strength and grit. Tolerable stress is severe and negative but is usually in response to a one-off event, like a death in the family. If managed with the help of a caring adult, a child can overcome tolerable stress. But toxic stress is different. It *is* toxic – literally poison. Medically defined as the 'extreme, frequent or extended activation of [the body's] stress response without the buffering presence of a supportive adult',[50] toxic stress is exactly what you would imagine is created by those ACEs. In the absence of enough compensating warmth, love and affection from at least one parent or primary caregiver, it creates physical, molecular changes in the brain.

When the body senses stress or anxiety, it activates defences that cause chemical and physical reactions. As it is temporary, positive or tolerable stress doesn't pose a problem. But repeated stress disables the ability to respond correctly. 'If you are growing up in an environment where there are constant threats, the brain adapts in a way that reacts to those threats,' explains Burke Harris. Children exhibit relatively minor symptoms like the inability to sit still. But as adults they become unable to cope and end up behaving destructively. 'When we were evolving, the threats were sabre-tooth tigers and lions and bears, and this made a ton of sense,' says Burke Harris. 'Whatever it is, you'd have to jump on it and beat the crap out of it in order to survive. Nowadays when you do that, you end up incarcerated or, if you're trying to sit still in a classroom and the kid next to you hits you or pokes you, then you end up getting kicked out of class. What we see in children who are experiencing toxic stress is tremendous difficulty in self-regulation.'[51]

Children with toxic stress have higher levels of the long-term stress hormone, cortisol, in their brains. This is particularly problematic for younger children because of neuroplasticity, the way our brains physically change and evolve. Neuroplasticity isn't unique to stressed children – everyone's brain architecture and chemistry are affected by experiences. But children younger than five years old are especially vulnerable to environmental stressors. This is because there are two types of neuroplasticity. One is synaptic plasticity (the strength of connections between brain cells), which occurs throughout our lifetimes. The other is cellular plasticity (the number of those connections), which occurs primarily in the first five years of a child's life. The elevated levels of cortisol from toxic stress disrupt that development and can cause long-term damage. For children, failure to inhibit the stress hormones in their brain inhibits their own maturation. This permanent, toxic stress leads not just to bad health outcomes for children but to bad life outcomes that are at the heart of the fight against poverty.

The costs of poverty

Welfare costs the UK £120 billion per year.[52] Addiction costs £36 billion.[53] Child poverty costs £29 billion.[54] Educational failure costs £20.2 billion.[55] Crime costs £17.1 billion for the criminal justice system and an additional £24 billion in social and economic costs.[56] These social problems, almost by definition, are overwhelmingly concentrated among the poor. As the saying goes, some of this 'will always be with us.' But so many of these costs would be reducible, avoidable, if we took more interest in their deep, structural causes rather than just (expensively) addressing the symptoms. This would mean addressing poverty on a more human level, concentrating on the individual person from their very earliest days and how they end up part of a 'social problem'. All those big numbers – the costs of welfare, crime, addiction – are composed of individual people with their own stories and circumstances. And one thing we can now say with confidence is that for a vast majority of them, adverse childhood experiences – and the toxic stress that goes with them – are part of their story and circumstances.

We typically attempt to intervene after kids commit crime or drop out of school, but we fail to prevent these problems in the first place. By the time the 'system' even realises someone like Sasha exists, she is already deeply in crisis and needs lots of costly help to get out. But if we look at where ACEs mostly arise, it's at home, in the family context. That's not surprising: the family is the core unit of life. Families care for each other, teach each other, play together, eat together, love together. Most importantly, families raise children. Generally, happy and successful children tend to come from stable, loving families; troubled children tend to come from troubled homes.

There are caveats, of course. Some people who are extremely successful – and sometimes even happy – grew up in homes that were far from being stable and loving. There's a theory that overcoming early adversity was for many of the world's most successful people a direct spur to their accomplishments. But what we don't know – and will never know – is: What if the adversity wasn't a spur but a harness, that they achieved amazing things *despite* the difficulties they experienced at an early age? Imagine how much more might have been possible. And remember, it's not just about avoiding social costs; it's about the benefits too, the benefits to all of us if children develop in the right way from an early age.

Family first

Here's the big idea. The easiest, most effective, most cost-effective way to end poverty, reduce inequality, promote better health and well-being, cut crime and antisocial behaviour, spur entrepreneurship and innovation; the best way to achieve the outcomes we all want for our society and economy; the single most valuable thing we can do in government and outside it to make the world a better place for all … is to invest in the infrastructure that matters most: the human infrastructure of the family.

Most families work well. In their own ways they do a good job of preparing their children to succeed as adults. All we need to do is help the minority of families where that's not happening to get their act together – to become at least as good as average. That single change would do more to end poverty and improve our society and economy than anything else. And it is possible. We have done much harder things than this. We have mobilised resources on a much bigger scale, more quickly, than would be needed for this. We have invaded countries. We have put a man on the moon. Now we can end poverty – the human way.

We are getting this so wrong at the moment. We leave it far too late to pay attention to the things that matter. Altering a child's path is a little like steering a large ship. Shifting 1 degree at the start is much easier than making a 90-degree course correction later on, hundreds of miles away from harbour. For children, acting early to make sure they're on track means fewer kids will get into trouble as teenagers or young adults. It's a lot harder to help a delinquent youth or a dropout than it is to help a toddler. Social problems begin early and then multiply. Stress, as other recent studies have found, is contagious, adding to cycles of toxic stress in struggling families.[57] And one of the biggest sources of stress is family structure itself, specifically in the form of children raised without their father, or a consistent father figure, in the home. Men who don't stay around to raise their children are one of the primary causes of social breakdown. In the UK, some 76 per cent of young offenders come from households without dads.[58] Families break at different points, but many do so in part because of the stress of having children. And the experience of family breakdown, combined with the circumstances of poverty, leaves an often indelible imprint on the children affected.

Recall David Robinson of Community Links in East London and the boy with eleven caseworkers. That story doesn't just make the case for streamlining social services for families; it also points to a broader issue. Even when government tries to help people living in poverty, it often does so haphazardly. The problems of poverty don't neatly stack into whatever programme we've created to tackle them.

We've seen throughout this book that in many policy areas we try to compensate for their complexity by putting them into neat boxes – 'silos' in policy-speak – thinking that by simplifying or neatly packaging and assigning them to a particular agency, law or programme, everything will be made easier. This is inherently not human; the human world is a messy place, and most things are interconnected. Many chapters in this book overlap with each other, and that's not a coincidence. After all, you can't solve unemployment without thinking about education; you can't think about health without thinking about food. And no social issue can be solved without thinking about our most fundamental social unit, the family.

Instead of helping the East London boy piecemeal – in school, through his probation officer, or in his after-school programme – those efforts should have been put into a broader context: What is his family situation? What is his home physically like? What were his ACEs? Is he suffering from toxic stress? To turn around the lives of troubled children and help them escape poverty for good, we don't just need to streamline the help we give them; we need to provide the right infrastructure for them to succeed. We need to help their entire family.

If we fail to take a broad view of a family and its problems, solutions will only be patches that treat symptoms rather than the underlying cause. Poverty stems from multiple things going wrong: perhaps the stress of a difficult relationship or a break-up leads to substance abuse and the loss of a job; perhaps someone who has received government assistance and training can't get a job because she can't afford childcare or transport to work. These problems are all related, and those who suffer them are often least equipped to handle them. If you have a stable income or a good social-support network, a break-up or substance abuse can be overcome. But if several of these things happen at once, that missing support network exacerbates the severity of each problem. Children born into families living under these circumstances are swimming against the tide even before their birth.

All this is made much worse, of course, by the scale and distance of government. The parts of government that typically provide services for families are local authorities responsible for many hundreds of thousands of people. It's no surprise that these large bureaucracies end up putting their own systems and procedures first – often in the name of 'efficiency'– and the individual circumstances of real people a distant second.

That's why we need organisations like David Robinson's Community Links and why we should give them a much bigger role in fighting poverty. Community Links has two great strengths. First is its multifaceted 'hub' approach, combining many services in one place. 'Within the hub model there is no wrong door.' According to Robinson, this improves service and reduces the cost for both the individual and the state.[59] That doesn't mean it does everything, but it is an entry point that allows people who need services to access them in a convenient way in a comfortable setting with people they know and trust. This is the other critical strength of Community Links: relationships matter, and they are more easily built and maintained when not spread across a dozen agencies. They're even more powerful when they are organic and come from a person's own volition. No one is mandated to come to Community Links, and so it's a source of trusted counsel rather than suspicion.

Promise Neighborhoods is a similar programme present in dozens of communities across the United States. Based on Harlem Children's Zone (HCZ), a now deservedly well-known programme in New York that aims to provide cradle-to-college services in a comprehensive fashion, Promise aims to bridge service providers. Rohan and I visited HCZ and met its inspiring, charismatic leader, Geoffrey Canada, while we were researching policy ideas in 2010. The HCZ model focuses programmes not only on children – its centrepiece is a series of charter schools – but also on the environment around them. Among the many programmes are parenting classes, coaches for teachers, healthy eating initiatives, tax preparation clinics, test-prep classes, and more. HCZ recognises the importance of early childhood, so it targets expectant parents and works with them and their children until college. Its Baby College gives parents tools and advice, whereas its Three-Year Journey programme works as a weekly support network to which parents bring their children. As the parents meet and take part in workshops, their children play together in a structured environment.

As children grow up, they and their families get age-appropriate support, from a recreation centre to an Employment and Technology Center, where, in addition to getting access to technology, youths can get tutoring and academic counselling. Tying all these programmes together is communication: rather than have dozens of agencies independently handling these tasks, a child or family works within a single network.[60] The result is an elimination of red tape as well as continuity and stability.

The goal of Promise Neighborhoods is to spread the HCZ model across the United States with grants from the Obama administration to existing local organisations in poor communities. The Promise Neighborhood Institute (PNI), meanwhile, provides training, tools for continuous feedback, and lessons from best practices across the country. In a way PNI exemplifies the localism I discussed in Chapter 2: local service delivery that helps communities solve their own problems, buttressed by a central infrastructure that provides support that can only be organised at scale.[61]

But in the end, however it's organised or delivered, it comes down to the individual, human level: one person working with one family to help its members get their lives back on track. These services flourish on the basis of simplicity: having one counsellor, adviser or advocate is better than ten. That simple idea was the starting point for one programme I'm especially proud of having helped start in government in the UK.

We knew intuitively – and then, once we took office, had the detailed research to back it up – that a relatively small group of completely broken families suffers and creates the most problems in British society. These families, around 120,000 of them, cost taxpayers some £9 billion annually (£75,000 per family on average).[62] Their interconnected problems – unemployment, debt, substance abuse, violence, educational failure – read like a template for the adverse childhood experiences Nadine Burke Harris sees in San Francisco. For decades government at all levels had failed to get a grip on these deep problems, and I was determined that we would be different. I also knew that a traditional bureaucratic approach would never work. We needed something more human, and I knew exactly the person for the job.

If you want to meet the personification of a 'human' civil servant, meet Louise Casey. A former deputy director of the British homeless charity Shelter, she came to prominence when Tony Blair appointed her head of the Rough Sleepers Unit in 1999 to solve the decades-old problem of homeless people sleeping out on the streets of London. She succeeded – and then went on to take a number of high-profile positions in government. Her Wikipedia entry describes her as 'known for being outspoken'. You can say that again.

In 2011 we asked Louise to lead a new Troubled Families Unit with a dedicated budget and very clear brief: £448 million in funding over three years to turn around the lives of those 120,000 most chaotic, dysfunctional families by the end of the Parliament in 2015.[63] The crucial difference was the approach: a more human one, focusing a family worker on each of these families. The family workers would be given the training and discretion to respond creatively to the very different, human needs of the people they were trying to help. 'On the whole most politicians think there are two ways to get something done in government. One is to pass laws through Parliament. Of course, you can get some change through passing laws,' Louise explains, 'but it's a blunt instrument. The other way is through fiscal change. When it comes to poverty or families, either they think they need to change the laws, that is, introduce a measure to tackle antisocial behaviour, or they think the thing to do is tax credits.'[64]

'Large institutions,' she says, 'operate around numbers and targets; they don't operate around people, behaviour and change.' But that institutional setting is especially problematic for troubled families and their plethora of problems. 'My families have an average of nine very significant problems and multiple agencies around them, each operating within their own systems. It's no shock to me that you can often find over fourteen different agencies running around them.' The approach Louise's team takes is to try to work with families to get to the root of their problems. They recognise that these problems are not based in government, so neither are the solutions; instead, they try to understand the exact context of a family's situation, in all its complexity. They work on the family's terms, not the government's. For instance, in many cases a family might be receiving state services that are either unhelpful or counterproductive, so the Troubled Families Unit will stop them. In other cases they work with local councils, the police, and the health, voluntary and community sectors to ensure coordinated, unduplicated services for families. As with David Robinson's Community Links, taking complexity out of people's lives is one of the best antidotes to their problems.

Perhaps most importantly, instead of being reactive, the unit tries to be proactive, asking how it can prevent a family from falling into further crisis. 'I met this girl who lived a life of abuse, handing it on to her three children. [Because she was a drug abuser, the social workers] said 'prevention' and prescribed her methadone so she doesn't go out and shoplift anymore. That's not prevention!' Louise exclaims. 'That is too late and not enough done. The problem is no one wants to go about it directly. People think that's judging families: some on the Left don't like it because they think it's judging the poor; some on the Right don't like it because they can't accept that these people need help getting back on their feet and it's not just about getting a job.'

This is the whole point: we need to get out of an ideological mindset and think about these people as they are, not as our grand political theories paint them. 'I profoundly think that when you're dealing with people like my families, they need an inspirational, sometimes judgemental mentor,' Louise says. 'You need a human being to enter their lives skilfully, lovingly, and to create a connection with them where everyone else has otherwise failed to connect.'

Sometimes the best person can be found within the family itself. Louise's most profound insight into how best to help troubled families is simple: most parents – even abusive ones – love their children and are their best hope for a successful childhood. 'I can predict the families that have histories of abuse; they have a lack of boundaries: no sense of what's right and wrong, no sense of how to create relationships with people, how to love well. People beat people even though they love them.' Although there is a line to be drawn and children should be protected from abusive parents, the default reaction shouldn't be for government to swoop in and alienate them. A child's relationship with their parents is the most important relationship in their life, and to sever it without working to repair it first is dangerous and short-sighted. That's why we need a different model that works as much as possible within the communities in which children live, a model that avoids making ideological and presumptuous pronouncements. That is the point of the Troubled Families Unit and its shift to a more human policy approach. It is already showing results: by June 2015, 99 per cent of families it has worked with had turned their lives around; in the 2015 Queen's Speech, the Government announced an expansion of the programme to 400,000 families.[65]

There are many more families where children are growing up in intergenerational poverty than the truly chaotic and dysfunctional families who are the focus of Louise's work. Without action, we can be pretty sure that the children in those families will be the ones who end up on welfare, in the criminal justice system, or, at the very least, lacking the opportunities most of us take for granted. As my former colleague in government, Liberal Democrat policy adviser Richard Reeves, puts it, 'The bigger challenge is to help the millions of parents who are not directly threatening their children, but are nonetheless damaging their long-term life chances by raising them poorly. Targeted interventions often seem to make the most sense in terms of making the best use of limited resources. But precisely because they are targeted, they run the risk of creating a stigma.'[66] When I was thinking about our family policies and how to help this wider group without stigmatising them, an answer came to me in the most personal possible way, in the form of one of the great British inventions, an innovation we can trace all the way back to Greater Manchester over 150 years ago.

The human face of social policy

In 1862 the first health visitors were employed by the municipality of Salford, known in those days as 'sanitary visitors', and introduced in response to the high levels of infant mortality and poor living conditions in nineteenth-century working-class areas. The idea was for trained workers to come into people's homes and develop a trusting relationship with families over time, proffering advice on nutrition, health, looking after young children – whatever a family needed. In 1929 health visiting was made a universal statutory service, and it has evolved considerably over time, including its incorporation into the world of professional nursing in 1945 and then fully into the NHS in 1974. But it was my personal, human experience of health visiting at the time of the birth of my first son that convinced me that Britain's long tradition of health visitors could be the centrepiece of a modern revitalisation of family policy.

The key, as with so many of the most successful policy interventions, is the human touch. Health visitors, who first come into your home at a time of great stress and anxiety – the birth of a child – have the potential to become the single best way to help families with problems, way beyond the immediate pressures of caring for a newborn. As with Louise Casey's approach in the Troubled Families Unit, it's all about the human, personalised connection. I know that many families (particularly those living in big cities) have far from positive experiences of health visiting. Despite its rich and proud history, the service has become inconsistent as budget cuts, a rise in caseloads and a lack of sufficient recruits has eviscerated the ability of many health visitors to provide anything beyond perfunctory assistance. With a ratio that has grown from an average of one health visitor for every twenty families to one for every 362 – and in some cases as many as 1,142 – they can scarcely develop a rapport with families, let alone become trusted advisers.[67] After an initial check or two, their overwhelming workloads often rule out any meaningful interventions except for the worst cases. But this is clearly something that can be changed. Home visiting can be much more than an early-warning system; it can be a central component of a more human family policy.

Home visitors could offer a lot more than just checking that a baby is well fed and looked after; they should be trained for the fully fledged family work that the best of them already perform. They can identify relationship problems, parenting problems, substance-abuse problems, mental health issues – and then direct families to locally available help and support. It's natural for home visitors to be the primary connection between the state and families. They are already in the home, and not because anything's gone wrong. And unlike other agents of government, they are trusted: the bonds they've forged with parents and children can be built upon. They are the human face of social policy.

We know this approach really works. From its origins in Victorian Britain, home-visiting services have been emulated in many other countries. One of the world's most evaluated social policy interventions is the Nurse-Family Partnership (NFP) service first developed by David Olds, professor of paediatrics, psychiatry and preventive medicine at the University of Colorado in Denver. It is very similar in intent to the concept of health visiting in Britain, although in the United States it has been focused on low-income families since its conception in the early 1970s. Studies show that it works: one by the RAND Corporation showed that children in the programme end up being arrested less, while their mothers have fewer children and spend less time on welfare. For high-risk mothers each dollar invested in NFP produced $5.70 in value.[68]

Children in NFP or similar programmes perform better academically and are less likely to live in a home with safety hazards – and thus require fewer emergency treatments for injuries. Later on they are less likely to abuse drugs or alcohol or break the law. Meanwhile parents are less likely to have more children, fathers are more involved in child-rearing, and families use less welfare.[69]

We've seen that families living in poverty are already overburdened with too many social workers and state agents. A health visitor can be a coordinator of care – when operating properly, a guide to the best that the state, voluntary and private sectors have to offer and the definition of a more human public sector. That's why, in government in the UK, we chose to overhaul the health-visitor service by investing in recruitment, training and organisation. If we reinvigorate the programme with a new sense of purpose, along with the resources and staff to bring down the visitor–family ratio, we could revolutionise the help that families get, creating a practical, effective – and cost-effective – ladder out of poverty.

To ensure it remains the truly life-changing – and long-term cost-saving – programme it should be, caseloads for each home visitor *must* be capped, allowing for a proper amount of time to be dedicated to each child and family. And when I say 'proper time', I mean it: daily visits for the first two weeks of a child's birth, weekly for the first three months, monthly for the rest of the year, and then quarterly until enrolment in preschool or kindergarten. This is the level of investment required. Anything short of that will almost certainly degenerate into an expensive waste – and a missed opportunity to end poverty in Britain while transforming the opportunities for all children, not just the poorest.

If we're serious about giving every British child an equal shot, this is what we have to do.

I wrote in Chapter 2 about the terrible waste caused by government's short-term approach. Our children are not line items on budgets; their childhoods are not measurable in quarterly increments. The early interventions I've described in this chapter are the most effective – and, for those who count money, cheapest – way to solve big social problems. But they don't mesh well with the political calendar. Poverty is a complex, difficult issue that takes time, effort and resources to solve. The old bureaucratic approach has made little headway – except to expand the bureaucracy. A more human way is better: in the short term, a business-friendly living wage to make sure no one who works full-time is poor. For the long term, fighting the causes of poverty with one-to-one help for the families for whom poverty is a cycle that needs to be broken.

Central to fighting poverty is avoiding the glib and patronising assumption that if only the poor acted like the rich, they would be better off. Yes, wealthier parents often practise better habits, but it's not because they are more loving or better parents. They're certainly not 'better' in any moral sense. It's because they have built-in advantages, both economic and social resources, often inherited and entrenched for generations. Poor parents, however, as we've often seen, have to struggle against impossibly difficult, seemingly immutable circumstances that they themselves might have been born into. Those circumstances are frequently rooted in broader social ills, from institutional racism to the failures of past anti-poverty programmes. It's not just a matter of telling them they should try harder. Thus, society has dual responsibilities: first, to extend a hand to help people overcome the obstacles they face, and then to work to fix those structural obstacles in the long run. 'When the evidence is overwhelming that we fail kids before they fail us, when certain programmes would actually save public money while elevating personal responsibility,' writes Nicholas Kristof, 'isn't it also time to stop making excuses for our own self-destructive behaviours as a society?'[70]

Building the right support for families is like the construction of great physical infrastructure: you won't see results immediately, but in the end it will be hugely effective and worthwhile. That's how we will end poverty for good.

CHAPTER 9

INEQUALITY

In many ways Sebastian Thrun personifies Silicon Valley. A German computer scientist, his career spans success in academia as a Stanford professor, in industry as an engineer at Google and founder of its Google X lab, and now in start-ups as the founder of Udacity, a business aiming to revolutionise how we learn. He is responsible for technology – from self-driving cars to wearable computing – that represents the future. Sebastian is among the world's foremost authorities on artificial intelligence and automation, and he's worried. On the one hand, technology will make us so productive that the cost of goods, Sebastian speculates, could approach free. We have the potential to reach new heights of human creativity as a result. On the other hand, there will be a significant cost: 'The thing I can't wrap my head around with artificial intelligence is its effect of doing away with the value you bring to the table in terms of labour. The ability to contribute is diminishing. There are fewer and fewer jobs where people can go home satisfied in the evening and say I did something amazing today.' That, he thinks, is 'eating into the middle class, eating into employment', and will have serious social, economic and political ramifications. 'The world where people can contribute productively is limited to a small number.'[1]

Sebastian's uncertainty reflects the central economic question of our time: What can we do about stalled social mobility and our increasingly unequal society?

The symptoms of inequality

I believe in the positive power of business and the market economy. But something has gone wrong. Capitalism doesn't seem to be working at the human level, even though statistics can tell a positive story. Economic growth no longer lifts household incomes the way it used to. Since the financial crisis, GDP has recovered (surpassing its pre-crisis size) but median income remains flat. The wealthiest 10 per cent, however, are capturing a greater share of the pie.[2]

Even with current wage growth, the economic forecasters at EY Item Club still predict that median pay in real terms will be £17,827 by 2017 – down from £18,852 in 2008.[3] Despite falling unemployment and rising employment statistics, more and more people lack fulfilling, steady work: they are working part-time (and having to rely on a second job or benefits to make ends meet)[4] or are underemployed in jobs that don't use the skills they acquired in the education system.[5] Meanwhile, the prospects for long-term, secure job growth are dim: long-term unemployment is still abnormally high as unemployed workers find it harder and harder to return to work.[6] The British economy might have jobs, but these jobs won't fill the long-term void left by an economy hobbled by increasingly low worker productivity[7] and stagnating wages.[8] And those who do work are getting less of its gains: workers' share of income is trending downwards[9] as it declines in favour of returns to those who own capital.[10]

It's not just income; inequality of wealth is worsening as well. In America, the middle class grew its wealth along with the rich in the post-war years. But now there is a divergence. According to economists Emmanuel Saez and Gabriel Zucman, the share of household wealth controlled by the top 0.1 per cent grew from 7 per cent in the 1970s to 22 per cent in 2012, a figure that nears inequality levels at the peak of the Gilded Age. Since the financial crisis, as the rich have largely recovered their wealth, the wealth of the bottom 90 per cent has stagnated at mid-1990s levels. And according to Saez and Zucman, the trend in income inequality fuels the trend in wealth inequality. As real wages for the top 1 per cent have grown, the rich have been able to save more of their income and convert it to wealth. But as wages for the rest have stagnated, the middle class and poor have not been able to save. 'Today, the top 1 per cent families save about 35 per cent of their income,' they write, 'while [the] bottom 90 per cent families save about zero.'[11] Overall the top one-tenth of the richest 1 per cent own almost as much wealth as the bottom 90 per cent.[12]

Fifty years ago the low-skilled and undereducated shifted from stable decent-paying jobs in the fields to stable slightly better-paying jobs in factories, right out of school. The labour market was 'more flexible', according to Tyler Cowen, 'because the technologies of those times often relied on accompanying manual labour'.[13] Few new jobs today are like that. In studying the long-term unemployed, Princeton economists Alan Krueger, Judd Cramer and David Cho describe them as a new permanent class for whom the main economic policy levers – like tax cuts or interest rate changes – simply don't work because they lack the skills to do the jobs available.[14] Meanwhile, higher education isn't guaranteeing success either. According to one report, as many as a third of university graduates are working in jobs that don't require the degree they have.[15]

This shift in the type and number of jobs available – and, by extension, inequality – is going to get worse. The twin forces of globalisation and technology have already wiped out jobs in manufacturing. That will soon be matched in the clerical, administrative and professional classes – doctors and lawyers too. (Despite the training and specialisation that goes into them, many of these careers will be made obsolete by off-shoring, replacement by robots or an algorithm, or both.) A report by Oxford economists Carl Frey and Michael Osborne estimates that some 47 per cent of America's jobs will eventually be lost to automation over the next decade or two.[16] And of the jobs that remain, many, according to LSE anthropologist David Graeber, will be 'bullshit jobs'. They will be

> the kind of jobs that even those who work them feel do not really need to exist. A lot of them are made-up middle management – you know, I'm the 'East Coast strategic vision coordinator' for some big firm, which basically means you spend all your time at meetings or forming teams that then send reports to one another ... And then think about the ancillary workers that support people doing the bullshit jobs: here's an office where people basically translate German formatted paperwork into British formatted paperwork or some such, and there has to be a whole infrastructure of receptionists, janitors, security guards, computer maintenance people, which are kind of second-order bullshit jobs, they're actually doing something, but they're doing it to support people who are doing nothing.[17]

Another factor is the way businesses account for investment. In the same way government invests myopically, as we saw in

Chapter 2, business does too, according to the world's leading management guru Clay Christensen, and this myopia is central to the link between business innovation and jobs. He describes three types of innovations. *Empowering innovations* create new sectors of the economy, bringing products and services to the masses, leading to many new jobs. Think Ford's Model T or Intel's chips. A *sustaining innovation* is neutral; it improves the empowering innovation but creates few new jobs because it basically replaces it. 'Whenever Toyota sells a Prius,' Christensen says, 'they don't sell a Camry.' The third type, *efficiency innovations,* are what he believes are at the heart of our problems. Efficiency innovations allow firms to make the same product for the same customer, but more cheaply. Although Walmart, according to Christensen, lowers costs by about 15 per cent, it also lowers retail employment in the areas it enters by around the same amount. This is good for consumers but harms the overall economy.

In the 1980s the spreadsheet was introduced into the daily life of businesses. For the first time, management consultants could pinpoint the different ways to profit: invest in innovations that profit over time or those that profit quickly. Empowering innovations take years to develop; efficiency innovations might return capital in a year or two. Unsurprisingly, executives – with their pay linked to short-term share-price gains – chose the latter. More profits, but fewer jobs and long-term investments. Banks are 'awash with capital', but small businesses can't get funded to expand their enterprises, and our economic recoveries generate fewer jobs each time. According to Christensen, it's the accounting software that has misdirected investment in this way. Higher rewards for shareholders, lower rewards for workers, fewer jobs created.[18] So if you want someone to blame for inequality, blame Dan Bricklin, the inventor of the spreadsheet. A bit, anyway.

These problems of economic inequality are exacerbated by something else: structural inequality. In recent decades we saw the emergence of something close to a meritocracy in which the best could rise to the top and anyone who worked hard could have a stable, middle-class life. But that security has gone. And now those who succeed in this new world are piling on their advantages and cementing them for their children through marriage, parenting and education choices. Those who have 'made it' are inadvertently shutting down opportunity for the rest of society. We need solutions to this structural, family-based inequality too.

The big trends

So we know the problems. We see these giant, overwhelming forces that seem to be way beyond the control of any country or government, and we wonder whether anything can be done, whether we just have to accept our fate and do what we can to help people cope with the worst effects. We get angry. Over the last few years, as I've seen some of the terrible failings and destructive consequences of global capitalism, I too have been tempted by the arguments of the anti-capitalist, anti-globalisation movement. On many occasions I have felt emotionally on their side. So are they right?

Let's see. Paradoxically, as inequality has risen dramatically in the West, global inequality is at its lowest rates ever; the number of people in poverty worldwide has been halved in twenty-five years.[19] So to 'stop' or even 'slow down' globalisation – whatever that means – because we fear its impact on ourselves, would be selfish and short-sighted. Remember how deep a human instinct it is to trade: we would hurt ourselves not just economically but also in our evolution as humans, reversing centuries-long progress in which economic cooperation brought humanity closer. Inhibiting globalisation would mean closing ourselves off and moving backwards: less connected, less empathetic, less human. I sometimes feel like lashing out at the faceless money-shuffling global corporations and going back to some blissful prelapsarian state. But it's really not the answer. It's not rational. Even if it were possible, it would do more harm than good: people would be hurt, mostly poorer people in other countries who are desperate to participate in the global economy that we so lightly disparage.

Does the answer to inequality lie in stopping technology, then, or at least checking its remorseless advance? This is also an easy conclusion to reach, especially for me, someone who refuses to have a mobile phone (much to the irritation of those close to me) and who is prone to emotionally charged rants about how technology is 'ruining our lives'.[20] Trying to tame technology may also seem the obvious conclusion from the very idea of this book; after all, if we want things to be 'more human', if we're 'designing a world where people come first', surely we should put human beings and the decent, well-paid jobs they need ahead of the latest 'inhuman' technology? Right?

Wrong. Again, it's important not to let emotions lead us down a self-defeating path. We need to take a step back from whatever contemporary concerns we may have about technology and look at the big picture. We need to remember our history. The moment when I really understood the impact of technology on humanity was when I read the first volume of Robert Caro's biography of Lyndon Johnson, *The Path to Power*, specifically, Chapter 27. There you will find a description of life in the Hill Country of Texas in the 1920s, where the future president grew up, before electricity. It is a vivid portrayal of life's 'drudgery', especially for women – before technology intervened:

Without electricity, even boiling water was work ... If the source was a stream, water had to be carried from it to the house, and since, in a country subject to constant flooding, houses were built well away from the streams, it had to be carried a long way. If the source was a well it had to be lifted to the surface – a bucket at a time. It had to be lifted quite a long way: in the hills it was a hundred feet or more. And so much water was needed! ... the average family farm used 200 gallons, or four-fifths of a ton, of water each day – 73,000 gallons, or almost 300 tons, in a year ... On the average, the well was located 253 feet from the house – [so] to pump by hand and carry to the house 73,000 gallons of water a year would require someone to put in during that year 63 eight-hour days, and walk 1,750 miles.[21]

Worse, without electric heaters, they also had to haul wood to fuel their stoves. Then there was laundry day: laundry was done outside by hand in a tub. Imagine physically scrubbing clothes, 'agitating' them like an electric washer, carrying them in heavy wet tubs (three tubs of water per load – and remember how hard it is to get water), then wringing them out, then 'punching' the clothes. This was hard, physical, onerous labour. 'Living – just *living* – was a problem,' Caro was told by one person who endured it. 'That was farm life for us. God, city people think there was something fine about it. If they only knew.'[22]

Any time you think technology is a bad thing for humanity, just read those passages and be thankful that you are alive now. Technological progress can free us to spend time on things that are more pleasurable and creative than domestic and professional drudgery. Think about the incredible impact even basic technology, like the washing machine, had on the lives – and life chances – of women. The early- and mid-twentieth century's wave of household innovation meant more time to be human. There is no reason to believe that the technology of today and tomorrow will be different.

Human productivity

So despite sometimes being emotionally drawn to the notion that the answer to rising inequality is to stop, slow down, or reverse the powerful forces (globalisation and technology) that have contributed to it, that's not what I think. On balance, they are positive for humanity. So what *is* the answer?

Over the last few years the debate has focused on education and skills – increasing the individual productivity of workers, and the overall productive capacity of the economy. We have a dearth of skilled workers for the jobs at the top, and too many underskilled – but, more often than might be expected, overeducated – people fighting for positions at the bottom. This results in a paradox of not enough competition for the most highly paid jobs (driving high wages for the few even higher) and tremendous oversupply of low and unskilled workers at the bottom (driving low wages for the many even lower). Our inability to match skills to economic needs is one of the biggest factors driving income inequality.

None of this is news. For as long as I can remember, politicians on all sides have been reciting the mantra that we need to equip people with the skills to do well in the economy of the future. Well, yes. Policies have come and gone, funded and organised by governments, by the private sector, in partnerships between them. The trouble is, none of it seems to have made any difference.

The person who has the clearest insights on this is Rohan. In a documentary for the BBC's *Panorama* series he argues that a big part of the answer to inequality is something that is very much a poor relation in our politics, a subject that rarely gets debated in our election campaigns, Westminster salons or the editorial pages of our newspapers, that never leads the agenda on news programmes, something much less vivid a concept than 'inequality': training. His view is that we need to think about training completely differently, in a more human way. Not as a policy but as a way of life – everyone's life.[23] We need an infrastructure that makes it possible for every adult to benefit from repeated bursts of training. More importantly, we need to understand that the barriers are often in the mind, in people's attitude to training. So we need a total change of culture; a shift in which self-improvement isn't just for TV reality shows but rather a constant process for everyone; we have to normalise readjustment and reinvention throughout life.

As I write this, I am in the midst of my own career shift, from policy implementation at 10 Downing Street to teaching at Stanford University and creating a technology business in Silicon Valley. My experience shows how the idea that still dominates education today – that we get trained for our careers in our late teens and early twenties and then are done – is preposterously antiquated. I could never have predicted where I'd be today when I was at university. We are ill served by a system and a culture that assumes we've filled our brains once we're finished with secondary or higher education. Changing this should not be a burden: to learn is one of the most human qualities there is. Game designers worked this out a long time ago – video games are addictive precisely because they constantly challenge players to improve, and reward them when they do. Once you've mastered a new level – usually having failed a couple of times first – it's that sense of accomplishment, being recognised for a newly improved ability, that keeps players going, not to mention a temporary high when the chemical dopamine is released in the brain.[24]Achieving competency is an innate psychological need, directly related to well-being.[25] This is learning in action. And it's one of the most distinguishing characteristics between humans and other animals.

But in Britain we start with a cultural disadvantage: the idea that training is more for the tradesman than everyman; it's the plumber who trains, not the chief executive. Where American executives attend business school and executive education to learn and reinvent themselves, for British executives, seeking more education is too often an admission of inadequacy. This attitude starts at the top. The cultural norm in the highest echelons of British society is to glorify the gifted amateur and innate ability; if you work too hard, it's a sign that you aren't talented or clever enough – it's 'bad form' to show you've tried. Honestly. If we ever want people to improve themselves so they can make the most of their potential, we have to move beyond this complacency, this idea that people are 'set' once they finish school or university and start their careers.

The anti-training culture has pernicious effects on all aspects of British society, from politics and the competence of government and administration to the performance of the national football team. Every human has within them a desire to learn and improve and it's a terrible competitive disadvantage if the national culture is to mock or denigrate this instinct. If we could get over this hang-up, we would have a better chance of solving so many problems we seem to be stuck with, and could look confidently towards the rest of this century instead of grumpily fearing the worst. We have to normalise readjustment and reinvention throughout life. This is the key to social mobility.

A serious assault on inequality means drastically changing the way training is provided, to make it as malleable and dynamic as the world of work now is. That won't happen unless we design training with people's real lives in mind. In further education the debate is always about fees and funding. But for those who drop out or don't even start, the real barriers are more complex: things like difficulty getting to class, family obligations, health problems, pregnancy, even the burdens of a current, unfulfilling job. And the intriguing possibility is that many of these barriers can now be overcome by the very thing that automates jobs away: technology.

'Nanodegrees'

Back to Sebastian Thrun. He was an early pioneer of what we now know as MOOCs – massive, open, online courses. In 2012 he decided to put his Stanford Artificial Intelligence course online and was astonished to see 160,000 participants within days. It gave him the idea for his next venture. 'A lot of people in life are stranded because of the lack of lifelong learning,' Sebastian says. In his view, though, learning is only one piece of the puzzle. Accreditation is just as important. Imagine, he says, a teacher who also has computer science skills and wants to leave education to work at a tech company. 'You might be a really great software engineer, but you will never get a job at a company like Facebook because your CV will say "high school, high school, high school". So the model today buckets people in life, with the choices they make early on restricting choices they make later, leading to social immobility.' That's why training is such a vital weapon in the fight against inequality. We just have to rethink how it is designed and delivered.

Sebastian's solution: Udacity's 'nanodegrees'. Nanodegrees are for those who have neither the time nor the inclination to pursue a conventional degree programme. They are short, online courses for people who want to learn or improve on a specific skill. Many are created in partnership with employers – so nanocourse users know that the skills they learn will improve their employability. Nanocourses are structured with the utmost flexibility: you go at your own pace, on your own devices, and can repeat sections as often as you want. 'Learning for a dedicated period of time in a dedicated physical location is something we can only really afford in our youth when we have no obligations: no family, no kids, no mortgage,' Sebastian says. Nanocourses benefit from technology that allows learners to overcome distance – the first hurdle – but, more than that, overcome the pace of the traditional classroom, which forces students to go through a course at the same time as everyone else. 'Ideally,' Thrun says, 'you have a teacher-student ratio of one to one, but in any setting right now that's uneconomic.' But with so many users on each course, Udacity can make the best professors available to everyone.

Such flexibility enables incremental learning anytime and anywhere. Thrun likens it to 'toothbrush technology', borrowing a term from Google co-founder Larry Page: something you do for a short time at least twice a day, anywhere – 'on the toilet even!' he says.[26] Here is an instance where technology could help create a new social norm: like going to the gym, gaining skills and knowledge should be one of those things you just do throughout your life as part of a regular routine, a practical step towards a more mobile society and less unequal economy.

Though the promise of Udacity is that it gives individuals autonomy over their own skills development, employers can do their part as well. Here's an example. Like most large retail stores, John Lewis has armies of delivery drivers bringing online orders and bulky items to customers' doors. As appliances have become more complicated, shoppers have started to pay for items not just to be delivered but installed as well. John Lewis thought: who better to install something than the person already on site, carrying it from the van to the front door? Many delivery drivers have therefore been trained to install the products they carry. Such specialised training 'increases the contribution they are able to make', which, according to chairman Charlie Mayfield, means John Lewis is 'able to pay them more'.[27] It's a simple, practical example of the principle of lifelong training being put into practice.

Even so, just as the skills we use will change with ever greater frequency, so too will our careers. Rather than bemoan this fact, we should design policies that help. Danish policymakers get this, aiming not for job security but employment security. Labour law makes it intentionally easy to hire and fire employees; it's a two-way street. Though this results in a large number of dismissals during downturns, it allows firms to adapt to changing circumstances and workers to end up where they can add the most value. A quarter of Danish private-sector workers change jobs each year, but to smooth these transitions the unemployed are guaranteed a relatively generous benefit (up to 90 per cent of a normal salary for the lowest-paid workers[28]) as well as education, skills training, or subsidised work placement, if not placement in a new job.[29] To prevent firms from under-investing in skills development, one downside of high employee turnover, 'continuing vocational training,' a hallmark of the Danish Flexicurity system, is generously funded by the state. Individuals can work toward part-time degrees or certificates at universities or training centres.[30] No wonder Denmark has one of the lowest rates of inequality in the world.[31]

Because it allows people flexible jobs and the ability to make money from assets they aren't using, the 'sharing economy' has been widely trumpeted as a modern answer to wealth inequality and social mobility. Assuming regulators update employment rules to make it as easy for 'gig' employees to access some of the benefits full-time employees are used to – such as affordable insurance and workers' compensation in the event of in-work disability – this could indeed be the case for some. But there are companies frequently described as being part of the sharing economy in which people are 'sharing' not an unused asset but simply their labour: companies like DoorDash, which brings food from restaurants, and TaskRabbit, which lets people outsource errands and small tasks. Although this may be convenient for users of the services, let's not fool ourselves into thinking that this is going to help in the fight against inequality – it may in fact make it worse. As journalist Leo Mirani deftly explains, this part of the 'gig economy' is the latest incarnation of an old-fashioned service relationship in places with a large-enough concentration of rich people who are willing to pay for mobile convenience:

Of the many attractions offered by my hometown, a west coast peninsula famed for its deep natural harbour, perhaps the most striking is that you never have to leave the house. With nothing more technologically advanced than a phone, you can arrange to have delivered to your doorstep, often in less than an hour, takeaway food, your weekly groceries, alcohol, cigarettes, drugs (over-the-counter, prescription, proscribed), books, newspapers, a dozen eggs, half a dozen eggs, a single egg. I once had a single bottle of Coke sent to my home at the same price I would have paid had I gone to a shop myself.

The same goes for services. When I lived there, a man came around every morning to collect my clothes and bring them back crisply ironed the next day; he would have washed them, too, but I had a washing machine.

These luxuries are not new. I took advantage of them long before Uber became a verb, before the world saw the first iPhone in

*2007, even before the first submarine fibre-optic cable landed on
our shores in 1997. In my hometown of Mumbai, we have had
many of these conveniences for at least as long as we have had
landlines – and some even earlier than that.*

*It did not take technology to spur the on-demand economy. It
took masses of poor people.*[32]

San Francisco, where many of these services originate and
are now based, Mirani points out, has more severe income
inequality than Mumbai. So let's not kid ourselves: much of
the sharing economy is simply a modern version of the service
economy. Although parts of it can indeed give people a stake
in the economy, it will only ever be a part of the solution.

Training, lifelong learning – even parts of the sharing
economy – might alleviate some of the problems associated
with rising inequality. But our digital, globalised fate is
inevitable, and the increasing precariousness of employment
may require us to consider a new kind of safety net, like
Danish-style Flexicurity, which combines the best of a vigorous,
'employment-at-will' US approach with a more European
emphasis on social stability. Either way, we will need to ensure
that workers are given the skills, tools and training that will
allow them to adjust to whatever comes next.

The third cause of inequality

Like poverty, inequality has symptoms and causes. An
economy-wide skills mismatch is a symptom whose solution
is more and better training, but its causes are much deeper,
and we've already discussed two of them: technology and
globalisation. There is a third cause of inequality, though,
potentially more pervasive than the other two combined. It
is structural, often family based, and warrants vigorous attack.

Today's debate around inequality often focuses on 'the 1 per cent', the bankers and CEOs making millions or billions of dollars for often no justifiable reason. Although they certainly contribute to inequality overall, they represent just a small part of the problem. The wider affluent classes – the lawyers, doctors, engineers and middle-tier executives – often products of public schools and Oxbridge – also contribute to inequality, but their contribution is less financial than cultural and behavioural. They are entrenching privilege for their children. With all their environmental advantages – from safe neighbourhoods to good nutrition to access to tutors, music lessons, extracurricular activities and travel – the children of the rich are lapping their poorer peers, even when the latter are naturally brighter. As the British economist Leon Feinstein has shown, although students from privileged backgrounds with innate ability maintain their trajectory, similar students from less-privileged backgrounds don't just regress over time; they are eventually overtaken by initially low-achieving but richer peers.[33] Affluent children are not succeeding just because of nepotism – although there's plenty of that around – but their success is undeniably a function of the family and social infrastructure into which they are born, an infrastructure that enables them to be exceptionally well prepared for the challenges of the modern economy. The world remains merit based, but it's a meritocracy in only a partial sense of the word. Yes, the winners are qualified for their positions, but too many losers fall short not for lack of effort or intellect but because they start so far back that they're never even competing.

Some of this 'affluent glass ceiling' is explicit. Consider professional licences. Although a doctor or lawyer should obviously be licensed, it is increasingly common for even moderately skilled jobs like childcare or teeth whitening to require a licence. In the 1950s only one in twenty workers needed a licence in America; now three in ten do.[34] Why might this be? Well, as author and commentator Reihan Salam argues, professionals don't want the competition; dentists want to maintain the exclusive right to clean teeth, so they have erected an artificial barrier to those who wish to do it. As a result, those who might enter slightly higher-skilled fields for better opportunities find themselves facing expensive credential schemes and onerous requirements.[35] This has made mobility more difficult while entrenching the privileges of those already occupying these higher-status professions.

Inequality is further ingrained when the affluent marry each other. Their 'assortative mating', as it has been called, results not only in high-earning two-income families but also in brighter offspring who, by inheriting brainy genes from brainy parents, inevitably do well in the educational rat race themselves (test scores, remember, near perfectly correlate with income).[36]

As a result, those who are on the winning side of technology and globalisation enjoy those benefits now and pass them along to their children, creating what *The Economist* calls a 'hereditary meritocracy'.[37] For those displaced in today's economy, the outlook is grim: where your economic station is inherited, the consequences of being adversely affected by technology and globalisation don't just damn you; they damn your children and grandchildren. As with poverty, inequality has the regrettable feature of worsening itself. So in the same way, we need to come back to the real source of the inequality: what goes on at home, in the family. Children not born into affluence need better schools and, eventually, better training. But even more, they need better support from the start. If we're going to fight inequality, chucking bricks at the '1 per cent' will be largely futile; we have to narrow the gap by raising up those being left behind.

Family, again

What do the inequities look like in practice? They're small things, really, but they start early and can quickly add up to a profound impact before children even get to primary school. For instance, research shows that hearing lots of words – both in quantity and variety – is important for a child's development. More affluent and educated families speak to their children significantly more often and with a larger vocabulary than their poorer and less educated counterparts. By the age of three, rich kids have heard some 30 million more words than their poorer peers, creating a 'word gap' that leaves poor children academically and developmentally behind.[38]

Early interactions, developmental psychologists tell us, can make a huge difference to a child's well-being. According to developmental psychologist Ann Bigelow, something as simple as skin-to-skin contact between a baby and its mother is incredibly valuable: 'it helps calm babies: they cry less and it helps them sleep better. There are some studies that show their brain development is facilitated – probably because they are calmer and sleep better.' And it helps the mothers (and fathers) too: they are less depressed, more sensitive to their babies' cues, and gain better responsiveness from the babies. Another important interaction: simply by responding to infants, usually by repeating motions back to them, parents show their children that they are causal agents and have an interactive role to play in the world. According to Bigelow: 'Seeing [their behaviour] reflected back helps [babies] understand themselves. ... The more experience babies have with someone who is going to be emotionally engaged with them, the better off they're going to be.'[39] It's easy to airily assume that all this is known by and comes naturally to every parent. Not at all. Educating, encouraging and helping parents to interact with their children in constructive ways is step one on the road to a more equal society. We know now that the quality and style of parenting received by a child is a better predictor of success than anything else, including the economic circumstances of the family.

There is not – nor should there be – one 'ideal' family or parenting approach. But there are some circumstances that are more ideal than others. Of course, it's about making sure children grow up in a loving home, but a word that comes up over and over again in any discussion of child development and family policy is 'stable'. Stability is what gives children the structure within which to grow and develop and thrive; it is one of the best things we can give children, both for their own happiness and flourishing and for that of our society and economy too.

That's why marriage is so important and central to the argument on inequality. Studies have consistently shown that children whose parents are married or who live together and marry later do better in behavioural, cognitive and health outcomes than those who just live together.[40] Both groups do better, though, than children whose parents divorce or who never marry at all. Children born into families with delinquent dads fare the worst.[41] And yet stability increasingly eludes us as today's adults often put their needs before those of their children. Family breakdown in the UK has risen dramatically: according to the Office of National Statistics, the divorce rate has nearly doubled since 1971 from 5.9 divorces per thousand married population to 10.8 per thousand. (If you go back further, things really have changed: in 1858, there were only 24 divorces across all of Britain.)[42] And as we're divorcing more, we're marrying less: compared to fifty years ago, the marriage rate has dropped from 67 marriages per 1,000 unmarried men to 22.1, and 52.4 marriages per 1,000 unmarried women to 19.9.[43] Parents (mostly mothers), are increasingly comfortable bringing up children not only outside marriage, but on their own.

Disastrously for inequality, marriage is increasingly the preserve of the university educated and well off.[44] Working-class and non-university-educated women who still want children are now more willing to have them without a father in the home. Although many judge women for bringing children into the world in less-than-ideal circumstances, think about their situation – especially when compared to their university-educated peers – before judging: 'College-educated young adults can see a good future, where they're likely to find a good partner, pool two incomes, and they're willing to wait to have kids till they can do that,' says Andrew Cherlin, a sociologist who's studied long-term family and social trends. Less-educated women, however, 'don't see the possibility of finding partners with good incomes. And many are unwilling to give up the opportunity to have a child by waiting.'[45] For some of those without a university or even high-school education and with sparse hopes for career advancement, it doesn't matter: parenthood is the one marker of adulthood they can attain.

What this means is that affluent children, on average, start life with the benefit of a lot more emotional as well as financial stability. It's no wonder they leap ahead. For the vast majority of children lacking the in-built advantages of wealthy and educated parents, instability is especially acute. This is why anyone who cares about inequality needs to care about finding ways to help parents maintain their relationship in the first place, so broken homes can be avoided. It all goes back to Louise Casey's point from the previous chapter: a child's parents are the best agents for good in that child's life, no matter how imperfect. And as simple a fact as that is, our culture today has tacitly approved separated families. Because the issues involved are so highly personal and intimate, we have hesitated to take a position or make a judgement. If two adults in a couple decide they can no longer live together, well, that's their business and no one else's, right? Wrong – not if they have young children. When the costs and benefits affect everyone, as they do, we can't just privatise this issue. It's a matter of social responsibility, not just personal choice. Of course, it's true that raising a family is immensely challenging. But it seems as if, increasingly, the socially acceptable position is to prioritise the experience of the parents. That's important, but it's the wrong priority. If you care about future opportunity and a more equal society, the interests of children should be the priority.

When the evidence shows that it's better for people – and society – when children grow up in stable, loving homes, then a more human way of tackling inequality means accepting that marriage is a vital issue of public policy. But this has often been misunderstood – or deliberately distorted – as a simplistic assertion that married couples make better parents than their unmarried counterparts. Of course that's not true. The argument is about family stability. Marriage is what social scientists call a commitment device. It creates inertia in the relationship, making it more likely that couples will stay together in the face of the inevitable stresses and pressures, providing a more stable set of relationships – and stable relationships lead to better life chances for children.

Of course, it's possible that married parents are more likely to stay together because they're likelier to have the characteristics of a more stable couple in the first place. But that still tells us something. Wealthier and better educated parents wait to have children until they are married and in a stable position. They don't rush into commitments – either relating to marriage or to children. For them, marriage is a mark of maturity in a relationship, a signal that they are ready to take on more responsibilities together. If we want to encourage all potential parents to think about their readiness for children – and we should – marriage is as good a tool as any.

The value of that commitment device is never tested more than during the unprecedented stress that arrives with children; child-rearing, studies tell us, directly contributes to making already unstable relationships even less stable.[46] 'Children do seem to increase happiness [while] you're expecting them, but as soon as you have them, trouble sets in,' Harvard psychologist Dan Gilbert explains. 'People are extremely happy before they have children and then their happiness goes down, and it takes another big hit when kids reach adolescence. When does it come back to its original baseline? Oh, about the time the children grow up and go away.'[47] Although having children strains all couples' relationships with each other, the commitment device of wedding vows helps keeps them together,[48] and this is overwhelmingly in the interests of children unless something terrible is going on. Although 37 per cent of cohabiting couples split up by their child's fifth birthday, less than 6 per cent of married couples do. And though marrying after the birth of a child helps, those couples still have a significant gap with couples who were already married before. Put differently, two in three children born to cohabitating couples will see their biological parents break up by age twelve, compared with only one in four in married-couple families.[49]

By the way, what we feel – and, increasingly, scientifically know – about child development in the context of family structure is one of the reasons we should support marriage equality. Encouraging marriage is not about promoting some traditional or moral view about what's right or wrong for adults; it's about what's best for children. And the evidence suggests that children are better off being raised by a married gay couple who provide a stable, loving home than by an unmarried – and unstable – straight couple.[50]

But even if you're not persuaded by the evidence in support of the collective, societal benefits of marriage, there's now a strong body of work highlighting the individual benefits. It turns out that marriage is just better for you than the alternative. According to Gilbert, married couples are on average happier, healthier, wealthier, live longer, and even have better sex.[51] (How does he know?) A 2014 paper using data from the UK's Annual Population Survey showed that, even taking premarital happiness levels into account, 'the married are still more satisfied' and that marriage helps people through midlife dips in unhappiness.[52] According to co-author Shawn Grover, 'Marriage may be most important when there is that stress in life and when things are going wrong.'[53] Spouses are friends, and that friendship helps get each other through difficult times. 'The biggest benefits [of marriage] come in high-stress environments,' says John Helliwell, the study's other co-author. 'People who are married can handle midlife stress better than those who aren't because they have a shared load and shared friendship.'[54]

Married couples are happier, happier couples are more stable, and homes that are more stable give children a better chance in life. That's why the growing marriage gap between the rich and the rest is so alarming.

It goes without saying that there are circumstances when single parenthood is the better option. A parent in an abusive relationship should get out of it, in the interests of both themselves and their child. But we need to work to avoid those drastic outcomes. Being in a relationship is hard; being a parent is harder and more stressful. Although children can bring out the best in us, they can also bring out the worst, especially when there are underlying tensions between a couple that bubble to the surface.

So if richer, better educated, more successful prospective parents are getting married, and the poorer, worse educated, less successful ones aren't, how do we get the latter to marry before having children – or at least to wait until they're in a stable relationship? The go-to policy response has typically been tax incentives. That may help in a symbolic sense, signalling the value society places on marriage, but from a practical perspective, past efforts have fallen flat.[55] Instead, we urgently need to enlist the help of behavioural science experts and practitioners of human-centred design. There aren't many areas where an effective 'nudge' would make more difference than this.

One of the worst aspects of the welfare state bureaucracy is the way it has worked as an anti-family programme, incentivising couples to have and raise children apart. At the same time, by stigmatising and treating fathers as 'unhelpful', 'deadbeat' or 'lay-about', we drive them away from playing a productive role in their children's upbringing, a role we know their children will benefit from. If given the chance, fathers can and will play constructive roles. 'The data does not indicate that during the first three years of the child's life, most low-income fathers are irresponsible,' says Ronald Mincy of Columbia University. 'Fathers are helping during the pregnancy, making financial contributions and visiting the child. But over time these informal contributions wane as the relationship between the couple deteriorates. The father becomes discouraged and the mother gets annoyed. The father's inability to make financial contributions seems part of that deterioration. Static will be introduced in the relationship that will serve to bar fathers from seeing their kids.'[56] Although 'delinquent dads' certainly aren't blameless, it's not enough just to chastise them.

Around 24 million children in the United States – about one in three – live without their biological fathers,[57] and this leads to overwhelmingly worse life outcomes for those children. Boys with absent fathers are more likely to go to prison;[58] girls are more likely to become pregnant as teenagers.[59] Meanwhile, children who grow up with contact with their fathers have better social and emotional health and perform better academically; [60] one study found that a father's involvement is associated with a higher likelihood of getting mostly As.[61] Clearly delinquent dads have different circumstances that require different solutions. And any reform of family policy needs to incorporate the criminal justice system too, given the devastating impact on American family life wrought by the mass incarceration of young men. The important point is that we need to focus on ways to forge productive relationships between all parents and their children, not just for the present generation but for future generations too. As the saying goes, when you bring up a child, you bring up a parent.

In some cases courses specifically for fathers can work best. That's what one group in Baltimore, Maryland, is doing. Community worker Joseph Jones realised that because the vicious circle of poverty, drugs and crime robs many men of their fathers, they in turn have little experience of what being a good father actually looks like. So Jones created the Baltimore Responsible Fatherhood Project to give fathers the skills and tools to be responsible dads. The teachers, called fatherhood specialists, don't lecture but instead help lead discussions with groups of predominantly black fathers on how to overcome practical challenges in their lives. 'This is my sanctuary,' says forty-year-old LaKeeth Blackmon, 'a place where I can be myself and meet good people and not get caught up with what's going on in the streets.' Blackmon's experience is typical of the fathers who participate in the programme: he has six kids with three different mothers, has served time in prison, and is facing trial for dealing marijuana. But he hopes his participation in the Fatherhood Project will help him be a better father and set a positive example for his own children. After all, says Jones, 'How do you become a man if you've never seen somebody be a man, if the people in your life have abdicated their responsibilities and left you as a little person?'

It's not just about men, of course. Our social norms around family life have failed miserably to catch up with the progress women have made over the last few decades. This is the cause of much of the stress that undermines many marriages today. Women worry more about parenthood than men do and are more likely to change their career trajectories in anticipation of it.[62] As Anne-Marie Slaughter points out, whereas mothers feel obliged to put their families ahead of their work, men are often praised for their sacrifice of home life – and valuable time with their children – for the sake of their careers. 'Why should we want leaders who fall short on personal responsibilities?' Slaughter asks. 'Ultimately, it is society that must change, coming to value choices to put family ahead of work just as much as those to put work ahead of family.'[63] This is exactly right: professional culture must value family life for both mothers and fathers. We have to make it easier both for mothers to be professional women and for professional men to be fathers.

Generous paternity leave would be a good start. The first few weeks and months after a child is born are when domestic duties are renegotiated; if the mother is at home and the father at work, by default the mother often ends up taking over more domestic duties. By sharing those duties with fathers, mothers get a fairer deal in the long run.[64] Paternity leave also helps mothers avoid the stigma of new motherhood in the workplace. Mothers often face brutal challenges upon having children, with workplace policies and cultures that make it difficult if not impossible to resume their careers.

Those with access to paid maternity leave are likelier to return to their prior employer, and 97.6 per cent of them make the same salary or more upon returning. However, 30.6 per cent of women who have to change where they work experience a pay drop.[65]

But parental leave at birth isn't enough; we need to help parents spend time with their families throughout the years their children are growing up. If both parents – especially fathers – continue to make efforts to share parenting and household duties, it will make for a happier and more stable marriage, which, in turn, is good for their children.[66] This means better family leave and giving workers more control over their hours so they can choose what to prioritise. For example, although we know that a child's early years are crucial, we mustn't neglect other important stages. Parents with teenagers know that it's actually in those later years, when emotional and physical development can cause all sorts of problems as well as joys and opportunities, when children need their parents around just to talk to and spend time with. Inequality can be rooted in something as mundane as how often a family eats together.[67]

Employers tend to see paid family leave as harmful to business. But in a study of California's family leave law, the authors found that 'the vast majority of employers reported that it has had a minimal impact'; indeed, some employers even reported cost savings.[68] So although maternity leave doesn't hurt business, the lack of paternity leave does harm women. Many are cast aside for promotion ahead of time because their bosses know they might soon be taking off anywhere from a few months to a few years.[69] If fathers took similar leave, such discrimination would obviously decline: if both parents took leave, there would be less reason to discriminate against mothers who biologically have to. Obviously mothers (and fathers) might choose to remain at home in the long run – that's a perfectly valid choice – but in an age when women are breaking down barriers in the workplace, shouldn't the norms around parenting change too? Although maternity and paternity leave don't seem like issues of inequality, they really are: they can help close the gaps between upper-income and lower-income families and between men and women in the workplace.

Helping parents

Precisely because being a parent is so hard, there is not one parent who would not benefit from better information and support. To be more direct: there's not one family, not one parent, who wouldn't benefit from parenting education.[70] But the stigma associated with anything that sounds like 'parenting classes' is massive. What a terrible shame, a silly prejudice that directly affects inequality. Octavius Black, founder of an excellent new parenting programme in the UK, Parent Gym, observes that 'challenging someone's parenting skills is one of the strongest challenges to their identity';[71] it smacks of government intervention and the nanny state. But so many lives would be improved if it were as normal to learn about being a better parent as it is to learn how to drive. It's already seen as completely normal to buy parenting guides, to read the books and magazines – there are even parenting apps. Many mothers complain that they receive no medical advice on crucial questions like breastfeeding and where their baby should sleep.[72] But there's something about parenting classes that is socially unacceptable. People fear looking foolish in front of others, or look on it as an admission of incompetence, or even a punishment.

I saw this first-hand when I was developing our family-policy agenda in government. As you'd expect, I spoke to experts in the theory of parenting education and worked with some fine civil servants with fantastic knowledge and commitment. But nothing was as striking for me as attending some classes in person. Even though I was there for the purposes of policy research, I took part myself (I could hardly just sit at the back taking notes!). And I learned, even in a few two-hour sessions (courses usually run eight to ten weeks), incredibly useful tips and techniques that have made a real, practical difference in my own family. The most amazing thing, though, was talking to the other parents afterwards. Without exception they used the same phrase to describe the experience: 'This has changed my life.' Perhaps most interesting was the testimony of parents who had been sent to the classes by a court or local authority or some other arm of the state because their children were considered out of control. These parents were even more enthusiastic than those who had signed up voluntarily, but they all told me some version of the same story: 'I had to be dragged kicking and screaming to come to this, but after the first one I could see it would change my life.' That phrase again: 'I wish someone had told me about this years ago – it would have changed everything.' Another parent recounted through tears how her relationship with her seven-year-old son had completely transformed just over the course of the eight weeks she'd been going to the sessions. One reason seems to be a very human one: the fact that you're there with a small group of other parents. You can be honest about your anxieties and learn from each other. Everyone has trouble with parenting; there's great relief in realising you're no worse at it than most people.

There are many, many providers of parenting classes and, as you'd expect, some are great, some are all right, and some are terrible. What we need to see is a massive opening up and 'mainstreaming' of this market – a little like the exercise and fitness market, perhaps. There was a time when there were practically no gyms anywhere except in universities and army barracks; now they're everywhere. There was a time when having a personal trainer meant you were a Hollywood celebrity or multimillionaire. Now it is mainstream, and my question is: If it's socially acceptable to learn how to exercise, don't you think we might take the same approach when it comes to looking after our children?

In government we took a small step in that direction with a pilot programme in 2012. The idea was to help stimulate a market for parenting courses by giving people vouchers they could spend with approved providers in their area. To reduce the stigma and make the whole thing seem normal and not part of some welfare scheme, we worked with Boots, which helped give out the vouchers in their stores. The pilot was broadly successful, increasing both demand and supply for parenting courses, but perhaps more importantly, it did actually decrease their stigma.[73] Building on that success, the Prime Minister announced in January 2016 an expansion of the programme as part of a £70 million Life Chances Strategy.[74] Nonetheless, public awareness is still low, and we have much more work to do to create a culture more receptive to parenting support, as David Cameron argued in a thoughtful, wide-ranging speech setting out the Life Chances agenda. Here's the bottom line: we need to make parenting education aspirational. Instead of being seen as something done to you by the government because you're a bad parent, it needs to be something everyone chooses to do because it's part of being a good parent.

Parents can't be all things for all children, and as with any institution in which people are involved, we must recognise that all parents have their limitations. Many of the least well-off parents face difficulties that stem not from any personal fault but structural adversities in society, particularly institutional sexism and racism. It's incumbent upon us to fix those problems, but in the interim, society must do all it can to help those parents give their children better life chances.

In fact, if you look at the children and young people who succeed – especially those who overcome adverse circumstances – most of them have someone else looking out for them, be it a teacher, a coach or a mentor of some kind. Remember the adults – some of them middle-aged – taking the Starbucks college courses? Having a counsellor, a cheerleader, an adviser was one of the most important aspects of their success. In the same way that those students succeeded, in the same way that parents need a bit of mentoring, it's only natural to mentor children as well. For children of privilege or family stability, such mentor figures are often commonplace. If they don't have a supportive parent or teacher, they have a music teacher, football coach or tutor to provide support instead. Here, the worlds of education and technology collide to offer a potential solution. Technology could liberate teachers and coaches to focus on the interpersonal skills only a mentor can provide. Technology can't care, but people can.

Likewise, government can't raise children, but it can create the infrastructure necessary for them to flourish. Family stability, parental leave, parenting education – they're all about the same thing: giving children better chances by helping families of every circumstance do well. Combining such family interventions with a new approach to training would increase opportunity.

Failure to get this right will reinforce inequality, one of the most urgent questions of our times. Technology is making obsolete many tasks once done by people. And those who have the resources and education keep solidifying their advantages; those who don't, fall behind.

The former is an inescapable fact. The latter is not.

Rather than lament change, we should embrace it as an opportunity to make work more human and opportunity more abundant. In the face of technology's onslaught, 'a better strategy', according to Geoff Colvin in his book, *Humans Are Underrated*, is to ask: 'What are the activities that we humans, driven by our deepest nature or by the realities of daily life, will simply insist be performed by other humans, even if computers could do them?' We once washed clothes using wash boards; now we have washing machines. We once stoked furnaces by hand with coal; now we fuel furnaces through gas lines. Have we suffered for it? No. We've become only more prosperous. Let's forget those inhuman jobs and instead focus on the skills that are most human and create economies around *them*. 'It used to be that you had to be good at being machine-like,' notes Colvin. 'Now, increasingly, you have to be good at being a person.' This is wonderful news, he goes on to say: we're being asked 'to become more essentially human'.[75] People are innovative, creative, caring and nuanced. Let's create an economy that embraces these qualities. We should be happy to rid ourselves of the automated, mind-crushingly boring, administrative cubicle jobs and the back-breaking, dehydrating, physically dangerous factory and agricultural ones. Wouldn't those workers be the first to agree that they'd be better off if they did something that engaged them as people, not workhorses? They would be better off in terms of wealth, health and general well-being. As would the rest of us.

The debate around inequality is often focused on outcomes: who's rich and who's not. That's the wrong way to look at it. Instead, we should be examining mobility: Who is falling behind because they aren't getting a fair shot? Yes, this includes the workers who are dropping out of the labour force because of lack of skills, but it also includes their children – and those of the larger middle classes – who are losing out on the chance to get ahead because of their home and family lives.

No one wants to see a society with a few people at the top doing incredibly well while everyone else is struggling, yet that really seems to be where we're heading. As long as generational inequality persists, our society will fail to live up to the standard it has set for itself: that everyone be given the chance to compete fairly, on the same terms, in a true meritocracy.

We can go in a different direction, however, if we cast the inequality debate in more human terms, making it normal for every individual to train and gain skills all the way through life, strengthening marriage and families, and giving better support to parents so we bridge the gaps between the worst-off children and the best-off. That is the basis of a more human economy – a more human society – in which opportunity is more equal and prosperity more widely shared.

CHAPTER 10

CHILDHOOD

Children are vulnerable, so we protect them. Children need nurturing and guidance, so we put their needs first. These are basic, human instincts. But today we're getting childhood all wrong, simultaneously overprotecting and under-protecting.

It's human to fall in the playground and hurt yourself; it's human to be lost or bored. If we overprotect our children, we inhibit their development – mentally, physically and emotionally – and risk them developing unhealthy fears and behaviours. But it's also human to be a child during childhood, and although we're overprotecting children's play with ridiculous, risk-averse safety measures, we are at the same time under-protecting them, allowing them to experience the adult world prematurely because we're too lazy to properly invigilate or too weak to say no. We think we're being kind, but we're doing real and lasting harm.

There is a particular problem with technology. Devices have brought children entertainment and education, but they've also erased the boundaries between the child and adult worlds. We need to better police the border between children and technology because unconstrained, unlimited access to the Internet prematurely exposes children to unhealthy sexual norms, inhibits their cognitive abilities,

298 • MORE HUMAN

and disturbs normal social interactions. Perhaps worst of all, technology is resurrecting old ideas of misogyny, setting back one of our society's greatest recent achievements.

Let's not blame 'kids today' for these trends; it's our fault as adults for putting up senseless boundaries while failing to set up sensible ones. But it's not too late; we can turn things around. We need to – because children are humans, too.

Overprotection

Berkeley, California, is famous for its world-class university, periodic outbursts of student radicalism, and – if you care about food and where it comes from – Alice Waters's pioneering restaurant Chez Panisse (see Chapter 5). But there's something else Berkeley ought to be famous for: the most extraordinary and wonderful children's playground you've ever seen. The Berkeley Adventure Playground is built by the people who use it, constructed of salvaged wood, old rubber tyres, scraps of sails, all decorated with graffiti-like smears of paint. Enter with your young children, and you are handed a container of nails and a hammer. Walk around, and you'll see children as young as six and seven sawing pieces of wood. No safety equipment. No bossy rules. Just families having fun, being creative and, above all, being human. It's a little bit terrifying, and it's hard to believe you're still in America – the land of the waiver, lawsuit and helicopter parent.

The people who run the Berkeley Adventure Playground understand the true essence of children's play. Back in Britain, Prince Charles is championing another type of adventure playground. At Dumfries House – a Scottish estate his charities support – the trust has built one of its own, situated in the woodland surrounding the house. Rather than building and destroying, children who visit (at no charge) experience a different sort of physically and mentally stimulating play, with elaborate three-dimensional mazes (imagine a multi-storey structure of nets, ropes and wood), zip-lines, tunnel slides, climbing structures, and a circular netted swing that could hold three or four children. If only every child had easy access to such recreation.

But they don't. And it's only become worse in recent years. Whether as parents or policymakers, we have become so irrationally fearful of every risk that we've outlawed and restricted and regulated children's lives to the point at which things seem to be designed more for our peace of mind than our children's recreation and benefit.

This mindset has so conquered our collective psyche that those who want to give their children more leeway are ostracised, even penalised. Brooklyn mother Lenore Skenazy's nine-year-old son wanted to experience some independence, so she and her husband armed him with a MetroCard, some quarters for a phone, $20 in cash, and a map – and left him at a department store that sat directly above a station for their local subway line. Forty-five minutes later, exhilarated, he returned home. When she wrote up this positive experience, she was quickly dubbed 'America's Worst Mom'.[1]

Skenazy, a middle-class mother, was relatively lucky in that the only punishment she got was name calling. Consider the shocking experience of Debra Harrell, a single mother in Tennessee. Harrell is one of the millions of low-paid, overstressed workers we met in Chapter 8. She works hard to support herself and her daughter but can't afford childcare. Rather than having her nine-year-old daughter sit in the McDonald's where she works all day, Harrell gave her a cell phone and let her play in the local park down the street.

Park-goers, suspicious of a child playing by herself, reported her to the authorities. Harrell was arrested, charged with unlawful neglect of a child, and subsequently fired. Because Harrell is a single parent, her daughter was then taken from her home and placed in the care of local social services. Following a public outcry, Harrell thankfully got her daughter and job back. But imagine the ordeal she had to go through. Imagine how much worse off her daughter is, living forever with the experience of having her mother imprisoned and spending time in public-sector care. All this because a mother trusted her daughter and let her play outside.

This overprotective attitude is harming children. Whether it's aggressive bureaucracy removing any remotely challenging play equipment from playgrounds or panicking over the idea that a child might encounter a single germ or piece of dirt, we are cutting away at the basic humanity of childhood experience. By trying to create a risk-free existence for our children, we are gradually shutting them off from the world. Neighbourhoods friendlier to cars than kids, public space appropriated for shopping rather than playing, energy and investment going into superficially more captivating indoor alternatives, particularly involving technology. We ply our kids with electronics to keep them busy – and give us a breather – and we prevent them from playing outside because we fear what might happen to them. But we forget that an important part of many of our own childhoods involved engaging in the world, not being 'protected' from it.

Of course, to a certain extent, caution is natural and proper: our instincts and emotions guide us to protect our children, after all. But it's gone way too far. The dreary and soulless trend toward the avoidance of any risk reflects good instincts and good intentions that have been perverted by a culture of hysteria, lawsuits and puffed-up bureaucracies.

'Playground safety', for example, is mostly a solution in search of a problem, argues the play expert Tim Gill in his book, *No Fear*. Despite the occasional sensational headline, serious playground injuries are rare, deaths even more so. The facts show that a child has about a one-in-sixteen chance of being injured on a playground and only a one-in-200 chance of receiving an injury requiring medical attention.[2] Nonetheless, when something does go wrong, it is amplified disproportionately in the media: tragic accidents are emotional, and emotion makes for better stories. But although the over-dramatisation of danger to children may generate more clicks, sell more newspapers, keep a few more viewers from turning off the local news, it also breeds fear of previously uncontemplated risks. The result is an illogical debate that leads to unnecessary rules, irrational insurance policies, and a whole new miserable, exhausting world of paranoid language, bureaucracy and culture to enforce it all. Parents, terrified for their children, and insurers, terrified of lawsuits, have pushed for new guidelines and regulations on anything that touches children's lives. But because, as Gill writes, 'there was little or no attempt to look systematically at accident data or to place playground accidents in a wider context,' these trends merely 'reinforced the idea that playgrounds should be free of risk,' leading to policies that put the prevention of any injury whatsoever over the goal of having the best playgrounds for children.[3]

This is terribly wrong. We shouldn't ignore passionate parents, but we shouldn't make policy decisions to mollify them either, because rather than solving problems, parents' unjustified fears have created new ones. Go to any public playground today, and you'll see that the equipment is increasingly dull and uninspiring, making playtime less fun and less adventurous. This is not just a shame; it stunts crucial aspects of child development. Even worse, some safety rules have actually made children less safe. For example, it turns out that the cushioned safety surfacing often required to be in place to break children's falls is really only meant to prevent serious head injuries – an extremely rare occurrence – and in fact leads to more broken bones.[4]

What's more, safety surfacing is so expensive, it means that other more cost-effective ways of keeping children safe are ignored. A cost-benefit analysis done in the UK found that spending up to £250 million over five years on playground safety surfacing (the amount needed to install and maintain it for Britain's playgrounds) would have saved one child's life during that time. Of course, every child's life is incalculably precious. But imagine how much more agony could be spared if those resources were invested in ways of protecting children from genuine danger, such as road traffic, which typically kills well over 150 children and seriously injures around 10,000 over a comparable five-year period.[5] If you want to be statistically brutal – but accurate – about it, making our children infinitesimally safer at playgrounds condemns them to die elsewhere at a much higher rate.

Hard at play? Or hardly playing?

But play is being undermined and distorted in more places than playgrounds. Our society increasingly sees play as a neat and tidy occupation that should occur in prescribed ways. When children try to break out of these artificial shackles, they – especially boys – are deemed to be 'troublemaking' or 'antisocial' for perfectly innocent offences like making noise, hitting things (and occasionally each other) and climbing trees. Of course, there are risks for our children – there always have been and there always will be. But we should focus on the real hazards, not imagined ones. Society has worked itself into a frenzy that the world is ever more dangerous. But it's not true. Consider child abduction: compared to forty years ago, we perceive a growing threat, although it's no more likely to happen than it was in the 1970s. The odds of a child being kidnapped and murdered by a stranger are one in 1.5 million.[6] We fear that our children might be assaulted by strangers, but they are far likelier to fall victim to an abusive relative or family friend.[7] Instead of working harder to protect children from domestic abuse, we teach them to avoid strangers – the vast majority of whom would be a source of help should they ever need it.

'Today's children,' writes author Jay Griffiths, 'are enclosed in school and home, enclosed in cars to shuttle between them, enclosed by fear, by surveillance and poverty and enclosed in rigid schedules of time. These enclosures compound each other and make children bitterly unhappy.' Our children are virtual prisoners of their parents and caregivers. In 1971, 80 per cent of British seven- or eight-year-olds walked to school on their own; by 1990, it had dropped to 9 per cent. We instinctively distrust children, forgetting that they can handle themselves much earlier and far more effectively than we give them credit for. When parents do trust their children, society condemns them. In 2010, writes Griffiths, 'two children, aged eight and five, cycled to school alone and their headmaster threatened to report their parents to social services.'[8]

In our attempts to shield children from risk, we've not just made their play dull or wasted public money on largely pointless safety measures; we've also inadvertently hampered children's development. The life lessons that come with play are some of the most essential. Among other things, high-quality, unencumbered, imaginative and adventurous play teaches children resourcefulness, entrepreneurship, hand-eye coordination, creativity, cooperation and social skills. A sense of adventure is not only an integral part of being a child; it is essential for their biological, human development. When doctors want to inoculate a patient against a disease, they make a vaccine containing a bit of the disease so that the body can identify it and learn to overcome it; this is the only way vaccines work. Fear works in much the same way. A Norwegian study by early-childhood education professor Ellen Sandseter found that safe play is actually detrimental to the process of child development. She found that children were exhilarated when exposed to stimuli they had previously feared. As they gradually matured and mastered new skills and explored new environments, their natural – and perfectly healthy – inhibitions, which protected them from any serious danger, correspondingly declined. In other words, the thrill helped them overcome their phobia. If they didn't experience risky play, their natural phobias became pathologised and unhealthy later on. Sandseter concluded that lack of risky play might lead to an increase in psychopathy and neuroticism as children grow up.[9]

Play is essential, but not just to any one child's development; it's essential for the development of humanity itself. This is obvious to those who observe it up close. What is play but tinkering, trying new things, new combinations, new rules, new roles, new ideas? Play is the essence of experimentation, of risk taking, of innovation. Play leads to progress.

'Free-range kids'

The good news is that we don't have to do anything too radical to make play more human. The Berkeley Adventure Playground isn't the only example of enlightened thinking; advocates of authentic play – and the fantastic playgrounds they support – exist all around the world, and the movement is growing. But it is nonetheless still under attack, and we need to support those who are fighting back. Like London Play. As councils and communities eliminate adventure playgrounds or build dull new ones, organisations like London Play campaign against such moves while developing their own playgrounds that engage children and facilitate play in fun and educational ways. They have also sought to shed light on both real and imagined dangers. For example, knowing that cars are a legitimate concern, London Play has experimented with closing down streets for periods and setting up temporary play spaces (like a life-sized Monopoly board with each house on the street a different property).

Paul Hocker, London Play's development director, has been struck by how naturally play comes to children, even when they are exposed to new things. When London Play did its first street closure in 2009, kids were so excited, they couldn't wait to start. When they did, it was 'like something out of a Disney film', with children 'flying out' of their homes, 'dragging all sorts of objects and plunking them on the road'. Even though they'd never played on the street before, 'within about ten minutes, there was this very rich, stimulating play space that they had just created from bits and odds and ends they had. They didn't need to be told what to do. And that's the secret of the work,' Hocker says, 'to provide children with the space and the licence to play and play freely. As much as society changes around children, how children play remains the same.'[10]

So one solution is simply to create more permanent play spaces, both formal and informal. It just needs to be made more of a priority in the process of urban planning and property development. It is a choice that could be made. Of course, there needn't be just one model for reforming play. Adventure playgrounds often discourage parental involvement, the idea being that children better develop their independence away from the anxious eyes of overprotective mothers and fathers. For children without easy access to the outdoors, organised 'forest schools' have emerged whereby children regularly visit woodland sites, in all weather, not only to play in a way that provides healthy exposure to nature but also to learn skills in survival, ecology, craft, self-regulation and teamwork. Finding more ways for children to play outside is crucial. As Hocker says, 'The more kids are outside, the safer it is.'[11]

But even if we make playtime more human and convince the powers that be – from parents to policymakers – that real play is fine and needs to be supported with more and better play spaces, perhaps the biggest threat to play is the new rat race that discourages it altogether in favour of hyper-organised and didactic leisure activities. Although for many over-scheduled children of over-achieving and over-anxious parents in places like London and New York, 'leisure' is hardly the word. You have to feel sorry for these kids. Their parents have bought into the anxiety that football and even piano lessons aren't enough, so we have to add Mandarin Chinese lessons, the violin, ballet, extra maths – extra everything, with expensive tutors. And all of these activities must be structured and supervised with benchmarks and rankings. But as crazy as this sounds, parents are under immense pressure; we have been led to believe that if our children aren't doing everything, they won't do well in nursery or primary school or the endless standardised tests, and thus will fail to get into a good university. And then their lives are basically over.

Ironically, whereas rich and middle-class parents have scheduled healthy play out of their children's lives, poor children end up without it for different reasons. Recognising that poverty doesn't just contribute to stress (as we saw in Chapter 8) but that it also stops families from playing, especially in urban areas with limited space, we have to make sure a playful childhood is still accessible to all, even if that means fitting it among otherwise routine activities. KaBOOM!, an American charity that got started bringing communities together to build playgrounds for kids in need, has recently turned its focus to making sure play can happen throughout the day, especially in areas where 'trips to the playground' are few and far between. 'Cities across the country are beginning to make great strides in creating communities that foster walkability and bikeability,' KaBOOM! president James Siegal writes. 'Now it is time for cities to put kids first and embrace Playability.'[12] So yes, we need more parks, playing fields, and playgrounds ... but we also need more bus stops with swings, crosswalks with hopscotch marks, and games in waiting rooms.

Lenore Skenazy, the New York mother who let her son take the subway on his own, has started the Free-Range Kids movement to campaign for a less structured and supervised approach to parenting. In her book and on her website Skenazy draws attention to the social norms we've embraced as parents without really thinking through their ramifications. She points out that the idea of even having to define a 'free-range kid' is ridiculous: thirty, forty, fifty years ago being a kid and being a free-range kid were one and the same thing. But now parents are made to feel guilty about everything from not breastfeeding to not buying the right knee pad for playing outside. Meanwhile, we need to listen less to the hype about dangers to children and focus on the things that really threaten them. For example, the idea of 'stranger danger' is an outdated and unhelpful one. We need to teach our children how to talk to strangers so they know who to turn to in case of real danger.

This is not to say that there aren't some children who need better support and supervision. Education writer Paul

Tough points out that although risk is indeed elusive for the richest children, it is a daily occurrence for the poorest and most vulnerable kids. Whereas rich children can benefit from risk, poor children are overwhelmed, suffering adverse consequences like toxic stress. As one critic put it in a review of Tough's book, there are two childhood extremes: 'For rich kids, a safety net drawn so tight it's a harness; for poor kids, almost nothing to break their fall.' Helping children develop character by persevering through the challenges of childhood and adolescence is how we can help them succeed.[13]

We need to let children explore the world on their own terms. And we need to recognise that play is natural – naturally human. Rather than fight it, let's harness it productively. All of those involved with the upbringing of children – parents, policymakers, educators, coaches, neighbours – need to step back and think: Are we really protecting children, or are we allaying our own fears instead? Chances are, if you're a parent reading this, you had a carefree childhood. You survived. Your children will too.

Under-protection

A carefree childhood doesn't mean total freedom. There is an important sense in which we are not protecting children enough. It is bizarre that at a time when adult life is being extended in dramatic ways upwards – people are living longer, working longer, staying active longer – we also seem determined to extend adult life downwards, forcing – or, at best, allowing – children to become consumers earlier, to become sexual earlier, and to take on board at an earlier and earlier age the very adult burdens of stress and anxiety. Why? What's the hurry? Our culture mocks notions of childhood innocence. We don't treat children like children any more. We are, in fact, inhuman towards them because we treat them like something they're not: adults. This not only threatens the healthy development of an entire generation; it also stands to reverse one of society's most important advances of the last fifty years: women's emancipation.

Leaning out

At long last women are now taking up roles of power and influence, asserting equality at work, and claiming their place in areas previously the sole domain of men. We've seen the success of strong women who forged a path for others – pioneers like Virginia Woolf and Gloria Steinem, Germaine Greer and Betty Friedan – and those who have taken that path up, like Margaret Thatcher, Hillary Clinton, Christine Lagarde, Janet Yellen, Mary Barra. For the first time ever, in 2015 all the top jobs in an American city, Washington, DC – mayor, police chief, schools commissioner – were held by women. In Nordic countries gender equality has been the social norm and practical reality for decades. Obviously there's further to go. Pay inequality, offensive stereotypes, sexism and gender gaps persist. As of the 2015 election, only 191 members of the House of Commons were women – 29 per cent.[14] Just five women currently lead FTSE 100 companies.[15] Despite all the barriers she's broken, even Hillary Clinton had to put up with Barack Obama commenting on her clothes in a televised debate during her 2008 presidential bid.

Thankfully we have great champions today. As secretary of state and now presidential candidate, Clinton has been a tireless advocate for women's emancipation, economic empowerment and leadership. Pakistani teenager Malala Yousafzai continues her inspiring campaign for the rights of girls simply to go to school. One of the most prominent advocates for women can be found in Silicon Valley: with her book *Lean In*, Facebook executive Sheryl Sandberg calls on women to overcome the forces holding them back professionally. But there's some irony in the fact that the latest leader to carry the flag of gender equality is the chief operating officer of a technology giant. That's because one of the biggest threats to gender equality in the world today actually comes from technology, from something that is, literally before our eyes, reversing feminism's hard-fought gains: the smartphone.

The fundamental battle on gender equality is in the mind. Gender equality is rooted in people's attitudes, whether it's women's attitudes about their role in life, society and the economy; men's attitudes about theirs; or both about each other. In my generation that battle is being won. We are moving firmly away from obnoxious and anachronistic stereotypes of women as housewives, mothers and nothing more, and as sex objects, subordinate to men, defined by appearance rather than brains or talent. Those attitudes are just not socially acceptable any more.

But when we look at what's going on with young children and teenagers and ask whether progress is being made – let alone maintained – the answer is no. Young people are increasingly being exposed to depictions of and attitudes towards women that we thought we'd consigned to the history books: as sex objects defined by looks.[16] Children's clothing is ever more sexualised: one study found that almost 30 per cent of pre-teen clothing had 'sexual' characteristics that highlighted breasts, buttocks or slimness.[17] As cultural pressures including impossibly high standards in beauty, fashion and grooming are communicated across all age groups, they have a significant effect on impressionable girls.[18] This has real-world consequences. Self-objectification is common in young girls and women and has been found to impair cognitive function (because young women are so distracted by worrying about their body image) and to cause emotional distress.[19] Shame, anxiety and self-disgust regularly occur now in pre-teen girls.[20] And it is causing unnatural and frankly scary behaviour. Driven by images and videos of models, pop-culture icons and porn performers showing the perfect wax job, as well as the consequent expectations of boys, girls as young as eleven are starting to shave their pubic hair.[21]

The assault on gender equality is not happening in the political arena, where progress at the legislative and regulatory level – even the representative one – is steady, if slow. It's not happening in the workplace, where, despite the need for more change, as we saw in the previous chapter, women's equality is becoming gradually accepted. No, the assault on gender equality is most evident in the younger generation and its culture. And we can be even more precise than that. The potentially disastrous unwinding of progress towards equal treatment of men and women is happening in the place where young children spend more and more of their time: the online world. Specifically their gateway to that world: the smartphone and other mobile Internet-enabled devices (MIEDs). Nearly four decades after Susie Orbach published *Fat Is a Feminist Issue*, we can today identify the twenty-first-century update: phones are a feminist issue. For children, this is where we need more protection, not less.

Sexualised childhood

The average British child receives his or her first mobile phone at the age of twelve; nearly one in ten receives one before the age of five.[22] A third of children aged five to fifteen have a smartphone, and two-thirds of twelve- to fifteen-year-olds do; nearly half of three- to four-year-olds own some kind of device, while a majority of those aged eight to fifteen have three or more.[23]

Let me repeat: more than half of these children have at least three media devices. In a survey of mostly low-income parents visiting a medical centre in Philadelphia, three-quarters of children by age four had their own mobile device. (Tablets in particular were widely owned: 20 per cent of one-year-olds, 38 per cent of two-year-olds, and over half of three-year-olds had a tablet.) Astonishingly, 4 per cent of under-ones owned a smartphone; 60 per cent of parents reported letting their children use devices while they were out running errands.[24] So after that barrage of numbers, let's just agree the simple points: it is normal for young children to be inundated with technology, they're using smartphones and tablets to go online without supervision, and these trends are accelerating. True, many parents *say* they monitor their children on the Internet, which covers everything from asking them what they've been doing to actively checking their browser history or sitting beside them as they use it. But when the device in question is a mobile Internet-enabled device (MIED), then, of course, parents cannot always watch what their child is doing. Nor can they know what content their children are viewing on another child's MIED or when their child is not at home. Consider: a study commissioned by McAfee, an Internet security company, found that although many parents say they maintain some sort of vigilance, 61 per cent of teens feel confident they can hide whatever they're doing online from their parents.[25] In another survey 49 per cent of teens claim their parents do nothing to monitor their devices.[26] Meanwhile, according to Ofcom, 40 per cent of eight- to eleven-year-olds report no direct supervision when they're online – at home or elsewhere.[27] Parents, on the other hand, find limiting their children's technology activities is the most difficult behaviour to control – harder, even, than getting them to go to bed or complete their homework.[28]

The ubiquity of smartphones has enabled the ubiquity of pornography and other sexual or sexualised content (e.g., in music videos) not suitable for children. Over half of twelve- to fifteen-year-olds use the Internet to view sexually explicit material,[29] and a significant number of children are exposed to explicit content at ten or eleven years old.[30] This premature sexualisation gives children incorrect notions of healthy sex and relationship dynamics. It inculcates in young, impressionable minds – starkly and brutally – the idea we have fought to banish from our culture: that women's primary role is as the object of sexual gratification for men.

For many children pornography is what they think real-life sex is or should be. As most online porn is created for men and is often aggressive if not violent, MIEDs are creating in this generation absolutely shocking, dark patterns of expectation and behaviour when it comes to sex. Young girls think they have to look and behave like porn performers, shaving their bodies and taking part in sexual activity that is often painful and disturbing to them, like anal sex or sex with more than one boy at a time. (The silver lining in this very dark cloud is that the increased incidence of anal sex is leading to less teen pregnancy, according to anecdotal reports. But really, is this what we have become?) Boys, meanwhile, are freed from any moral or cultural restraint to treat girls with respect or affection. The shared understanding of what sex means today is the grim, inhuman, exploitative version that the porn industry has manufactured.

These concerns are real. Young people increasingly report that they learn about sex from pornography; some 45 per cent of young men believe it is educational, and three-quarters of young women believe it puts pressure on girls to act and look 'a certain way'.[31] Consequently young men expect girls to conform to the fantasised version of sex they see in porn and are themselves, unsurprisingly, more likely to be sexist.[32] Men who watch porn are more likely to see women as sexual 'playthings'.[33] Worse, that education is one of violence: in the years 2009 to 2012, 4,562 minors committed 5,028 sex offences in Britain.[34] The children, some of whom were as young as five, 'mimicked' behaviour seen in porn, often viewed online.[35] As many as one in three had victimised family members. More than one-third of sex offences committed against juveniles in the United States are by other children.[36] 'When you interview young women about their experiences of sex, you see an increased level of violence – rough, violent sex.' That, according to Professor Gail Dines, a leading anti-porn campaigner, 'is directly because of porn, as young boys are getting their sexual cues from men in porn who are acting as if they're sexual psychopaths.'[37] Men can be victims too: Irish and Canadian researchers have found that exposure to porn directly affects male perceptions of body image and self-esteem.[38] 'Pornography,' adds Dines, 'is sexually traumatising an entire generation of boys.'[39]

Yes, I know, porn has never exactly been good on this account. And yes, children have always happened across the proverbial copy of *Playboy* or *Hustler* or whatever in their father's drawer. But the scale and nature of it today is completely different from anything our society has ever seen before. At younger and younger ages, children are spending more and more time on smartphones. And it's on smartphones that porn today is being watched: 71 per cent of traffic at Pornhub, one of the Internet's most trafficked porn sites, in Britain comes from a mobile device; 64 per cent of

Pornhub's international traffic – 88 billion video views in total in 2015 – comes from a mobile device.[40] Before Internet porn there was regulation, of sorts. The kind of material available at the local sex shop or on the top shelf of the bookstore or on Page Three of the *Sun* might have degraded women, but it wasn't in the same league of depravity that any child can access today with a couple of clicks on their MIED.

We know that things are bad when it's the porn editors who say so. Martin Daubney is the former editor of *Loaded*, a men's magazine that features plenty of sexual imagery of women. Accused of peddling pornography, he 'agonised' that his 'magazine may have switched a generation onto more explicit online porn'. When he set out to investigate the effects of this culture on young people, it was worse than he imagined. 'I used to be sceptical that porn was as damaging a force as the headlines and David Cameron – who recently said it was 'corroding childhood' – suggest ... but what I saw ... changed my opinion of pornography forever,' he wrote in 2013.[41] He describes attending a panel of young teenagers assembled by sex-education consultant Jonny Hunt, who asked them to write A-to-Z lists of all the sexual terms they were familiar with. It turned out that it was the adults who had insufficient vocabulary.

'"Nugget, what's that?" asked Jonny,' Daubney recalls. '"A nugget is a girl who has no arms or legs and has sex in a porno movie," chortled one young, pimply boy, to an outburst of embarrassed laughter from some.' More shocking were the mundane answers. 'For example, the first word every single boy and girl in the group put on their list was "anal".' One teenage boy described a pornographic scene featuring bestiality (which is illegal in most places).

Porn, Daubney concludes, 'is the most pernicious threat facing children today'. Children are fed a steady diet of submissive and abused women as norms. Their idea of proper sexual behaviour is that boys can get away with whatever they want and girls think they should allow it. And although, in the well-known phrase, smartphones are the 'sewer not the sewage', these devices have done as much as anything in recent years to turn back the clock on feminism, as girls' images of themselves and their potential are reversed.

But the most tragic part of the triangle of sex, MIEDs and young people isn't even exposure to pornography; it's that they expose themselves. Law-enforcement officers around the world have long battled child pornography, but they are increasingly wondering how to battle child pornography committed by the victims. Technically minors who possess nude images of even themselves are falling foul of child pornography laws, but as one columnist put it, charging them as paedophiles 'makes as much sense as charging a kid who brings a squirt gun to school with possession of an unlicensed firearm'.[42] And so police officers, school administrators and parents are left in a grey area, desperate to communicate the severity of 'sexting', as the perky euphemism goes, without ruining their children's futures.

An otherwise unassuming rural region in central Virginia, Louisa County, became the centre of a firestorm in early 2014 when a sexting scandal erupted after a local high school girl saw her naked image on an online bulletin board and her mother reported it. Journalist Hanna Rosin of the *Atlantic* spent several weeks there to try to understand the ordeal that followed. Police started with the girls whose pictures were on the site and the boys who followed them on Instagram. Every interview yielded more names of high school students who had sent or received 'sexts'; the confiscated smartphones started to pile up. Donald Lowe, the police officer leading the investigation, said that his characterisation of the girls evolved from 'victims' to 'I guess I'll call them victims' to 'they just fell into this category where they victimised themselves'.[43]

The problem with smartphones is that they amplify and escalate normal 'teenagers being teenagers' behaviour into something much worse. As Rosin writes, technology has the power to turn an otherwise private experience into a public hell. Where once a girl might have flashed a boy she liked in an empty room and that was the end of it, now that 'flashing' has a permanent record. Kids who illicitly forward these pictures without permission are unquestionably committing sex crimes, and the majority who do so might know it's wrong, but they certainly don't think of themselves as criminals. Are these 'youthful indiscretions' any worse than anything that previous generations did? They may or may not be, but one thing is clear: because of the technology and its ubiquity, the consequences are far worse.

Today 52 per cent of teenagers use Instagram to share photos (61 per cent of girls), with an average of 150 followers; 41 per cent use Snapchat (51 per cent of girls).[44] The boys Lowe interviewed told him that sharing nude pictures was 'nothing unusual. It happens all the time.' When Rosin asked students how many of their peers they thought sexted, the answer was 'everyone'.[45] Boys now expect sexual pictures from girls, flattering and cajoling them until they cave in, but then immediately think of a girl as a *thot* ('that ho over there') – best translated as 'slut' or 'whore' – when she sends a picture. Last November over one hundred students at a Colorado high school were part of an elaborate 'sexting ring' in which participants gained points depending on which photos they collected.[46] A study of several high schools in Texas found that over half (57 per cent) of students have been asked to send a naked photo; 28 per cent have sent one, and almost a third have asked for sexts in return.[47] The ubiquity of phones and the Internet is bad enough when it exposes young people to porn and unhealthy and backward attitudes towards sex, violence and the opposite sex. But by eliminating all but the smallest barriers to communicating explicit material of oneself or another far and wide, MIEDs haven't just spurred this behaviour; they've often, as in sexting, created it.

'I'd like to learn how to have a conversation'

A common response to all this would be, 'Well, yes, I know, it's terrible, but really, what can we do about it? The Internet and phones and technology – they bring all these good things, but they bring some bad things too, and we just have to accept it and do the best we can to deal with the worst parts of it. You can't turn the clock back.'

'You can't turn the clock back.' 'You've got to take the rough with the smooth.' 'You can't put the genie back in the bottle.' These are some of the clichés that are bandied about in any discussion of the impact of the Internet on society. Generally I would say they're probably true. Generally it's true that the Internet is like all new technology that becomes widely adopted: it has become widely adopted because we find it useful and good and accept its downsides as part of the price we pay for the far larger upsides. Generally I agree that you can't and shouldn't try to turn the clock back. Generally.

But the issue I'm talking about in this chapter is not general. It's specific. The issue is of children having unsupervised access to the Internet. Not children using technology or children using tablets or smartphones or going on the Internet or even children owning mobile phones. The issue is *unsupervised access to the Internet.* That's a pretty narrow, specific issue. And there is something we can do about it. More to the point, I believe there's something we must do about it because MIEDs are putting at risk one of the best and most important social changes in human history: the empowerment of women. It's great that Sheryl Sandberg's Lean In Foundation created a partnership with Getty Images to create a new library of stock images showing women in traditionally male professional roles. Now let's see some action on smartphones too. As mobile phones became camera-phones and then smartphones connected to the Internet, it was like handing young people the keys to the drinks cabinet – it was only a matter of time before something went horribly wrong. Technology ran way ahead of our ability to handle it; for many young people, navigating the intersections of the Internet, mobile devices and social media has been a baptism by fire. Just as with alcohol, we need to keep it away from our children unless we're there to supervise, not least because phones aren't just a feminist issue. They are a developmental issue too.

We know what a good childhood looks like – and it turns out that modern brain science backs up what we knew by instinct all the time. The things that are generally associated with happy children who go on to be successful adults are human things, including time spent with people who love them, physical activity, walking in and spending time in nature, and playing.[48] Traditional toys, argues Brian Verdine, a postdoctoral fellow at the University of Delaware in Newark, are much better than 'electronic toys and apps' at helping children learn spatial skills. 'Skills, including early geometry and knowing the names of shapes, help kids learn the maths skills they pick up in kindergarten,' he says. 'And if they already have those (before they begin school), they are ahead of the curve.'[49] None of these things are provided by smartphones, tablets and other MIEDs, and yet an increasing – and alarming – proportion of children's time is being diverted from the positive things we know are good for them. One recent study found that 'educational' toys that light up, play music and talk back to children lead to 'decreased quantity and quality of language' compared to more human approaches.[50]

'Parents see that children will watch these screens and look like they understand, but they are not looking and perceiving in a way that is helping them learn,' says Marsha Gerdes, a psychologist at the Children's Hospital of Pennsylvania. 'Kids are not learning as much as when they are actually looking at their parent's face and listening to them sing a song when they are watching a pattern on a screen.'[51] Research has shown that children who play with blocks do better in maths later on,[52] and yet children are spending between two and four hours a day on screens.[53] It should alarm us that devices are now more popular than traditional toys.[54] As we saw earlier, the problem of overexposure to screens and tech is pretty evenly spread across the income groups. But the difference is that middle- and upper-class families at least have the money and the time to build positive physical – not screen-based – experiences into their children's lives. Not so for poor families, where the device can be a blessed relief from the stresses of parenting in difficult circumstances. You can understand why, but it doesn't make it right.

Studies are starting to tell us that when we allow children to shut out the world to focus on devices, we harm not just social relationships but basic human abilities as well. Chief among them is the skill of conversation. Sherry Turkle, a Massachusetts Institute of Technology (MIT) professor who studies the interaction between people and technology, recounts a recent conversation she had had in the course of her research: 'An eighteen-year-old boy who uses texting for almost everything says to me wistfully: "Someday, someday, but certainly not now, I'd like to learn how to have a conversation."'[55] Turkle found that people increasingly eschew conversations because they can't control what is said. In text messaging, email and social media, they can. What's more, people can customise their communications, tuning in and out without having to endure one second of content they don't care about. But there are costs. As Turkle puts it, 'You can end up hiding from each other, even as we're all constantly connected to each other.' And they – our children – are suffering the consequences: ironically, more connectivity dehumanises.

In her book *Alone Together* Turkle writes about an encounter she had with a teenager: '"There is a difference between someone laughing and someone writing that they're laughing." He says, "My friends are so used to giving their phones all the attention ... they forget that people are still there to give attention to."'[56] This phenomenon is leading to slightly tragic new rules of etiquette, like the number of people in a group who can acceptably be looking down at their screen at any one time.[57] Neglected friendships are one thing, but what about parents neglecting their children? When parents spend so much time on their devices, it is, Turkle says, problematic for their children. 'These kids are extremely lonely. We are giving everybody the impression that we aren't really there for them. It's toxic.'[58] A detailed 2015 survey of teens' media habits by Common Sense Kids Action revealed that American teenagers spend, on average, a total of nine hours a day on screens – not including any screen time at school.[59]

Although it's bad enough to be experimenting on ourselves with screens and devices, we run great risks that the connectivity enabled by technology will have magnified impact on impressionable children. As we learned with the work of Nadine Burke Harris in Chapter 8, children are especially affected by neuroplasticity. Keeping that in mind, imagine how much it affects you, then imagine your children, who now have to grow up in this toxic environment, unable to access any space that's technology-free or without a device. We're experimenting with their very ability to think.

We are not powerless

MIEDs are incredible inventions and fantastic tools for all sorts of things. They facilitate learning through education programmes and apps, allow parents to keep in touch with their children, save time and hassle, and enhance our daily lives. They can free us from drudgery to spend time on things of more value. Without question, children need to be comfortable with and adept at using the latest technology. But because there are undeniable adverse side effects, we should try to address them rather than assuming there's not really anything we can do about all this, that we 'have to take the rough with the smooth', 'can't turn the clock back', 'can't put the genie back in the bottle', and so on.

That response is weak, feeble, pathetic. Of course it's possible to protect our children while enabling them to successfully navigate our technologically advanced, connected society. This is not a generalised, existential problem with technology or the Internet; it is a highly specific, narrow, solvable problem: How do we prevent the negative social consequences of unsupervised child access to the Internet?

There are lots of well-meaning efforts. You now see a steady stream of books and articles on 'digital detoxing' and similar self-denying ordinances as well as advice to parents on how to limit their children's screen time. Turkle recommends we establish 'sacred spaces' at home and at work away from our devices so we can reflect on our thoughts and connect with others. An app called TeenSafe lets parents monitor their children's mobile activity, which is fine, but it doesn't exactly get to the root of the problem. (Besides, what parent wants to so blatantly spy on their children?) More promising are 'digital detox' apps like RescueTime and Anti-Social. But although these can help solve some of the problems of adult over-reliance on tech, I don't think the 'self-denying ordinance' approach comes close to being the solution we need for children.

One serious way forward lies in the design of tech products themselves. Many of the biggest tech companies have put huge amounts of effort into building versions of their core products that prevent children from seeing adult content on the Internet. Examples include Apple's Family Sharing, Google's SafeSearch, and YouTube's Safety Mode (full disclosure: my wife, Rachel, was a leading advocate for child-protection efforts when she worked at Google). There are also apps like Net Nanny that claim to offer the same kinds of protections. Another version of this argument is that parents should not give children smartphones with data plans, thus limiting their use to phoning and texting.

These are all positive steps to address the problems we've seen in this chapter. But they don't go far enough. First, phones and tablets are increasingly sophisticated, and although parents may have options for more control, children are often two steps ahead. There are too many stories of children easily getting around various child-protection controls for anyone to have confidence in this approach. One so-called 'vault app' used by students in the Colorado sexting ring hides illicit photos behind what looks like a calculator (into which children can surreptitiously enter their passwords).[60] But there's an even more serious objection, and it's rooted in a very human concept we've seen a few times already in this book: social pressure. This problem of children seeing adult content and being able to use the Internet to harm themselves and others, this phenomenon of phones as a feminist issue, phones as a developmental issue, phones as an antisocial issue – it's not a product issue or a technical issue. It's a behavioural issue.

It's not just about whatever controls or restrictions you as a parent put on your child's use; it's also about everyone else's children and their access to the Internet on whatever devices their parents have allowed them. However much some parents might not wish their children to have these devices outside the home or classroom, unsupervised, or whatever controls they successfully – or unsuccessfully – place on their own children's usage, they simply have no way of supervising their access to other children's devices. What do you do if you don't want your children to have an MIED? Should they be stigmatised or face peer pressure to get one?[61] I'm obviously alert to the risk that my own children might lose out because they aren't carrying the latest smartphone, tablet or 'wearable'. As a parent, I will be forced to decide between what I believe to be good for my children's emotional and neurological development and what is best for them socially. That's a terrible choice, for me and for all parents.

That's why we need a fundamental rethink: this problem is not an individual problem; it's a collective one, like pollution, and that's how we need to deal with it. Unconstrained, unsupervised Internet use by children is mental pollution, and there is a simple solution for that kind of thing, one we know well and are used to applying.

Here's a way we could make life easier for parents, better for children, and retain the benefits of technology while making life more human. We need to create a social norm that children should never have access to the Internet without supervision. Because the principal method through which children access the Internet unsupervised is through smartphones or other MIEDs, that's where we have to take the fight. Just as we've banned smoking or drinking for under-sixteens because we think those things are bad for them, we should ban smartphones and other mobile Internet-enabled devices for children too – to protect under-sixteens from unsupervised content. They could still have so-called feature phones to call their parents in an emergency or send text messages, but they would not be able to view pornography and other illicit video and photo content or to take and post pictures of themselves whenever they wanted. Establishing this as a norm would license parents' enforcement of what would be an (inevitably) unpopular rule: 'It's not my fault. It's the law.'

Of course, children should have the benefits of the Internet when they're learning, exploring and connecting with the world. As we saw in Chapter 3, technology can help students and teachers alike. But all of this can be achieved under supervision, in the home with parents and at school. If we allow uncontrolled use, devices will dominate our children's lives to the detriment of making friends, gaining tactile knowledge and playing outside – in short, everything that makes childhood so wonderful, vital, human. That's why we need more protection. That's why we need a ban.

I realise this might sound extreme or fanciful, but you can't tell me it's impossible. It's not. My family is living proof of it. Our sons do not have phones or tablets, only use a computer at school, and at home have perhaps a half-hour or so of screen time three or four days a week, watching videos, not TV. I myself do not have a smartphone, and no, I don't say this from some cabin in the woods but a few miles from Stanford and as the CEO of a tech start-up and husband of an Uber executive. I feel perfectly connected and perfectly happy not to be chained to screens.[62]

Some will say, 'How can you justify something as draconian as banning kids from having smartphones or tablets?' I think it's reasonable to put the burden of justification on them: 'Could you please explain why you want children to have unsupervised, unlimited access to the Internet?' For those who think my idea of a ban is unenforceable in a practical sense and who point to underage drinking and smoking despite similar bans, I'd say, of course, no ban ever achieves complete, 100 per cent compliance. But they can be made to be effective in the vast majority of cases, and perhaps most importantly, a ban helps set a social norm. It draws a line and upholds society's standards and collective sense of right and wrong.

As society adapts to the digital age we need to push back a bit and make the digital age adapt to us. On the one hand, technology, especially in the form of mobile devices, has built a whole new world of progress. On the other hand, devices have unintended and serious negative side effects that we need to recognise and address if we are to maintain a healthy relationship with technology and retain our humanity. Ending children's unsupervised access to the Internet is a step in the right – and more human – direction.

Being a parent has always been hard, and today seems ever harder. But as in so many other areas of life, we now have the evidence to know what our children need and what they don't. They need the freedom to play, to interact in the world, to discover themselves. They don't need the freedom to roam the Internet. We can't make childhood perfect, but we can set sensible rules and boundaries that best suit our children's very real limitations, needs and aspirations. We should allow children to have a childhood that's more human.

CHAPTER 11

SPACES

Walk down East London's famous Brick Lane, pulsing with life and energy at the intersection of the worlds of art and fashion and music and tech start-ups and waves of immigrants who have made this incredible place their home over the centuries, turn into Hanbury Street, and soon you'll come to a building as intriguing and important as any that have been created in the world these past few years.

The first things you'll see are trees – carefully selected to make sure one of them is flowering, whatever the season. Then you'll notice a strange, bubble-shaped orange wall emerging from the side of the building. Go in, and you'll be struck by the colours – amazing, bright colours. Poke around a bit. There's a café, desks, mid-century furniture, offices. But everywhere there are plants – not just stuck in pots, as you'll find in the beige-topia office buildings the world over, but plants that are actually growing up and along the walls and columns. Hydroponically, if you please. What is this place?

I'm so proud to say that it's the first Second Home, a business that Rohan started as an expression of his belief that our physical surroundings have a huge part to play in the quality of our lives – our personal lives and, as in the case of Second Home, our working lives. With his business partner

Sam Aldenton and two thrillingly inventive Spanish architects, José Selgas and Lucía Cano, Rohan is showing in a practical way what we can achieve by aiming higher when it comes to designing our surroundings. (The *Architectural Review* asked rhetorically whether Second Home is 'the best office in the world'.[1]) According to Selgas and Cano, 'Everything for us is related to how the brain works, whether that is a homespace or a workspace. The brain is more related to nature. If you are in an artificial rectangular space, your brain is restricted.'[2] As a result, Second Home is full of nature, and to reflect the natural world, there are no right angles in the whole building. As Rohan says, 'We didn't evolve with straight lines.'[3]

But Rohan's vision is not simply about melding nature and people. In his original building in London as well as in future Second Homes planned in America and around the world, it's also about making people more comfortable in their environment. 'Space is not just a commodity,' he says; it's about 'community and serendipity'. It has to be 'curated'. People want to interact with one another, so Second Home works to ensure a diverse community where people and ideas can cross-pollinate. But Rohan and Sam also understand that people want time and space for themselves. They've designed Second Home for both, enabling members to regulate their own social interaction. For example, side entrances and exits allow you to avoid seeing others if you just want to slip in and out.

Second Home is a living, contemporary manifestation of a phrase that has come to capture the essence of why spaces matter. In 1943 Winston Churchill was asked to comment on the design of the new House of Commons building in Westminster. He explained his view that the physical characteristics of the building would have a major influence on how the politicians who used it would behave and, ultimately, on the policies that resulted. He quipped, 'We shape our buildings, and afterwards our buildings shape us.'[4] Far too many architects and city planners have forgotten this essential truth – despite how obvious it seems. In Chapter 2 we looked at the idea of human-centred design in the context of government and public policy; in this chapter we're going to apply the same principle – human-centredness – to the design of the physical space around us.

Paradoxically, the more sophisticated we've become, the more our physical interactions with the world have become thoughtless and unnatural. Look at the buildings and public spaces we use every day. Why are so many of them so terrible? Why is so much of the man-made world seemingly designed without any regard for us, the people who actually have to live in it? We have settled for industrially designed and manufactured homes and offices, suburbs that are 'good enough', but our inhuman attitudes towards the built environment make many aspects of our lives, from education and healthcare to childhood play, much worse. We need places that work on a human scale and a human level.

In 1931 German psychologist Kurt Lewin proposed what would come to be known as Lewin's equation: $B = f(P, E)$ – that is, human behaviour is a function of a person and his or her environment. This was groundbreaking at the time: most psychologists assumed a person's habits and behaviours were a result simply of the type of person they were. Lewin thought otherwise. 'Only by the concrete whole which comprises the object and the situation are the vectors which determine the dynamics of the event defined,' he remarked when the theory was first (so clearly) proposed.[5] Several decades later psychologists would coin the term 'situationism' to describe the overwhelming influence that external factors have on a person's behaviour, as opposed to internal characteristics like mood, personality and preferences. In the ensuing decades experiment after experiment in the lab as well as in the real world has proved this to be the case, lending even more weight to those wartime words of Winston Churchill. Our surroundings play such an important role in determining how happy, healthy and productive we are. It's time we made them more human.

Homes, not housing

The most obvious place to start is where we should most feel 'at home': our actual homes. Home is where we rest and recharge, raise our families, bond with friends. Home is an intimate place; it should be the haven from which you make your daily adventures into the world. Of course for many around the world, even the rudimentary basics of a home like dryness, warmth and running water are still unattainable luxuries. And homelessness remains a shocking problem in the developed world, too. But for the vast majority who live in basic, structurally sound dwellings, home – in its deepest sense – is still an elusive concept.

Britain suffers from two problems where homes are concerned. First, there aren't enough of them. There are some 1.7 million households on waiting lists in the UK[6] despite enough readily available land for at least 1.5 million.[7] A quarter of adults under thirty-five still live in their childhood bedrooms, even though 72 per cent of them are working.[8] Only 142,390 homes have been built on average annually in the past four years – far fewer than the 240,000 needed each year.[9] In 2013, fewer homes were built in England than in any year since 1949,[10] except for 2010.[11] Moreover, the idea that there's 'not enough land' is a myth: urban landscape accounts for only 10.6 per cent of English land, 3.4 per cent of Northern Ireland, 1.9 per cent of Scotland and 4.2 per cent of Wales.[12]

The second problem is with what's being built. They are barely homes at all. They are factory houses. Consider this: 31 per cent of homeowners today would not choose a home built in the last ten years;[13] British homes are on average the smallest in Western Europe.[14] The average new home is only 818 square feet. (In Australia, it's 2,217 square feet; Denmark: 1,475. Even crowded Japan's average is more than 70 per cent larger than in the UK.)[15] Even worse, because the number of bedrooms is used as a key metric when selling houses, developers increasingly take advantage of the fact by carving additional useless rooms into already small spaces. They have no problem charging more for the extra walls.[16] But what use is a child's 'bedroom' without a table for building toys or doing homework, without shelves for books, without room to play?

Both these problems – not enough homes, not good enough homes – are structural. They are caused by the nature of the market, dominated by fewer and fewer big housebuilders, whose dominance continues to grow. Medium-sized companies have closed down at the rate of 60 per cent since the recession and small builders have declined by half.[17] The five largest builders were responsible for 20 per cent of house completions in 2008–9. In 2012–13, their share rose to 33 per cent.[18] This is not a proper market; these are not proper businesses. They are bureaucracies, just like the ones we met in Chapter 6, manipulating and lobbying their way to dominance while giving people a worse and worse service. The factory houses they build sell because there's little choice and there's a housing shortage. As a result, the houses are also getting more expensive. Property prices increased

4,268 per cent between 1971 and 2012. The authors of a report by KPMG and Shelter point out that if chicken prices increased at a similar rate, a typical supermarket broiler would now cost £51.33.[19] And the industrial housebuilders' market power means they have no need to care about what people actually want from their homes.

A report from Ipsos MORI and RIBA found that many homeowners find the 'feel' and 'character' of a home to be more important than many practical considerations.[20] Developers and politicians might dismiss this as sentimental, but how a home feels to you strongly affects how you feel in it. This is vital for physiological as well as psychological well-being. Human-centred design principles teach us that homes ought to be flexible, both for different everyday uses and for the long term. And it's obviously a fallacy to think that every person and family, in all their uniqueness, would want the same thing: people are different. Yet the houses built by the big developers are all the same. How is it that we can customise things as trivial as our burgers or cars, yet have almost no say over our homes unless people have the money to pay for extensive (expensive) remodelling? We need a complete shake-up of the so-called housing 'market' so people can choose what they want rather than meekly accept whatever the big bureaucratic housebuilders offer. It's absurd that people keep referring in Britain to a 'housing market'. The market for new homes is no more a market than the GUM store in Communist Moscow was a 'supermarket'.

As a product-design student at the Royal College of Art in the early 2000s, Bruce Bell had nearly unlimited access to the latest in manufacturing technology. Hundreds of different machines, from punch presses (that cut holes in things), to routers (that hollow out areas of a surface), to wire benders (that bend wires), were his to experiment with. In the last decade or so these already powerful machines have been extraordinarily enhanced by technology, by digital control. Product designers can now achieve precision that could only have been dreamt of before. Now, you can get any idea you want test manufactured on a one-off basis at high quality and low cost, in very little time.

But Bell didn't go into industrial design; he went to an architecture firm, building homes, not products – and still in very old-fashioned ways. Having just learned cutting-edge manufacturing techniques at the RCA, it killed him that he would draw something to the millimetre on the computer and 'the contractor would still be using a hammer and saw, measuring things with a tape measure'. He wanted to find a way to replicate the magic he had experienced with digital fabrication, where the product would materialise in real life just as precisely as it was illustrated on the screen. Bell set out to transform the way we build houses.

After experimenting with different machines and techniques, he settled on one simple tool: a CNC router (CNC stands for 'computer numerical control'), which basically cuts shapes out of timber boards by 'drawing' the design with a mechanical cutting bit that moves up and down from above. Now it would be possible to 'print' the whole house: the walls, doors, window frames, floors and ceilings could all be cut out of specially engineered wood and 'joined' together with practically no gaps in between, like Lego blocks. After some prototyping, a process was created and a London-based company, Facit Homes, was born. They soon discovered a second advantage to the CNC machine: it was easily transportable. This was revolutionary: bringing the machine to site meant the architect, builder and homeowner could be standing next to the house in progress, notice something they didn't like, change a component's design, and have it manufactured and placed almost immediately. 'We can stay flexible and not be restricted by the tools that we create. We can respond to any design scenario, any client situation,' Bell says.

What Bruce Bell and Facit have done is far more consequential than any of the individual homes they've designed and built. They're showing that the future of housing really can have people at its centre. Rather than vainly exhorting the massive bureaucratic homebuilders to change their practices to adopt human-centred design, Facit's technology makes it possible for every home to be an act of personal expression, based on the needs, desires and circumstances of individual people and families.[21]

A more human future for housing is one where we become a nation of 'self-builders' – a country that allows individuals and families to pull together the land, financing, design and construction of their own homes. 'Self-building' doesn't mean that you literally have to build your own house. It could mean hiring a firm like Facit to give you total personalisation of your home. Self-building meets the needs of those who will actually live in the house and liberates them from the homogenising dictates of local planners and 'volume' builders. But today only 10 per cent of new homes in the UK are self-built. In Austria it's 80 per cent; in Germany, Belgium, Italy, Sweden, Norway and France it's around 60 per cent.[22] Why are we so uniquely standardised and centralised? We have a fond self-image in Britain as a creative, entrepreneurial nation of rebels and upstarts compared to the bland, boring, sheep-like dullards of Europe. When it comes to housing, it's completely the other way round. We are the ones who pathetically submit to the grey tyranny of the identikit house, while the rest of Europe enjoys the freedom of domestic self-expression. Again, why? It's not a simple question, but the overwhelming reason – and the reason the big housebuilders have been able to achieve their baleful dominance – is the limited availability of land. In other countries, local councils have to make space available for development by people and not just big housebuilding companies.

Consider the Homeruskwartier district in Almere, a city of 200,000 people half an hour east of Amsterdam.[23] The local authority drew up street plans in 2006 and then made plots – ranging from under 86 square metres to 1,200 – available to local people to buy their own plot and design whatever they wanted.[24] Over 1,000 homes have already been built, with thousands more on the way.[25] The project has drawn comparisons to the neighbourhoods that run along Amsterdam's famous canals: 'They did the same as we are trying to do,' explains Jacqueline Tellinga, a driving force behind Homeruskwartier. 'The plots were parcelled out, the buyers were given a few guidelines over things such as height, but after that it was left to the individual.'[26] The result? The most incredibly quirky, interesting, human neighbourhood you can imagine. Each house not only fulfils the needs of those who live within; it is an outward expression of their personalities. One house, painted bright red, is set up as a beach house, with sand and lounge chairs in the back yard. One row of homes imitates Amsterdam's canals, with the bottom floor even forming the wall of a canal along the back. In another house, the owner decided to use strips of Teflon as the side facade. People got homes that suited their needs precisely. For one family, that was a garage large enough for their boat. For another, it was an attached granny flat. Each resident received an A4 sheet of paper that specified their plot, its dimensions and a few restrictions – nothing about design, though. 'We wanted to give the people complete freedom in aesthetics as part of our ideology of trusting people,' Tellinga explains. 'Who are we to decide what kind of aesthetic they have to use?'[27]

Another Dutch city, Nijmegen, has been similarly inspired. With a little more restriction, it's offering residents a choice of twenty-nine 'flat-pack' designs. In addition to giving local architects work (over twenty local firms collaborated with the city to contribute to the catalogue), the fact that each can be easily assembled helps keep costs down without sacrificing design quality.[28] Local architects understand the community and its complexity. They understand local needs; they get its vernacular. Moreover, employing local architects keeps whatever profits are made in the community, rather than having them siphoned off to some housebuilder's corporate headquarters.

In the UK, such a wonderful way of building a neighbourhood is made impossible for no other reason than weak political will. It's certainly not cost (self-built homes in the UK cost about 60 to 75 per cent of their final value),[29] nor is it lack of demand. According to an Ipsos MORI survey, there are more than 6 million people in the UK looking to get involved in a custom-build project in the next year.[30] There's plenty of land, but you can't just buy a plot and build a house. Instead, the land is portioned off in large chunks and sold to one of the handful of volume homebuilders who hold them in land banks. Barratt, Berkeley, Persimmon and Taylor Wimpey – the four largest developers – collectively held 450,000 plots as of December 2015.[31] Many plots that receive permission for building on remain vacant. In 2013, the Local Government Association estimated that across the UK, there were some 380,000 plots altogether that had achieved planning permission but on which the houses had yet to be completed,[32] of which 152,000 hadn't been even started (by

January 2016, there were some 475,000 plots without homes that had the requisite permission).[33]

You might think this makes the marketplace ripe for rival start-ups, but housebuilding is as much locked up by policy and government as by the big private firms involved. Planning rules make it very hard to enter the market, since you need to begin siting land and seeking approval years in advance. When authorities make land available to build on, they tend to do so in large tracts – tens of thousands of plots at a time – making them functionally available only to huge firms for huge developments. But even once the land title changes hands, slow approval holds things up. It's so complicated and takes so long that only a large, bureaucratic developer can interact with the planning bureaucracy itself.

People on both sides argue about who's to blame. The industry says it's moving as fast as it can – that it's government that slows them up. People in government say that the homebuilders carefully calibrate the pace of their building to maximise profits, rather than the number of people moving into homes. But the truth is that the whole system is wrong and needs to be replaced with one that puts people first. Just as with banks and supermarkets, we've allowed a too-big-to-fail system to dominate an industry that is more important than most: it's providing fundamental infrastructure for living.

Meanwhile, localised not-in-my-back-yard sentiments prevent affordable housing from being built in many towns and villages – the very affordable housing those areas need to stop their economic decline. Of course, if you already have a home, the system's working great. But it's people who don't yet live somewhere who need the homes built. That's why real neighbourhood control of housing needs to be accompanied by financial incentives for those neighbourhoods to accept new housing. Once you allow your mind to wander outside the bizarre, centralised paradigm that is the housebuilding system of today, the solution is really quite simple. Land that's sited or zoned for houses – regardless of who owns it (non-builders own 45 per cent of the permitted home sites in London)[34] – has to be opened up. We must commit not just to building more homes but to making them affordable and human-centred. The best way to do this is to break open the bureaucratised planning and building process. If individuals and families or small and medium-sized firms have the financing, they should be as free to build on housing plots as the large developers. Innovations – whether it's new policies, development models, or design and construction technology itself – that move us in this direction have to be encouraged. We desperately need to make the housing system more human.

Space and the quality of everyday life

Home might be where the heart is, but when it comes to the communities in which we live and work, many urban planners and architects seem to have followed only their heads. Obsessed with their own notions of how a perfectly rational society would look and function, they spent the twentieth century experimenting with our neighbourhoods, often with awful results. There is no more iconic example of inhuman architecture than the work of Swiss architect Le Corbusier, who inspired many of France's urban housing projects in the mid-twentieth century – high-rises that have mostly served to isolate poor individuals from the rest of the community. The very term he used to describe his buildings is exactly what's wrong with them: 'machines for living in'. It's hard to imagine a less human approach. One of this style of architecture's best critiques was offered by Jane Jacobs, who had studied social housing as a reporter for *Architectural Forum* in the 1950s. As Canadian journalist Robert Fulford reports,

> *On paper [the housing developments] looked fine, but when Jacobs visited them she discovered that the open spaces were empty of people. Planners had segregated residences, retail stores, business offices and schools, an arrangement that was tidy but also inhuman and uninteresting. An environment created out of goodwill and careful thought had turned out to be boring, dangerous and ultimately unliveable. The new developments had literally been planned to death: they left no room for happy accidents, and no room for life.*[35]

If ever there were an advocate of human-centred design, it was Jacobs. In her classic – and now thankfully influential – book, *The Death and Life of American Cities*, she lays out both her critique of and antidote to the 'visionary' planning that typified public projects in the mid-twentieth century (and government programmes more generally today). Jacobs's legitimacy derived not from theory, which she ignored, or any advanced degree, which she lacked, but from street-level observations of people themselves and how buildings and streets influenced their interaction. She was only concerned about how cities worked 'in real life', as she put it, because that was the only way to understand how to plan, rebuild or develop a neighbourhood for economic and social success.[36] For 'planners' to be captivated by their own visions of order and beauty was to forget about how people actually lived. If you pick up her book, which reads as much as a work of literature as an urban planning guide, you might be surprised at the simplicity of many of her suggestions and the length she devotes to each. There's an entire chapter discussing the need for short street blocks (with many possible routes to any given destination, an area 'opens up'), another on old buildings, and four chapters on sidewalks. To many these are trivial features that merely enhance a city's functions; to Jacobs they were central to its fundamental vitality. These issues are brilliantly brought to life in that most iconic of cities, Paris. It is a place that tells a powerful tale of contrasts, providing a juxtaposition between a human, Jane Jacobs, world and an inhuman, Le Corbusier, one.

When he seized power as emperor in 1852, Napoleon III had an almost 'messianic' plan for Paris.[37] To build his vision, he appointed Baron Georges-Eugène Haussmann, a Parisian native who had been prefect in various other French cities, to be the new 'Prefect of the Seine'. Paris had many ills. The medieval streets were difficult to navigate and often impassable, paved with stones that 'offered an uncertain footing for pedestrians and horses alike', and made of dirt that the 'slightest rain … turned into black mud.'[38] Paris was, according to French writer Maxime du Camp, 'on the point of becoming uninhabitable. Its population [was] suffocating in the tiny, narrow, putrid and tangled streets in which it had been dumped. As a result of this state of affairs, everything suffered: hygiene, security, speed of communication and public morality.'[39] Much of this stemmed from lack of good plumbing and sanitation; sewers overflowed and emptied into the Seine, which was in turn a source of drinking water.

Napoleon and Haussmann were determined to modernise Paris. They knew that a city, as a physical space, encompassed a complex ecosystem. Accordingly, writes historian Colin Jones, they 'saw themselves as physician-urbanists, whose task was to ensure Paris's nourishment, to regulate and to speed up circulation in its arteries (namely, its streets), to give it more powerful lungs so as to let it breathe (notably, through green spaces), and to ensure that its waste products were hygienically and effectively disposed of.'[40] Haussmann channelled his patron's dictatorial powers by aggressively attacking the city in order to change it. In one sense his reforms were the epitome of inhumanity: instead of rebuilding piecemeal, he demolished whole neighbourhoods to recreate Paris in a neater grid, building wide avenues on straight axes to ease movement in the city. The new apartments that lined them were uniform and modern, in the now-famous Haussmannian style. But they were in the service of human outcomes: Haussmann created wide avenues so pedestrians could have spacious promenades, he built new buildings to modernise living spaces and allow light to come to the streets, and he constructed several huge new parks to give all Parisians access to green space, 'green lungs' for the overcrowded and polluted city.[41] He fulfilled some of Parisians' most basic human needs – creating a modern plumbing system that brought fresh water from outside the city while disposing of waste in a sanitary manner – but he also promoted their aspirational ones by building the Opéra Garnier as a monument to culture. There's no doubt today that Paris is a beautiful, modern city.

That is, at its centre. When you contrast the centre of Paris with its *banlieues*, or suburbs, full of housing projects (called *Habitation à Loyer Modéré*, or 'rent-controlled housing') inspired by Le Corbusier, you find a different, sadder story. These built-up 'utopias' are cruel traps: residents have sunlight and fresh air but are left in thrall to whichever gang controls the lifts. More fundamentally, Le Corbusier forgot that as people move through life, they want different kinds of residences – urban apartments for young people, then space for raising a family, and then a pleasant retreat for retirement. 'If you don't vary the housing units in a given neighbourhood – if you fill entire quarters of the city with standard-issue monoliths – you condemn upwardly mobile people to constant movement,' observes American journalist Christopher Caldwell, who has studied the *banlieues* in great depth. 'The only people who develop any sense of place are those trapped in the poverty they started in.'[42] At first glance Haussmann's Napoleon-era reforms and the construction of the Le Corbusier–inspired high-rises seem similar: both stemmed from the top-down visions of hubristic planners, but both, too, had 'more human' goals at their centres.

However, despite the inhuman process, Haussmann's vision in Paris worked. The *banlieues* did not. Central Paris is beautiful, with plentiful transport connecting mixed-use buildings everywhere. On almost every street the ground floor is a shop or business with offices and housing above. The *banlieues*, on the other hand, have become synonymous with disaster, most recently burdened by massive riots in 2005. The rioters, mostly first- and second-generation North Africans, had plenty of grievances: unemployment, racism, France's failure to integrate them into society. But their grievances were exacerbated by the inhuman architecture of the *banlieues*. By concentrating the city's poorest, most desperate and most violent residents, French planners inadvertently created a powder keg that duly burst when three youths from a *banlieue*, thinking they were being chased by the police, hid in a power station and were electrocuted. Two died, a third was gravely injured, and an entire community of young people rose in rebellion against the society they felt was responsible. Neighbourhood design did not cause the weeks of ensuing riots, but the daily indignities of inhuman architecture and planning certainly contributed to them.

The reason central Paris 'works' is because with different types of people using the same streets at all times of day,

Haussmann inadvertently created a 'Jacobsian' city: there are always, in her famous phrase, 'eyes on the street' to watch over it. The *banlieues*, with their isolated, single-use buildings dominated by gangs, are the precise, inhuman opposite.

One of the marks of a great, human neighbourhood is that you can't really tell where it begins or ends – one area just flows into the next. Sooner or later you know you're somewhere special, but the precise moment never really announces itself.

For decades it was pretty easy to know when you had entered St Lawrence, Toronto. Situated close to the bustling downtown, Toronto Harbor, and the Canadian national railways yard, the neighbourhood had once been a busy port area, but by the 1960s it had grown blighted and vacant. But affordable housing was high on the agenda of 1970s mayor David Crombie, and despite its grittiness, St Lawrence offered prime real estate in the heart of the city. The city-hall bureaucrats were nervous about any sort of large new development; prior years and decades had already been scarred by grand efforts at urban renewal in the style of Le Corbusier and like-minded city planners around the world. Toronto's leaders had fresh memories of their own: Regent Park, a 1950s 'tower in the park' housing project near downtown, had fallen into disrepair and crime after ten years, and the 1960s high-rise development of St James Town just to the north is ridden with crime to this day.

But 1970s Toronto would be different. Jane Jacobs moved there from New York in 1968 and had already begun influencing its activists and politicians alike. Mayor Crombie and Michael Dennis, the city's housing commissioner, were eager pupils of her ideas and prepared to throw out the existing textbooks on urban planning in favour of a completely new approach. Their first move with St Lawrence was to bring in an outside architect, Alan Littlewood, at Jacobs's recommendation (perhaps his appeal was precisely that he had no formal planning degree). From the start he saw the project as a process of 'invisible mending';[43] that is, rather than raze entire city blocks and rebuild a 'utopian' community, Littlewood kept as much of the neighbourhood's original features – and historic brick character – as possible, tucking new housing in where he could among its existing roads and buildings as well as its treasured mid-nineteenth-century structures like the wedge-shaped Gooderham flatiron building, the Cathedral Church of St James, St Lawrence Hall, and St Lawrence Market, which now houses what *National Geographic* magazine has called the world's best food market.[44]

St Lawrence would come to typify the recommendations Jacobs had made in her seminal book a decade earlier. It would be more human. To prevent the *banlieue* problem à la Paris, the neighbourhood was built to appeal to a broad spectrum of individuals and families, using a variety of dwelling types – apartments, condominiums, houses – to meet the needs of residents of all ages and incomes, as both market and social housing were intermixed. And unlike most new developments at the time, which kept traffic strictly separated from pedestrians with long and wide 'superblock' roads next to large parks and plazas, St Lawrence preserved its nineteenth-century street grid of short, frequent blocks. This allows for the type of serendipitous 'street ballet' adored by Jacobs. She writes,

> *Under the seeming disorder of the old city, wherever the old city is working successfully, is a marvellous order for maintaining the safety of the streets and the freedom of the city. It is a complex order. Its essence is intricacy of sidewalk use, bringing with*

it a constant succession of eyes. This order is all composed of
movement and change, and although it is life, not art, we
may fancifully call it the art form of the city and liken it to the
dance ... an intricate ballet in which the individual dancers and
ensembles all have distinctive parts which miraculously reinforce
each other and compose an orderly whole.[45]

St Lawrence has been successful because the long-term
realities of people were put before the – often short-sighted –
needs of planners, developers and bureaucrats. Unlike many
ego-driven projects, the place is special precisely because it
doesn't immediately appear to be anything special; it's the
people who live there, flourishing, who take centre stage.[46]
Not a machine, but a neighbourhood for living.[47]

Of course, it's not feasible for most cities to rebuild themselves,
but municipal leaders needn't make large changes to their
civil infrastructure to make their neighbourhoods more
human; small improvements can have a transformative
effect. Consider dense and bustling New York. Mayor Mike
Bloomberg saw an opportunity to reduce traffic fatalities
while improving the health and happiness of cyclists and
pedestrians by adopting 'complete streets' through parts of
Manhattan. Now not only do many streets have bike lanes,
but parked cars have also been moved to their street side to
serve as a barrier between auto and bike traffic.

Meanwhile his planning commissioner, Amanda Burden,
approached the city with a new philosophy to 'tap into [her]
humanity', asking herself of public spaces: 'Would you want
to go there? Would you want to stay there?' Her answer was
a series of unique projects throughout the city to make it
more liveable and connected, transforming an old elevated
railway trestle into the High Line, a one-and-a-half-mile park

through the heart of three neighbourhoods in Manhattan's West Side, as well as over 300 acres of dilapidated waterfront into dynamic new parks.[48] She worked with transport commissioner Janette Sadik-Khan, who took the lead in experimenting with the creation of pedestrian- and cyclist-friendly streets, even closing some to create car-free plazas. Her best tactic? Designating with temporary materials, like paint, 'so if it worked better for traffic, if it was better for mobility, if it was safer, better for business, we would keep it, and if it didn't work, no harm, no foul, we could put it back the way that it was,' she says. There is 'much less anxiety when you think that something can be put back. But the results were overwhelming.'[49]

Space and function

Today, even as our public spaces on the outside give the appearance of having evolved beyond Le Corbusier cubes, the facades of most buildings merely obscure the ugly truth within: that we are living and working in machines as much as – if not more than – ever before. Too much of our built environment, both public and private, is designed to maximise overall 'efficiency' and minimise cost rather than serve our most human needs.

This inhuman approach to space contributes to any number of problems – from environmental harm and social unrest, as in Paris's *banlieues*, to poor workplace productivity. Marlon Nieuwenhuis, a psychologist at Cardiff University, found that adding plants to otherwise spartan offices increased productivity 15 per cent.[50] (Second Home London has a thousand of them.) A study by Northwestern University and the University of Illinois at Urbana-Champaign found that office workers with window exposure to natural light slept longer and better, were more physically active, and enjoyed better overall quality of life than their counterparts without.[51] Of those spaces that aren't explicitly 'broken', many just serve their minimal function – think of windowless classrooms, soulless offices, treeless streets – processing people through the day rather than providing the setting in which they can lead happier and more fulfilled lives. In a twist of irony, the machine-type spaces we live and work in are often designed to better serve other machines – cars, trucks, computers – than humans.

According to Carlo Ratti, a designer and architect who works on the nexus of technology and the physical world at MIT, technology could help change this. The original computers were so large that, to use them, people had to work in large, dark, air-conditioned rooms, often squirrelled away in basements. 'The machine determined the physical condition of the space around it,' he says. 'It was 90 per cent machine, 10 per cent human.' Now technology has literally untethered us. The advent of small, powerful and mobile devices coupled with ubiquitous wireless Internet allows us to work anywhere – even outside. And this 'ubiquitous computing' marks a profound shift in how we design spaces. There is a paradox, Carlo says, in that when technology is all around us, 'we can focus much more on the architecture, on the human side of things, and design offices, homes and buildings around people instead of around machines.'[52] Indeed, the whole reason we can discuss open-plan offices or flexible homes is because technology is no longer the limiting factor in building spaces. We can focus on our environments in other ways, like helping us to be healthier, more productive, more creative – in short, more human. And we are getting better and better at it.

Around the world school administrators, factory owners and office managers observe first-hand the difference that can be made by space designed with people in mind. It can even be a competitive advantage: Steve Jobs famously insisted that the toilets at Pixar Studios (creator of hits like *Toy Story* and *Finding Nemo*) be located in the centre of the building so people from different departments would run into each other throughout the day, sparking spontaneous human interaction and creative collaboration.

If any company understands the importance of putting people at the centre of the design process, it's furniture manufacturer Herman Miller, which makes some of the most ergonomic furniture in the world. For many years, though, the human-first principles they applied to their furniture making didn't extend to their workers. After a transformative factory redesign – infusing both the manufacturing and office areas with natural light; connecting different parts of the building by an indoor bamboo-plant-lined 'boulevard'; and adding and expanding operable windows throughout the plant – they saw employee happiness and sense of belonging skyrocket and productivity significantly improve.[53] The executives of SnowPeak, a Japanese camping-gear company, thought they would create better products if they could observe their customers using them. So the company adapted the concept of a factory store: they created a 'factory camping ground'. When they built their headquarters, they sacrificed large amounts of land around the building so loyal – and, perhaps, curious – customers could come and camp in view of the windows. As a result, product designers and makers can see exactly how their equipment is used and better understand what works and what doesn't. SnowPeak's commitment to transparency works both ways. There are no opaque walls or doors – all is glass. No space is off limits, so staff and customers can fully see what's going on and can give feedback. And although everyone can see in, all you need to do is turn toward an outside 'wall' to see the beautiful mountains beyond, a constant reminder of the company's mission to connect customers with nature.[54]

Although some aspects of space design are unequivocally 'better', different spaces suit different needs, especially in the workplace. Companies that want internal groups to work together effectively and creatively will likely want an open plan; those that want to mix up employees from different departments might add flexible seating. But where individuals need to be productive on their own, companies might want to keep the traditional model, or at least a more enlightened variant of it.[55] That means considering employees' needs, not just the corporate view. Open-space offices might boost creativity, but they can also create anxiety, with employees paranoid that their bosses are watching what they're up to. Balancing open and private space is critical; employees need room for themselves, whether to think, work, or simply have a phone call without fear of eavesdroppers. In one recent survey 88 per cent of the most satisfied workers were those who could work where they wanted.[56] The key, as Rohan is showing in Second Home, is to give workers a choice so they can adjust to their own preferences.

The power of space to enhance creativity, productivity or employee health needn't be limited to the workplace, though. Thoughtful architects have shown that extending more human design to our schools can improve pupils' performance as well. It should come as no surprise that in Finland, whose excellent schools we discussed in Chapter 3, educators are equally thoughtful about school design. School architects in Helsinki consider questions such as whether the structure allows pupils and staff to break their routines and try new things; whether the environment fosters creativity, enabling observation and investigation of everyday phenomena; whether the building protects against violence and bullying; and even whether the school welcomes visiting parents.[57]

Space as solution

Spaces, as we have seen, can have an immense impact on daily life and can help us be more human in our homes, workplaces and play spaces. But they can also help solve social and environmental problems. In 1982 James Q. Wilson and George L. Kelling put forward their famous 'broken windows' theory – that visible, physical signs of disorder signal crime as an acceptable norm, perpetuating further crime. Small fixes to the physical environment, such as cleaning up graffiti and litter as well as repairing broken street furniture like park benches, can have more of an impact on crime than direct police intervention or increased social services.[58]

In Lowell, Massachusetts, authorities identified thirty-four crime 'hot spots' and proceeded to clean half of them up. They found that in the half where litter was collected and debris removed, there was a 20 per cent drop in police calls.[59] At the University of Groningen in the Netherlands psychologists repeatedly left an envelope with a €5 note clearly visible inside half-sticking out of a postbox. When the street was orderly, 13 per cent of passers-by took it (the rest pushed it back in); when litter surrounded the area, 25 per cent took it; and when the postbox itself was covered in graffiti, the number increased to 27 per cent. Disorder on the street doubled the propensity of passers-by to become thieves.[60/61]

Street-level nudges can be remarkably effective for other problems as well. Sweden's Vision Zero programme, which

aims to eliminate road deaths, has given Sweden one of
the best road-safety records in the world.[62] Since it started
in 1997, annual road deaths have come down by four-fifths
compared to 1965, despite a doubling of traffic.[63] Vision
Zero has a simple but radically human-centred message: 'In
every situation a person might fail, the road system should
not.'[64] The Swedes have thus tried to design a road system
nationwide that aims to maintain and increase mobility but
never at the expense of people's lives. They understand that
people make mistakes, but they believe that death should
not be the consequence. This is not, the Swedes argue, any
different from how we approach other systems: 'If you take a
nuclear power station, aviation, a rail system, all of them are
based on the idea that they are operated by people who can
make a mistake,' says Claes Tingvall of the Swedish National
Road Administration. With that in mind, roads are designed
in Sweden so that although mistakes might cause an accident,
there are no fatalities or serious injuries. 'You have to take the
human in our behaviour into account when you design the
road transport system. It is understanding that we will never
be perfect,' says Tingvall. For example, knowing that drivers
will try to overtake other cars on two-lane roads, Sweden has
installed '2+1' roads, where each direction of traffic takes
turns using a middle third lane to overtake. In its first decade
that one improvement saved 145 lives.[65]

My favourite example of more human design for public
space is from the Netherlands. Consider how Amsterdam
became one of the most bike- and pedestrian-friendly cities
in the world, with cars used for only 22 per cent of all trips
(the rest are by bike, public transport or foot).[66] In the
early 1970s Amsterdam was like most urban environments
around the world: traffic clogged and dangerous. At rush
hour streets resembled car parks, and the air was choked

with exhaust fumes. Car accidents killed more than 3,000 people annually across Holland in the early 1970s, including over 500 children.[67] In 1972 one group of children living in central Amsterdam had had enough. The neighbourhood called De Pijp ('the pipe') was about a hundred years old, five times denser than the rest of the city, and not built for the cars that the 40,000 inhabitants brought with them and filled the streets with.[68] Pupils at one of the local schools started a petition to make the streets less convenient for cars and safer for children like them, launching a campaign that quickly outgrew the tiny classroom from which it started. They even took matters into their own hands, temporarily closing a street to physically demonstrate the need for a safe place to play.

This was part of the birth of a larger movement, Stop de Kindermoord ('stop child murder'), that would transform streets in Amsterdam and greater Holland. It wasn't easy – there's a famous video of an irate driver picking up and throwing aside a roadblock which children had erected to turn a small part of a street into a car-free zone. Despite the violent backlash against the anti-car campaign, the children, supported by their teacher, stuck to their guns. All they wanted was a safe place to play. And through their action they started a worldwide urban design movement that today has mainstreamed pedestrian zones, bike lanes, street furniture, tree planting and so on. The children recognised that the space they lived in was not designed for their human needs – to play, to walk to school, and to socialise with their friends and families – and they did something about it. One group of children, in one school in Amsterdam. What a lovely, inspiring tale of more human social change.

In many cases making space more human is really just about recognising how people actually behave in certain contexts – as opposed to how we assume they do – and designing our environments with this in mind. A Stanford University project that Jason (the Jason who, along with his brother Scott, helped me write this book) was involved in, designing a 'concept home' that would be net-zero-energy, shows how a human-centred approach can help solve environmental problems too. Jason first mapped all the places where people interact with their homes in ways that consume energy – light switches, thermostats and so on. His team's key insight was that few people actually want to waste resources; we just do so because there are small, seemingly insignificant barriers that, for reasons of forgetfulness, lack of attention or even just laziness, get in our way. If the team could remove as many of these barriers as possible, people's intention to either save money, do good for the environment or simply avoid waste would be less impeded.

Of the handful of innovative products his team developed and built in the house, my favourite was a 'room switch' that would make the people at Nest (producers of beautiful and practical home services like thermostats) blush. 'We wanted to rethink the whole idea of the light switch,' Jason says. There are all sorts of different electronic items plugged into the wall that draw energy, even when they're off – device chargers, televisions, kitchen appliances. Jason and his team wanted to design a 'light' switch that worked for the whole room, one that could turn everything off, not just the lights. 'Simplicity was important – part of the reason people don't unplug things is because it's a pain.' The solution, as is so often the case, lay right in front of them. Most of the team had Apple laptops, which have what are called 'trackpads'. Inspired, they built a similar control in place of where a light switch would normally be: instead of a toggle switch or even a screen, you touch an opaque surface. As Jason puts it, 'You can achieve an incredible amount of functionality based on your gestures and how many fingers you use to draw them, all without automating away users' agency.' Yet most importantly, with any 'room switch', it just took one touch to turn off every electrical appliance in a room or even put the whole house 'to sleep'.

Spaces and human impact

'First life, then spaces, then buildings – the other way around never works.' At seventy-nine years old, Danish architect Jan Gehl still has strong opinions about the way our cities are designed. He's spent the past fifty years developing the principles of what makes a city 'liveable' and leading an unwavering campaign for 'architecture that considers human scale and interaction'.[69]

I was fortunate to be introduced to Gehl's work by Richard Rogers, who, along with the great British architect, Thomas Heatherwick, has taught me so much about architecture and urban design and is a fantastic champion for the future of cities. 'Cities – like books – can be read, and Jan Gehl understands their language,' he writes in the foreword to Gehl's book, *Cities for People*. 'The street, the footpath, the square, and the park are the grammar of the city; they provide the structure that enables cities to come to life, and to encourage and accommodate diverse activities, from the quiet and contemplative to the noisy and busy. A humane city – with carefully designed streets, squares and parks – creates pleasure for visitors and passers-by, as well as for those who live, work, and play there every day.' Denser and more sustainable cities, Rogers adds, are the future, but only if we build them with space to walk, cycle and breathe in, with 'beautiful public spaces that are human in scale, sustainable, healthy and lively'.[70] Like the thinking of Jane Jacobs, Rogers's and Gehl's philosophies of cities resonate with me deeply.

It turns out that Gehl might not have learned the language of cities at all had love not intervened. It was 1960, and like all formally trained architects at the time, he was perfectly prepared to build exactly those types of 'modern cities' that Jane Jacobs would soon complain about, cities that, in his words, were full of 'high rises and a lot of lawns and good open space – good windy spaces'.[71] Had he not met Ingrid Mundt, a psychologist who would become his wife, his life might have turned out drastically different. As someone who studied 'people rather than bricks' as Gehl puts it, Mundt inspired a host of conversations among their combined peers. Why weren't architects interested in people? Why weren't they paying attention to how architecture could 'influence people's lives'? Why couldn't they work out how to make cities that would make people happier?

Gehl's philosophy was forever changed. 'Brasilia, the capital of Brazil, is a great example,' he said. 'From the air it's very interesting. It's interesting for a bird or eagle. From the helicopter view, it has got wonderful districts with sharp and precise government buildings and residential buildings. However, nobody spent three minutes to think about what Brasilia would look like at the eye level ... Nobody was responsible for looking after the people.'[72]

In 1965 they created the PSPL, a 'public space/public life' survey in Siena, Italy. The initial goal was simple: keep track of the number of people in a public space and what they were using it for.[73] Such 'street-level' observations would inform recommendations for improvements to various neighbourhoods. Fast-forward half a century, and Gehl has now surveyed cities around the world. His focus is almost entirely on considering the city, however large, at the human scale. To him that's the only way to understand the effect architecture ultimately has on people.

From São Paulo and Amman to Brighton and New York, Gehl and his team spend weeks surveying people at all times of day, watching how they interact with the urban space in question – where they walk, where they spend time, what they do. Just as in Siena, he and his firm can take this base knowledge and use it to advise clients on questions of urban design and master-planning. In all these years his goal remains the same: create 'cities for people'. Through this work Gehl has created a list of twelve criteria for any public space, based on what he and his colleagues believe are the things people need from their urban environments. They span three categories: *protection* (from traffic, crime and pollution); *comfort* (to be able to walk, stand or sit, converse and play without impediment), and *enjoyment* (of the weather – hot, cold, rain or snow – and of aesthetic qualities). Their approach is meticulous, combining highly studious ethnography with traditional surveys to capture every on-the-ground detail. In one project aimed at improving London's walkability, surveyors counted thousands of pedestrians, measured precise distances between kerbs and pavement obstacles, like rubbish bins and street poles, and keenly observed every sort of behaviour they could catalogue, from mothers enlisting passers-by to help carry a pushchair down steps, to how many people cross against a red signal. They even compare measurements between weekdays and weekends, summer and winter. Though they don't provide a score per se, their reports are exhaustive, combining qualitative and quantitative elements, including photographs, charts and annotated maps to give planners a sense of where they are strong and where they are deficient in each category.[74]

To do this for every space, from schools to offices, houses to neighbourhoods, would be extreme. But Gehl is on to something. We don't need specific measurements or a points system to be able to assess whether a space fulfils human needs; acknowledging them during its design is half the battle. So here's a simple way for us to make our spaces more human. Today every building that's constructed has, at the very least, basic safety standards it has to pass as well as extra hurdles like environmental impact reports. On top of that, almost every type of space is subject to seemingly endless rules and regulations, standards and requirements.

What I propose is far simpler: a report, nothing too long or onerous – let's call it a Human Impact Report. No specific regulations or requirements. Just a short, straightforward statement of how any development – home, office, city block or neighbourhood redevelopment – fulfils each of Gehl's twelve criteria. In the spirit of 'nudging' outlined in Chapter 2, the point here is not to create another layer of burdensome bureaucracy; rather, if architects, planners, designers, builders and engineers are prompted to start thinking along these lines, that simple act will end up making a difference – because it will make people think. It will make people think about people. And when this becomes part of the planning vernacular, when buyers, tenants, residents, citizens, and everyone else who occupies a space is exposed to these questions – and how builders answer them – 'human-ness' will become a real competitive advantage. Imagine that: a system in which developers and builders and architects and urban planners compete with each other to make the world around us more human.

That's a world I'd want to call home.

CHAPTER 12

NATURE

There's a classic speech that American park rangers deliver whenever they catch a child trying to make off with a 'natural' souvenir. 'You are supposed to calmly kneel down and say, "I saw you picking the flower. That is so pretty! Now think about what would happen if every child picked a flower,"' explains Matthew Browning, a former park ranger at North Carolina's Mount Mitchell State Park. 'And then they are supposed to have this moment of guilt.' One day in 2009 Browning saw a fellow ranger give the speech to a boy, about eight years old, in the park's restaurant. Instead of picking flowers, the boy had picked up a small handful of 'rocks'. In fact, it was gravel that the rangers had bought at the local supply store to spread over the road. Browning had an epiphany. 'It made me sick. The boy was crestfallen. He was so excited about coming to the park that he wanted to take a little memento back with him. More than feeling empowered or excited to protect the natural world, now he is going to associate going to state parks with getting into trouble.'[1]

But it's not just picking flowers and rocks that get you into trouble. Mount Mitchell – and most parks, for that matter – prohibit all sorts of things: going off the official footpath, climbing trees, shouting, playing with sticks, digging holes …

you name it. Disillusioned, Browning left the park and enrolled in graduate school to study the recreational use of natural areas. Hearing about so-called nature play areas in Europe where children are allowed to play with abandon, he set off to Sweden to observe some first-hand. He ended up finding one near just about every primary school he visited (Sweden has a lot of forests). 'They all had plenty of forest and plenty of kids playing in the woods.' Browning didn't interact much with the children, preferring to observe rather than interrupt. But one day he met a twelve-year-old boy. 'He was talking about how he would break branches and build forts and throw rocks,' Browning said. 'He had a knife with him. He said: "I carve sticks into spears and stuff like that."' So Browning asked him whether he would ever stick the knife into a tree. The boy was shocked: '"No! It would hurt the tree; it would hurt the tree just like it would hurt me."'

This twelve-year-old's instinct highlights the human instinct of wanting to connect with nature. In 1984 the world's leading evolutionary biologist E. O. Wilson introduced the biophilia hypothesis: the human 'urge to affiliate with other forms of life'.[2] He uses it to explain the fact that for much of human history, we've surrounded ourselves with plants and animals, either domesticated in our homes, gardens and communities, or close by in adjacent parks. You even see it in zoos, where animals exhibit unnatural behaviour when their pens don't mimic the natural environments from which they come.[3] It's an inborn desire we all share.

Indeed, study after study has substantiated the important beneficial effects of nature on human health and well-being. Views of nature and natural settings reduce stress and improve attention – walking in it even more so.[4] Though running reduces anxiety and depression wherever it is done, Swedish researchers have found the effects are amplified when it is done in nature.[5] In a Pennsylvania hospital, patients with a view of trees had shorter stays, by almost a day on average, and required fewer pain medications than those in rooms facing a brick wall.[6]

Unnatural behaviour

Despite nature's great importance to us, for most of our history we've gone out of our way to conquer the natural world. We've tilled the land, hunted and then domesticated animals, cut down forests, dammed rivers, mined mountains, built cities. Now we're manipulating genetics with biotechnology and even toying with the idea of engineering the climate – to fix the damage we ourselves have inflicted. We have tried to bend nature to human will. We have tried to make nature ... more human.

For generations this relationship worked because the scale and power of nature so exceeded that of human civilisation. Our efforts to surmount nature enabled our survival and progress as a species without, it seemed, doing nature much harm. But that has changed as we have become more mechanised and industrialised. As humanity began to outpace its natural context, the costs of our way of doing things became apparent. We saw pollution, spoilt landscapes and filthy cities. In 1952 London was hit by the Great Smog, a combination of cold weather and windless conditions that trapped air pollution, mostly from burning coal, for four days in and around the city, creating smog so thick that it is estimated to have prematurely killed at least 4,000 people.[7] A similar event killed nineteen people in Donora, a small mill town in southwestern Pennsylvania, just four years before that. There, weather conditions led to toxic smoke from the town's steel and zinc mills blanketing the town for five days in a row.[8]

We reacted, the pendulum swung a bit toward conservation, and we cleaned things up. A bit. Earlier progressives like John Muir and Theodore Roosevelt had championed the cause of nature, greatly expanding its protection through the National Park system.[9] But the inexorable march of industry went on throughout the twentieth century. A decade that saw a high-water mark of environmental awareness and activism in the 1960s and 1970s – Earth Day, the Environmental Protection Agency, the *Clean Air* and *Water Acts*, and, of course, the publication of Rachel Carson's *Silent Spring* – then receded into an era of cheap plastics, mass manufacturing, and ever-growing urban sprawl and fossil-fuel consumption. As quickly as we learned our lessons, it seems, we forgot them. So today we live with a tomorrow that has never been more at risk.

Humanity's hubris – our hubris – was thinking that we could endlessly extract from nature with little or no adverse consequences. Our fundamental mistake, according to the influential twentieth-century economist E. F. Schumacher, was to treat nature like an infinite bank account from which we could forever make withdrawals. But such an adversarial relationship is a fallacy: if man won his battle with nature, 'he would find himself on the losing side'.[10] Despite our best efforts, there's just no way to bend all of nature's vast, incomprehensible complexity to our human rules and institutions. We have to realise that nature isn't just humanity's support structure; humanity is a part of nature. Our careless manipulation of it is not only unnatural; it is irrevocably harmful both to nature and, ultimately, to ourselves.

We've now destroyed nearly one-fifth of the Amazon rainforest – more than three times the land area of the entire UK.[11] We lose over 20 million acres of tropical forest per year.[12] We dump an estimated 4 to 12 million tons of plastic into our oceans every year.[13] Rather than biodegrade – the way organic material would – plastic just breaks down into smaller and smaller pieces, devastating the wildlife that ingests it. Coral reefs occupy less than a quarter of 1 per cent of the marine environment but house a quarter of known fish species. In the 1970s live coral covered half of the Caribbean's reefs; today it covers 8 per cent of them.[14] According to the International Union for Conservation of Nature's latest Red List of Threatened Species, 41 per cent of amphibians and 26 per cent of mammals are currently under threat of extinction. Precision is difficult, as many species are still undiscovered, but estimates suggest we are losing between 500 and 36,000 species each year.[15]

One of the most impactful meetings I ever had was when Rohan took me to meet E. O. Wilson at Harvard University. He is one of the first theorists to discuss and advocate for 'biodiversity' – that is, variation among genes within species, species within ecosystems, and ecosystems among each other. As he puts it, we risk losing '"genetic encyclopedias" millions of years in the making',[16] embodying countless medical, biotechnical and agricultural opportunities (e.g., 49 per cent of cancer-fighting drugs are derived from nature).[17] According to Wilson, we stand to reduce at least half of the Earth's remaining plant and animal species to extinction or critical endangerment by the end of the century. Such cataclysms – of which the Earth has had five so far, the last one having brought an end to the dinosaurs – take 5 to 10 million years to repair. 'We are, in short, flying blind into the environmental future,' Wilson says.[18]

To forestall the sixth mass-extinction event of which he speaks, we have to get more serious about conservation. According to a December 2014 assessment by the science journal *Nature*, a loss of 690 species per week, the upper end of estimates, would bring such an event about by the year 2200.[19] Wilson's bold vision – what he calculates is necessary to avoid ruinous biodiversity loss[20] – is to set aside half of the Earth for conservation or restoration ('Half Earth'). Crucially, it's not just making sure that land already out of civilisation's way remains protected (though this is important); it's making sure that all of the world's ecosystems have at least some protected areas where nature can 'do its thing'. In some cases this will require restoration; in others it might mean paying landowners to ensure parts of their land remain undeveloped but still accessible for light use. It also means threading these protected areas together so that as habitats shift with a changing climate, wildlife is able to migrate – perhaps hundreds or even thousands of miles through accessible 'corridors', like the White Hawk Project adjoining the Corcovado National Park in Costa Rica.[21] In order to preserve the park's incredible biodiversity – some 2.5 per cent of the world's total – the White Hawk Project purchases and maintains land abutting the park in order to create wildlife corridors using conservation easements, which restrict development and land use for ecological benefit.

When our family, along with Rohan and his wife, Kate, vacationed near the park in April 2015, we learned about the White Hawk Project first-hand from Lana Wedmore, our ecolodge's owner and the project's founder. What is so amazing – but equally frustrating – about Lana's work is that compared to the massive sums spent by government (often ineffectively) fighting climate change, she's asking for a pittance. And yet here is a solution that not only contributes to global climate efforts but also conserves land for ever and tangibly saves species from extinction – today. Even more tangibly, visiting the Corcovado National Park exposed all of us to the rainforest and showed us first-hand the true value of nature and its protection. This kind of direct exposure to nature has got to be the best way to instil in everyone – especially children – a conservation ethos that lasts a lifetime.

It seems hardly necessary by now to justify why this would be worthwhile. The unknown human value that will one day derive from the biodiversity preserved – and stimulated – by a globally connected wilderness alone makes ambitions like Half Earth and projects like White Hawk easy to justify. But it's also the benefit of having truly natural nature (such a phrase would seem ridiculous if it weren't necessary) local to everyone. We would be infusing our modern, sophisticated landscape with pristine nature, side by side, everywhere.

Throughout this book I've discussed how we need to make our world more human. But when it comes to nature, we've already made the world too human. We've distorted our idea of what nature is and should be because we've misunderstood our part in it. So now we need to fundamentally rethink humanity's relationship with the natural world and move the pendulum back towards the system of our ancestors, in which we benefit from nature while simultaneously giving back to and coexisting with it.

Natural capital

Nature isn't just beautiful; it's practical. Nature can help us prevent floods, dampen tidal waves, filter water and clean the air. Engineers – not just environmentalists – are increasingly recognising nature as a way to provide essential services we otherwise would trust to machines and concrete and steel. It actually has a term devoted to it: green infrastructure. Nature provides many 'services' to us when left in its natural state. For example, it saves our lives and communities in times of natural disaster. Flooding and storm surges can be softened, if not stopped, by wetlands and marshes that absorb the brunt of the impact. When authorities built sea walls to protect against annual floods in the Humber estuary in Yorkshire and in Lincolnshire, they inadvertently killed off the wetlands that had formed natural barriers. So when flood waters hit, the walls held back some water but, without the wetlands to block the storm surge, flooding was actually worse. To solve the problem, sea walls have now been deliberately breached so that the wetlands can return to their natural state, a move that will create around £11.5 million of net benefit over the next fifty years in terms of saved farmland and property compared to the damage the standing sea wall would have led to.[22] In Boston the Army Corps of Engineers found that annual flooding of the Charles River would cost $17 million a year if not for wetlands protecting the city.[23] Wetlands can be particularly crucial during extreme events: a long-standing rule of thumb holds that for every 2.7 miles of wetlands, a hurricane storm surge can be reduced by as much as a foot.[24] When Hurricane Katrina hit New Orleans in 2005, it found a city built out too far to the ocean's edge, with 1,900 square miles of natural wetlands having been destroyed and developed between true land and the Gulf of Mexico.[25] Without these natural shock absorbers, the flooding wasn't just destructive; it was devastating. Thankfully some wetlands were still intact; scientists estimate that if there had been none left, the flood waters would have been 1 to 2 metres higher.[26]

Although some environmentalists might scoff at putting a price on nature, not to do so is to completely devalue it and let others take advantage – and destroy – its enormous wealth. Depleting natural resources might not cost money, but it isn't 'free'. Take, for example, the conversion of mangrove swamps in southern Thailand into shrimp farms. One report found that such conversions yield around $1,220 a hectare. But these profits fail to consider the costs of losing the mangroves. After five years the farm is depleted, requiring intensive and expensive rehabilitation. And while they are being used as shrimp farms, the mangrove swamps fail to provide wood for local communities, nurseries for local fish farming and a barrier against storms. In total, one study found the implicit costs equal $12,392 a hectare, over ten times more than the profits reaped from shrimp farming.[27] Yet because the costs are borne by the 'public' while the profits are earned privately, the decision was a foregone conclusion: profits were made, natural capital was lost, the community suffered. The argument – and a compelling plan – for rigorously accounting for nature is brilliantly set out in *Natural Capital*, the latest book published by economist Dieter Helm (my tutor at Oxford). Simply implementing his approach would make more practical difference than any number of international environmental conferences.

Nature doesn't only mitigate the impacts of future disasters; it also provides us with essential services every day, often cheaper and more reliably than man-made infrastructure can. In the American state of Maine about 15 per cent of the population, mostly in the greater Portland area, gets its water from Sebago Lake. The lake covers 30,000 acres, and the area that supplies it is more than fifty miles long.[28] Because of the area's pristine condition, the Portland Water District has long operated under a federal waiver allowing it to draw its water without many of the typical filtration requirements that are otherwise necessary in other geographies. Recently, though, the lake's water quality has deteriorated, as run-off from upstream land development and population growth has increased. The typical approach would be to invest in 'grey' infrastructure, so-called because of the colour of the excessive cement usually involved – in this case, 'membrane filtration' technology. An analysis by the World Resources Institute found that this would cost between $102 million and $146 million. Investing instead in conservation and restoration of the surrounding forest ecosystem – green infrastructure – at a cost of between $34 million and $74 million would deliver $70 million in savings.[29] It turns out that natural forest land is just more efficient at keeping our water clean (one study estimates that for every 10 per cent increase in forest cover in a source area, there is a corresponding decrease of about 20 per cent in water treatment costs).[30] And yet our human habits, Australian ecological economist Robert Costanza estimates, destroy $23 trillion each year of the $142.7 trillion in these 'services' that our natural ecosystems provide us – not just clean air and water and storm protection but also waste decomposition, crop pollination, renewable energy sources and raw materials, to name a few.[31]

Despite these powerful arguments, the environmental movement is losing. People understand what they can see, hear, touch and smell. At that level I think most people really do care about the environment, even if they hate green politics and can't stand talk of climate change. I've yet to meet someone who is in favour of dirty air and water, dead forests or poisoned landscapes. Or someone who doesn't enjoy, if they get the chance, spending time in the mountains, at a lake or at the beach. Behaviour that could be described as 'environmentalist' is really just showing our love of nature. Pretty much everyone is in favour of that. But by branding and politicising environmentalism, we've made good stewardship a question of saving the entire planet: an unrelatable idea.

So although our local actions do indeed have global impacts, these impacts have to be talked about at the human scale, otherwise their real meaning becomes obscure.

Climate change doesn't mean 'global sea-level rise' (though this may happen); it means that farmers lose their crops and livelihoods, entire species of animals and plants are lost forever, and the sea will wipe out centuries-old villages.

The other problem with the big global-environmental argument is that it diffuses responsibility. Elinor Ostrom won the Nobel Prize in economics for demonstrating the tragedy of the commons, in which behaviour that benefits the individual at the group's expense leads to everyone doing it until the whole group is out of luck. This phenomenon is exacerbated when problems are made to seem big; the individual actions we take to both create and to solve the problems have the illusion of insignificance. Noble as fighting for 'parts per million' is, it just doesn't mean anything if you're not a scientist. We have to make sure nature is accessible to everyone, so everyone can have their own experiences, their own memories to draw from, their own reason to care that we don't destroy it all.

As much as the communications revolution – not to mention high-definition television – has enabled us to more vividly experience exotic ecosystems and animals across the world, there is no substitute for the real thing. The key to making us environmentalists, conservationists, good stewards – or, really, just conscientious human beings – is exposure to what we otherwise wouldn't care about. So the answer to the threat to nature is not a new law, a new government programme, an ad campaign, or any of the other traditional levers of bureaucratic action; it's something more human than all of that. It's the simple act of being in nature, walking in nature, playing in nature, getting out into nature, seeing the world's wonder. When you begin to comprehend your place on the planet in the midst of everyone and everything else, it all suddenly comes into perspective. But of course, this theme has been true throughout the book: empathy through human connection and experience.

This is what politicians and conservationists have got wrong. Although often well meaning, their efforts have morphed the environmental movement into Big Green, the bureaucracy and politics of which have needlessly made the environment a contested and partisan issue. The environment should not be a battlefield of Left versus Right; it's actually about loving the world we live in, our home. People – all people – want blue skies and clean air and safe water, but you'll never convince people to be greener if you make it all about carbon dioxide or a couple of degrees Celsius. We have to highlight how nature can actually, tangibly help us in our own daily lives. 'Green' means animals, parks, the countryside. It's about where people want to go on vacation or spend free time with their families. It's about the joy of fresh air and beautiful scenery.

'Shopping is not a hobby'

Connecting people with nature will become ever more urgent as humanity continues to urbanise. Since 1950 the urban population has increased from 30 per cent of the global population to 54 per cent today, and it is expected to reach 66 per cent by 2050.[32] Cities represent a prosperous and, in some respects, more sustainable future. But for all its modern, hipster vibe, urbanisation comes with a significant drawback: the more we live in cities, the further we are from nature and the closer we get to forgetting its importance altogether. We risk what some are calling 'nature deficit disorder'.[33]

But how do you persuade people to change? At the moment we fail miserably at distilling nature into human terms, resulting in dangerous abstraction. We need to bring people's interaction with nature back to a human, visceral level. Nature must be experienced by the human touch.

But getting people into nature is a big hurdle. I've seen it at first-hand. When I grew up, spending time in nature was not the social norm. Now, here in Northern California, where it is very much part of the culture, I've chosen, for the first time in my life, to do strange things for a confirmed urbanite – like go camping. Camping! How horrific. Actually not. It is no exaggeration to say that our children and their friends are never happier than when they are out in the woods or wherever we go in nature. It is cheaper – and better – than any number of toys or trips to theme parks or visitor attractions.

That's why we should start with children. It's not just about a respect for and understanding of the natural world, its importance to us, and the necessity of sustainability and conservation. It also helps child development. Children need to engage in the world if they are to be properly educated. As we saw in Chapter 10, a significant part of their development comes from exploration and adventure, and there is no better place to do that than out in nature.

Many parents understand this but don't know how to go about it. There are too many barriers to getting their children into nature, many of which are simply inherent in our inhuman world today: families live too far away from natural spaces, parents have unrealistic fears of the outdoors, teachers lack enthusiasm for leaving the classroom, technology too easily entertains and distracts.[34] The key is to start the process early, with a proper communication of the interconnection between nature and society. Jason and Scott fondly remember their grandparents sending them the magazines *Your Big Backyard* and *Ranger Rick*, published by the National Wildlife Federation in America, which, by helping them understand the importance of nature as children, made them lifelong environmentalists. Those magazines worked because they explained nature in children's terms.

The same principle guides author Christiane Dorion, who has developed a creative way to communicate complex environmental and scientific concepts through her pop-up children's books. 'Children are naturally interested in the natural world,' she explains, so she tries to identify 'the questions they are interested in learning about'. And it turns out that children are indeed fascinated by the water cycle and weather patterns – just not when described in those words. Instead, Dorion poses questions that children have actually asked her: Where does rain come from? What's inside the Earth? How do plants live? She then answers them in surprisingly rich detail while keeping it all age accessible. They might not understand biodiversity loss or climate change, but they come to intuit how small things in their lives connect directly to a wider world.[35]

If applied correctly, technology, like Dorion's books, can play a helpful role too. Researchers at Stanford, MIT and Harvard are working on various projects to create virtual-reality simulators that put users directly into otherwise inaccessible natural circumstances. One simulation created at Stanford transforms users into a pink coral, so they can see what happens to reefs over time. During the simulation, sea urchins, sea snails and fish interact around 'you'. Over the course of thirteen minutes the simulation progresses through a century, and the environment changes around the reef as it is degraded by acidification, an urgent problem currently facing all the world's oceans.[37] Species present at the start disappear, and even the pink coral skeleton that the users embody disintegrates. Early studies suggest that conveying the gravity of human effects on the environment in such a personal way has a significant impact on attitudes, which the researchers confirmed in follow-ups with participants afterwards.[38] 'One can viscerally experience disparate futures and get first-hand experience about the consequences of human behaviour,' says Jeremy Bailenson, the director of Stanford's Virtual Human Interaction Lab, which ran the simulation.[38] And with the advent of virtual-reality headsets like Oculus VR, zoos, parks and schools can increasingly use these technologies to complement their real-world programmes.

The studies done around virtual reality prove that we need to empathise with nature to care about it. But it's also pretty ridiculous that we have to reduce nature to a virtual-reality headset. All the book learning in the world won't change the simple fact that children need to touch nature for themselves. It must be palpable, emotional and experienced first-hand. That's why programmes like Vida Verde are so crucial to this effort.

Vida Verde is an educational camp and organic farm in California's Santa Cruz Mountains dedicated to getting children from all backgrounds into nature. 'There are thousands of children who live thirty miles from the ocean, and they've never actually seen it,' explains Laura Sears, who founded the organisation with her husband, Shawn, in 2001. 'We've seen kids who come to Vida Verde who've never spent time walking on uneven surfaces.' Shawn and Laura bring groups of children from different inner-city schools in the San Francisco area for three days and two nights to their 23-acre property. The children learn experientially, classifying plants and animals on walks, learning about mammals while milking the resident goats, as well as birds while collecting hens' eggs, and understanding the sea while running barefoot in the sand (many for the first time in their lives) or exploring rock pools – all in the same lesson, of course. 'It's a beautiful thing to let these children start to discover and explore and let their guard down,' Laura says, 'and just be in this gorgeous environment that they maybe never thought they'd ever get to be in.'

'Kids do really well being outside, using all their senses and bodies to learn, not just reading something or hearing it,' Shawn explains. Being there and doing it makes it real for them. For the first time they can really connect to the place where they live, and from then on their teachers can use this in the classroom to connect lessons to real life. Teachers report that children engage in their studies as they haven't in the past. Perhaps more importantly than this, nature can be harnessed as a tool for teaching very human lessons about relationships, trying new things, determination and working together. In one activity, the goat hike, small groups of students use teamwork to herd resident goats across a river, through the thistles and up a mile-long hill on a steep, sometimes tricky path. 'It's a physical challenge. They simply have to work together to make it,' says Shawn. 'You see students who don't necessarily talk or hang out with each other otherwise doing it because it's needed. People just breaking down and treating each other like human beings – and walking away from the experience with fresh eyes for those around them and new friends.'[39] Such programmes are so important. Jason and Scott – Northern Californians themselves – remember that when they were sixth graders (they're twins), everyone in their grade went to a place like Vida Verde, where many of them camped for the first time. They spent a week hiking, exploring marshland, running basic experiments in the forest, not to mention growing emotionally by being away from their parents for the first time. Nearly every public school in the region participates in such programmes, providing a valuable link to nature for countless schoolchildren.

You can predict the objections. 'Well, that's all very well if you live in Northern California in one of the richest and most naturally beautiful places on Earth, but what about the real world where you don't have incredible nature on your doorstep? Or incredible wealth to preserve it? Or incredibly rich families who can pay to send their kids to experience it?'

Well, here's the thing: none of this is pre-ordained or determined by geography, finances or anything else. It's about priorities.

At the moment, across the world, consumerism is the social norm and nature is not. We choose to build Westfield shopping centres. Why? Why do we need more of those? Why do we think it's acceptable for children to spend a weekend afternoon going shopping? As my sister-in-law, Kate Whetstone, once pithily remarked, 'Shopping is not a hobby.' But for many people in rich countries today, that's exactly what it is. We can change that. The norm has certainly flipped before: when workers spent most of their time in the fields, bronzed by the sun, the elite stayed inside. But with the advent of the factory and then the office cubicle, that norm switched. Once workers' skins grew pale under artificial lights, the rich jumped at any chance they could to develop a tan, setting themselves apart – the 'leisure' class. Now people with money buy homes in the country, houses by the beach, lodges in the mountains, villas on the lake. The rich have made nature fashionable, with eco-tourism and luxury brands and philanthropy. They wouldn't think of keeping their kids inside all the time. But the outdoors shouldn't be a function of fashion; it should be something everyone enjoys, from the richest to the poorest, that everyone rightly feels entitled to experience as a human, without stigma. We must choose to make this a priority; we must choose to collectively pay for it; we must choose to require it. Nature should be a fundamental part of our human experience. More than anything else, nature should unify us.

But right now it divides us. The second you suggest that everyone else should get better access to nature, it's suddenly just that – a luxury, a waste of money that we can't afford – because, gosh, what would happen to those SAT scores? Why? Why is nature a necessity for rich people but a luxury for poor people? Why is nature less important for students than maths or art or history?

One of the many reasons I would love to be mayor of a city is to show what can happen when we take a radically different – a revolutionarily different – approach to land use. When it comes to the physical presence of nature in our lives, we could easily incorporate woodlands and wetlands and natural habitats right in the middle of our towns and cities. Not just parks, but real, wild nature. There are some great examples: in Los Angeles I visited the Ballona Wetlands near Playa del Rey. Here, where you'd least expect it – in bustling LA, surrounded by a highway to the east, private homes to the south, a strip mall to the north, and a tourist beach to the west – are 600 acres of open space that state officials are trying to restore to their former glory. The wetlands here once stretched for miles in either direction up and down the coast but were carved out into developments around fifty years ago. Even in Ballona there is hardly any wetland left. For centuries Berliners have enjoyed the Grunewald forest, covering more than 7,000 acres in the western part of the German capital. In Knoxville, Tennessee, locals recently championed the preservation of 1,000 acres of forest along the Tennessee River waterfront. Just three miles from downtown, residents and visitors there can use its more than forty miles of trails to walk, mountain bike, run or just explore. And of course, there's London's Hampstead Heath, 790 acres of rambling hills and woodland, dearly loved by dogs and visitors alike.

But these are exceptions. How about designing a world where they're not?

If we do make space for nature in the midst of our modern world, how do we make sure children grow up in it, not through a once-a-year field trip, but all the time? Well, we know exactly how to do it – we just need to make the choice. There are countless national and local organisations, notably the Scouts and Cubs and Girl Guides, dedicated to giving children fun experiences in nature. We could easily make nature an expectation for every child, just as we expect them to learn maths or, now, coding. It's actually more important than either of those or any other academic subject, because the kinds of experiences you gain when you spend time in nature, with others, help build your character in ways that are far more useful in the twenty-first century than anything academic.[40] But instead we insist on locking children up in windowless, soulless boxes from eight in the morning for the rest of the day. Madness. But amid the strange priorities that have infected today's world, it's the argument I'm making – that we should expect all children to spend time in nature as a basic, substantial part of their education – that's more likely to be seen as crazy.

Nature must be made more accessible in another way too. Remember North Carolina park ranger Matthew Browning and the twelve-year-old boy he saw being chastised for playing in nature? The way things stand now, nature is a museum, where we can look but not touch. How do we expect to get excited about nature if we can't engage with it? The typical sheltered life of the twenty-first-century family might make us feel safer, but we are not better off as a result. We cannot survive without nature; we are inextricably linked. Nature is not harmless, but it is far from harmful. We must engage with it, understand it and raise our children in it. And if we do, not only will we improve everyone's happiness and well-being today, but we will also do something much more significant: we will bring up a generation of people who really understand and respect nature and humanity's place within it.

Because when it comes to the natural world around us, it's time we were a little bit ... less human.

CONCLUSION

This book has ranged across many aspects of life. From food to government, from the economy to healthcare, I've argued that we need to redesign, reorganise and reconsider our world in terms more suited to the way we truly, naturally, humanly are. From the beginning I haven't promised to cover everything. But I hope that the idea behind *More Human* will help give you a framework for thinking about your own life and how you relate to everything from your civic participation, to your interaction with the light switch, to your lunch. I've talked about how to make our institutions more human, our products and services more human, even our buildings more human. But what about the essence of our humanity – our relationships with one another? How do we make those more human as well?

To be human is to love, to accept and to empathise with each other, but it seems as if it is just as human to hate, ostracise and blame. Witness the ethnic, sectarian and nationalist tensions across the globe today. For all the progress we've made, we still live in a world of the scapegoat, of the 'other' – whether that's Poles being blamed for economic ills in Britain or all Muslims being blamed for the thoughts and actions of some.

Obviously, overcoming difference is most keenly felt at home where de facto segregation and misunderstandings sometimes result in subtle – and not so subtle – discrimination and conflict. Lack of mutual understanding can lead to grave injustices, but when those differences fester, as is happening around the world, we see something worse: terrorism, war and genocide.

Britain is lucky to have the ability to be an actor on the world stage, and we have come to the aid of many under existential threat, from the people of Kuwait to those of Sierra Leone, Bosnia and Libya. Engaging in armed conflict is a decision that should be made with a heavy heart, and clearly the answer should not always be 'yes'. But by remembering that we have a heart, we can make a substantial difference to the lives of millions. We can distribute humanitarian aid; we can rebuild communities; we can advise nascent governments. We have to remember that we are all flesh and blood. We all suffer. We are all human.

One of the greatest instances of human suffering today is the European refugee crisis. Driven mostly from the interminable Syrian civil war as well as instability and chaos in the wider Middle East and strife in Iraq, Afghanistan, Africa and central Asia, millions are displaced and living in camps, hundreds of thousands of refugees have made their way towards Europe, tens of thousands have crossed through it, and thousands have died in transit.

Some politicians welcome Syrian refugees, but many citizens resist, creating a political crisis on top of a humanitarian one. Unlike anything since the Cold War, Europe faces a catastrophe that is pitting countries against one another and citizens against their leaders. We have seen the worst of humanity: drowned children on beaches, smugglers leaving their charges to die in trucks and boats – but also immigrants abusing their welcome in disgusting ways. We have seen the best, too: governments inviting refugees in, humanitarians rescuing the distressed, and townspeople welcoming the tired with food, water, song, applause – even into their own homes. These good Samaritans exemplify the best of humanity, a common spirit of empathy, solidarity and hope. Although refugees cannot be allowed in without limit, the West has a responsibility to do its part. And given its responsibility for the Iraq War, whose aftermath helped give rise to ISIS, it's scandalous that some American politicians propose barring Syrian refugees, particularly on religious grounds.

The conflicts in the Middle East and Africa and the ensuing refugee crisis are not about to end; they are only going to get worse. There will be more Syrias. National leaders, the foreign policy establishment, the NGOs and the UN must take true responsibility. For years the international community dithered when it came to Syria, letting the civil war there smoulder. Countries across the Middle East are collapsing upon themselves, the chaos partly the result of either our cack-handed intervention or the lack of any intervention at all. There is no perfect solution, and yet somehow the international community waits for one, imparting half-measures that accomplish nothing. Powerful countries cannot engage in the world and then retreat from it when their actions have unintended consequences. Britain and America might be wary of further intervention in the Middle East, but a bad intervention in Iraq does not invalidate all future ones. The fact that military intervention might not always be the right answer doesn't mean it never is.

Moreover, this fight is not simply a 'conventional' war for land or power; it is a fight against grave evil committed both in the Middle East and across the world. ISIS is a group that is perpetrating unspeakable barbarism, especially on women and children, a group whose thirst for brutality is equal to the worst twentieth-century dictators; a group whose very raison d'être is to provoke an ideological confrontation on a biblical scale. It's like fighting the Nazis and Communists at the same time – ISIS is the nadir of our humanity. That is why our fight is a moral one and, like the Cold War, will be long and gruelling. Although we cannot be sure of any military campaign's success, sometimes, when fighting to salvage humanity from itself, the fight is all there is.

But even if we vanquish ISIS militarily – as I believe we must – there will be the further, in many ways more difficult, battle against an ideology of hate, one that we have to undermine and discredit at every instance of its occurrence. Violent extremism within Islam is obviously a perversion of that faith. But we must accept that although few Muslims support the murder, torture and abuse practised by ISIS (or would wish to live under its yoke), the worldview it promotes is the extreme conclusion of a belief system to which many Muslims are nevertheless sympathetic. That ideology we might usefully describe as 'Caliphism' – not Islam itself but a very specific misreading of Islam that demands the implementation of a Muslim Caliphate under Sharia law.[1]

Even to non-Muslim observers, it is evident that Islam is in the throes of an identity crisis, one which cannot be solved by the West for the Muslim world. But Western leaders can give cover to the moderates who are now outshouted by the extremists. We have to create the space for the reform of Islam that is so clearly necessary. To start, we can take oxygen away from its sources in places like Saudi Arabia and especially Qatar. That our allies in these countries also promote the most extreme religious fundamentalism – and even on occasion its most violent manifestation – should not be allowed to continue just because it is diplomatically correct. But we also have to build up the positive version of Islam. We have to ask ourselves: how do we help create Islamic societies more like Indonesia, the world's largest Muslim country, where Nahdlatul Ulama, the world's largest Islamic group, has launched a campaign against the ideology that ISIS represents? As that campaign seeks to do, fighting ISIS means delegitimising Caliphism at home and abroad.

There will always be those for whom twisted ideologies determine all, but disaffection lets radicalism take root, whether it be Caliphism (the most dangerous of the moment), nationalism, neo-fascism, or any other form of ethnic, religious, racial or ideological chauvinism. This is especially true in an era in which communications through social media can reach so many people so easily across any distance. We must better police the channels through which terrorists and other extremists lure our youth, and we must use creativity and all our technological know-how to give them better alternatives. But we must also offer them an aspirational path.

The inevitable conclusion? We need a concerted, aggressive effort to advance the basics of a decent human life, an inoculation against extremism: basics that have always and are everywhere underpinned by the institutions of a market economy and a free society: property rights, the rule of law, an independent judiciary, a free press, accountable democratic processes. The lack of these institutions is at the root of many of the problems that beset us.

Reactionaries from Putin in Russia to Erdogan in Turkey have proposed an alternative narrative, erecting authoritarian 'illiberal states'. They posit that not every country should be a democracy or a market economy. But these leaders are dangerously misguided. There is no society that doesn't need accountability, representation or the rule of law. There is no people that doesn't deserve to rule themselves. Living in a liberal society, in the form of democracy and a market economy, is the right of every person. As I've shown throughout this book, when done right, these are the most human ways to order our lives.

So we must double down and insist on them, using every weapon in our military, political, economic, diplomatic and cultural arsenals. The West's invention of democracy and markets doesn't make them exclusively ours. It is our human responsibility – not to mention in our own self-interest – to help spread them around the world. We must insist that all people everywhere are accorded the basic human rights due to them. We must incentivise leaders – even the most recalcitrant – to adopt the institutions that are the foundation of true human flourishing, and if they refuse, we must try harder, use more pressure; never stop until it's done and we ensure that every citizen everywhere enjoys the birthrights we take for granted. This is not imposing 'Western' values on the world; it is treating every person with the humanity they are intrinsically due.

Diplomats, economists and NGO do-gooders have been addressing these issues for years, of course. They have had some successes. But their failures have been glaring. Concerned more with decorum and political correctness than on-the-ground results, they have let down too many people in too many places, allowing their noble intentions to protect them from critical accountability. Our engagement must be based on what actually works, and that means listening to how people – citizens and rulers alike – actually behave and respond to our efforts and then adjusting them until we get it right. Just as such human-centred approaches are vital – as we've seen in this book – to the design of baby incubators or urban spaces, the same care, humility and empathy must be applied to building the most fundamental of democratic institutions, even when starting from scratch.

The millions who rose up in the Arab Spring or in Ukraine did so because they lacked a future in their homelands: no jobs, no education, certainly no stake in the political process. Such disenfranchisement in Arab countries, bereft of legitimate institutions, allowed the plague of ISIS to develop when the Arab Spring and Syrian civil war created power vacuums. But the disenfranchisement had been there for decades before, and helped spawn the dystopian Caliphism of which ISIS is just the latest and most abominable example.

Anthropologist Scott Atran has spent years immersing himself among what many would consider our very worst enemies: the Western youth who have joined ISIS. Testifying before the UN Security Council, he insists that the key to stopping young people from self-radicalisation is to deeply empathise with them. No, that doesn't mean agreeing with them. It means recognising that although there is no archetype for an extremist, we will only be able to prevent the arrival of what will almost surely be a next generation of terrorists if we first understand what motivates them to the brink.

Only when we have overcome the blind spot that has brought a seemingly distant war to the hearts of our cities can we create an alternative narrative that engenders the same passion and dedication that leads them to ISIS. We are losing some of our young people at their most vulnerable moments, and as much as we must stop those who prey upon them, we must also work to address the causes of their disillusionment, be they moral, economic or social. Most ISIS fighters aren't necessarily true believers, but rather lost youth looking for something, anything to believe in – to live (and die) for. In the West, especially in countries like France and Belgium where young Muslims feel apart from society, Caliphism provides a way to express agency over their own lives. Yes, we need to humiliate the source of their misplaced inspiration. But, more than that, we need to give them an alternative hope.

As we work to bring marginalised people and societies everywhere into the fold, we must remember that helping others build up their own capacity to help themselves requires tremendous humility. Along with our insistence that all countries are free and fair, we have to listen closely to their people to truly understand what that means for them. We have to be nimble. We have to be respectful. But we do have to be persistent.

Sometimes fulfilling those obligations will come in grand gestures and actions; sometimes, in order to enforce civilised norms and uphold international order, we will need to impose sanctions on other countries – or at the very least on their leaders. But where possible we should look to bolster ways of relating to one another that avoid conflict and reduce strife. Not just economic ties (whose importance we saw in Chapter 6) but also things like the informal diplomacy between academics, artists, students, civil-society groups and tourists in countries around the world, including rogue states like North Korea, Iran, Russia and China. Exchanges, visits and conferences – personal, human contact – should underpin important international relationships. When world leaders spend time at summits, they don't just negotiate; they also develop rapports that can enhance future relations and nip brewing crises in the bud.

Despite the supposed urgency to discuss other matters, our leaders must never lose sight of what is truly important. In the short-term , trade and security cooperation can easily seem like overriding priorities. But for long-term economic success and long-term security, the rule of law, human rights, and the institutions of a market economy and a free society matter more – and Western leaders must remind autocrats of their necessity at every possible moment. We've tried patience with countries like China (and Russia and Saudi Arabia) and yet too often let other considerations get in the way. We are lucky to live in countries that are wealthy, powerful, free and safe all at the same time. We must not shirk the responsibilities those privileges entail.

Given the depth and breadth of problems across the globe, supporters of human understanding might look at the world today and sink into despair, wondering whether we have learned anything from the horrors of our past. But the terrible version of ourselves that we see in all those war-torn, chaotic or even just economically depressed places is not the true us. It is the anxious us, the ignorant us, the fearful us. And the funny thing is that although rhetorically or theoretically we might blame someone else for our problems – the immigrant or the minority – in practice, on a day-to-day basis, in our real human lives, we do not.

Proximity and contact are the ultimate antidotes against insularity and prejudice, a point proven by the steady evolution of public opinion on gay rights. It turns out that once people realise that one of their neighbours, friends, colleagues or relatives is gay, their homophobia turns into tolerance and then acceptance and then comradeship. It's easy to hate strangers on TV and in far-away parades; it's much harder to hate a group to which your son or daughter belongs. When confronted on their prejudices by their own children, people tend to evolve and overcome them; after all, if you can't empathise with your child, who can you empathise with?

Gay people are relatively lucky in that anyone might be gay; even ardent homophobes might end up with a lesbian cousin or a gay nephew. But for those of different ethnic, racial, national and religious backgrounds, such genetic serendipity is impossible. And although we have come further than ever before in human history, we need to push ourselves to always engage with those who are different.

Being more human with one another is crucial to bridging cultural divides and living in a more peaceful world. If we are to be a successful global society, this is imperative. But it's sometimes much more basic than that. We need to ask ourselves what it is to interact with each other meaningfully on a daily basis. Civility is not just for the advice columns; it is incumbent upon us all to practise it. And in a world in which technology has rapidly changed social interactions, litigating technology's role would be a good start. As we have seen, mobile phones and the Internet have fundamentally altered how we communicate with each other, for good and for bad. Technology helps us learn in our own time, with courses customised to our needs. Mobile phones give parents the comfort of letting their children push the boundaries of independence. And Skype connects distant friends and relatives across oceans, time zones and continents. Through the advent of big data, we now have more capacity to understand and control our own existences than ever before. But technology has its problems. It can be manipulated by nefarious actors, like terrorists seeking impressionable recruits. It has led to the scourge of pre-teen and teenage sexting. It is changing our neurology. Perhaps most importantly, it is changing how we live our lives. Too many people, it seems, now live not for the moment but for the 'likes' and 'retweets'; they would too often rather hang out online than in person. Staying connected to others is wonderful, but not if its cost is disconnecting from reality and actual people.

In technology as in so many other areas, you could say, 'No, the status quo is human.' You could ask, as we did at the beginning of this book: Why is a world designed by humans not already, by definition, 'more human'? Well, in much the same way that all the social-science theories that explain human behaviour as rational fail to take into account our own irrationalities, our institutions fail to live up to their own standards too. Sometimes when we created our institutions, we simply didn't know what was or wasn't human. Behavioural science is a rather novel field, and until recently many of us really did believe that people were perfectly rational. But because we weren't – and still aren't – even our 'rational' institutions turn out imperfectly. We fell victim to the hubris – another human trait – that we could outsmart nature, that we could outsmart even ourselves. Cities were built based on how planners believed we should live, not how we actually would. Education systems were designed based on how we once thought children learned and what they needed for success, not on what actually matters now and for the future. That's why it's so important to embrace the science – the human insights – in fields like behavioural economics, neuroscience, psychology and biology that allow us to better know ourselves, to better pinpoint interventions, and to better help people flourish.

That's not to say that we shouldn't theorise or experiment until we get it right – tinkering is human too, after all – but we should understand the limits of designing any system, product, service or environment without connecting with the people who will be involved in it on a daily basis as consumers, providers, recipients, residents, patients or students. We are on the cusp of transcending 'just theory' in many fields simply because we increasingly have easy access to all the data.

We must also remember that everything is interconnected: children don't just need good families, wholesome play and limits on mobile Internet-enabled devices; they also need liveable homes and safe streets, access to nature, and food and schools not made in or designed as factories. For our economy to flourish, we need to not only treat workers as humans, require fair competition and enable people to fulfil their potential, but also plan for the long term, combat poverty at its roots, better educate our future workforce, and lessen the stranglehold of special interests over our regulatory regimes.

As we saw, some themes are woven through everything. Although we must be wary of technology, we must also allow for its near-limitless possibilities. And we must remember that the importance of families pervades every issue, from education to poverty to jobs to inequality, which is why government should redouble its efforts at early and comprehensive family interventions. Government itself is formally covered in Chapter 2, but government, regulation and public policy play a role in every issue in this book. The best way to make change, after all, is through our political system, as I argued in Chapter 1 and will reprise in the Postscript.

In fact, as I said from the outset, in many ways we need a revolution in our society to counteract its many ills. Some are obvious – dissatisfaction with government, unfair wages, the power of rich elites – but others are less so, like the surreptitious harm of smartphones, the attack on proper play, and the absence of human-centred design in policymaking. There is an increasing divide between elites and everyone else in Western societies, and it is a dangerous gap. We need sweeping institutional changes, like bans on factory farms, and sweeping attitudinal changes, like how we relate to nature. Above all, we need a more human world to be accessible to everyone, not just the elites, which is why we need to reinvigorate our democracy.

More – or less – human?

In this book I've argued that more human values, scale, design, products and policies are all good things; that we should aspire to make everything in our lives as human as possible. I've just argued for a revolution in doing so. But although we know what a more human world would mostly look like, there's an interesting exception emerging, a field in which, as it gets more human, the result is more *in*human.

This is the field of robotics and artificial intelligence. Artificial intelligence (AI), simply defined, is the field of trying to create intelligence synthetically. We already have many basic versions of it, from IBM's Watson to Apple's Siri to Google's self-driving cars. Perhaps the ultimate expression of AI is the 'singularity' hypothesis which, as articulated by futurist Ray Kurzweil, predicts 'the union of human and machine, in which the knowledge and skills embedded in our brains will be combined with the vastly greater capacity, speed, and knowledge-sharing ability of our own creations.'[2]

If this sounds like science fiction, you're right. But excitingly – or alarmingly, depending on your view – reality is in many ways already catching up with science fiction. Think about Steven Spielberg's 2002 film *Minority Report*. Although our world doesn't yet resemble his, we have developed many of the technologies his characters use, like automated cars, facial-recognition software, personalised advertising, predictive crime fighting (they used mutated psychics called precogs; we use big data and analytics), gesture-based computer interfaces, and even jet packs.[3] As exciting as that may be, it also means that the future is arriving sooner than we think. And we have to determine what we want it to look like.

Technological optimists like Kurzweil and Google's Larry Page believe that automation and robotics will free us up for more human endeavours. There is certainly a good argument for this; after all, as we saw in Chapter 9, even basic technologies have saved people from the most difficult and arduous tasks. Surely keeping people occupied in that way is inhuman? And surely liberating them to do more meaningful tasks or to spend more time in leisure is the more human alternative? Maybe AI is simply tomorrow's version of a mundane task that can be automated. We don't fear our washing machines – why fear whatever's coming next? As Rollo Carpenter, the founder of AI software firm Cleverbot, says, 'We cannot quite know what will happen if a machine exceeds our own intelligence, so we can't know if we'll be infinitely helped by it, or ignored by it and sidelined, or conceivably destroyed by it … I believe we will remain in charge of the technology for a decently long time and the potential of it to solve many of the world's problems will be realised.'[4] For some roboticists, replacing people has never been the goal. 'There are seven billion people in the world, and almost all of them are very good at being people,' says Helen Greiner, co-founder of iRobot, which made the Roomba vacuum-cleaning robot, and CEO of CyPhyWorks. 'We're not trying to duplicate people. We're trying to help them; make them more efficient, better at their jobs; empower them to do more with robotic technology.'[5] To naturalist and science writer Diane Ackerman, 'Surpassing human limits is so human a quest, maybe the most ancient one of all',[6] and AI is simply the next limit. Indeed, pushing the boundaries of AI might be one of the most human things we can do. In her latest book, *The Human Age*, she writes,

> *I find it touchingly poetic to think that as our technology grows more advanced, we may grow more human. When labour, science, manufacturing, sales, transportation, and powerful new technologies are mainly handled by savvy machines, humans really won't be able to compete in those sectors of the economy. Instead we may dominate an economy of interpersonal or imaginative services, in which our human skills shine.*[7]

On the other side of the argument, technological pessimists like Elon Musk and Stephen Hawking believe that for every great technological advance, we take a step towards human obsolescence. 'With artificial intelligence, we are summoning the demon,' Musk says. 'You know all those stories where there's the guy with the pentagram and the holy water and … he's sure he can control the demon. It doesn't work out.'[8] For example, scientists are building robots that can literally feed (power) themselves: engineers at Bristol Robotics Laboratory are building the EcoBot III, which can convert flies into fuel, and the US Defense Department-funded EATR (energetically autonomous tactical robot) uses cameras and sensors to find organic matter such as leaves, which it can then pick up and burn as fuel.[9] Perhaps while robots perform mundane tasks, this is perfectly fine, but what happens when we can't stop a robot from overpowering us because we've taught it to power itself? These pessimists fear that, at best, AI will supplant jobs – fuelling inequality by leaving the working class with nowhere to go – and challenge the boundary between life and artificiality. But at their worst they fear the very supplanting of humanity as a species. 'The development of full artificial intelligence,' Hawking warns, 'could spell the end of the human race.'[10]

We therefore have to ask ourselves real questions about AI's potential impact. In the short term, artificial intelligence could cause inequality on a massive scale, more even than we have seen so far with automation, globalisation and family disparities. It could permanently lock out huge segments of society from the economy. Today robots enhance things we can't do, like compute, position us by using satellites, perform dangerous tasks, connect to a grid. They are largely unthreatening. But what if computers start to do what we've thought of as essentially human tasks – thinking critically, creating, caring, or applying values and reason? What if computers become more like us?

And what if they become more like us but lack central human qualities? 'Ultimately,' writes Sherry Turkle, whose life's work has involved human interactions with machines, 'the question is not whether children will love their robotic pets more than their animal pets, but rather, what loving will come to mean. [Think of] the young woman who was ready to turn in her boyfriend for a "sophisticated Japanese robot". Is there a chance that human relationships will just seem too *hard*?'[11]

Perhaps even more profound a question is: What does it mean if robots don't die? In his 2005 commencement speech at Stanford, Apple founder Steve Jobs spoke of death's great power: 'Death is very likely the single best invention of Life. It's Life's change agent.'[12] Despite Ray Kurzweil's insistence that humans will achieve immortality through biotechnology and advanced medicine, death is, for now, one of humanity's defining traits. Although human qualities like love and death might be the great divider between humans and artificial intelligence, a dearth of such characteristics – particularly if robots have many other unfathomable powers and abilities – might be dangerous. What if, like dystopian visions of the future in film and literature, artificial intelligence overtakes us because it exploits those differences or sees them as weaknesses? If it comes down to it, can humans with hearts beat machines with just brains?

If that's the case and AI is inevitable in the long term, we have to ask ourselves how much we could even control it. Stephen Hawking doesn't think we could. AI, he warns, 'would take off on its own and re-design itself at an ever increasing rate ... Humans, who are limited by slow biological evolution, couldn't compete, and would be superseded.'[13] We might literally bring about the means to our own destruction, locking humanity out of our own society. These are obviously vast, deep questions, and I don't pretend to know the answers to them. (But I don't feel too bad about that because the brightest minds in the field don't either.) That's why the debate about artificial intelligence is important: it's about not just the future of humanity but its definition. And yet that debate is cloistered in Silicon Valley and biotech and medicine and nanotech; it is not taking place in public forums, in Congress, in the public eye. We hardly know it is happening – how can we have an opinion about it? As futuristic technologies become more and more available, people will want them. Although not all will result in an artificial intelligence per se, new technologies that merge man and machine carry with them vast implications that need to be considered.

Take the work of Hugh Herr, an MIT scientist and engineer who lost both legs below the knee in a rock-climbing accident. He used that accident as inspiration for what has become his life's work. 'I reasoned that a human being can never be broken. Technology is broken. Technology is inadequate. This simple but powerful idea was a call to arms to advance technology for the elimination of my own disability and ultimately the disability of others.' At his lab at MIT and in his private company Herr has developed incredibly advanced prosthetics that are customised in every sense of the word.

> *I began by developing specialised limbs that allowed me to return to the vertical world of rock and ice climbing. I quickly realised that the artificial part of my body is malleable, able to take on any form, any function, a blank slate through which to create perhaps structures that could extend beyond biological capability. I made my height adjustable. I could be as short as five feet or as tall as I'd like. Narrow, wedged feet allowed me to climb steep rock fissures where the human foot cannot penetrate, and spiked feet enabled me to climb vertical ice walls without ever experiencing muscle leg fatigue. Through technological innovation, I returned to my sport stronger and better. Technology had eliminated my disability and allowed me a new climbing prowess.*[14]

Herr recognises the potential to improve our quality of life across the board. He and others have started to experiment with exoskeletons, applying the same technology that has made him a better climber to perfectly healthy people. And although his work is confined to prosthetic limbs, he sees on the horizon relief for all sorts of disabilities and other physical impairments. 'It's not well appreciated,' he says, 'but over half of the world's population suffers from some form of cognitive, emotional, sensory or motor condition, and because of poor technology, too often, conditions result in disability and a poorer quality of life. Basic levels of physiological function should be a part of our human rights. Every person should have the right to live life without disability if they so choose – the right to live life without severe depression; the right to see a loved one in the case of seeing impaired; or the right to walk or to dance, in the case of limb paralysis or limb amputation.' And he is optimistic that this will soon come to pass. 'We the people need not accept our limitations, but can transcend disability through technological innovation,' he says. 'Indeed, through fundamental advances in bionics in this century, we will set the technological foundation for an enhanced human experience, and we will end disability.' When Rohan and I met him in Cambridge, Massachusetts, the conversation left a profound impression. And the seed of an idea for a policy response.

Ending disability would be great, but how will we grapple with adding extra ability? What will it mean to compete in sport? How much of a human is it ethical to replace? Should we be allowed to amputate limbs to obtain new artificial ones?

These are all important questions about the rapidly approaching future in AI, robotics and biotechnology, questions that bring up an important axiom: Just because we can, should we? Elon Musk, along with other Silicon Valley leaders Reid Hoffman, Peter Thiel and Sam Altman, came together late last year to launch a non-profit research institute, OpenAI, dedicated to ensuring that artificial intelligence is developed in a measured and responsible manner. 'We could sit on the sidelines or we can encourage regulatory oversight,' said Musk, 'or we could participate with the right structure with people who care deeply about developing AI in a way that is safe and is beneficial to humanity.'[15] Similarly, Stanford University has announced a century-long study of the effects of AI on society.[16] 'Artificial intelligence is one of the most profound undertakings in science, and one that will affect every aspect of human life,' says Stanford president John Hennessy. 'Given Stanford's pioneering role in AI and our interdisciplinary mindset, we feel obliged and qualified to host a conversation about how artificial intelligence will affect our children and our children's children.'[17] Hennessy is right: this is a necessary conversation, but it's one we need to bring out in the open. And although Musk and others are providing a healthy counter to the unquestioning attitude of others in Silicon Valley, they're still in Silicon Valley. Stanford is still Silicon Valley. We need more discussion generally, and we need it to be more informed and more integrated into daily life and debate. I don't know the answer, but I definitely want to do that most human thing: argue about it.

Britain has provided a precedent for situations such as these. After the world's first baby conceived by *in vitro* fertilisation (IVF) was born in 1978, the British government assembled a committee in 1982 to examine the ethical considerations of this new advance. The committee, chaired by philosopher Mary Warnock, delivered a report that managed a consensus on the ethical framework for IVF without judging or making moral pronouncements.[18] After the report, the government established the Human Fertilisation and Embryology Authority (HFEA) in 1990, a public body that now independently regulates IVF treatment, human embryo research, and human cloning.[19]

As we grapple with the challenging existential questions that artificial intelligence and robotics present, I think we need to establish a body like the HFEA to study it intelligently, carefully, delicately and, above all, publicly. That's the conclusion Rohan and I came to after meeting Hugh Herr at MIT. The HFEA has worked precisely because it has not overstepped its bounds and has avoided moralising, preaching or presuming to set political priorities. Similarly, any such body for AI could be an impartial arbiter to moderate the discussion among our best minds – not just engineers and scientists but also philosophers, ethicists, doctors and policymakers – making sure that whatever we do, we walk into the future with the best possible knowledge of its implications.

Even if it is on bionic legs.

POSTSCRIPT

In this book I've discussed many changes. Some we can each start doing individually, like spending more time in nature with our children, and others, businesses can make, like choosing to pay a living wage. But most of the changes proposed in this book are things that will have to come from government – even where the change means government doing less or giving its power away. It still needs government to act. That's not surprising: much of my thinking on the issues in this book has taken place either in or preparing for government. It's also how it should be: in a democracy our political system is the only institution that truly represents us – our wishes, our rights, our aspirations. All governments make rules, limit excess, lock up wrongdoers, preserve what should be protected, and forge ahead where progress is needed. Democracies are different, though, in that their legitimacy stems not from force or birthright but from the authority of our votes. That is democracy's promise – and why democracy must be the solution.

But because of people's almost total lack of confidence these days that our political system in Britain can really change much of anything, I understand that the arguments in the book could seem out of reach. How are we supposed to transform all of these things? Where do we even start?

The first step is fixing our democracy

The Park Slope Food Co-Op is a neighbourhood grocery store in Brooklyn, New York. My friend Chloe Wasserman, who lives nearby with her family, first took me there around fifteen years ago, and I fell in love with it instantly. Each of its 16,000 members contributes to the community by working in the shop once every four weeks for a total of two hours and forty-five minutes in a squad that almost always works together as a close team. Every member must contribute equally in time but can participate in a variety of tasks. All co-op members are entitled to play a role in the store's governance. Not only is it a close-knit community, but by saving on labour costs, the co-op can provide its members with high-quality organic, local food at a 20 to 40 per cent discount.

What can a grocery store teach us about fixing our broken democracy? It shows us that if you humanise the process, members of a community are happy to give their time to the common good, working alongside others in all sorts of areas of life, especially if they get something concrete out of it, like lower grocery costs. But when it comes to community engagement through the political system, it's a completely dehumanised process: an anonymous trip to the polling station once every few years and the payment of local taxes. That's it. No wonder people feel alienated from politics.

We could change that. We could strengthen a neighbourhood's social fabric by actively bringing residents into the civic sphere through the concept of 'civic service'. This would be a little like jury service, except more predictable and regular. Let's identify useful roles in communities that could be provided by local residents, and then invite – or even require – them to give two or three hours of service a month, just like the members of the Park Slope Food Co-Op. It would help people connect with their neighbours and increase their sense of belonging and social responsibility.

Civic service is a natural, human complement to neighbourhood government. The aim should be to make local service a social norm, make it easier to do by specifying the time, place and people to do it with, and offer some kind of tangible incentive, such as perhaps a small discount on local taxes. Even with a compulsory version of civic service, which might seem extreme, just as with the Park Slope Food Co-Op, if the benefits are clear and the social connections strong, people will love it; they will love being of service and love the engagement with their neighbourhood and their community.

Of course, civic service is an idea that calls for experimentation. In his terrific book on civic innovation, *Citizenville*, Gavin Newsom writes about Manor, Texas, which used an innovative gaming and points system to encourage civic service. The authorities there created a mobile game app in which residents earn points for participation, like submitting ideas to improve the city. A suggestion gets 1,000 'Innobucks', and its adoption and implementation earn 100,000. These points weren't a real currency, but they did allow residents to access perks within the city, like police ride-alongs or discounts at local retailers.[1] Although Newsom concedes that gaming is a strange way to organise a voluntary service system, it is actually an expression of human-centred design. 'We have to meet the people where they are,' writes Newsom. And where they are right now is playing games and spending time on social-networking sites.'[2] Rather than compete with faceless avatars, Manor's residents competed with their neighbours – for bragging rights over who was the most active citizen.

Let's shift that kind of thinking one step further – not just expressing an opinion about how things should be run but getting involved directly, a couple of hours a month. That's what I mean by civic service. Even if it was compulsory, getting people physically – not just politically – engaged in local services would make them feel more committed. Civic service needn't – and shouldn't – feel like a chore. By meeting people where they are, letting people choose how they serve, and making it enjoyable, local governments can infuse duty with passion.

For a system of government that has increasingly lost the trust of its own people, simple, human, practical involvement of this kind would be a small step towards rehabilitation. But there's something else we can do. Something you can do.

It goes right back to the first chapter of this book: politics. Fixing our democracy is the first step in moving towards a more human world. We need to take power out of the hands of the insiders and put it back where it belongs – in the hands of the people. End the stranglehold of the political machines on the left and right. Make it easier for more independent and independent-minded candidates to run for office. Give people confidence that it's worth getting involved. Make the representatives we have, actually represent us. As long as the same people control the conversation in the town hall, county council or Westminster, things will stay the same. So we need more grass-roots, interactive, accountable politics. We need to make politics more human.

That's where you come in. If you agree with the ideas in this book and want to see them happen, I can tell you exactly what you need to do. You won't necessarily like the answer, but I'm going to tell you anyway.

Of course it means backing candidates for elected office – especially state and local – who are truly committed to change, to overthrowing the systems of governance that have helped precipitate the problems we face today. But the trouble is, there aren't enough such candidates. So, you need to run for office. Run for the local council. Run for mayor – if that's an option where you live. Run for Parliament. But one way or another, get your hands on the levers of power. If enough of us do it, we can really change things. One independent-minded person who wants to see more human politics enacted, on their own, is not going to change anything. But a handful on a council – just like the 'flat pack democracy' gang in Frome? Now you're talking. A couple of hundred in Parliament? That's a revolution.

We can do this. We really can. We can take back our democracy and make the world more human. But it will only happen if you – *yes, you* – take that first step and run for office. I know it's daunting. I know it's off-putting. I know you'll be worried about the kind of people you'll have to deal with, becoming a public figure, having actual responsibility for things. But that's what democracy is. And the trouble is, we've allowed it to be captured by the insiders and the vested interests and the people with money and influence. They're counting on you to be put off by it all, to be put off by the hassle, the complexity, the difficulty. That's their bet – that you don't actually care that much. That you don't really want change.

Prove them wrong.

Take back our democracy.

Make the world more human.

The first step? Right now, go to crowdpac.co.uk

ACKNOWLEDGEMENTS

Number one: my amazing wife, Rachel Whetstone, whom I love and respect in equal measure and without whom my recent adventures – moving to California, teaching at Stanford, founding a tech start-up – would literally not have been possible. I also appreciate her putting up with days of family disruption during the production of this book – especially Christmas in Beaver Creek, 2014 (Jody and Vivienne, thanks to you too). And of course, Ben and Sonny, who have forever changed how I see the world.

One more thing on Rachel. As everyone who knows us is aware, we have strong opinions and tend to express them. But we try to hold back – in public at least – when it comes to each other's work. When I was in government Rachel had clear views on what we were doing but never aired them. It's the same with me and Uber, where Rachel works today, and I hope you will understand that for the most human of reasons – family harmony! – I'd prefer to express my views in private. Sorry to disappoint, but there are few references to Uber in these pages.

That I have a platform to write this book is something I owe to one person above all others: David Cameron. I will always be grateful to him for giving me the incredible honour of working in government. He and Sam are remarkable people and true friends. His strong, steady leadership and remarkable sense of duty were justly rewarded in the British general election of 2015, and I am so immensely proud that he was the first Conservative party leader in well over a century to increase both share of the vote and number of seats in Parliament. I'm thrilled he won the majority he so deserved.

There are too many good friends and former colleagues in government to thank here personally, but I want to single out George Osborne, Michael Gove and Oliver Letwin for their special contribution to my political and policy education; Michael Heseltine, Michael Howard, David Young and Ken Baker – heroic political figures, all four – for the immense privilege of working with them and the inspiration they have given me; and Andrew Lansley, who helped me take that first vital step into this strange but fascinating world. I will never be able to thank Maurice Saatchi, Jeremy Sinclair, Bill Muirhead, and the wider Saatchi 'family' enough for all they've done for me personally and in everything I've been able to achieve professionally.

Also essential in developing the ideas in this book: my friend and former business partner Giles Gibbons. Our time working together at the company we founded, Good Business, was a hugely fertile one for my understanding of the social problems addressed in *More Human* and how they might be solved.

Many people helped turn *More Human* into reality. Gail Rebuck at Penguin Random House first encouraged me to write this book and helped me hone its theme. The team at WH Allen – Ed Faulkner, Elen Jones, Lucy Oates and copyeditor Mary Chamberlain – have been amazing partners; I can't quite believe how smoothly (most of) it has happened, and in record time. Georgina Capel and Rachel Conway at Capel & Land; Rae Shirvington, Shona Abhyankar and Caroline Butler at Ebury Publishing, and Fiona McMorrough and her team at FMcM have been a pleasure to work with and invaluable on the business and promotional side.

Writing on so many topics has meant reaching out to experts, thinkers and doers in all of these areas. Jason, Scott and I feel privileged for having been able to talk to people doing such awe-inspiring work. Many are cited, but some provided feedback and insights without expectation of credit, and I'd like to thank them here.

My first teaching assistant at Stanford, Chelsea Lei, was extremely helpful in constructing an early case study. Sarah Stein Greenberg has proven an indispensable colleague at the Stanford d.school and, along with Mel Kline Lee, Jenny Stefanotti and Brent Harris, helped us consider the possibilities of human-centred design in government. The enthusiasm of Maya Shankar, who has set up and now leads the White House's own 'nudge' unit, is contagious. Francis Fukuyama at Stanford provided valuable feedback on our government chapter and the history of bureaucracy. Bill Eggers of Deloitte, and William Simon of Columbia University likewise affirmed our thinking on government reform. Charlotte Alldritt discussed with us the fascinating findings of the RSA's City Growth Commission. Sir Simon Jenkins usefully critiqued our arguments on localism and schooling. Parliamentary researcher Mark Sandford kept us current on the exciting adoption of new mayoral authorities.

Lucy Heller of Ark, Sir Anthony Seldon of Wellington College, and Barbara Chow of the William and Flora Hewlett Foundation were insightful and provocative on education. Jamie Heywood's inspiring journey and thoughtfulness were instrumental to our healthcare thesis. Sten Tamkivi and

Daniel Vaarik educated us on Estonia's advances in e-health; Jason Oberfest of Mango Health did the same for the intersection of health and mobile devices; Camilla Cavendish helped us understand key aspects of the structure of the NHS. I'm extremely grateful to Liz Kendall for pointing us towards the need to discuss end-of-life care. Patrick Holden of the Sustainable Food Trust and Peter Melchett of the Soil Association helped clarify our thinking on agriculture and food policy. Conversations with Matt Rothe directed us to some of the latest and most interesting innovations in sustainable food. Isabel Oakeshott gave valuable feedback on the food chapter manuscript. Philip Lymbery of Compassion in World Farming provided detailed and timely answers to our numerous questions on factory farm conditions.

John Fingleton, former head of the UK Office of Fair Trading; John Gibson, my former No. 10 colleague now at Nesta; and Christine Varney, former US assistant attorney general for antitrust, proved stimulating sparring partners when discussing competition and helped us create a more rigorous chapter on capitalism. Louise Casey, one of Britain's most inspiring advocates for families and children, helped us set the tone for our poverty chapter; David Robinson of Community Links was similarly inspirational, as was Taryn Gaona, a former teacher and now my children's wonderful nanny. Michael McAfee of PolicyLink gave us a close look at the complexities surrounding the education of a child in poverty. Neil Jameson and Sarah Vero of the Living Wage Foundation, Michael Kelly at KPMG, Conor D'Arcy of the Resolution Foundation, Steve Mobbs of Oxford Asset Management, and Marianne Levine of Politico helped us understand the debate around low pay. Sir Charlie Mayfield, chairman of the John Lewis Partnership, provided tremendous insight into the challenges of improving low-paid workers' skills and compensation. Sebastian Thrun, founder and CEO of Udacity, proved extraordinarily thoughtful on the issue of workers and technology as well as artificial intelligence.

James O'Shaughnessey, another former colleague at No. 10, helped us greatly with our arguments in the chapter on spaces. Former Toronto mayor David Crombie, Alan Ricks of MASS Design, Nash Hurley of VITAL Environments, and Carlo Ratti of MIT proved similarly inspirational on architecture and design. Ben Schwegler of the Walt Disney Company, former Pentagon official Paul Stockton, Scott Jacobs of Generate Capital, Teryn Norris formerly of the US Department of Energy, Ryan Satterlee of Accenture, John Thorpe of Thameswey Energy, and Will Dawson and Giles Bristow of Forum for the Future helped us think through our complicated relationship with energy. Sarah Butler-Sloss of the Ashden Trust and David Beach at Stanford provided keen insight and incredibly useful examples and contacts for case studies. Our conversation with children's author Christiane Dorion on teaching nature remains one of the most delightful of the entire writing experience.

A number of people had valuable insights into our themes writ large, including Matthew Taylor or the RSA, Adam Lent of Ashoka, Jim Adams at Stanford, Nick Pearce of IPPR, Geoff Mulgan of Nesta, David Halpern of the Behavioural Insights Team, retired diplomat Sir David Manning, and Nassim Nicholas Taleb of New York University.

A handful of people went above and beyond in their assistance. Richard Young of the Sustainable Food Trust spent a huge amount of time offering technical assistance to help us understand agricultural policies and the effects of antibiotic use on farms. Mark Schurman at Herman Miller is as close to a living library on the subject of office design as there can be and was exceptionally generous with his time and knowledge. London mayoral candidate Zac Goldsmith helped steer us in the right direction many times across a number of issues.

Jason and Scott want to thank the ever-perspicacious Todd Johnson of Jones Day, Banny Banerjee of Stanford ChangeLabs, and Paul and Iris Brest of Stanford Law School and the Creative Commons Foundation, respectively. Thanks to Peter, Lisa and Julianne Cirenza, who welcomed us into their London home during our travels, and Peter, for his astute observations and feedback on the financial sector. Finally, thanks to Paul and Sheri Bade – Mom and Dad – whose support, understanding, guidance and love is the very human foundation of this, one of our proudest accomplishments.

There are three people who have inspired me personally and professionally in more ways than they know and whose names I'm completely thrilled to see on the jacket of this book: Mike Bloomberg, Arianna Huffington and Nassim Taleb. They are all major public figures with strong views on many topics – and it's important to point out that the views expressed in this book are entirely mine and not endorsed by them in any specific detail.

I want to thank those who laboured through early drafts to give me great feedback: Jenni Russell, who also spent an inordinate amount of effort connecting us with people to talk to; Dieter Helm, my tutor at Oxford, who helped me think through the broad themes of the book as well as the technical aspects of infrastructure and competition; and Kate MacTiernan.

Jason and Scott have been a double joy to work with. (Everyone should have twins helping them with their book!) They complemented each other and me in the best ways as they helped me research and write *More Human*, diving into the project head first – and putting up with me for over two years of it. This book couldn't have been produced without them, and I'm so grateful for their hard work.

And then, finally, I must thank the person who has been central to this book throughout its life: from the years we spent together developing and working on many of the ideas in *More Human*, to the confidence he gave me that this was a project worth pursuing, to the book's structure and comments on drafts at every stage – my closest friend and former colleague in government, Rohan Silva, to whom this book is dedicated.

NOTES

Introduction

1   JetBlue has acknowledged and apologised for this incident. The dialogue is not a verbatim transcript but is based on Devereaux's recollection as expressed in various media appearances since the incident. For more, watch her interview at Jennifer Devereaux, interview by Tamron Hall, *NewsNation with Tamron Hall*, MSNBC, 19 June 2014.

2   HRC quote: Dan Merica, 'Black Lives Matter Video, Clinton Campaign Reveal Details of Meeting', CNN Politics, 18 August 2015, www.cnn.com/2015/08/18/politics/hillary-clinton-black-lives-matter-meeting.

3   Jeremy Rifkin, *The Empathic Civilization: The Race to Global Consciousness in a World in Crisis* (New York: Jeremy P. Tarcher/Penguin, 2009).

4   For more on the nuanced and complicated history of bureaucracy, see Francis Fukuyama, *Political Order and Political Decay* (New York: Farrar, Straus and Giroux, 2014), 15–18, 68–71.

5   Alfred D. Chandler Jr., *The Visible Hand: The Managerial Revolution in American Business* (Cambridge, MA: Harvard University Press, 1977).

6   Michael A. Mitt, David King, Menna Krishnan, Marianna Makri, Mario Schjren, Katsuhiko Shimizu, and Hong Zhu, 'Creating Value Through Mergers and Acquisitions: Challenges and Opportunities', in *The Handbook of Mergers and Acquisitions*, eds. David Faulkner, Satu Teerikangas, and Richard J. Joseph (Oxford, England: Oxford University Press, 2012), 71–113.

7   Evgeny Morozov, *To Save Everything, Click Here: The Folly of Technological Solutionism* (New York: Public Affairs, 2013), xii.

8   Since 2007 hourly wages have declined even for workers with a bachelor's or advanced degree. For more, see Elise Gould, *2014 Continues a 35-Year Trend of Broad-Based Wage Stagnation* (Washington, DC: Economic Policy Institute, 2015), www.epi.org/publication/stagnant-wages-in-2014.

Chapter 1

1   Francis Fukuyama, *Political Order and Political Decay* (New York: Farrar, Straus and Giroux, 2014), 455–548.

2   According to political scientists Martin Gilens and Benjamin Page, 'When a majority of citizens disagrees with economic elites or with organised interests, they generally lose.' For more, see Martin Gilens and Benjamin I. Page, 'Testing Theories of American Politics: Elites, Interest Groups, and Average Citizens', *Perspectives on Politics* 12, no. 03 (2014): 564–81, 576.

3   'Election 2015 Results', *BBC News*, http://www.bbc.com/news/election/2015/results.

4   Tony Blair, *A Journey: My Political Life* (New York: Vintage Books, 2011), xi.

5   Patrick Macfayden and Mike Dudley-Jones, quoted in John Harris, 'How Flatpack Democracy Beat the Old Parties in the People's Republic of Frome', *Guardian*, 22 May 2015, http://www.theguardian.com/politics/2015/may/22/flatpack-democracy-peoples-republic-of-frome.

6   Lawrence Lessig, 'We the People, and the Republic We Must Reclaim', TED Talk, 27 February 2013, Long Beach, California, www.ted.com/talks/lawrence_lessig_we_the_people_and_the_republic_we_must_reclaim/transcript?language=en.

Chapter 2

1   Alex Singleton, 'Obituary: Sir John Cowperthwaite', *Guardian*, 8 February 2006, www.theguardian.com/news/2006/feb/08/guardianobituaries.mainsection.

2   Diane Coyle, 'GDP Is a Mirror on the Markets. It Must Not Rule Our Lives,' *Guardian*, 20 November 2014, www.theguardian.com/commentisfree/2014/nov/20/gdp-markets-short-term-victorians-value.

3   Dieter Helm, interview by authors, Menlo Park, CA, 21 November 2014.

4   Anthony King and Ivor Crewe, *The Blunders of our Governments* (London: Oneworld Publications, 2013), 243.

5   Jane Jacobs, *The Death and Life of Great American Cities* (New York: Vintage Books, 1961), 13.

6   World Health Organization, 'Preterm Birth (Fact Sheet 363)', www.who.int/mediacentre/factsheets/fs363/en.

7   Linus Liang, interview by authors, Stanford, CA, 20 November 2014.

8   'Who Are We?' Embrace, 2015, http://embraceglobal.org/who-we-are/our-story.

9   Sadly, Tversky died before their joint work was recognised, so technically Kahneman is the laureate, though he accepted it on behalf of them both. For their seminal paper, see Daniel Kahneman and Amos Tversky, 'Choices, Values, and Frames', *American Psychologist* 39, no. 4 (1984): 341.

10   Ronald G. Fryer Jr., Steven D. Levitt, John List, and Sally Sadoff, 'Enhancing the Efficacy of Teacher Incentives Through Loss Aversion: A Field Experiment', no. w18237, National Bureau of Economic Research, 2012.

11   David Brooks, 'The Character Factory', *New York Times*, 1 August 2014, www.nytimes.com/2014/08/01/opinion/david-brooks-the-character-factory.html.

12   Robert B. Cialdini, Linda J. Demaine, Brad J. Sagarin, Daniel W. Barrett, Kelton Rhoads, and Patricia L. Winter, 'Managing Social Norms for Persuasive Impact', *Social Influence* 1, no. 1 (2006): 3–15.

13   David Brooks, 'Stairway to Wisdom', *New York Times*, 15 May 2014, www.nytimes.com/2014/05/16/opinion/brooks-stairway-to-wisdom.html.

14   Editorial board, 'Mr. Bratton Reverses to Go Forward', *New York Times*, 12 September 2014, www.nytimes.com/2014/09/13/opinion/mr-bratton-reverses-to-go-forward.html.

15   US Department of Justice, Civil Rights Division, 'Investigation of the Ferguson Police Department', 4 March 2015, 62.

16   US Department of Justice, 'Investigation of the Ferguson Police Department', 3.

17   'Measure for Measure', *Economist*, 30 November 2013, www.economist.com/news/united-states/21590954-can-asking-better-questions-reduce-americas-prison-population-measure-measure.

18   Peel, who later served as prime minister, founded the Metropolitan Police in 1829 while he was home secretary. British police officers are affectionately called 'bobbies' in his honour. He has been associated with the so-called Peelian Principles, which revolutionised the policing profession by laying down the field's first set of ethical guidelines. Also known as 'policing by consent', it is grounded in the idea that the police draws its power, in the words of the British Home Office, from 'the common consent of the public', See Home Office, 'Freedom of Information Release: Policing by Consent', 10 December 2012, www.gov.uk/government/publications/policing-by-consent.

19   Richard H. Thaler, *Misbehaving: The Making of Behavioral Economics* (New York: W. W. Norton & Company, 2015), 320.

20   Rohan Silva, interview by authors, London, 17 September 2014.

21   Ibid.

22   Lena H. Sun, 'Johns Hopkins Team Wins U.S. Award for Improved Suit to Fight Ebola', *Washington Post*, 13 December 2014, www.washingtonpost.com/news/post-nation/wp/2014/12/13/johns-hopkins-team-wins-u-s-award-for-improved-suit-to-fight-ebola; Julie Hirschfeld Davis, 'Adviser Guides Obama into Google Age', *New York Times*, 4 January 2015, www.nytimes.com/2015/01/04/us/politics/her-task-weaning-the-white-house-off-floppy-disks.html.

23   Karen Courington, interview by authors, Menlo Park, CA, 1 July 2015.

24   Ken Tatham, interview by authors, Menlo Park, CA, 16 December 2014.

25   'Local Elections', *France in the United States*, Embassy of France in the United States, 20 December 2013, http://www.ambafrance-us.org/spip.php?article518.

26   Polly Curtis, 'French Civil Servant's Confession Strikes a Chord in Drive to Shrink State', *Guardian*, 23 March 2011, http://www.theguardian.com/world/2011/mar/23/french-civil-servant-bored-workforce.

27   Irène Couzigou, 'France: Territorial Decentralisation in France: Towards Autonomy and Democracy', in *Local Government in Europe: The 'Fourth Level' in the EU Multi-Layered System of Governance*, eds., Carlo Panara and Michael R. Varney, (New York: Routledge, 2013), 75.

28   In England, the average electorate of a council authority in 2014 was around 161,000. For more details, see this table published by The Local Goverment Boundary Commission for England: https://www.lgbce.org.uk/__data/assets/excel_doc/0006/22839/NEW-Copy-of-Counties-Pivot-Table-2014.xlsx.

29   'BBC Poll: One in Five "Disillusioned" with Westminster', *BBC News*, 21 October 2014.

30   Nicco Mele, *The End of Big: How the Internet Makes David the New Goliath* (New York: St. Martin's Press, 2013), 29.

31   For more, see Peter Schuck, *Why Government Fails So Often: And How It Can Do Better* (Princeton, NJ: Princeton University Press, 2014), 193.

32   House of Commons Committee of Public Accounts, Department of Health: The National Programme for IT in the NHS; Twentieth Report of Session 2006–07, HC 510 (London: The Stationery Office, 2007), EV 18.

33   Ibid., EV 19; Nicholas Timmins, 'The NHS Electronic Records Are Two Years Late', *Financial Times*, 29 May 2006.

34   Anthony King and Ivor Crewe, *The Blunders of our Governments* (London: Oneworld, 2013), 195–200.

35   House of Commons Committee of Public Accounts, Department of Health, Review of the Final Benefits Statement for Programmes Previously Managed Under the National Programme for IT in the NHS (London: National Audit Office, 2013); Department of Health, National Audit Office, The National Programme for IT in the NHS. An Update on the Delivery of Detailed Care Records Systems (London: The Stationery Office, 2011).

36   King and Crewe, 195–200.

37   Alan Milburn quoted in Fraser Nelson, 'Milburn: How I Can Help Gordon Brown', *Spectator*, 19 May 2007.

38   There are 16 authorities that currently have directly elected mayors. Some are a legacy of the Local Government Act 2000. When the Coalition came to government, it wanted to devolve more power to cities, so the largest ten cities in England after London (Birmingham, Leeds, Sheffield, Bradford, Manchester, Bristol, Wakefield, Coventry, Nottingham and Newcastle-upon-Tyne) were obliged to hold referendums on whether to adopt elected mayors or not. The councils of Leicester and Liverpool adopted the mayoral system in December 2010 and February 2012. The ten cities held a referendum in May 2012; only one, Bristol, decided in favour of a directly elected mayor. Since then, in an agreement between Chancellor George Osborne and its ten local councils, Manchester will hold elections for a metropolitan mayor in 2017. Similar agreements to Manchester have been reached in several other metropolitan areas including Sheffield City Region, Tees Valley, West Midlands, North-East, and potentially 'North Midlands'. All of these metropolitan areas are expected to hold mayoral elections in 2017. Meanwhile, two more mayoral referendums are expected in 2017: one on establishing a mayor in the authority of Bath and North East Somerset, another on abolishing the mayor in Torbay. For more see: House of Commons, Directly-Elected Mayors, by Mark Sandford,

SN/PC/5000 (London: House of Commons Library, 2015); 'English Mayoral Elections and Referendums', BBC News, 4 May 2012;'George Osborne: Greater Manchester to Have Elected Mayor', BBC News, 3 November 2014; and Mark Sandford, email to authors, 13 January 2016.

39   When activists tried to prevent Muslims from building a community centre in Manhattan near the site of the 9/11 attacks, Bloomberg took the politically risky but morally correct stand for religious freedom.

40   'Local Elections', *France in the United States.*

41   Charlotte Wildman, 'The "Chicago of Great Britain": Growth and Urban Regeneration in Liverpool', in *The History Boys: Lessons from Local Government's Past*, Simon Parker and Joe Manning, eds. (London: New Local Government Network, 2013), 29–37.

42   Martin Fackler, 'District in Tokyo Plans to Extend Rights of Gay Couples', *New York Times*, 13 February 2015.

43   Robin I. M. Dunbar, 'Neocortex Size as a Constraint on Group Size in Primates', *Journal of Human Evolution* 22, No. 6 (1992): 469–93.

44   Jan De Ruiter, Gavin Weston and Stephen M. Lyon, 'Dunbar's Number: Group Size and Brain Physiology in Humans Reexamined', *American Anthropologist* 113, no. 4 (2011): 557–68.

45   Drake Bennett, 'The Dunbar Number, From the Guru of Social Networks', *Bloomberg Businessweek*, 10 January 2013.

46   See note 36 of this chapter.

47   Jerry Sternin, 'The Viet Nam Story', www.positivedeviance.org/about_pd/Monique%20VIET%20NAM%20CHAPTER%20Oct%2017.pdf.

48   Mauricio Lim Miller, 'When Helping Doesn't Help', *Huffington Post*, 7 May 2012, www.huffingtonpost.com/maurice-lim-miller/when-helping-doesnt-help_b_1497038.html.

49   Ibid.

50   Ibid.

51   Anne Stuhldreher and Rourke O'Brien, *The Family Independence Initiative: A New Approach to Help Families Exit Poverty* (Washington, DC: New America Foundation, 2011).

52   David Bornstein, 'Out of Poverty, Family-Style', *New York Times*, 14 July 2011, http://opinionator.blogs.nytimes.com/2011/07/14/out-of-poverty-family-style/?_r=0.

53   Stulhdreher and O'Brien, *The Family Independence Initiative.*

54   Lim Miller, quoted in Bornstein, 'Out of Poverty, Family-Style'.

Chapter 3

1   Se-Woong Koo, 'An Assault upon Our Children', *New York Times*, 3 August 2014, www.nytimes.com/2014/08/02/opinion/sunday/south-koreas-education-system-hurts-students.html.

2   Data from Statistics Korea, as reported in Yewon Kang, 'Poll Shows Half of Korean Teenagers Have Suicidal Thoughts', *Wall Street Journal*, 20 March 2014, http://blogs.wsj.com/korearealtime/2014/03/20/poll-shows-half-of-korean-teenagers-have-suicidal-thoughts.

3   Ibid.

4   Julie Lythcott-Haims, *How to Raise an Adult: Break Free of the Overprinting Trap and Prepare Your Kid for Success* (New York: Henry Holt and Co., 2015), 100–1.

5   In the last six years there have been two major suicide clusters at Palo Alto high schools. From 2009 to 2010 five teens killed themselves by stepping in front of trains. Between October 2014 and May 2015 another four did the same. See 'In Palo Alto's High-Pressure Schools, Suicides Lead to Soul-Searching', NPR, 10 May 2015, www.npr. org/2015/05/10/405694832/in-palo-altos-high-pressure-schools-suicides-lead-to-soul-searching.

6   Lythcott-Haims, *How to Raise an Adult.*

7   Julie Lythcott-Haims, interview by authors, Palo Alto, CA, 5 August 2015.

8   All quotes from Jason Pittman are from his interview by authors, Mountain View, CA, 5 November 2014.

9   Jessica Lahey, *The Gift of Failure: How the Best Parents Learn to Let Go So Their Children Can Succeed* (New York: HarperCollins, 2015), 27.

10   Jeff Sandefer, e-mail to authors, 3 September 2014.

11   Jason Tanz, 'The Tech Elite's Quest to Reinvent School in Its Own Image', *Wired*, 26 October 2015, www.wired.com/2015/10/salman-khan-academy-lab-school-reinventing-classrooms.

12   Palo Alto High School and Gunn High School, Palo Alto's two public high schools, are widely regarded as being among the best in the nation. Although I am no fan of such ranking systems, Gunn is ranked 38th and Palo Alto High is ranked 56th nationally by *Newsweek*, which puts both above the 99.7th percentile in the United States. For more, see 'America's Top Schools 2014', *Newsweek*, www.newsweek.com/high-schools/americas-top-schools-2014.

13   Emerging economies to be sure, but certainly not comparable to two economic superpowers. For the most recent (2012) PISA scores, see 'Snapshot of Performance in Mathematics, Reading and Science', PISA, www.oecd.org/pisa/keyfindings/PISA-2012-results-snapshot-Volume-I-ENG.pdf.

14   JouachimWuttke, 'Uncertainty and Bias in PISA', in *Pisa According to Pisa: Does Pisa Keep What It Promises?*, eds. Stefan Thomas Hopmann, Gertrude Brinek, and Martin Retzl (Vienna, Austria: Lit Verlag, 2007), 241–63.

15   William Stewart, 'Is Pisa Fundamentally Flawed?' *TES Connect*, 27 September 2014, www.tes.co.uk/article.aspx?storycode=6344672.

16   Aleksander P. J. Ellis, Bradford S. Bell, Robert E. Ployhart, John R. Hollenbeck, and D. R. Ilgen, 'An Evaluation of Generic Teamwork Skill Training with Action Teams: Effects on Cognitive and Skill-Based Outcomes', *Personnel Psychology* 58, no. 3 (2005): 641–72.

17   Angela L. Duckworth and Martin E. P. Seligman, 'Self-Discipline Outdoes IQ in Predicting Academic Performance of Adolescents', *Psychological Science* 16, no. 12 (2005): 939–44.

18   'IBM 2010 Global CEO Study: Creativity Selected as Most Crucial Factor for Future Success', IBM, 18 May 2010, www-03.ibm.com/press/us/en/pressrelease/31670.wss.

19   Tony Wagner and Ted Dintersmith, *More Likely to Succeed: Preparing Our Kids for the Innovation Era* (New York: Simon and Schuster, 2015), 73.

20   Joshua Wolf Shenk, *Powers of Two: How Relationships Drive Creativity* (Boston, MA: Eamon Dolan, 2009).

21   Jenni Russell, 'Let's Put Character Above Exam Results', *The Sunday Times*, 5 June 2011.

22   Willem Kuyken, Katherine Weare, Obioha C. Ukoumunne, Rachael Vicary, Nicola Motton, Richard Burnett, Chris Cullen et al., 'Effectiveness of the Mindfulness in Schools Programme: Non-Randomised Controlled Feasibility Study', *British Journal of Psychiatry* 203, no. 2 (2013): 126–31.

23   Allyson P. Mackey, Amy S. Finn, Julia A. Leonard, Drew S. Jacoby-Senghor, Martin R. West, Christopher F. O. Gabrieli, and John D. E. Gabrieli, 'Neuroanatomical Correlates of the Income-Achievement Gap', *Psychological Science* 26, no. 6 (June 2015): 925–33.

24   Barbara Chow, interview by authors, Menlo Park, CA, 18 June 2015.

25   The Juárez Correa story is heavily adapted from Josh Davis's profile of him in *Wired*. Josh is one of the greatest unearthers of amazing human stories. For the original article, see Joshua Davis, 'A Radical Way of Unleashing a Generation of Geniuses', *Wired*, 15 October 2013, www. wired.com/2013/10/free-thinkers.

26   Marjukka Liiten, 'Top Favourite: Teaching Profession' (in Finnish), Helsingin Sanomat, 11 February 2004, cited in Pasi Sahlberg, *Finnish Lessons: What Can the World Learn from Educational Change in Finland?* (New York: Teachers College Press, 2010), 72.

27   Sahlberg, *Finnish Lessons*, 125.

28   Ibid., 127.

29   Ellen Gamerman, 'What Makes Finnish Kids So Smart?' *Wall Street Journal*, 28 February 2008, www.wsj.com/articles/SB120425355065601997. See also Sahlberg, *Finnish Lessons*, 65.

30   OECD, 'Education at a Glance: OECD Indicators', www.oecd.org/edu/Education-at-a-Glance-2014.pdf.

31   Anthony Seldon, *An End to Factory Schools: An Education Manifesto 2010–2020* (Surrey, UK: Centre for Policy Studies, 2010), 9–10.

32   *Asking Students About Teachers* (Measures of Effective Teaching Project, 2012).

33   See, for example, Pearson Learning, www.pearson.com/learning.html; Disney Education Programs, http://dep.disney.go.com; McGraw-Hill Education, www.mheducation.com; Houghton Mifflin Harcourt, www. hmhco.com.

34   Peter Hill and Michael Barber, *Preparing for a Renaissance in Assessment* (London: Pearson PLC, 2014).

35   Editorial Board, 'Small Schools Work in New York', *New York Times*, 18 October 2014, www.nytimes.com/2014/10/18/opinion/small-schools-work-in-new-york.html.

36   Rebecca Unterman, *Headed to College: The Effects of New York City's Small High Schools of Choice on Postsecondary Enrollment* (MDRC, 2014), www. mdrc.org/sites/default/files/Headed_to_College_PB.pdf.

37   William T. Harris, 'Elementary Education', *North American Review* (1895): 538–46, 15.

38   Perhaps one of the reasons there are so many standardised tests is the
      money they make: Pearson made $85 million per year from 2010 to
      2015 just in the state of Texas on test administration. College Board,
      the private 'non-profit' company responsible for the SAT, makes over
      three-quarters of a billion dollars in revenue annually. For more,
      see Matthew M. Chingos, *Strength in Numbers: State Spending on K–12
      Assessment Systems* (Washington, DC: Brown Center for Education at the
      Brookings Institution, 2012); and *Agenda Materials: College Board Forum
      2015* (The College Board, 4–6 November 2015).

Chapter 4

1   This original figure came from data analysis reported by the
      HealthCare Commission. Subsequent investigations in the public
      inquiry determined that a specific number couldn't be established
      with certainty but that the level was much higher than it should
      have been. The head of the public inquiry explained that while
      he was asked to conduct individual investigations for everyone
      that died, he deemed this 'impracticable'. There were, however,
      investigations of three of the cases referenced in this paragraph.
      See: Robert Francis, *The Mid Staffordshire NHS Foundation Trust
      Inquiry: Independent Inquiry Into Care Provided by Mid Staffordshire
      Foundation Trust*, January 2005 – March 2009, vol. 1 (London: The
      Stationery Office, 2010), section C.

2   These anecdotes from the Mid-Staffs scandal are from the following
      sources: Claire Ellicott, 'NHS Hospital Scandal Which Left 1,200
      Dead Could Happen Again, Warn Campaigners', *Daily Mail*, 9
      November 2010; Sarah Boseley, 'Mid Staffordshire NHS Trust Fined
      for "Avoidable and Tragic Death"', *Guardian*, 28 April 2014; 'Stafford
      Hospital: The Victims of the Hospital Scandal', *BBC News*, 6 February
      2013; 'Stafford Hospital: Q&A', *BBC News*, 25 March 2013; and Tracy
      McVeigh, 'Scandal of NHS "Death Factories"', *Observer*, 11 August
      2002.

3   Henry Taylor, 'Who Is the Biggest Employer?' *World Economic Forum*, 17
      June 2015.

4   Quotes from *The King's Fund Report* and Joyce Robins (of the charity,
      Patient Concern), quoted in: 'Hospitals "Are Medical Factories"', *BBC
      News*, 3 December 2008.

5   'Hospitals "Are Medical Factories"'.

6   Ibid.

7   Jeremy Hunt quoted in Randeep Ramesh, 'Give Each NHS Hospital
      Patient a Single Consultant, Says Jeremy Hunt', *Guardian*, 23 January
      2014.

8   Joanna Goodrich and Jocelyn Cornwell, *Seeing the Person in the Patient*
      (London: The King's Fund, 2008), 9.

9   In addition to the sentiments of the patients, advocates and politicians
      quoted above, similar conclusions were reached by *The King's Fund
      Report*, *The Darzi Report*, and *The Cavendish Review*. For more, see:
      Goodrich and Cornwell, *The King's Fund Report*; Ara Darzi, *High Quality
      Care For All: NHS Next Stage Review Final Report* (The Darzi Report), 7432
      (London: The Stationery Office, 2008); and Camilla Cavendish, *The*

Cavendish Review: An Independent Review into Healthcare Assistants and Support Workers in the NHS and Social Care Settings (London: Department of Health, 2013).

10 Abraham Verghese, 'A Doctor's Touch', TEDGlobal 2011: The Stuff of Life, Edinburgh, Scotland, September 2011, www.ted.com/talks/abraham_verghese_a_doctor_s_touch?language=en.

11 'Introducing the Vscan Family', GE Healthcare, 2015, https://vscan.gehealthcare.com/introducing-vscan-family.

12 Priit Kruus, Peeter Ross, Riina Hallik, Reelika Ermel, and Ain Aaviksoo, *Wider Implementation of Telemedicine in Estonia* (Tallinn, Estonia: Praxis/Center for Policy Studies, 2014).

13 Responding to author's question at speech: Toomas Ilves, 'Evolving into a Genuinely Digital Society', presentation, Green Library, Stanford University, Stanford, CA, 23 May 2014.

14 Ali Parsa, phone interview by authors, 28 October 2014.

15 Jason Oberfest, interview by authors, San Francisco, CA, 27 August 2014.

16 James Heywood, phone interview by authors, 9 October 2014.

17 Nassim Nicholas Taleb, *Antifragile: Things That Gain from Disorder* (New York: Random House Trade Paperbacks, 2014), 338.

18 Alice G. Walton, 'Steve Jobs' Cancer Treatment Regrets', *Forbes*, 24 October 2011, www.forbes.com/sites/alicegwalton/2011/10/24/steve-jobs-cancer-treatment-regrets.

19 Julie Steenhuysen, 'Overuse of Heartburn Drugs is Risky: Study', *Reuters*, 10 May 2010; Health and Social Care Information Centre, National Statistics, *Prescriptions Dispensed in the Community: England 2004-2014*, (2015), 56–7.

20 Ian Forgacs and Aathavan Loganayagam, 'Overprescribing Proton Pump Inhibitors', *BMJ* 336: no. 7634 (2008): 2–3.

21 Kenneth E. L. McColl, 'Effect of Proton Pump Inhibitors on Vitamins and Iron', *American Journal of Gastroenterology* 104 (2009): S5–S9; Nigam H. Shah, Paea LePendu, Anna Bauer-Mehren, Yohannes T. Ghebremariam, Srinivasan V. Iyer, Jake Marcus, Kevin T. Nead et al., 'Proton Pump Inhibitor Usage and the Risk of Myocardial Infarction in the General Population', *PloS One* 10, no. 6 (June 2015): e0124653.

22 Taleb, *Antifragile*, 342.

23 Jeanne Whalen, 'How Glaxo Marketed a Malady to Sell a Drug', *Wall Street Journal*, 25 October 2006, www.wsj.com/articles/SB116174246339602800.

24 Steven Woloshin and Lisa M. Schwartz, 'Giving Legs to Restless Legs: A Case Study of How the Media Helps Make People Sick', *PLoS Medicine* 3, no. 4 (2006): e170.

25 Health and Social Care Information Centre, National Statistics, *Prescription Cost Analysis England 2013*, (3 April 2014), 109; *Health and Social Care Information Centre, National Statistics, Prescriptions Dispensed in the Community: England 2003–13* (2014), 28.

26 Murray Aitken, *Medicines Use and Spending Shifts: A Review of the Use of Medicines in the U.S. in 2014* (IMS Institute for Healthcare Informatics, April 2015); Murray Aitken, *Medicines Use and Spending Shifts: A Review*

of the Use of Medicines in the U.S. in 2013 (IMS Institute for Healthcare Informatics, April 2014).

27 Michael Anderson, quoted in Alan Schwarz, 'Attention Disorder or Not, Pills to Help in School', *New York Times*, 9 October 2012, www.nytimes.com/2012/10/09/health/attention-disorder-or-not-children-prescribed-pills-to-help-in-school.html.

28 Nancy Rappaport, quoted in ibid.

29 Ibid.

30 John N. Mafi , Ellen P. McCarthy, Roger B. Davis, and Bruce E. Landon, 'Worsening Trends in the Management and Treatment of Back Pain', *JAMA Internal Medicine* 173, no. 17 (2013): 1573–81.

31 Victoria Sweet, 'The Efficiency of Inefficiency', TEDxMiddlebury, Middlebury, Vermont, 9 March, 2013, www.youtube.com/watch?v=VA08kzp7tSg.

32 Victoria Sweet, *God's Hotel: A Doctor, a Pilgrimage, and a Journey to the Heart of Medicine* (New York: Penguin, 2013), 49–50.

33 Sweet, 'The Efficiency of Inefficiency'.

34 Francis W. Peabody, 'The Care of the Patient', *Journal of the American Medical Association* 88 (1927): 876–82.

35 Sweet, 'The Efficiency of Inefficiency'.

36 Department of Health and Human Services, *Medicare Atypical Antipsychotic Drug Claims for Elderly Nursing Home Residents* (Office of the Inspector General, May 2011).

37 Although the US government sponsors Medicare for all senior citizens, many also have private medical insurance.

38 Daniel R. Levinson, *Medicare Atypical Antipsychotic Drug Claims for Elderly Nursing Home Residents* (Department of Health and Human Services, May 2011), http://oig.hhs.gov/oei/reports/oei-07-08-00150.pdf.

39 Ina Jaffe and Robert Benincasa, 'Nursing Homes Rarely Penalized for Oversedating Patients', NPR, 9 December 2014, www.npr.org/sections/health-shots/2014/12/09/368538773/nursing-homes-rarely-penalized-for-oversedating-patients.

40 The Pathstone story is heavily adapted from Ina Jaffe's reporting for NPR: Ina Jaffe and Robert Benincasa, 'This Nursing Home Calms Troubling Behavior Without Risky Drugs', NPR, 9 December 2014, www.npr.org/sections/health-shots/2014/12/09/368539057/this-nursing-home-calms-troubling-behavior-without-risky-drugs.

41 'Woman Dies After Farewell to Horse at Wigan Hospital', *BBC News*, 7 November 2014, www.bbc.com/news/uk-england-manchester-29951094.

42 While the figures vary across different surveys, a majority prefer to die at home. The National Audit Office puts the figure between 56 per cent and 74 per cent (see: National Audit Office, *End of Life Care* (London: The Stationery Office, 2008) 5; while a report by the non-profit Cicely Saunders International puts the figure in England at 63 per cent (see: Barbara Gomes, Natalia Calanzani, and Irene J. Higginson, *Local Preferences and Place of Death in Regions within England 2010* (London: Cicely Saunders International, 2011), 11.

43 Barbara Gomes et al., *Local Preferences*.

44 NAO.

45   Dennis McCullough, *My Mother, Your Mother: Embracing 'Slow Medicine',
      the Compassionate Approach to Caring for Your Aging Loved Ones* (New York:
      Harper, 2008), 48.

46   Charles Leadbeater and Jake Garber, *Dying for Change* (London,
      Demos, 2010).

47   Irene J. Higginson, Ilora G. Finlay, Danielle M. Goodwin, Kerry Hood,
      Adrian G. K. Edwards, Alison Cook, Hannah-Rose Douglas and Charles
      E. Normand, 'Is There Evidence that Palliative Care Teams Alter End-
      of-Life Experiences of Patients and Their Caregivers?', *Journal of Pain
      and Symptom Management* 25, no. 2 (2003): 150–68.

48   Leadbeater and Garber.

49   Keshia M. Pollack, Dan Morhaim, and Michael A. Williams, 'The
      Public's Perspectives on Advance Directives in Maryland: Implications
      for State Legislative and Regulatory Policy', *Health Policy* 96, no. 1
      (2010): 57–63.

50   'Advance Care Planning: National Guidelines', *Concise Guidance to Good
      Practice* 12 (Royal College of Physicians, 2009).

51   Chana Joffe-Walt, 'The Town Where Everyone Talks About
      Death', NPR, 5 March 2014, =www.npr.org/sections/
      money/2014/03/05/286126451/living-wills-are-the-talk-of-the-town-
      in-la-crosse-wis.

52   Baohui Zhang, Alexi A. Wright, Haiden A. Huskamp, Matthew E.
      Nilsson, Matthew L. Maciejewski, Craig C. Earle, Susan D. Block et al.,
      'HealthCare Costs in the Last Week of Life: Associations with End-of-Life
      Conversations', *Archives of Internal Medicine* 169, no. 5 (2009): 480–8.

53   '2011 Minnesota Statutes', The Office of the Revisor of Statutes, www.
      revisor.mn.gov/statutes/percent20?id=256B.0756&year=2011; Shana
      F. Sandberg, Clese Erikson, Ross Owen, Katherine D. Vickery, Scott T.
      Shimotsu, Mark Linzer, Nancy A. Garrett et al., 'Hennepin Health: A
      Safety-Net Accountable Care Organization for the Expanded Medicaid
      Population', *Health Affairs* 33, no. 11 (2014): 1975–1984.

54   Story drawn from 'Member Spotlight: Ron', Hennepin Health, http://
      content.govdelivery.com/accounts/MNHENNE/bulletins/be91e8.

55   Sandeep Jauhar, 'Bring Back House Calls', *New York Times*, 14 October
      2015, www.nytimes.com/2015/10/15/opinion/bring-back-house-
      calls.html.

56   Debra Umberson and Jennifer Karas Montez, 'Social Relationships
      and Health a Flashpoint for Health Policy', *Journal of Health and Social
      Behavior* 51, no. 1 suppl (2010): S54–S66.

57   For more, see Blue Zones, www.bluezones.com.

Chapter 5

1   Patrick Holden, e-mail to authors, 23 December 2014.

2   For British figures, see: 'Antimicrobial Resistance – Why the
      Irresponsible Use of Antibiotics in Agriculture Must Stop', *Alliance
      to Save Our Antibiotics* (June 2014), 5. For American figures, see
      PolitiFact's analysis in Becky Bowers, 'Rep. Louise Slaughter Says 80%
      of Antibiotics Are Fed to Livestock', *Tampa Bay Times*'s PolitiFact.com,
      15 October 2013.

3   Antibiotics don't work for every disease on factory farms. Porcine epidemic diarrhoea, a virus, emerged and spread so quickly that some workers resorted to pureeing the intestines of dead piglets and feeding it back to the mothers in order to 'vaccinate' them. I imagine access to pasture, more humane conditions and a natural diet would have been equally effective at keeping them healthy, but this almost certainly would have been less profitable. See Nick Kristof, 'Is That Sausage Worth This?' *New York Times*, 20 February 2014. See also 'Fight Cruelty: Chicken FAQ', ASPCA, 2015, www. aspca.org/fight-cruelty/farm-animal-cruelty/chicken-faq; 'Welfare Issues for Meat Chickens', Compassion in World Farming, 2014, www.ciwf.org.uk/farm-animals/chickens/meat-chickens/welfare-issues; and Robert F. Wideman and Rhonda D. Prisby, 'Bone Circulatory Disturbances in the Development of Spontaneous Bacterial Chondronecrosis with Osteomyelitis: A Translational Model for the Pathogenesis of Femoral Head Necrosis', *Frontiers in Endocrinology* 3 (February 2012).

4   Tom Frieden, *Antibiotic Resistance Threats in the United States, 2013* (Centers for Disease Control and Prevention, US Department of Health and Human Services, 2013), 11.

5   For more, see Maryn McKenna, 'How Your Chicken Dinner Is Creating a Drug-Resistant Superbug', *Atlantic*, 11 July 2012, www.theatlantic. com/health/archive/2012/07/how-your-chicken-dinner-is-creating-a-drug-resistant-superbug/259700; and Cólín Nunan and Richard Young, 'E. coli Superbugs on Farms and Food', *The Use and Misuse of Antibiotics in UK Agriculture* 6 (Bristol, England: Soil Association, 2012).

6   Liam Donaldson, *150 Years of the Annual Report of the Chief Medical Officer: On the State of Public Health 2008* (London: Department of Health, 2009): 32–9.

7   L. Trasande, J. Blustein, M. Liu, E. Corwin, L. M. Cox, and M. J. Blaser, 'Infant Antibiotic Exposures and Early-Life Body Mass', *International Journal of Obesity* 37, no. 1 (2013): 16–23; Illseung Cho, Shingo Yamanishi, Laura Cox, Barbara A. Methé, Jiri Zavadil, Kelvin Li, Zhan Gao et al., 'Antibiotics in Early Life Alter the Murine Colonic Microbiome and Adiposity', *Nature* 488, no. 7413 (2012): 621–6.

8   To its credit, Perdue, a major chicken manufacturer, announced in late 2014 that it would greatly reduce the use of antibiotics 'medically important to humans' on its farms. McDonald's and Foster Farms have made similar moves. Although these are steps in the right direction and should be encouraged, general antibiotic use is still profligate (in at least 95 per cent of meat sold in the United States), even among these producers.

9   Although E. coli, mad cow, salmonella, and other such outbreaks are indeed likelier to happen in concentrated animal feedlots than on less dense pastures, food disease is always an inevitability, however humane or sustainable the operation is.

10 James R. Johnson, Michael A. Kuskowski, Kirk Smith, Timothy T. O'Bryan, and SitaTatini, 'Antimicrobial-Resistant and Extraintestinal

Pathogenic Escherichia coli in Retail Foods', *Journal of Infectious Diseases* 191, no. 7 (2005): 1040–9.

11   For emergency investigations, see: 'Poultry Processors and Retailers Respond to the Campylobacter Claims', *Guardian*, 23 July 2014. For campylobacter figures in Britain, see: 'Campylobacter', Food Standards Agency, https://www.food.gov.uk/science/microbiology/campylobacterevidenceprogramme.

12   Felicity Lawrence, Andrew Wasley, and RaduCiorniciuc, 'Revealed: The Dirty Secret of the UK's Poultry Industry', *Guardian*, 23 July 2014.

13   Howard Moskowitz, quoted in Michael Moss, 'The Extraordinary Science of Addictive Junk Food', *New York Times* magazine, 24 February 2013, http://www.nytimes.com/2013/02/24/magazine/the-extraordinary-science-of-junk-food.html.

14   'Müller Corner Fruit Strawberry', *Müller UK & Ireland*, 2015, https://www.muller.co.uk/nc/our-brands/mueller-yogurt-desserts-brands/product-details.html; 'KitKat Collection: 4 Finger Milk Nutritional Information', *Société des Produits Nestlé S.A*, 2015, http://www.kitkat.co.uk/content/kitkatcollection/FourFinger.

15   Larry Hand and Madeline Drexler, 'Public Health Takes Aim at Sugar and Salt', Harvard School of Public Health Review, Fall 2009.

16   '6-inch Low Fat Subs: Nutritional Information', *Subway*, http://www.subway.co.uk/assets/pdf/subway-nutritional-values-uk.pdf.

17   'Heinz Tomato Ketchup', *H.J. Heinz Foods UK Limited*, http://www.heinz.co.uk/en/Products/Tomato-Ketchup/Products/Heinz-Tomato-Ketchup.

18   Manny Fernandez, 'Cheese Whatevers, City Has Them by the Handful', *New York Times*, 4 August 2010, www.nytimes.com/2010/08/04/nyregion/04cheez.html.

19   Moss, 'The Extraordinary Science of Addictive Junk Food'.

20   Bryony Butland, Susan Jebb, Peter Kopelman, K. McPherson, S. Thomas, J. Mardell and V. Parry, Foresight: *Tackling Obesities: Future Choices, Project Report* (Government Office for Science, 2007).

21   This assumes a projected UK population of 77 million, per ONS estimations. In 2015, fewer than half the population paid personal income tax, so we conservatively estimate the tax base in 2050 at 40 million individuals. See Office for National Statistics, 'UK National Population Projections – Principals and Variants, 2012-2087', http://www.ons.gov.uk/ons/interactive/uk-nationalpopulation-projections--dvc3/index.html. and 'Number of Individual Income Taxpayers by Marginal Rate, Gender and Age, 1990–91 to 2014–15', https://www.gov.uk/government/system/uploads/attachment_data/file/404149/Table_2.1.pdf.

22   Niman Ranch, profiled in more detail on page 141.

23   Matt Rothe, quoted in Erik Olesund, 'How the Tractor Ruined Farming', *Green Grid Radio*, 28 June 2014; and from interview by authors, Stanford, CA, 24 October 2014.

24   *Soil: Protect European Soil from Environmental Damage* (European Environmental Bureau, 2015), www.eeb.org/index.cfm/activities/biodiversity-nature/soil.

25   Stephen Devlin, Thomas Dosch, Aniol Esteban and Griffin Carpenter, *Urgent Recall: Our Food System Under Review* (New Economics Foundation, November 2014).

26   Parliament of the United Kingdom, *Agricultural Incomes and Subsidies* (2012 Data).

27   'Soil Association 2014 Organic Market Report Reveals Growth in Organic Sales for the First Time in Four Years', *Soil Association*, 13 March 2014, http://www.soilassociation.org/news/newsstory/articleid/6650/soil-association-2014-organic-market-report-reveals-growth-in-organic-sales-for-the-first-time-in-fo. 50 per cent of the UK's total croppable area is dedicated to cereal production and 49 per cent of cereals are used to feed livestock. (Source: author's calculations from Department for Environment, Food and Rural Affairs, Department of Agriculture and Rural Development (Northern Ireland), The Scottish Government, Rural and Environment Research and Analysis Directorate, Welsh Assembly Government, The Department for Rural Affairs and Heritage, *Agriculture in the United Kingdom*, 2012 (National Statistics, 2013).)

28   Ilan Brat and Sarah Nassauer, 'Chipotle Suspends Pork Sales at a Third of Its Restaurants', *Wall Street Journal*, 13 January 2015, www.wsj.com/articles/chipotle-suspends-pork-sales-at-a-third-of-its-restaurants-1421194340.

29   Allison Aubry, 'Antibiotic-Free Meat Business Is Booming, Thanks to Chipotle', NPR, 31 May 2012, www.npr.org/sections/thesalt/2012/05/31/154084442/antibiotic-free-meat-business-is-booming-thanks-to-chipotle.

30   As defended by the pork industry. See Rick Berman, 'Commentary: Playing Chicken with Pork', PORK Network, 28 February 2013, www.porknetwork.com/pork-news/Commentary-Playing-chicken-with-pork-193903501.html?view=all.

31   Nathanael Johnson, 'Swine of the Times', *Harper's Magazine*, May 2006.

32   Paul Willis, phone interview by authors, 12 November 2014.

33   Anya Fernald, phone interview by authors, 20 October 2014.

34   Jay Rayner, 'Booths: The Honest Supermarket', *Observer*, 13 November 2011.

35   Geico Insurance, 'Free Range Chicken: It's What You Do', YouTube.com, 8 March 2015, www.youtube.com/watch?v=3v1wFKKWMCA.

36   Bedded space is technically defined as 'littered' space. While EU regulations require slightly more total space per bird, they make no requirements for its material. For more, see: Council Regulation (EC) 1999/74 of 19 July 1999 laying down minimum standards for the protection of laying hens [1999] OJ L203/53.

37   European Commission Decision No. 543/2008/EC (Poultrymeat Standards), 2008, O.J. L 157/46 Philip Lymbery, email to authors, 29 March 2015.

38   Michael Pollan, *Cooked: A Natural History of Transformation* (London: Allen Lane, 2013), 264; Allison Aubrey, 'Where's the Whole Grain in Most of Our Wheat Bread? ', NPR, 15 April 2014, www.npr.org/sections/thesalt/2014/04/15/301473319/wheres-the-whole-grain-in-most-of-our-wheat-bread.

39   Klaus von Grebmer, Amy Saltzman, EkinBirol, Doris Weismann, Nilam
      Prasai, Sandra Yin, YisehacYohannes et al., *Global Hunger Index: The
      Challenge of Hidden Hunger, Synopsis* (International Food Policy Research
      Institute, 2014), www.ifpri.org/publication/synopsis-2014-global-hunger-
      index-challenge-hidden-hunger; Catherine Price, 'Vitamins Hide the
      Low Quality of Our Food', *New York Times*, 15 February 2015, www.nytimes.
      com/2015/02/15/opinion/sunday/vitamins-hide-the-low-quality-of-our-
      food.html.

40   According to Dr Alex Richardson, a research fellow at Oxford
      University. See: Andrew Purvis, 'Running on Empty Carbs', *Guardian*,
      22 March 2009.

41   Leicester City Council, 'Council Meat Tests Highlight Labelling
      Concerns', 3 November 2014, http://news.leicester.gov.uk/
      newsArchiveDetail.aspx?Id=f2792.

42   Stephen Evans, 'Mislabelled Fish Slip Into Europe's Menus', *BBC News*,
      2 April 2013.

43   Various studies reported in: 'Seafood Fraud', Oceana, http://oceana.
      org/sites/default/fi les/euo/OCEANA_fi sh_label_english.pdf.

44   For Ireland, see: Dana D. Miller and Stefano Mariani, 'Smoke, Mirrors,
      and Mislabeled Cod: Poor Transparency in the European Seafood
      Industry', Frontiers in Ecology and the Environment 8, no. 10 (2010):
      517–521. For Paris figures, see: 'Seafood Fraud', Oceana.

45   Department of State, Department of Commerce, *Action Plan for
      Implementing the Task Force Recommendations* (Presidential Task Force on
      Combating IUU Fishing and Seafood Fraud, 2015).

46   Kimberly Warner, Walker Timme, Beth Lowell, and Michael Hirshfield,
      Oceana Study Reveals Seafood Fraud Nationwide (Oceana, February 2013),
      http://oceana.org/sites/default/files/reports/National_Seafood_
      Fraud_Testing_Results_FINAL.pdf.

47   Michael Pollan, quoted in Ezra Klein, 'Big Food', *Vox*, 23 April 2014,
      www.vox.com/2014/4/23/5627992/big-food-michael-pollan-thinks-
      wall-street-has-way-too-much-influence.

48   Kelly Brownell, quoted in Moss, 'The Extraordinary Science'.

49   Indeed, although I'm happy to excoriate soft drink companies, it
      does seem rather unfair to single them out while ignoring all the
      other junk food in our diets. Dietary Guidelines Advisory Committee,
      Scientific Report of the 2015 Dietary Guidelines Advisory Committee
      (Washington, DC: USDA and US Department of Health and Human
      Services, 2015).

50   Ami Sedghi, 'UK Tops Chart of EU Food Waste', *Guardian*, 22 May
      2015, http://www.theguardian.com/world/2015/may/22/uk-tops-
      chart-of-eu-food-waste.

51   Department for Environment Food & Rural Affairs, *Food Statistics
      Pocketbook 2015*, (London: National Statistics, 2015), 35.

52   For more, visit 'Animal Welfare', *Jeremy Coller Foundation*, http://www..
      jeremycollerfoundation.org/programmes/animal-welfare.

53   J. Kiley Hamlin, 'Moral Judgment and Action in Preverbal Infants
      and Toddlers Evidence for an Innate Moral Core', *Current Directions
      in Psychological Science* 22, no. 3 (2013): 186–193; Abraham Sagi and

Martin L. Hoffman, 'Empathic Distress in the Newborn,' *Developmental Psychology* 12, no. 2 (1976): 175.

54   Jeremy Bentham, *An Introduction to the Principles of Morals and Legislation*, ch. 17, para. 122 (1789).

55   Nicky Amos and Rory Sullivan, 'The Business Benchmark on Farm Animal Welfare: 2014 Report', *Business Benchmark on Farm Animal Welfare* (2014), 35.

56   *Farm Assurance Schemes & Animal Welfare: How the Standards Compare: 2012* (OneKind and Compassion in World Farming, 2012), www.ciwf. org.uk/media/5231246/standards_analysis_exec_summary.pdf.

57   'Philip Lymbery: Chief Executive', Compassion in World Farming, 2014, www.ciwf.org.uk/about-us/our-staff/philip-lymbery.

58   Jonathan Safran Foer, *Eating Animals*, 59 (New York: Back Bay Books, 2009).

Chapter 6

1   Priorities USA Action, 'Stage', YouTube.com, 23 June 2012, www. youtube.com/watch?v=oLo0Jwj03JU.

2   Angei Drobnic Holan and Nai Issa, 'In Context: Hillary Clinton and Don't Let Anybody Tell You That Corporations Create Jobs', *Tampa Bay Times*'s Politifact, 30 October 2014, www.politifact.com/truth-o-meter/   article/2014/oct/30/context-hillary-clinton-and-dont-let-anybody-tell.

3   Jonathan Sacks, *The Dignity of Difference: Avoiding the Clash of Civilizations* (Foreign Policy Research Institute, July 2002).

4   David Packard, quoted in James C. Collins and Jerry I. Porras, 'Building Your Company's Vision', *Harvard Business Review*, September 1996.

5   Estimates on farming vary and range from as recent as 6,500 to as early as 14,000 years ago. For various sources, see Felipe Fernández-Armesto, *The World: A History*, 2nd ed. (London: Prentice Hall, 2010), 31–56; Peter Watson, *Ideas: A History of Thought and Invention, from Fire to Freud* (New York: Harper Perennial, 2005), 53; *Collins Atlas of World History*, ed. Geoffrey Barraclough (Ann Arbor, MI: Arbor Press, 2003), 38. For trade, see Matt Ridley, 'When Ideas Have Sex', TED Global 2010, Oxford, England, July 2010, www.ted.com/talks/matt_ridley_when_ideas_have_sex?language=en.

6   Ridley, 'When Ideas Have Sex', details in ibid.

7   Stephen Machin, 'Real Wages and Living Standards: The Latest UK Evidence', *LSE Centre for Economic Performance*, 6 April 2015, http:// blogs.lse.ac.uk/politicsandpolicy/real-wages-and-living-standards-the-latest-uk-evidence/.

8   Median household income figures calculated from ONS data on median household income and the Bank of England's inflation calculator. For more information on median pay, see: Simon Lowe, 'Plotting A New Course to Improved Governance', *Corporate Governance Review 2014*, (Grant Thornton UK LLP, 2014), 32.

9   'FTSE 100 Directors' Total Earnings Jump By 21% in a Year', *Thomson Reuters* and *IDS*, London, 13 October 2014.

10   Office for National Statistics, *Annual Survey of Hours and Earnings, 2015 Provisional Results*, 2054, http://www.ons.gov.uk/ons/rel/ashe/annual-survey-of-hours-and-earnings/2015-provisional-results/stb-ashe.html.

11   Taking Stock – Review of 2016 AGM Season (PwC, 7 September 2015).

12   Data compiled by Robert Colvile from Income Data Services, FTSE, and Bloomberg. See Robert Colvile, 'Yes, CEOs Are Ludicrously Overpaid. And Yes, It's Getting Worse', *Telegraph*, 13 October 2014.

13   Sam Colt, 'Tim Cook's Total Pay for 2014 Was Over \$100 Million', *Business Insider*, 24 January 2015, www.businessinsider.com/heres-how-tim-cook-raked-in-over-100-million-in-2014-2015-1.

14   Reuters, 'A.I.G. Pays Its Ex-Chief \$47 Million', *New York Times*, 2 July 2008; author calculations from Yahoo Finance; Timothy G. Massad, 'Overall \$182 Billion Committed to Stabilize AIG During the Financial Crisis Is Now Fully Recovered', *Treasury Notes* (U.S. Department of the Treasury), http://www.treasury.gov/connect/blog/Pages/aig-182-billion.aspx.

15   Jenny Chu, Jonathan Faasse and P. Raghavendra Rau, 'Do Compensation Consultants Enable Higher CEO Pay?', *New Evidence from Recent Disclosure Rule Changes*, 23 September 2014.

16   Nassim Nicholas Taleb, *Black Swan: The Impact of the Highly Improbable Fragility* (New York: Random House, 2010), 182.

17   Rex Nutting, 'Transcript of Holder's Admission on Too-Big-to-Jail Banks', *Market Watch*, 7 March 2013, http://blogs.marketwatch.com/thetell/2013/03/07/transcript-of-holders-admission-on-too-big-to-jail-banks.

18   Peter Schroeder and Kevin Cirilli, 'Warren, Left Fume Over Deal', *The Hill*, 10 December 2014, http://thehill.com/regulation/finance/226638-democrats-balking-at-dodd-frank-changes-in-cromnibus.

19   Matt Fuller, 'Republican Champion of Dodd-Frank Changes Goes After Elizabeth Warren', *Roll Call*, 28 January 2015, http://blogs.rollcall.com/218/on-a-controversial-law-subtlety-is-key-for-kevin-yoder; 'Rep. Keven Yoder: Top 20 Industries Contributing to Campaign Committee', OpenSecrets.org, 2 February 2015, www.opensecrets.org/politicians/industries.php?cycle=2014&cid=N00031502&type=I&newmem=N.

20   Eric Lipton and Ben Protess, 'Banks' Lobbyists Help in Drafting Financial Bills', *New York Times*, 23 May 2013, http://dealbook.nytimes.com/2013/05/23/banks-lobbyists-help-in-drafting-financial-bills.

21   Andy Borowtiz, 'Citigroup to Move Headquarters to US Capitol Building', *New Yorker*, 13 December 2013, www.newyorker.com/humor/borowitz-report/citigroup-move-headquarters-u-s-capitol-building.

22   Steven Mufson and Tom Hamburger, 'Jamie Dimon Himself Called to Urge Support for the Derivatives Rule in the Spending Bill', *Washington Post*, 11 December 2014, www.washingtonpost.com/news/wonk/wp/2014/12/11/the-item-that-is-blowing-up-the-budget-deal.

23   Eric Lipton, 'For Freshman of the House, Seats of Plenty', *New York Times*, 11 August 2013, www.nytimes.com/2013/08/11/us/politics/for-freshmen-in-the-house-seats-of-plenty.html?_r=0.

24 'Barclays Appoints Hector Sants', *Barclays*, 12 December 2012, http://www.barclays.com/news/2012/12/barclays-appoints-hector-sants.html.

25 'Sir Jeremy Heywood, Cabinet Secretary and Head of the Civil Service: Biography', *British Goverment*, https://www.gov.uk/government/people/jeremy-heywood.

26 'Sir James Crosby Resigns from FSA', *BBC News*, 11 February 2009.

27 'About: Secretary of the Treasury Jacob J. Lew', US Department of the Treasury, 5 June 2014, www.treasury.gov/about/Pages/Secretary.aspx.

28 Philip Rucker and Joe Stephens, 'White House Economics Aide Summers Discloses Income', *Washington Post*, 4 April 2009, www.washingtonpost.com/wp-dyn/content/article/2009/04/03/AR2009040303732.html.

29 'Alan Greenspan to Consult for Deutsche Bank Corporate and Investment Bank', Deutsche Bank, 13 August 2007, www.db.com/presse/en/content/press_releases_2007_3606.htm.

30 Patrick Holden, 'The Price of Milk', *Sustainable Food Trust*, 16 January 2015, http://sustainablefoodtrust.org/articles/price-milk/.

31 Julia Glotz, 'Sainsbury's and Co-op Follow Tesco with Milk Price Cuts', *The Grocer*, 5 March 2014.

32 A *Guardian* investigation and analysis conducted in 2014. Simon Goodley and Leila Haddou, 'Revealed: Tesco Hoarding Land That Could Build 15,000 Homes', *Guardian*, 26 June 2014.

33 Competition Commission, *Market investigation into the Supply of Groceries in the UK* (London: UK Competition Commission, 2008), 11.

34 Goodley and Haddou, 'Revealed'.

35 Tanya Pilgrim, 'The End of the Supermarket Sweep?', *Pennington Manches*, 8 October 2012, http://www.penningtons.co.uk/news-publications/archivenews/2012/the-end-of-the-supermarket-sweep/.

36 'Great Britain Grocery Market Share (12 weeks ending)', *Kanter World Panel*, http://www.kantarworldpanel.com/en/grocery-market-share/great-britain.

37 Antony Seely, 'Supermarkets: Competition Inquiries into the Groceries Market', *House of Commons Library Standard Note: SN03653* (2012); Competition Commission, *The Supply of Groceries*, 72.

38 'Consumer Prices', *OECD*, 30 March 2015, https://stats.oecd.org/index.aspx?queryid=221.

39 Christine Tacon, 'Welcome from the Groceries Code Adjudicator' in *News from the Adjudicator*, 17 November 2015, https://www.gov.uk/government/uploads/system/uploads/attachment_data/file/477446/News_from_the_Adjudicator_Edition_5_final.pdf.

40 The researchers, Gerard Hoberg and Gordon Phillips, applied the widely accepted Herfindahl-Hirschman Index (HHI) to numerous companies and overall industries.

41 For information on many of these mergers, see Theo Francis and Ryan Knutson, 'Wave of Megadeals Tests Antitrust Limits in U.S.', *Wall Street Journal*, 18 October 2015, www.wsj.com/articles/wave-of-megadeals-tests-antitrust-limits-in-u-s-1445213306.

42   Mark Leibovich, *This Town: Two Parties and a Funeral—Plus, Plenty of Valet Parking!—in America's Gilded Capital* (New York: Penguin Random House, 2013), 330.

43   Paul Blumenthal and Ryan Grim, 'The Inside Story of How Citizens United Has Changed Washington Lawmaking', *Huffington Post*, 25 February 2015, www.huffingtonpost.com/2015/02/26/citizens-united-congress_n_6723540.html.

44   Through 2014. See 'Who's Up, Who's Down?', Open Secrets, 2015, www.opensecrets.org/lobby/incdec.php.

45   Elizabeth Warren, interview by Michael Krasny, *Forum*, 88.5 KQED FM, 7 May 2014.

46   Allison Fitzgerald, 'Koch, Exxon Mobil Among Corporations Helping Write State Laws', *Bloomberg*, 21 July 2011, www.bloomberg.com/news/articles/2011-07-21/koch-exxon-mobil-among-corporations-helping-write-state-laws.

47   John Oliver, 'Last Week Tonight with John Oliver: State Legislatures and ALEC' (HBO), YouTube.com, www.youtube.com/watch?v=aIMgfBZrrZ8.

48   Fitzgerald, 'Koch, Exxon Mobil'.

49   'Ag-Gag Laws Silence Whistleblowers', Moyers & Company, 10 July 2013, http://billmoyers.com/2013/07/10/alec-activists-and-ag-gag.

50   John Light, 'Frequently Asked Questions About ALEC', Moyers & Company, 28 September 2012, http://billmoyers.com/content/frequently-asked-questions-about-alec.

51   Christopher Snowdon, 'Who's Killing the British Pub?', *Institute for Economic Affairs Blog*, 10 December 2014.

52   Danny Hakim, 'Saving an Endangered British Species: The Pub', *New York Times*, 17 February 2014.

53   Mark Gilbert, 'British Pubs Cry in Their Beer', *BloombergView*, 12 December 2014.

54   Ofgem, The Revenues, Costs and Profits of the Energy Companies in 2013, Ofgem, 2013, https://www.ofgem.gov.uk/ofgem-publications/90701/css2013summarydocument.pdf, 7; Ofgem, Supply Market Indicator for April 2015, Ofgem, https://www.ofgem.gov.uk/gas/retail-market/monitoring-data-and-statistics/understanding-energy-prices-great-britain/supply-market-indicator.

55   That we dislike cheating is no surprise, of course, but it's telling that we will, as humans, give up some of our reward in a transaction if it means penalising someone who has cheated. In repeated versions of the 'Ultimatum Game', psychologists allow a participant to divide an amount of money between themselves and a second participant however they choose, with the caveat that if the second person rejects the offer, neither gets anything. Although the economically rational decision would be to accept any offer above 0, it's almost always the case that if the second participant feels short-changed, they are more likely to retaliate by rejecting the money – hurting themselves in order to punish the first participant.

56   Sutirtha Bagchi and Jan Svejnar, 'Does Wealth Inequality Matter for Growth? The Effect of Billionaire Wealth, Income Distribution, and

Poverty', *Journal of Comparative Economics* 43, no. 3 (August 2015): 505–30.

57 John M. Connor and Robert H. Lande, 'Cartels as Rational Business Strategy: Crime Pays', *Cardozo Law Review* 34, no. 427 (2012): 427–89, 430.

58 Stanford, who also served as California governor and represented the state in the US Senate, founded the university in 1885 with his wife, Jane, in honour of their late teenage son, Leland Stanford Jr.

59 Robert Reich, 'Big Tech Has Become Way Too Powerful', *New York Times*, 18 September 2015, www.nytimes.com/2015/09/20/opinion/is-big-tech-too-powerful-ask-google.html.

60 US Census Bureau, *Business Dynamics Statistics: Firm Characteristics Data Tables* (Washington, DC: Department of Commerce, 2015), www.census.gov/ces/dataproducts/bds/data_firm.html.

61 Taleb, 282.

62 Ibid., 291.

63 'Red Dress Boutique', *SharkTank Blog*, http://sharktankblog.com/business/red-dress-boutique.

64 Rolfe Winkler and Douglas MacMillan, 'The Secret Math of Airbnb's $24 Billion Valuation', *Wall Street* Journal, 17 June 2015, www.wsj.com/articles/the-secret-math-of-airbnbs-24-billion-valuation-1434568517.

65 Bastian Lehmann, quoted in Farhad Manjoo, 'Amazon Not as Unstoppable as It Might Appear', *New York Times*, 18 December 2014, www.nytimes.com/2014/12/18/technology/personaltech/amazon-not-as-unstoppable-as-it-may-appear.html.

66 Carolyn Said, 'Peers Helps Uber, Lyft Drivers Get Back on Road After Accidents', *San Francisco Chronicle*, 4 December 2014, http://sanfrancisco.suntimes.com/sf-business/7/74/42864/peers-helps-uber-lyft-drivers-get-back-on-road-after-accidents.

67 Mark Rogowsky, 'After the New Jersey Ban, Here's Where Tesla Can (and Cannot) Sell Its Cars', *Forbes*, 15 March 2014, www.forbes.com/sites/markrogowsky/2014/03/15/after-the-new-jersey-ban-heres-where-tesla-can-and-cannot-sell-its-cars.

68 'Michigan Becomes 5th US State to Thwart Direct Tesla Car Sales', *Reuters*, 22 October 2014, www.reuters.com/article/2014/10/21/tesla-motors-michigan-idUSL2N0SG2YE20141021.

Chapter 7

1 Mohammed Abdul Ali and Abdul Kader, quoted in Jim Yardley, 'Bangladesh Pollution, Told in Colors and Smells', *New York Times*, 15 July 2013, www.nytimes.com/2013/07/15/world/asia/bangladesh-pollution-told-in-colors-and-smells.html.

2 Emily Chang, 'China's Famed Pearl River Under Denim Threat', CNN, 27 April 2010, www.cnn.com/2010/WORLD/asiapcf/04/26/china.denim.water.pollution.

3 'Dye Industry: Fact Sheet', Green Cross Switzerland, 2012, www.greencross.ch/nc/en/print/news-info-en/case-studies/environmental-reports/ten-most-dangerous-sources-of-environmental-toxins-2012/2012/dye-industry.html.

4   Sajjad Hussein, 'Six Months After Bangladesh Factory Collapse, Workers Remain in Peril', CNN, 24 October 2013, www.cnn.com/2013/10/24/opinion/bangladesh-garment-workers.

5   Mark Spera, quoted in Angela Salazar, 'BeGood Clothing's New Line—Organic Cotton and Silk Basics', *SF Gate*, 12 September 2014, www.sfgate.com/style/article/BeGood-Clothing-s-new-line-organic-cotton-and-5629690.php.

6   As reported in Larry Buchannan, Josh Keller, and Haeyoun Park, 'Your Contribution to the California Drought', *New York Times*, 21 May 2015, www.nytimes.com/interactive/2015/05/21/us/your-contribution-to-the-california-drought.html?_r=0. For some original figures, see either Mesfin M. Mekonnen and Arjen Y. Hoekstra, 'A Global Assessment of the Water Footprint of Farm Animal Products', *Ecosystems* 15, no. 3 (2012): 401–15, or various estimates as assessed by the Pacific Institute.

7   'Water Conservation Tips', *NationalGeographic*, http://environment.nationalgeographic.com/environment/freshwater/water-conservation-tips.

8   Simon Head, *Mindless: Why Smarter Machines Are Making Dumber Humans* (New York: Basic Books, 2014), 42.

9   Journalist Carole Cadwalladr spent a week working in Amazon's Swansea, Wales, factory. She recounts her experience here: Carole Cadwalladr, 'My Week as an Amazon Insider', *Guardian*, 30 November 2013, www.theguardian.com/technology/2013/dec/01/week-amazon-insider-feature-treatment-employees-work.

10 Simon Head, 'Worse than Wal-Mart: Amazon's Sick Brutality and Secret History of Ruthlessly Intimidating Workers', *Salon*, 23 February 2014, www.salon.com/2014/02/23/worse_than_wal_mart_amazons_sick_brutality_and_secret_history_of_ruthlessly_intimidating_workers.

11 Jodi Kantor and David Streitfeld, 'Amazon's Bruising, Thrilling Workplace', *New York Times*, 16 August 2014, www.nytimes.com/images/2015/08/16/nytfrontpage/scan.pdf.

12 'Full Memo: Jeff Bezos Responds to Brutal NYT Story, Says It Doesn't Represent the Amazon He Leads', GeekWire, 16 August 2015, www.geekwire.com/2015/full-memo-jeff-bezos-responds-to-cutting-nyt-expose-says-tolerance-for-lack-of-empathy-needs-to-be-zero.

13 Spencer Soper, 'Amazon Workers Cool After Company Took Heat for Hot Warehouse', *Morning Call*, 3 June 2012, http://articles.mcall.com/2012-06-03/business/mc-amazon-warehouse-air-conditioning-20120602_1_warehouse-workers-air-conditioning-breinigsville-warehouse.

14 Spencer Woodman, 'Exclusive: Amazon Makes Even Temporary Warehouse Worker Sign 18-Month Non-Competes', *Verge*, 26 March 2015, www.theverge.com/2015/3/26/8280309/amazon-warehouse-jobs-exclusive-noncompete-contracts.

15 In addition to undercover investigations cited above, you can view video from another by the BBC's *Panorama*, 2013, www.bbc.co.uk/programmes/b03k5kzp. In its response, Amazon also said that it

'adhere[s] to all regulations and employment law'. Although its response is no longer posted on its website, it is quoted in Matthew Jarvis, 'Amazon Response to BBC Panorama Worker Criticism', *PCR*, 26 November 2013, http://www.pcr-online.biz/news/read/amazon-responds-to-bbc-panorama-worker-criticism/032581.

16   Portia Crowe, 'Disclosing Pay Gaps Make No Sense for Wall Street Banks', *Business Insider*, 9 August 2015, http://www.businessinsider.com/disclosing-pay-gaps-on-wall-street-2015-8.

17   Gretchen Morgenson, 'The Boss Actually Said This: Pay Me Less', *New York Times*, 18 December 2005, http://query.nytimes.com/gst/fullpage.html?res=9D01EFDC1630F93BA25751C1A9639C8B63.

18   Will Ashworth, 'RiskMetrics Two Years After IPO', *Investopedia*, 28 February 2010, www.investopedia.com/stock-analysis/2010/riskmetrics-two-years-after-ipo-riskmscimhptrifigacas0304.aspx.

19   Almuth McDowall, quoted in Emma Jacobs, 'Strategies for Calling Time on Long Hours', *Financial Times*, 18 August 2014.

20   Sir Richard Branson, 'Excerpt from: *The Virgin Way: Everything I Know About Leadership*', Virgin.com, 23 September 2014, www.virgin.com/richard-branson/why-were-letting-virgin-staff-take-as-much-holiday-as-they-want.

21   Anne-Marie Slaughter, 'Why Women Still Can't Have It All', *Atlantic*, 13 June 2012, www.theatlantic.com/magazine/archive/2012/07/why-women-still-cant-have-it-all/309020.

22   Heather Boushey, 'Family Policy: The Foundation of a Middle-Out Agenda', *Democracy* no. 29 (Summer 2013).

23   Peter H. Villanova, John Bernardin, Sue A. Dahmus, and Randi L. Sims, 'Rater Leniency and Performance Appraisal Discomfort', *Educational and Psychological Measurement* 53, no. 3 (1993): 789–799.

24   Sam Culbert, quoted in Melissa Dahl, 'It's Time to Kill the Performance Review', *New York Magazine*, 1 June 2015, http://nymag.com/scienceofus/2015/05/time-to-revamp-the-performance-review.html.

25   Thomas Krommenacker and Ben Robinson, *Metro Bank: Breaking the Mould but Breaking the Malaise?* (Geneva, Switzerland: Temenos Headquarters SA, 2011), 13.

26   Mary Beth Quirk, 'Zappos CSR's Kindness Warms Our Cold Hearts', *Consumerist*, 17 January 2011, http://consumerist.com/2011/01/17/zappos-customer-service-reps-kindness-warms-our-cold-hearts.

27   Armando Roggio, 'The Zappos Effect: 5 Great Customer Ideas for Smaller Business', *Practical Ecommerce*, 21 March 2011, www.practicalecommerce.com/articles/2662-The-Zappos-Effect-5-Great-Customer-Service-Ideas-for-Smaller-Businesses.

28   Nathan Vardi, 'How "The Outsiders" Became One of the Most Important Business Books in America', *Forbes*, 8 May 2014, www.forbes.com/sites/nathanvardi/2014/05/08/how-the-outsiders-became-one-of-the-most-important-business-books-in-america.

29   William Thorndike, *The Outsiders: Eight Unconventional CEOs and Their Radically Rational Blueprint for Success* (Boston, MA: Harvard University Press, 2012), xii.

30   Ibid., 202.

31 Ibid., 70, 73.

32 Ibid., 23.

33 William Weldon, interview, *Knowledge@Wharton*, 25 June 2008, http://knowledge.wharton.upenn.edu/article/johnson-johnson-ceo-william-weldon-leadership-in-a-decentralized-company.

34 Bridget Kelly, Jason CG Halford, Emma J. Boyland, Kathy Chapman, Inmaculada Bautista-Castaño, Christina Berg, Margherita Caroli et al., 'Television Food Advertising to Children: A Global Perspective', *American Journal of Public Health* 100, no. 9 (2010): 1730-6.

35 McGinnis, Gootman, and Kraak, *Food Marketing to Children and Youth*.

36 Emma J. Boyland, Sarah Nolan, Bridget Kelly, CatrinTudur-Smith, Andrew Jones, Jason CG Halford, and Eric Robinson, 'Advertising as a Cue to Consume: A Systematic Review and Meta-analysis of the Effects of Acute Exposure to Unhealthy Food and Nonalcoholic Beverage Advertising on Intake in Children and Adults', *The American Journal of Clinical Nutrition* (2016): ajcn120022.

37 Christina A. Roberto, Jenny Baik, Jennifer L. Harris, and Kelly D. Brownell, 'Influence of Licensed Characters on Children's Taste and Snack Preferences', *Pediatrics* 126, no. 1 (2010): 88–93.

38 Emma J. Boyland, Emma, Melissa Kavanagh-Safran, and Jason CG Halford, 'Exposure to 'Healthy Fast Food Meal Bundles in Television Advertisements Promotes Liking for Fast Food but Not Healthier Choices in Children', *British Journal of Nutrition* 113, no. 06 (2015): 1012-18.

39 Xiaomei Cai and Xiaoquan Zhao, 'Click Here, Kids!' *Journal of Children and Media*, 4, no. 2 (2010): 135–54.

40 Jennifer Culp, Robert A. Bell, and Diana Cassady, 'Characteristics of Food Industry Web Sites and "Advergames" Targeting Children', *Journal of Nutrition Education and Behavior*, 42, no. 3 (2010): 197–201.

41 CSM, 8.

42 Harry Wallop, 'Food Companies Play Games with Children's TV Advertising Ban', *Telegraph*, 30 May 2014, http://www.telegraph.co.uk/news/health/children/10865263/Food-companies-play-games-with-childrens-TV-advertising-ban.html.

43 'Information to Make Choices: Dietary Guidelines'.

44 Emma Halliwell, Alice Easun, and Diana Harcourt, 'Body Dissatisfaction: Can a Short Media Literacy Message Reduce Negative Media Exposure Effects Amongst Adolescent Girls?' *British Journal of Health Psychology* 16, no. 2 (2011): 396–403.

45 Anna Holmes, 'Untouched Cover Photos Wanted: $10,000 Reward', *Jezebel*, 21 May 2007.

46 Victoria Rideout, *Advertising to Children and Teens: Current Practices* (San Francisco, CA: Common Sense Media, 2014), 15.

47 Neala Ambrosi Randi, 'Perception of Current and Ideal Body Size in Preschool Age Children', *Perceptual and Motor Skills* 90, no. 3 (2000): 885–9.

48 Girl Scouts and the Dove Self-Esteem Fund, 'Girls and Body Image', www.girlscouts.org/content/dam/girlscouts-gsusa/forms-and-documents/about-girl-scouts/research/beauty_redefined_factsheet.pdf.

49   Ray Anderson, quoted in Emily Langer, 'Ray Anderson, "Greenest CEO in America," Dies at 77', *Washington* Post, 10 August 2011, www.washingtonpost.com/local/obituaries/ray-anderson-greenest-ceo-in-america-dies-at-77/2011/08/10/gIQAGoTU7I_story.html.

50   'Press Release: Interface Reports Fourth Quarter and Fiscal Year 2014 Results', *Interface*, 18 February 2015, http://www.interfaceglobal.com/Investor-Relations/Press-Releases.aspx.

51   'Ray Anderson, Interface Chairman and Sustainability Leader, Dies at 77', Environmental Leader, 9 August 2011, http://www.environmentalleader.com/2011/08/09/ray-anderson-interface-chairman-and-sustainability-leader-dies-at-77.

52   Steve Hilton and Giles Gibbons, *Good Business: Your World Needs You*, (London: Texere Publishing, 2002), 56–8.

53   Liam Casey, interview by Piers Fawkes, *PSFK 2015*, 18 May 2015.

54   David Bonbright, interview by authors, Palo Alto, CA, 24 October 2014.

55   Elon Musk, 'All Our Patent Are Belong to You [*sic*]', Tesla Motors, 12 June 2014, www.teslamotors.com/blog/all-our-patent-are-belong-you.

56   Natasha Jones, 'Funding Circle and Santander Announce Partnership to Support Thousands of UK Businesses', Funding Circle, 18 June 2014, www.fundingcircle.com/blog/2014/06/funding-circle-santander-announce-partnership-support-thousands-uk-businesses.

57   Mark Kleinman, 'Temasek Snaps Up Stake in UK's Funding Circle', *Sky News*, 2 April 2015, http://news.sky.com/story/1457480/temasek-snaps-up-stake-in-uks-funding-circle.

58   'What Is a Benefit Corporation?' B Lab, 2015, http://benefitcorp.net.

59   Ainsley O'Connell, 'Most Innovative Companies 2015: Revolution Foods', *Fast Company*, 2015, www.fastcompany.com/3039619/most-innovative-companies-2015/revolution-foods.

60   Sarah Perez, 'AOL Co-Founder Steve Case Invests $30 Million into School Lunch Company, Revolution Foods', *TechCrunch*, 5 June 2014, http://techcrunch.com/2014/06/05/aol-co-founder-steve-case-invests-30-million-into-school-lunch-company-revolution-foods.

61   'How We Work', Andela, 2015,www.andela.co/how-we-work.

62   Allie Bidwell, 'An African Company Pays People to Learn Computer Science', *U.S. News & World Report*, 14 May 2015, www.usnews.com/news/stem-solutions/articles/2015/05/14/andela-an-african-company-paying-people-to-learn-computer-science.

63   Christine Magee, 'Backed by Spark Capital, Andela Will Develop a Continent of Tech Talent', *Techcrunch*, 25 June 2015, http://techcrunch.com/2015/06/25/backed-by-spark-capital-andela-will-develop-a-continent-of-tech-talent.

Chapter 8

1   David Robinson, interview by authors, London, 24 September 2014.

2   The amount spent on welfare in Britain annually. For more, see Andrew Hood and Paul Johnson, 'What Is Welfare Spending?' *Institute for Fiscal Studies*, 4 November 2014, http://www.ifs.org.uk/publications/7424.

3   Roughly $8 at 2003 exchange rates.

4   Abdul Durrant, quoted in Nick Cohen, 'A Tale of Two Cities', *Guardian*, 19 October 2013, www.theguardian.com/politics/2003/oct/19/socialexclusion.london.

5   Adam Corlett and Laura Gardiner, 'Low Pay Britain 2015', Resolution Foundation, 5 October 2015, www.resolutionfoundation.org/publications/low-pay-britain-2015.

6   'Press Release', Resolution Foundation, 1 October 2014, http://www.resolutionfoundation.org/media/press-releases/a-record-1-2-million-workersto-benefit-from-first-real-terms-minimum-wage-rise-for-six-years-today/.

7   Matthew Bolton, quoted in Dominic Casciani, 'Secret Life of the Office Cleaner', *BBC News*, 19 September 2005.

8   Sendhil Mullainathan, quoted in Maria Konnikova, 'No Money, No Time', *New York Times*, 15 June 2014, http://opinionator.blogs.nytimes.com/2014/06/13/no-clocking-out.

9   Sendhil Mullainathan and Eldar Shafir, *Scarcity: Why Having Too Little Means So Much* (New York: Time Books, 2013), 160.

10   Mullainathan, quoted in Konnikova, 'No Money, No Time'.

11   Johannes Haushofer, quoted in Nicholas Kristof, 'It's Not Just About Bad Choices', *New York Times*, 14 June 2015, www.nytimes.com/2015/06/14/opinion/sunday/nicholas-kristof-its-not-just-about-bad-choices.html.

12   Peter Hotez, quoted in Kristof, 'It's Not Just About Bad Choices'. For the study, see Peter J. Hotez, 'Neglected Infections of Poverty in the United States and Their Effects on the Brain', *JAMA Psychiatry* 71, no. 10 (2014): 1099–1100.

13   Kayte Lawton and Matthew Pennycook, *Beyond the Bottom Line: The Challenges and Opportunities of a Living Wage* (London: IPPR and Resolution Foundation, 2013).

14   Tom MacInnes, Hannah Aldridge, Sabrina Bushe, Peter Kenway, and Adam Tinson, *Monitoring Poverty and Social Exclusion, 2013* (York, England: Joseph Rowntree Foundation, 2013).

15   Alfred Deakin, quoted in Marilyn Lake, 'Minimum Wage Is More than a Safety Net, It's a Symbol of Australian Values', *The Age* (Melbourne), 10 April 2014, www.theage.com.au/comment/minimum-wage-is-more-than-a-safety-net-its-a-symbol-of-australian-values-20140409-zqsii.html.

16   Winston Churchill, Hansard House of Commons Debates, 28 April 1909, vol. 4, cols. 342–411.

17   Alan Manning, 'The UK's National Minimum Wage', CentrePiece, Autumn 2009.

18   Labour economists David Card and Alan Krueger found that a minimum wage in one jurisdiction they studied increased hiring by 13 per cent. See: David Card and Alan B. Krueger, 'Minimum Wages and Employment: A Case Study of the Fast Food Industry in New Jersey and Pennsylvania', *National Bureau of Economic Research*, no. w4509, 1993.

19   Manning.

20   See Card and Krueger, 'Minimum Wages and Employment'.

21   Jack Kennedy, Tim Moore and Annabel Fiddes, 'Living Wage Research for KPMG: Structural Analysis of Hourly Wages and Current Trends

in Household Finances', 2014 Report (Henley on Thames, England: Markit, 2014), 5.

22   Adam Corlett and Matthew Whittaker, *Low Pay Britain 2014*, (Resolution Foundation, 2014), 29.

23   The other low wage earners work part-time. Lawton and Pennycook, *Beyond the Bottom Line*.

24   HM Revenue & Customs, Child and Working Tax Credits Statistics: Finalised Annual Awards in 2012–13 (London, National Statistics, 2014).

25   'Working Paper: Uprating the UK Living Wage in 2014', Centre for Research in Social Policy, Loughborough University, 2014.

26   'What Is the Living Wage?' *BBC News*, 2 November 2014.

27   Lake, 'Minimum Wage Is More than a Safety Net'.

28   These are a selection of the almost 1,200 Living Wage employers as of January 2016. For a comprehensive list, see http://www.livingwage.org.uk/employers.

29   Cameron Tait, *Work That Pays: The Final Report of the Living Wage Commission* (London Living Wage Commission, 2014), 33.

30   'Global Powers of Retailing 2015: Embracing Innovation', Deloitte, 2015, www2.deloitte.com/au/en/pages/consumer-business/articles/global-powers-of-retailing.html.

31   Unless otherwise noted, all facts and quotes related to Costco come from Brad Stone, 'Costco CEO Craig Jelinek Leads the Cheapest, Happiest Company in the World', *BloombergBusiness*, 6 June 2013, www.bloomberg.com/bw/articles/2013-06-06/costco-ceo-craig-jelinek-leads-the-cheapest-happiest-company-in-the-world.

32   'Costco Wholesale Corp', *MarketWatch*, 13 January 2016, www.marketwatch.com/investing/stock/cost/financials.

33   William Lazonick, 'Profits Without Prosperity', *Harvard Business Review*, September 2014, https://hbr.org/2014/09/profits-without-prosperity.

34   Henry Ford and Samuel Crowther, *The Great Today and Greater Future* (Sydney: Cornstalk Publishing, 1926; reprint: Whitefish, MT: Kessinger Publishing, 2003), 198–9.

35   Jack Welch, quoted in Francesco Guerrera, 'Welch Condemns Share Price Focus', *Financial Times*, 12 March 2009.

36   Paul Polman, quoted in Eric Reguly, 'Time to Put an End to the Cult of Shareholder Value', *Globe and Mail* (Toronto), 26 September 2013, www.theglobeandmail.com/report-on-business/rob-magazine/maybe-its-time-for-ceos-to-put-shareholders-second/article14507016.

37   Cameron Tait, *Work That Pays: The Final Report of the Living Wage Commission* (London Living Wage Commission, 2014), 18.

38   Lawton and Pennycook, *Beyond the Bottom Line*, 18.

39   Richard Stringer, quoted in Citizens UK, 'Living Wage Week 2013', YouTube, 3:48, 3 November 2013, https://www.youtube.com/watch?v=7Xz0ylCLBgE.

40   See Molly Dahl, Thomas DeLeire, and Jonathan Schwabish, 'Stepping Stone or Dead End? The Effect of the EITC on Earnings Growth', *National Tax Journal* (2009): 329–346; Nada Eissa and Hilary W. Hoynes, 'Behavioral Responses to Taxes: Lessons from the EITC and Labor

Supply', *Tax Policy and the Economy*, vol. 20 (Cambridge, MA: MIT Press, 2006): 76–110; Raj Chetty and John N. Friedman, 'New Evidence on the Long-Term Impacts of Tax Credits', *Proceedings: Annual Conference on Taxation and Minutes of the Annual Meeting of the National Tax Association* 104 (2011): 116–24.

41 Jesse Rothstein, *The Unintended Consequences of Encouraging Work: Tax Incidence and the EITC* (Princeton, NJ: Center for Economic Policy Studies, Princeton University, 2008).

42 HM Revenue & Customs, Child and Working Tax Credits Statistics, 13 (author's calculations).

43 Tait, 25.

44 Lawton and Pennycook, 38.

45 *An Unhealthy Dose of Stress: The Impact of Adverse Childhood Experiences and Toxic Stress on Childhood Health and Development* (Center for Youth Wellness).

46 Paul Tough, 'The Poverty Clinic', *NewYorker*, 21 March 2008, www.newyorker.com/magazine/2011/03/21/the-poverty-clinic, 25–32.

47 This story is drawn from Jane Ellen Stevens, 'The Adverse Childhood Experiences Study—The Largest, Most Important Public Health Study You Never Heard of Began in an Obesity Clinic', *ACES Too High News*, 3 October 2012, http://acestoohigh.com/2012/10/03/the-adverse-childhood-experiences-study-the-largest-most-important-public-health-study-you-never-heard-of-began-in-an-obesity-clinic.

48 Nadine Burke Harris, 'The Chronic Stress of Poverty: Toxic Stress to Children', *The Shriver Report*, 12 January 2014, http://shriverreport.org/the-chronic-stress-of-poverty-toxic-to-children-nadine-burke-harris; Vincent J. Felitti, Robert F. Anda, Dale Nordenberg, David F. Williamson, Alison M. Spitz, Valerie Edwards, Mary P. Koss et al., 'The Relationship of Adult Health Status to Childhood Abuse and Household Dysfunction', *American Journal of Preventive Medicine* 14 (1998): 245–58.

49 Those who suffer from toxic stress are 2.2 times as likely to suffer from ischemic heart disease, 2.4 times as likely to have a stroke, 1.9 times as likely to suffer from cancer, 1.6 times as likely to suffer from diabetes, 12.2 times as likely to attempt suicide, 10.3 times as likely to use injection drugs, and 7.4 times as likely to be an alcoholic. For more, see 'An Unhealthy Dose of Stress'. For the original study, see Felitti et al., 'The Relationship of Adult Health Status'.

50 As defined by the American Academy of Pediatrics. For more, see Sara B. Johnson, Anne W. Riley, Douglas A. Granger, and Jenna Riis, 'The Science of Early Life Toxic Stress for Pediatric Practice and Advocacy', *Pediatrics* 131, no. 2 (2013): 319–27.

51 Nadine Burke Harris, interview by authors, San Francisco, CA, 6 October 2014.

52 Andrew Hood and Paul Johnson, 'What Is Welfare Spending?' Insitute for Fiscal Studies, 4 November 2014, http://www.ifts.org.uk/publications/7424.

53 'No Quick Fix: Exposing the Depth of Britain's Drug and Alcohol Problem', part of *Breakdown Britain II*, (Centre for Social Justice, 2013).

54   Note that this figure includes spending on welfare services to address the consequences of child poverty, loss of income, and tax receipts of workers who earn less for having been impoverished as children, and benefits spent on them as adults. It likely overlaps with welfare, child poverty, and educational failure costs. For more, see: Donald Hirsch, 'An Estimate of the Cost of Child Poverty in 2013', Child Poverty Action Group, 5 June 2013.

55   As noted earlier, a report published by National Numeracy and Pro Bono Economics written by analysts from the National Audit Office estimated the costs of innumeracy to be £20.2 billion, with a low estimate of £6.7 billion and a high estimate of £32.6 billion. For perspective, the £20.2 billion figure represents about 1.3 per cent of the British economy. See 'Cost of Outcomes Associated with Low Levels of Adult Numeracy in the UK', National Numeracy and Pro Bono Economics, 2014.

56   National Audit Office, The Criminal Justice System: Landscape Review (Report by the Comptroller and Auditor General) (National Audit Office, 7 March 2014), http://www.nao.org.uk/wp-content/uploads/2015/03/The-Criminal-Justicesystem-landscape-review-summary1.pdf.

57   Veronica Engert, Franziska Plessow, Robert Miller, Clemens Kirschbaum, and Tania Singer, 'Cortisol Increase in Empathic Stress Is Modulated by Emotional Closeness and Observation Modality', *Psychoneuroendocrinology* 45 (2014): 192–201.

58   Fractured Families: Why Stability Matters (London: Centre for Social Justice, 2013), 60.

59   David Robinson, Out of the Ordinary: Learning from the Community Links Approach to Social Regeneration (London: Community Links, 2010), 19.

60   Harlem Children's Zone, HCZ.org, 2015.

61   Michael McAfee, e-mail to authors, 4 September 2014.

62   Department for Communities and Local Government, 'Tackling Troubled Families', British Government, 15 December 2011, www.gov.uk/government/news/tackling-troubled-families.

63   'Troubled Families', Local Government Association, 29 January 2015, www.local.gov.uk/community-budgets/-/journal_content/56/10180/3691966/ARTICLE.

64   Louise Casey, phone interview by authors, 7 November 2014.

65   'PM Praises Troubled Families Programme Success', *Department for Communities and Local Government*, 22 June 2015, https://www.gov.uk/government/news/pm-praises-troubled-families-programme-success.

66   Richard Reeves, 'Bringing Up Baby', *New Statesman*, 29 January 2009.

67   'Helping New Families: Support in the Early Years through Universal Health Visiting', (Conservative Research Department), https://www.conservatives.com/~/media/Files/Downloadable%20Files/Helping%20new%20families.ashx.

68   See Nicholas Kristof, 'The Way to Beat Poverty', *New York Times*, 12 September 2014, www.nytimes.com/2014/09/14/opinion/sunday/nicholas-kristof-the-way-to-beat-poverty.html, which discusses the

study or the study itself: Lynn A. Karoly, M. Rebecca Kilburn, and Jill S. Cannon, *Early Childhood Interventions: Proven Results, Future Promise* (Santa Monica, CA: RAND Corporation, 2005).

69   See Harriet J. Kitzman, David L. Olds, Robert E. Cole, Carole A. Hanks, Elizabeth A. Anson, Kimberly J. Arcoleo, Dennis W. Luckey et al., 'Enduring Effects of Prenatal and Infancy Home Visiting by Nurses on Children: Follow-Up of a Randomized Trial Among Children at Age 12 Years', *Archives of Pediatrics & Adolescent Medicine* 164, no. 5 (2010): 412–18; David L. Olds, Charles R. Henderson, and Harriet Kitzman, 'Does Prenatal and Infancy Nurse Home Visitation Have Enduring Effects on Qualities of Parental Caregiving and Child Health at 25 to 50 Months of Life?' *Pediatrics* 93, no. 1 (1994): 89–98; David L. Olds, Charles R. Henderson Jr., Robert Cole, John Eckenrode, Harriet Kitzman, Dennis Luckey, Lisa Pettitt et al., 'Long-Term Effects of Nurse Home Visitation on Children's Criminal and Antisocial Behavior: 15-Year Follow-Up of a Randomized Controlled Trial', *JAMA* 280, no. 14 (1998): 1238–44; David L. Olds, Charles R. Henderson, Robert Tatelbaum, and Robert Chamberlin, 'Improving the Delivery of Prenatal Care and Outcomes of Pregnancy: A Randomized Trial of Nurse Home Visitation', *Pediatrics* 77, no. 1 (1986): 16–28; Edward Rodrigue and Richard V. Reeves, 'Home Visiting Programs: An Early Test for the 114th Congress', Brookings, 5 February 2015.

70   Kristof, 'It's Not Just About Bad Choices'.

Chapter 9

1   Sebastian Thrun, interview with authors, Mountain View, CA, 11 November 2014.

2   'Global Wealth Databook 2014', *Credit Suisse Research Institute*, October 2014, https://publications.credit-suisse.com/tasks/render/file/?fileID=5521F296-D460-2B88-081889DB12817E02, 126.

3   'EY ITEM Club special report on the outlook for consumer spending', *EY Item Club*, September 2014.

4   From August–October 2009 to August–October 2015, the number of people needing second jobs rose while number of overall jobs increased. Meanwhile, we've also seen increases in the number of part-time workers who couldn't find full-time positions. See: Office for National Statistics, *Labour Market Statistics, December 2015: Unemployment by Age and Duration*, 2015, http://www.ons.gov.uk/ons/taxonomy/index.html?nscl=Labour+Market#tab-data-tables.

5   Office for National Statistics, *Underemployment and Overemployment in the UK, 2014*, 2014, http://www.ons.gov.uk/ons/dcp171776_387087.pdf.

6   World Bank, Long-Term Unemployment (% of Total Unemployment), 2015, http://data.worldbank.org/indicator/SL.UEM.LTRM.ZS?order=wbapi_data_value_2012%20wbapi_data_value%20wbapi_da_tavalue-last&sort=asc.

7   Office for National Statistics, *Labour Productivity, Q3 2015*, 2015, http://www.ons.gov.uk/ons/rel/productivity/labour-productivity/q3-2015/index.html.

8   Office for National Statistics, *Annual Survey of Hours and Earnings, 2015 Provisional Results* (2015), http://www.ons.gov.uk/ons/rel/ashe/

annualsurvey-of-hours-and-earnings/2014-provisional-results/stb-ashe-statisticalbulletin-2014.html.

9   'Nonfarm Business Sector: Labor Share', Federal Reserve Bank of St. Louis, 9 February 2015, https://research.stlouisfed.org/fred2/series/PRS85006173.

10   Loukas Karabarbounis and Brent Neiman, 'The Global Decline of the Labor Share', *Quarterly Journal of Economics* 129, no. 1 (2014): 61–103.

11   Emmanuel Saez and Gabriel Zucman, 'The Explosion in U.S. Wealth Inequality Has Been Fueled by Stagnant Wages, Increasing Debt, and a Collapse in Asset Values for the Middle Classes', *LSE*, 29 October 2014, http://blogs.lse.ac.uk/usappblog/2014/10/29/the-explosion-in-u-s-wealth-inequality-has-been-fuelled-by-stagnant-wages-increasing-debt-and-a-collapse-in-asset-values-for-the-middle-classes. See their paper at Emmanuel Saez and Gabriel Zucman, *Wealth Inequality in the United States Since 1913: Evidence from Capitalized Income Tax Data*, no. w20625 (National Bureau of Economic Research, 2015), http://gabriel-zucman.eu/files/SaezZucman2014.pdf.

12   Saez and Zucman, 'Wealth Inequality'.

13   Tyler Cowen, 'Automation Alone Isn't Killing Jobs', *New York Times*, 6 April 2014, www.nytimes.com/2014/04/06/business/automation-alone-isnt-killing-jobs.html?_r=0.

14   Alan B. Krueger, Judd Cramer and David Cho. 'Are the Long-Term Unemployed on the Margins of the Labor Market?'. *Brookings Papers on Economic Activity* (2014), 229–280

15   Jaison R. Abel, Richard Deitz, and Yaqin Su, 'Are Recent College Graduates Finding Good Jobs?' *Current Issues in Economics and Finance*, 20, no. 1 (2014).

16   Carl Benedikt Frey and Michael A. Osborne, 'The Future of Employment: How Susceptible Are Jobs to Computerisation?' 17 September 2013, www.oxfordmartin.ox.ac.uk/downloads/academic/The_Future_of_Employment.pdf.

17   David Graeber, quoted in Thomas Frank, 'David Graeber: "Spotlight on the Financial Sector Did Make Apparent Just how Bizarrely Skewed Our Economy Is in Terms of Who Gets Rewards"', *Salon*, 1 June 2014, www.salon.com/2014/06/01/help_us_thomas_piketty_the_1s_sick_and_twisted_new_scheme.

18   Clayton Christensen, 'The Capitalist's Dilemma', lecture, RSA, London, 23 September 2013.

19   Laurence Chandy and Geoffrey Gertz, *Poverty in Numbers: The Changing State of Global Poverty from 2005 to 2015* (Brookings Institution, 2011), www.brookings.edu/~/media/research/files/papers/2011/1/global%20poverty%20chandy/01_global_poverty_chandy.pdf.

20   See Steve Hilton, 'I run a Silicon Valley start-up – but I refuse to own a cellphone', *Guardian*, 11 January 2016, http://www.theguardian.com/technology/2016/jan/11/steve-hilton-silicon-valley-no-cellphone-technology-apps-uber.

21   Robert Caro, *The Years of Lyndon Johnson*, vol. 1: *The Path to Power* (New York: Vintage, 1981; reprint: London: Pimlico, 2003), 504.

22   Ibid., 513.

23   Rohan Silva, 'Could a Robot Do My Job?' BBC *Panorama*, 18 September 2015, http://www.bbc.co.uk/programmes/b06cn1wv.

24   Matthias J. Koepp, Roger N. Gunn, Andrew D. Lawrence, Vincent J. Cunningham, Alain Dagher, Tasmin Jones, David J. Brooks, C. J. Bench et al., 'Evidence for Striatal Dopamine Release During a Video Game', *Nature* 393, no. 6682 (1998): 266–8.

25   Richard M. Ryan and Edward L. Deci, 'Self-Determination Theory and the Facilitation of Intrinsic Motivation, Social Development, and Well-Being', *AmericanPsychologist* 55, no. 1 (2000): 68.

26   Sebastian Thrun, interview by authors, Mountain View, CA, 11 November 2014.

27   Charlie Mayfield, interview by authors, 22 October 2014.

28   For up to two years as long as the worker's unemployment insurance contribution has been paid.

29   'Flexicurity', Denmark: The Official Website of Denmark, http://denmark.dk/en/society/welfare/flexicurity.

30   Thomas Bredgaard and Arthur Daemmrich, 'The Welfare State as an Investment Strategy: Denmark's Flexicurity Policies', July 2012, http://ilera2012.wharton.upenn.edu/RefereedPapers/BredgaardThomas%20ArthurDaemmrich.pdf.

31   'OECD Income Distribution Database: Gini, Poverty, Income, Methods, and Concepts', OECD, 19 June 2014, www.oecd.org/social/income-distribution-database.htm.

32   Leo Mirani, 'The Secret to the Uber Economy: Wealth Inequality', *Quartz*, 16 December 2014, http://qz.com/312537/the-secret-to-the-uber-economy-is-wealth-inequality.

33   Leon Feinstein, 'Very Early', *CentrePiece*, Summer 2003, http://cep.lse.ac.uk/pubs/download/CP146.pdf.

34   Morris Kleiner, *Reforming Occupational Licensing Practices* (Washington, DC: Brookings Institute: Hamilton Project, 2015), 5.

35   Reihan Salam, 'The Upper Middle Class is Ruining America', *Slate*, 30 January 2015, www.slate.com/articles/news_and_politics/politics/2015/01/the_upper_middle_class_is_ruining_all_that_is_great_about_america.html.

36   'America's Elite: An Hereditary Meritocracy', *Economist*, 24 January 2015, www.economist.com/news/briefing/21640316-children-rich-and-powerful-are-increasingly-well-suited-earning-wealth-and-power, 17.

37   'America's New Aristocracy', *Economist*, 24 January 2015, www.economist.com/news/leaders/21640331-importance-intellectual-capital-grows-privilege-has-become-increasingly, 9.

38   Betty Hart and Todd R. Risley, 'The Early Catastrophe: The 30 Million Word Gap by Age 3', *American Educator* 27, no. 1 (2003): 4–9.

39   Katherine Harmon, 'How Important Is Physical Contact with Your Infant?' *Scientific American*, 6 May 2010, www.scientificamerican.com/article/infant-touch.

40   Susan L. Brown, 'Family Structure and Child Well-Being: The Significance of Parental Cohabitation', *Journal of Marriage and Family* 66 (2004), 351–67.

41 Terry-Ann Craigie, Jeanne Brooks-Gunn, and Jane Waldfogel, *Family Structure, Family Stability and Early Child Wellbeing*, no. 1275 (2010), http://crcw.princeton.edu/workingpapers/WP10-14-FF.pdf.

42 Figures come from Table 3a. See Office of National Statistics, *Divorces in England and Wales, 2012*, http://www.ons.gov.uk/ons/rel/vsob1/divorces-inengland-and-wales/2012/stb-divorces-2012.html.

43 Office of National Statistics, *Marriages in England and Wales (Provisional), 2012* (Office for National Statistics, 2014).

44 Ibid.

45 Cherlin, quoted in Olga Khazan, 'The Luxury of Waiting for Marriage to Have Kids', *Atlantic*, 17 June 2014, www.theatlantic.com/business/archive/2014/06/why-poor-women-dont-wait-for-marriage-to-give-birth/372890.

46 Jean M. Twenge, Keith W. Campbell, and Craig A. Foster, 'Parenthood and Marital Satisfaction: A Meta-Analytic Review', *Journal of Marriage and the Family* 65 (2003), 574–83.

47 Dan Gilbert, quoted in Kate Devlin, 'Marriage Without Children the Key to Bliss', *Telegraph*, 9 May 2008, www.telegraph.co.uk/news/1941195/Marriage-without-children-the-key-to-bliss.html.

48 Niko Matouschek and Imran Rasul, 'The Economics of the Marriage Contract Theories and Evidence', *Journal of Law and Economics* 51, no. 1 (2008): 59–110.

49 John Hayward and Guy Brandon, 'Cohabitation: An Alternative to Marriage?' Jubilee Centre, June 2011, www.jubilee-centre.org/cohabitation-alternative-marriage-john-haywood-guy-brandon.

50 Ellen C. Perrin, Benjamin S. Siegel, James G. Pawelski, Mary I. Dobbins, Arthur Lavin, Gerri Mattison, John Pascoe et al., 'Promoting the Well-Being of Children Whose Parents Are Gay or Lesbian', *Pediatrics* 131, no. 4 (2013): e1374–e1383.

51 Dan Gilbert, quoted in Devlin, 'Marriage Without Children'.

52 Shawn Grover and John F. Helliwell, *How's Life at Home? New Evidence on Marriage and the Set Point for Happiness*, no. w20794 (National Bureau of Economic Research, 2014), http://faculty.arts.ubc.ca/jhelliwell/papers/w20794.pdf.

53 Shawn Grover, quoted in Claire Cain Miller, 'Study Finds More Reasons to Get and Stay Married', *New York Times*, 8 January 2015, www.nytimes.com/2015/01/08/upshot/study-finds-more-reasons-to-get-and-stay-married.html.

54 John F. Helliwell, quoted in ibid.

55 For example, President George W. Bush's Healthy Marriage Initiative. See US Department of Health and Human Services, *The Community Healthy Marriage Initiative Evaluation: Impacts of a Community Approach to Strengthening Families* (Washington, DC: Office of Planning, Research and Evaluation, 2012).

56 Ronald Mincy, quoted in Suzy Hansen, 'The Myth of the Deadbeat Dad', *Salon*, 9 August 2001, www.salon.com/2001/08/09/black_fathers.

57 Rose Marie Kreider, *Living Arrangements of Children, 2004* (US Department of Commerce, Economics and Statistics Administration, US Census Bureau, 2008).

58   Cynthia C. Harper and Sara S. McLanahan, 'Father Absence and Youth Incarceration', *Journal of Research on Adolescence* 14 (September 2004): 369–97.

59   Specifically, girls raised by single mothers. See Jay D. Teachman, 'The Childhood Living Arrangements of Children and the Characteristics of Their Marriages', *Journal of Family Issues* 25 (January 2004): 86–111.

60   Kimberly S. Howard, Jennifer E. Burke Lefever, John G. Borkowski, and Thomas L. Whitman, 'Fathers' Influence in the Lives of Children with Adolescent Mothers', *Journal of Family Psychology* 20, no. 3 (2006): 468.

61   Christine Winquist Nord and Jerry West, *Fathers' and Mothers' Involvement in Their Children's Schools by Family Type and Resident Status*, NCES 2001–032. (Washington, DC: US Department of Education, National Center for Education Statistics, 2001), http://nces.ed.gov/pubs2001/2001032.pdf.

62   Brooke Conroy Bass, 'Preparing for Parenthood? Gender, Aspirations, and the Reproduction of Labor Market Inequality', *Gender & Society* 29, no. 3 (2015): 362–85.

63   Slaughter, 'Why Women Still Can't Have It All'.

64   Liza Mundy, 'Daddy Track: The Case for Paternity Leave', *Atlantic*, January/February 2014, www.theatlantic.com/magazine/archive/2014/01/the-daddy-track/355746.

65   US Census Bureau, *Maternity Leave and Employment Patterns of First-time Mothers: 1961–2008* (Washington, DC: Department of Commerce, 2011).

66   Heather Boushey and Sarah Jane Glynn, *The Effects of Paid Family Medical Leave on Employment Stability and Economic Stability* (Washington, DC: Center for American Progress, 2012), www.americanprogress.org/wp-content/uploads/issues/2012/04/pdf/BousheyEmploymentLeave1.pdf, 3.

67   According to the OECD, children whose families eat their main meal together are less likely to be truant in school. See *Who Are the School Truants?* (PSIA in Focus, January 2014), www.oecd.org/pisa/pisaproducts/pisainfocus/PISA-in-Focus-n35-(eng)-FINAL.pdf.

68   Eileen Appelbaum and Ruth Milkman, *Leaves That Pay: Employer and Worker Experiences with Paid Family Leave in California* (Washington, DC: Center for Economic and Policy Research, 2011), www.cepr.net/documents/publications/paid-family-leave-1-2011.pdf.

69   Mundy, 'The Daddy Track', 16.

70   Indeed, feeling overwhelmed and unprepared is common for parents. See Susanne N. Biehle and Kristin D. Mickelson, 'Preparing for Parenthood: How Feelings of Responsibility and Efficacy Impact Expectant Parents', *Journal of Social and Personal Relationships* 28, no. 5, (2011): 668–83.

71   Octavius Black, quoted in Amelia Gentleman, 'Do We Need Parenting Classes?' *Guardian*, 31 March 2012, www.theguardian.com/lifeandstyle/2012/mar/31/do-we-need-parenting-classes.

72 Staci R. Eisenberg, Megan H. Bair-Merritt, Eve R. Colson, Timothy C. Heeren, Nicole L. Geller, and Michael J. Corwin, 'Maternal Report of Advice Received for Infant Care', *Pediatrics* 136, no. 2 (2015): e315–e322.

73 Geoff Lindsay, Mairi Ann Cullen, Stephen Cullen, Vaso Totsika, Ioanna Bakopoulou, Susan Goodlad, Richard Brind et al., *CANparent Trial Evaluation: Final Report Research Report* (Department for Education, University of Warwick, 2014), www.gov.uk/government/uploads/system/uploads/attachment_data/file/332182/RR357_-_CANparent_trial_evaluation_final_report__09_07_14_.pdf.

74 The funding it includes is also going towards the expansion of the Troubled Families Unit. For more, see: 'PM: Families Are the Key to Tackling Poverty', *Prime Minister's Office*, 10 January 2015, https://www.gov.uk/government/news/pm-families-are-the-key-to-ending-poverty.

75 Geoff Colvin, *Humans Are Underrated: What High Achievers Know That Brilliant Machines Never Will* (New York: Portfolio/Penguin, 2015).

Chapter 10

1 Lenore Skenazy, 'Free-Range Kids: FAQ', Free Range Kids, https://freerangekids.wordpress.com/faq.

2 David Ball in Tim Gill, *No Fear: Growing Up in a Risk Averse Society* (London: Calouste Gulbenkian Foundation, 2007), www.gulbenkian.org.uk/pdffiles/–item-1266-223-No-fear-19-12-07.pdf, 26–7.

3 Gill, in ibid., 37–8.

4 David Yearley in ibid., 25–6.

5 David Ball in ibid., 29; Department for Transport, 'Reported Casualties by Road User Type, Age and Severity, Great Britain, 2011', (Table RAS300002) in *Transport Studies* (2012). https://www.gov.uk/government/statistics/reported-road-casualties-great-britain-main-results-2011.
   See also David J. Ball, 'Policy Issues and Risk–Benefit Trade-offs of "Safer Surfacing" for Children's Playgrounds', *Accident Analysis & Prevention* 36, no. 4 (2004).

6 'Stressed Parents: Cancel That Violin Class', *Economist*, 26 July 2014, www.economist.com/news/united-states/21608793-helicopter-moms-and-dads-will-not-harm-their-kids-if-they-relax-bit-cancel-violin.

7 A Home Office report found that only 7 per cent of murdered children were killed by a stranger. See Research, Development and Statistics Directorate, *Reducing Homicide: A Review of the Possibilities*, by Fiona Brookman and Mike Maguire (London, Home Office, 2003), 16.

8 Jay Griffiths, *A Country Called Childhood* (Berkeley, CA: Counterpoint, 2014), 54 and 57.

9 Ellen B. H. Sandseter, 'Children's Risky Play from an Evolutionary Perspective: The Anti-Phobic Effects of Thrilling Experiences', *Evolutionary Psychology* 9, no. 2, (2001): 257–84.

10 Paul Hocker, interview by authors, London, 26 September 2014.

11 Ibid.

12 James Siegal, 'Kids First: What's Good for Kids Is Good for Cities', *Medium*, 4 March 2015, https://medium.com/@kaboom/kids-first-what-s-good-for-kids-is-good-for-cities-73811301165f.

13 Annie Murphy Paul, 'School of Hard Knocks: "How Children Succeed" by Paul Tough', *New York Times Sunday Book Review*, 26 August 2012, www.nytimes.com/2012/08/26/books/review/how-children-succeed-by-paul-tough.html.

14 While the May 2015 election represented a large increase in the number of women MPs, Britain is still far from gender parity in the House of Commons. See: Ed Lowther and Charlotte Thornton, 'Election 2015: Number of Women in Parliament Rises by a Third', *BBC News*, 8 May 2015.

15 Catherine Neilan and Chris Parmenter, 'FTSE 100 CEOs: These Are the Men (and a Few Women) Who Run Britain's Biggest Companies', *City A.M.*, 20 March 2015.

16 Emma Rush and Andrea La Nauze, *Corporate Paedophilia: Sexualisation of Children in Australia* (Canberra: Australia Institute, 2006).

17 Samantha M. Goodin, Alyssa Van Denburg, Sarah K. Murnen, and Linda Smolak, '"Putting On" Sexiness: A Content Analysis of the Presence of Sexual-izing Characteristics in Girls' Clothing', *Sex Roles* 65, no. 1–2 (2011): 1–12.

18 APA Task Force on the Sexualization of Girls, *Report of the APA Task Force on the Sexualization of Girls* (Washington, DC: American Psychological Association, 2010), www.apa.org/pi/women/programs/girls/report.aspx.

19 Barbara L. Fredrickson, Tomi-Ann Roberts, Stephanie M. Noll, Diane M. Quinn, and Jean M. Twenge, 'That Swimsuit Becomes You: Sex Differences in Self-Objectification, Restrained Eating, and Math Performance', *Journal of Personality and Social Psychology* 75, no. 1 (July 1998), 269–84.

20 Kathrine D. Gapinski, Kelly D. Brownell, and Marianne LaFrance, 'Body Objectification and "Fat Talk": Effects on Emotion, Motivation, and Cognitive Performance', *Sex Roles* 48, nos. 9–10 (2003): 377–88.

21 Beverley Turner, 'Pubic Hair Is Back Ladies. The Men Don't Care and the Women Can't Be Bothered', *Telegraph*, 15 November 2013, www.telegraph.co.uk/women/womens-life/10452327/Pubic-hair-is-back-ladies.-The-men-dont-care-and-the-women-cant-be-bothered.html; Heidi Stevens, 'Your 11-Year-Old Daughter Wants to Shave. Everywhere', *Chicago Tribune*, 10 July 2012, http://articles.chicagotribune.com/2012-07-10/features/sc-fam-0710-tween-wax-20120710_1_hair-removal-daughter-body.

22 'One in Ten British Kids Own A Mobile Phone by the Age of Five', uSwitch, August 2013, http://www.uswitch.com/mobiles/news/2013/08/one_in_ten_british_kids_own_mobile_phone_by_the_age_of_five/.

23 Ofcom, *Children and Parents: Media Use and Attitudes Report* (2014), http://stakeholders.ofcom.org.uk/market-data-research/other/research-publications/childrens/children-parents-oct-14, 29 and 32.

24   Hilda K. Kabali, Matilde M. Irigoyen, Rosemary Nunez-Davis, Jennifer
       G. Budacki, Sweta H. Mohanty, Kristin P. Leister, and Robert L. Bonner
       Jr., 'Exposure and Use of Mobile Media Devices by Young Children',
       Pediatrics 136, no. 6 (December 2015): 1044–50.

25   'The Digital Divide: How the Online Behavior of Teens Is Getting Past
       Parents', McAfee, June 2012, www.mcafee.com/us/resources/misc/
       digital-divide-study.pdf.

26   *2014 Teen Internet Safety Survey* (Atlanta: Cox Communications, 2014),
       www.cox.com/wcm/en/aboutus/datasheet/takecharge/tween-
       internet-safety-survey.pdf.

27   Ofcom, 199.

28   "Unplugging" from Technology', *Action for Children*, 6 January 2016,
       https://www.actionforchildren.org.uk/news-and-opinion/latest-
       news/2016/january/unplugging-from-technology/.

29   Jane D. Brown and Kelly L. L'Engle, 'X-Rated Sexual Attitudes and
       Behaviors Associated with US Early Adolescents' Exposure to Sexually
       Explicit Media', *Communication Research* 36, no. 1 (2009): 129–51.

30   Patricia Romito and Lucia Beltramini, 'Watching Pornography: Gender
       Differences, Violence and Victimization: An Exploratory Study in Italy',
       Violence Against Women 17, no. 10 (October 2011): 1077801211424555.

31   'Young People Sexual Relationships', IPPR, www.ippr.org/assets/
       media/publications/attachments/youngpeoplesexrelationships.jpg.

32   Michael Flood, 'The Harms of Pornography Exposure Among Children
       and Young People', *Child Abuse Review* 18, no. 6 (2009): 384–400.

33   Tori DeAngelis, 'Web Pornography's Effect on Children', *American
       Psychological Association Monitor* 38, no. 10 (November 2007): 50.

34   People Who Abuse Children (An NSPCC Research Briefing),
       NSPCC, 2014, http://www.nspcc.org.uk/global/assets/documents/
       information-service/researchbriefing-people-who-abuse-children.pdf.

35   Wesley Johnson, 'Children, Some Age Five, Commit Thousands of
       Child Sex Offences', *Telegraph*, 4 March 2013, www.telegraph.co.uk/
       news/uknews/crime/9905727/Children-some-aged-five-commit-
       thousands-of-child-sex-offences.html.

36   David Finkelhor, Richard Ormrod, and Mark Chaffin, *Juveniles Who
       Commit Sex Offenses Against Minors* (Washington, DC: US Department of
       Justice, December 2009), www.ncjrs.gov/pdffiles1/ojjdp/227763.pdf.

37   Gail Dines, quoted in Martin Daubney, 'Experiment That Convinced
       Me Online Porn Is the Most Pernicious Threat Facing Children Today:
       By Ex Lads' Mag Editor Martin Daubney', *Daily Mail*, 25 September
       2013.

38   Todd G. Morrison, Shannon R. Ellis, Melanie A. Morrison, Anomi
       Bearden, and Rebecca L. Harriman, 'Exposure to Sexually Explicit
       Material and Variations in Body Esteem, Genital Attitudes, and Sexual
       Esteem Among a Sample of Canadian Men,' *Journal of Men's Studies* 14,
       no. 2 (Spring 2006): 209–22.

39   Daubney, 'Experiment That Convinced Me'.

40   'Pornhub's 2015 Year in Review', *Pornhub Insights*, 6 January 2016,
       http://www.pornhub.com/insights/pornhub-2015-year-in-review.

41   Daubney, 'Experiment That Convinced Me'.

42   Sally Kalson, 'Sexting ... and Other Stupid Teen Tricks', *Pittsburgh Post-Gazette*, 29 March 2009, www.post-gazette.com/opinion/sally-kalson/2009/03/29/Sexting-and-other-stupid-teen-tricks/stories/200903290190.

43   Donald Lowe, quoted in Hanna Rosin, 'Why Kids Sext', *Atlantic*, November 2014, www.theatlantic.com/magazine/archive/2014/11/why-kids-sext/380798, 67.

44   Amanda Lenhart, 'Mobile Access Shifts Social Media Use and Other Online Activities', Pew Research Center, 9 April 2015, www.pewinternet.org/2015/04/09/mobile-access-shifts-social-media-use-and-other-online-activities.

45   Rosin, 'Why Kids Sext', 68.

46   Kassondra Cloos and Julie Turkewitz, 'Hundreds of Nude Photos Jolt Colorado School', *New York Times*, 6 November 2015, www.nytimes.com/2015/11/07/us/colorado-students-caught-trading-nude-photos-by-the-hundreds.html?_r=0.

47   Jeff R. Temple, Jonathan A. Paul, Patricia van den Berg, Vi Donna Le, Amy McElhany, and Brian W. Temple, 'Teen Sexting and Its Association with Sexual Behaviors', *Archives of Pediatrics & Adolescent Medicine* 166, no. 9 (2012): 828–33.

48   'Physical Activity Guidelines for Children and Young People,' NHS Choices, www.nhs.uk/Livewell/fitness/Pages/physical-activity-guidelines-for-young-people.aspx; Susan Strife and Liam Downey, 'Childhood Development and Access to Nature: A New Direction for Environmental Research', *Organ Environment*, 22, no. 1 (March 2009): 99–122.

49   Brian Verdine, quoted in Allison Bond, 'Blocks, Puzzles Help Kids Prep for School', *Reuters*, 20 March 2014, www.reuters.com/article/2014/03/20/us-puzzles-kids-idUSBREA2J1LN20140320.

50   Anna V. Sosa, 'Association of the Type of Toy Used During Play With the Quantity and Quality of Parent-Infant Communication', JAMA Pediatrics, (2015): 1–6.

51   Marsha Gerdes, quoted in Bond, 'Blocks, Puzzles Help Kids Prep for School'.

52   Brian N. Verdine, Roberta M. Golinkoff, Kathryn Hirsh Pasek, Nora S. Newcombe, Andrew T. Filipowicz, and Alicia Chang, 'Deconstructing Building Blocks: Preschoolers' Spatial Assembly Performance Relates to Early Mathematical Skills', *Child Development* 85, no. 3 (2014): 1062–76.

53   Pooja S. Tandon, Chuan Zhou, Paula Lozano, and Dimitri A. Christakis, 'Preschoolers' Total Daily Screen Time at Home and by Type of Child Care', *Journal of Pediatrics* 158, no. 2 (2011): 297–300. See also 'Zero to Eight: Children's Media Use in America 2013', Common Sense Media, Fall 2013.

54   'Touch Screens', Michael Cohen Group LLC, 17 February 2014, www.mcgrc.com/wp-content/uploads/2015/03/MCGRC_Digital-Kids-Presentation_022014.pdf.

55   Sherry Turkle, 'Connected, But Alone?' TED, April 2012, www.ted.com/talks/sherry_turkle_alone_together?language=en.

56   Sherry Turkle, *Alone Together: Why We Expect More from Technology and Less From Each Other* (New York: Basic Books, 2011), 268.

57   'The Dos and Don'ts of Using Your Phone at a Party', *Huffington Post*, 26 September 2014, www.huffingtonpost.com/2014/09/26/dinner-party-etiquette-phones-at-dinner_n_5884418.html.

58   Sherry Turkle, quoted in Catherine de Lange, 'Sherry Turkle: "We're Losing the Raw, Human Part of Being with Each Other"', *Guardian*, 5 May 2013, www.theguardian.com/science/2013/may/05/rational-heroes-sherry-turkle-mit.

59   'The Common Sense Census: Media Use by Tweens and Teens', Common Sense Media Kids Action, Fall 2015, www.commonsensemedia.org/research/the-common-sense-census-media-use-by-tweens-and-teens.

60   Katie Rogers, 'The Vault Apps That Keep Sexts a Secret', *New York Times*, 6 November 2015, www.nytimes.com/2015/11/07/us/the-vault-apps-that-keep-sexts-a-secret.html.

61   Justin Higginbottom, 'Growing Number of Children with Cellphones Adds Pressure to Purchase', *Desert News*, 22 April 2012, www.deseretnews.com/article/765570742/Growing-number-of-children-with-cellphones-adds-pressure-to-purchase.html?pg=all.

62   See Steve Hilton, 'I run a Silicon Valley start-up – but I refuse to own a cellphone', *Guardian*, 11 January 2016, http://www.theguardian.com/technology/2016/jan/11/steve-hilton-silicon-valley-no-cellphone-technology-apps-uber.

Chapter 11

1   Will Hunter, 'The Best Office in the World? Selgas Cano's New Work Space in London', *Architectural Review*, 29 January 2015, www.architectural-review.com/buildings/the-best-office-in-the-world-selgas-canos-new-work-space-in-london/8677631.article.

2   José Selgas and Lucía Cano, quoted in 'Future of Work', *Courier* 5 (August 2014), 5.

3   Interview with Rohan Silva.

4   Winston Churchill, Hansard House of Commons Debate, 28 October 1943, vol. 393, cols. 403–73.

5   Yuichi Shoda, 'Individual Differences in Social Psychology: Understanding Situations to Understand People, Understanding People to Understand Situations', in *The Sage Handbook of Methods in Social Psychology*, ed. Carol Sansone, Carolyn C. Morf, and Abigail T. Panter (Thousand Oaks, CA: Sage Publications, 2004), 119–21.

6   Office for National Statistics, *Live Tables on House Building* (Table 209: Permanent Dwellings Completed, by Tenure and Country (London: Office for National Statistics, 19 November 2015), https://www.gov.uk/government/uploads/system/uploads/attachment_data/file/477837/LiveTable209.xlsx .

7   *Building in a Small Island – Why We Still Need the Brownfield First Approach* (Kemsing, Kent: Green Balance [for the Campaign to Protect Rural England], 2011), 4.

8   Pete Jeffrys, Toby Lloyd, et al., *Building the Homes We Need: A Programme for the 2015 Government* (KPMG and Shelter, 2014), 4 and 25.

9   'Building Blocks', *Economist*, 22 December 2014.

10   Jeffrys and Lloyd, *Building the Homes We Need*, 18.

11   Department for Communities and Local Government, *Live Tables on Housing Building*, https://www.gov.uk/government/statistical-data-sets/live-tables-onhouse-building#discontinued-tables.

12   Robert Watson, Steve Albon, et al., *UK National Ecosystem Assessment: Synthesis of the Key Findings* (Cambridge, England: UNFP-WCMC, 2011), 60.

13   Rebecca Roberts-Hughes, *The Case for Space: The Size of England's New Homes*, Will Fox and Anna Scott-Marshall, eds. (RIBA, 2011), 8.

14   'Future Homes Commission Report', 33.

15   Jeffrys and Lloyd, 19.

16   Roberts-Hughes, 8.

17   Jeffrys and Lloyd, 43.

18   Tom Archer and Ian Cole, 'Over-Reliance on Private House Builders is Fuelling UK's Housing Crisis', *Guardian*, 12 September 2014.

19   Jeffrys and Lloyd, 22.

20   Stephen Finlay, Isabella Pereiva, Ella Fryer-Smith, Anne Charlton and Rebecca Roberts-Hughes, *The Way We Live Now: What People Need and Expect From Their Homes* (London: Ipsos MORI and RIBA, 2012), 11.

21   Bruce Bell, interview and correspondence by authors, October/November 2014.

22   Jeffrys and Lloyd, 42.

23   'Bevolkingsontwikkeling; regio per maand', *CBS Statline* (in Dutch), 26 June 2014.

24   Patrick Collinson, 'Self-Build: It's Time to Go Dutch', *Guardian*, 25 November 2011; Elizabeth Hopkirk, 'The Netherlands' Almere Leads the Way on Self-Build Communities', *bdonline*, 6 June 2011.

25   'Almere, Holland', *The Self-Build Portal*, 2015 http://www.selfbuildportal.org.uk/homeruskwartier-district-almere, 2015.

26   Jacqueline Tellinga, quoted in Collinson.

27   ——, quoted in Hopkirk.

28   Ian Steadman, 'Dutch City Gives Residents a Self-Build Affordable Housing Catalogue', *Wired*, 18 April 2013.

29   Ed Monk, 'The Ultimate DIY Investment', *This Is Money.co.uk*, 8 November 2013.

30   'Survey of Self-Build Intentions', *Ipsos-Mori*, 12 March 2013.

31   According to an investigation conducted by the *Guardian*. See: Graham Ruddick, 'Revealed: Housebuilders Sitting on 600,000 Plots of Land', *Guardian*, 30 December 2015.

32   Jeffrys and Lloyd, 57.

33   '475,000 Homes with Planning Permission Still Waiting to Be Built', Local Government Association, 7 January 2016, http://www.local.gov.uk/web/guest/media-releases/-/journal_content/56/10180/7632945/NEWS.

34   Tim Craine, *Barriers to Housing Delivery: What Are the Market-Perceived Barriers to Residential Development in London?* (London: Greater London Authority and Molior London Ltd, December 2012), http://www.london.gov.uk/sites/default/files/Barriers%20to%20Housing%20Delivery.pdf.

35   Robert Fulford, *Accidental City: The Transformation of Toronto* (Canada: MacFarlane, Walter & Ross, 1995), 77.

36   Jane Jacobs, *The Death and Life of Great American Cities* (New York: Vintage Books, 1961), 4.

37   As characterised by the author; Napoleon III, quoted in Colin Jones, *Paris: A History* (New York: Penguin Books, 2004), 301

38   David Pinkney, *Napoleon III and the Rebuilding of Paris* (Princeton, NJ: Princeton University Press, 1972), 18.

39   Maxime du Camp, quoted in Jones, *Paris*, 304.

40   Jones, *Paris*, 301.

41   Georges-Eugène Haussmann, quoted in Friedrich Lenger, *European Cities in the Modern Era, 1850–1914*, trans. Joel Golb (Leiden, Netherlands: Koninklijke Brill NV, 2012), 22.

42   Christopher Caldwell, 'Revolting High Rises,' *New York Times Magazine*, 27 November 2005, www.nytimes.com/2005/11/27/magazine/revolting-high-rises.html.

43   Fulford, *Accidental City*, 85.

44   Nadine Kalinauskas, 'St Lawrence Market in Toronto Named World's Best Food Market by National Geographic', *Shine On*, 5 April 2012, https://ca.shine.yahoo.com/blogs/shine-on/st-lawrence-market-toronto-named-world-best-food-145127435.html.

45   Jacobs, *Death and Life*, 50.

46   Dave LeBlanc, '35 Years on, St Lawrence Is a Template for Urban Housing', *Globe and Mail*, 6 February 2013, www.theglobeandmail.com/life/home-and-garden/architecture/35-years-on-st-lawrence-is-a-template-for-urban-housing/article8296990.

47   David Crombie, phone interview by authors, 17 September 2014.

48   Amanda Burden, 'How Public Spaces Make Cities Work', TED Talk, April 2014, www.ted.com/talks/amanda_burden_how_public_spaces_make_cities_work?language=en. Background information from interview with Amanda Burden, New York, 16 October 2015.

49   Janette Sadik-Khan, 'New York's Streets? Not So Mean Anymore', TED Talk, September 2013, New York, www.ted.com/talks/janette_sadik_khan_new_york_s_streets_not_so_mean_any_more?language=en. Background information from e-mail to author, 25 October 2015.

50   'Why Plants in the Office Make Us More Productive', *Science Daily*, 1 September 2014, www.sciencedaily.com/releases/2014/09/140901090735.htm.

51   Mohamed Boubekri, Ivy N. Cheung, Kathryn J. Reid, Chia-Hui Wang, and Phyllis C. Zee, 'Impact of Windows and Daylight Exposure on Overall Health and Sleep Quality of Office Workers: A Case-Control Pilot Study', *Journal of Clinical Sleep Medicine: JCSM: Official Publication of the American Academy of Sleep Medicine* 10, no. 6 (2014): 603.

52   Carlo Ratti, phone interview by authors, 13 October 2014.

53   Judith Heerwagen, 'Green Buildings, Organizational Success and Occupant Productivity', *Building Research & Information* 28, nos. 5–6 (2000): 353–67.

54   Kimberly Bradley, 'Model Factories: Fagus-GreCon', *Monocle* 69, no. 7 (December 2013–January 2014): 133–4.

55   Christine Congdon, Donna Flynn, and Melanie Redman, 'Balancing "We" and "Me": The Best Collaborative Spaces Also Support Solitude',

Harvard Business Review, October 2014, https://hbr.org/2014/10/balancing-we-and-me-the-best-collaborative-spaces-also-support-solitude.

56   'Power of Place', *Steelcase 360°*, no. 68 (2014): 17.

57   Kaisa Nuikkinen, 'Vision of the Helsinki City School Building Program: Healthy and Safe School Building', presentation at the American Institute for Architects' Schools in a Flat World conference, Helsinki, Finland, 11 September 2008.

58   Kees Keizer, Siegwart Lindenberg, and Linda Steg, 'The Spreading of Disorder', *Science* 322, no. 5908 (2008): 1681–5.

59   Anthony A. Braga and Brenda J. Bond, 'Policing Crime and Disorder Hot Spots: A Randomized Controlled Trial', *Criminology* 46, no. 3 (2008): 577–607.

60   Unfortunately, misinterpretation of the theory has been used to support other, only partially related policies. Critics use (far too-frequent) occasions of abusive police overreaction as an indictment of 'broken-windows' policing writ large. Such criticism is an inaccurate conflation of two completely different phenomena. Yes, broken-windows theory suggests it's important to police petty crime. But it also suggests that community policing – more human policing, whereby officers walk the beat and actively foster relationships – is the answer. A proper application of broken-windows policing is community engagement, not creating an authoritarian police state.

61   Keizer et al., 'Spreading of Disorder'.

62   OECD, *Road Safety Annual Report 2015* (OECD Publishing, 2015), DOI: 10.1787/irtad-2015-en, 11

63   Ibid., 436. See also 'Why Sweden Has So Few Road Deaths', *Economist*, 26 February 2014, www.economist.com/blogs/economist-explains/2014/02/economist-explains-16.

64   'Vision Zero Initiative: Traffic Safety by Sweden', Swedish Government and Business Sweden, www.visionzeroinitiative.com/en.

65   'Why Sweden Has So Few Road Deaths'.

66   'Cycling Facts and Figures', IAmsterdam, 2015, www.iamsterdam.com/en/media-centre/city-hall/dossier-cycling/cycling-facts-and-figures; Amanda Buck, 'Transparency: The Most Dangerous Cities for Walking', *GOOD Magazine*, 3 September 2010, http://magazine.good.is/infographics/transparency-the-most-dangerous-cities-for-walking.

67   Statistics Netherlands, 'Traffic Deaths Down Again', 18 April 2011, www.cbs.nl/en-GB/menu/themas/gezondheid-welzijn/publicaties/artikelen/archief/2011/2011-029-pb.htm; Ben Fried, 'The Origins of Holland's "Stop Murdering Children" Street Safety Movement', StreetsBlog Network, 20 February 2013, http://streetsblog.net/2013/02/20/the-origins-of-hollands-stop-murdering-children-street-safety-movement.

68   'Amsterdam Children Fighting Cars in 1972', *Bicycle Dutch*, https://bicycledutch.wordpress.com/2013/12/12/amsterdam-children-fighting-cars-in-1972.

69   'Jan Gehl: Biography', Project for Public Spaces, www.pps.org/reference/jgehl.

70   Richard Rogers, 'Forward', in Jan Gehl, *Cities for People* (Washington, DC: Island Press, 2010), ix.

71   Jan Gehl, quoted in Ellie Violet Bramley, 'Is Jan Gehl Winning His Battle to Make Our Cities Liveable?' *Guardian*, 8 December 2014, www.theguardian.com/cities/2014/dec/08/jan-gehl-make-cities-liveable-urban-rethinker.

72   Jan Gehl, quoted in 'Interview with Jan Gehl', American Society for Landscape Architects, www.asla.org/ContentDetail.aspx?id=31346.

73   Bramley, 'Is Jan Gehl Winning His Battle?'

74   *Towards a Fine City for People* (Copenhagen, Denmark: Gehl Architects, June 2004), http://issuu.com/gehlarchitects/docs/issuu_270_london_pspl_2004/0.

Chapter 12

1   Matthew Browning, quoted in Emma Marris, 'Let Kids Run Wild in the Woods', *Slate*, 25 May 2014, www.slate.com/articles/health_and_science/science/2014/05/kid_play_zones_in_parks_leave_no_trace_inhibits_fun_and_bonding_with_nature.html.

2   Edward O. Wilson, *Biophilia* (Cambridge, MA: Harvard University Press, 1984), 85.

3   David Hancocks, 'Bringing Nature into the Zoo: Inexpensive Solutions for Zoo Environments', *International Journal for the Study of Animal Problems* 1, no. 3 (1980): 170–7.

4   Roger S. Ulrich, Robert F. Simons, Barbara D. Losito, Evelyn Fiorito, Mark A. Miles, and Michael Zelson, 'Stress Recovery During Exposure to Natural and Urban Environments', *Journal of Environmental Psychology* 11, no. 3 (1991): 201–230; Chen-Yen Chang and Ping-Kun Chen, 'Human Response toWindow Views and Indoor Plants in the Workplace', *HortScience*, 40, no. 5 (2005): 1354–1359; Terry Hartig, Gary W. Evans, Larry D. Jamner, Deborah S. Davis, and Tommy Gärling, 'Tracking Restoration in Natural and Urban Field Settings', *Journal of Environmental Psychology* 23, no. 2 (2003): 109–23.

5   Maria Bodin and Terry Hartig, 'Does the Outdoor Environment Matter for Psychological Restoration Gained Through Running?' *Psychology of Sport and Exercise* 4, no. 2 (2003): 141–53.

6   Roger S. Ulrich, 'View Through a Window May Influence Recovery Surgery', *Science*, New Series 224, no. 4647 (27 April 1984): 420–1.

7   'The Great Smog of 1952', Met Office, 10 June 2014, www.metoffice.gov.uk/education/teens/case-studies/great-smog.

8   Louis Bainbridge to James T. Duff, October 31, 1948, in 'The Donora Smog Disaster October 30–31, 1948', Pennsylvania Historical & Museum Commission, www.portal.state.pa.us/portal/server.pt/community/documents_from_1946_-_present/20426/donora_smog_disaster/999079.

9   'Theodore Roosevelt', in *The National Parks: America's Best Idea*, PBS, 2009, www.pbs.org/nationalparks/people/historical/roosevelt.

10   E. F. Schumacher, *Small Is Beautiful: A Study of People as If People Mattered* (New York: Harper Perennial, 2010), 14.

11   Rhett Butler, 'Brazil', Mongabay.com, 13 July 2014, http://rainforests.mongabay.com/20brazil.wtm; 'Coordenaçã-Geral de

Observção da Terra—OBT: ProjectoProdes: Monitoramenot da FlorestaAmazônicaBrasileiraporSatélite' (in Portuguese), Ministério da Ciêcia e Technologia e Inovação e Minstério do MeloAmbiente, 2014, www.obt.inpe.br/prodes/index.php.

12   'Measuring the Daily Destruction of the World's Rainforests', *Scientific American*, 19 November 2009, www.scientificamerican.com/article/earth-talks-daily-destruction.

13   Jenna R. Jambeck, Roland Geyer, Chris Wilcox, Theodore R. Siegler, Miriam Perryman, Anthony Andrady, Ramani Narayan, and Kara Lavender Law, 'Plastic waste inputs from land into the ocean', *Science* 347, no. 6223 (2015): 768-71.

14   'Coral Reefs: Facts and Figures', IUCN, 20 March 2013, www.iucn.org/media/facts_and_figures/?12680/Coral-reefs--Facts-and-figures.

15   Richard Monastersky, 'Life: A Status Report', *Nature* 516 (11 December 2014): 159–61.

16   Edward O. Wilson, quoted in 'Edward O. Wilson: "The Loss of Biodiversity Is a Tragedy"', UNESCO Media Services, 2 September 2010, www.unesco.org/new/en/media-services/single-view/news/edward_o_wilson_the_loss_of_biodiversity_is_a_tragedy/#.Vlxh4dKrTDc.

17   David J. Newman and Gordon M Cragg, 'Natural Products as Sources of New Drugs over the 30 Years from 1981 to 2010', *Journal of Natural Products* 75, no. 3 (2012): 311–35.

18   Edward O. Wilson, 'My Wish: Build the Encyclopedia of Life', TED   2007,   www.ted.com/talks/e_o_wilson_on_saving_life_on_earth?language=en.

19   Monastersky, 'Life'.

20   Tony Hiss, 'Can the World Really Set Aside Half of the Planet for Wildlife?' *Smithsonian Magazine*, September 2014, www.smithsonianmag.com/ist/?next=/science-nature/can-world-really-set-aside-half-planet-wildlife-180952379.

21   I encourage you to learn more about their amazing work at www.whitehawkproject.org.

22   Daniela Russi, Patrick ten Brink, Andrew Farmer, Tomas Badura, David Coates, Johannes Förster, Ritesh Kumar et al., *The Economics of Ecosystems and Biodiversity for Water and Wetlands: Executive Summary* (Institute for European Environmental Policy &Ramsar Secretariat, 2013),   www.teebweb.org/publication/the-economics-of-ecosystems-and-biodiversity-teeb-for-water-and-wetlands, 50.

23   Environmental Protection Agency, Office of Water, *Wetlands: Protection Life and Property from Flooding* (May 2006), http://water.epa.gov/type/wetlands/ outreach/upload/Flooding.pdf.

24   There has been debate in the scientific community about the validity of this number, as there have been some instances in which the presence of intact wetlands do not reduce storm surge. For a thoughtful analysis, see Jeffrey Masters, 'Storm Surge Reduction by Wetlands', *Weather Underground*,   www.wunderground.com/hurricane/surge_wetlands.asp?MR=1. We acknowledge that the impact wetlands can have on reducing storm surges can't be generalised to all scenarios, but the benefit they have had and can have in many others is undeniable. See

also Corps of Engineers, US Army Engineer District, New Orleans, *Interim Survey Report, Morgan City, Louisiana and Vicinity*, no. 63 (New Orleans, LA: US Army Engineer District, November 1963).

25   Robert G. Dean, 'New Orleans and the Wetlands of Southern Louisiana', *Bridge* 36, no. 1 (2006): 35–42.

26   Donald F. Boesch, Leonard Shabman, L. George Antle, John W. Day Jr., Robert G. Dean, Gerald E. Galloway, Charles G. Groat et al., *A New Framework for Planning the Future of Coastal Louisiana After the Hurricanes of 2005* (Cambridge, MD: University of Maryland Center for Environmental Science, 2006), http://ian.umces.edu/pdfs/ian_report_333.pdf, 16.

27   Edward B. Barbier, 'Valuing Ecosystem Services as Productive Inputs', *Economic Policy* 22, no. 49 (2007): 178–229.

28   'Sebago Lake', Portland Water District, www.pwd.org/environment/sebago/sebago.php.

29   John Talberth, Erin Gray, Evan Branosky, and Todd Gartner, *Insights from the Field: Forests for Water* (Washington, DC: Water Resources Institute, 2012), http://pdf.wri.org/insights_from_the_field_forests_for_water.pdf.

30   Caryn Ernst, *Protecting the Source: Land Conservation and the Future of America's Drinking Water* (San Francisco: The Trust for Public Land, 2004).

31   Robert Costanza, Rudolf de Groot, Paul Sutton, Sander van der Ploeg, Sharolyn J. Anderson, Ida Kubiszewski, Stephen Farber et al., 'Changes in the Global Value of Ecosystem Services', *Global Environmental Change* 26 (2014): 152–8.

32   United Nations, Department of Economic and Social Affairs, Population Division, *World Urbanization Prospects: The 2014 Revision, Highlights* (ST/ESA/SER.A/352), http://esa.un.org/unpd/wup/highlights/wup2014-highlights.pdf, 1.

33   The term was coined by the writer Richard Louv in his book *Last Child in the Woods: Saving Our Children from Nature-Deficit Disorder* (Chapel Hill, NC: Algonquin Books, 2005).

34   *Reconnecting Children with Nature: Findings of the Natural Childhood Inquiry* (The National Trust, 2012), www.nationaltrust.org.uk/document-1355773744553.

35   Christiane Dorion, interview by authors, London, 26 September 2014.

36   Jeremy Bailenson, 'Virtual Reality Could Make a Real Difference in Environment', *San Francisco Chronicle*, 15 August 2014, www.sfgate.com/opinion/article/Virtual-reality-could-make-real-difference-in-5691610.php.

37   Sun Joo Grace Ahn, Jeremy N. Bailenson, and Dooyeon Park, 'Short- and Long-Term Effects of Embodied Experiences in Immersive Virtual Environments on Environmental Locus of Control and Behavior', *Computers in Human Behavior* 39 (2014): 235–45.

38   Jeremy Bailenson, quoted in Amy Westervelt, 'Can't Picture a World Devastated by Climate Change? These Games Will Do It for You', *Smithsonian Magazine*, 21 July 2014, www.smithsonianmag.com/science-nature/cant-picture-world-devastated-climate-change-these-games-will-do-it-you-180952104.

39   Shawn and Laura Sears, interview (San Gregorio, CA) and e-mail correspondence with authors, October 2014.

40   Outdoor play, studies show, is pivotal for a child's development and well-being. See Peter Gray, 'The Decline of Play and the Rise of Psychopathology in Children and Adolescents', *American Journal of Play* 3, no. 4 (2011): 443–63.

Conclusion

1   There have, of course, been historical examples of tolerant and even multicultural caliphates. Under Sultan Bayezid II, the Ottoman Empire, a professed caliphate, sent its naval fleet to Spain to evacuate Jews from the Inquisition. However, those who pine for a caliphate today seek the oppressive, violent, millenarian version of a caliphate rather than history's more enlightened examples. And as 'Caliphism' does not unhelpfully conflate Islam with its extremist, bastardised forms, it is still a preferable term to alternatives such as 'Islamism', or 'jihadism' – or worse still, terms like 'violent extremism', which euphemistically – and falsely – try to avoid making any connection with Islam at all.

2   Ray Kurzweil, *The Singularity Is Near: When Humans Transcend Biology* (New York: Viking, 2005).

3   Michael Howard, 'The Movie That Accurately Predicted the Future of Technology', Esquire.com, 23 September 2014, www.esquire.com/entertainment/movies/a30140/minority-report-tech-is-real-now.

4   Rory Cellan-Jones, 'Stephen Hawking Warns Artificial Intelligence Could End Mankind', BBC News, 2 December 2014, www.bbc.com/news/technology-30290540.

5   'She, Robot: A Conversation with Helen Greiner', *Foreign Affairs* 94, no. 1 (January–February 2015), 21.

6   Diane Ackerman, *The Human Age: The World Shaped by Us* (New York: W. W. Norton & Co., 2014), 225.

7   Ibid., 221–2.

8   Matt McFarland, 'Elon Musk: "With Artificial Intelligence We Are Summoning the Demon"', *Washington Post*, 24 October 2014, www.washingtonpost.com/news/innovations/wp/2014/10/24/elon-musk-with-artificial-intelligence-we-are-summoning-the-demon.

9   Susannah F. Locke, 'Robots That Eat Bugs and Plants for Power', *Popular Science*, 9 October 2009, www.popsci.com/military-aviation-amp-space/article/2009-09/robots-eat-bugs-and-plants-power.

10   Stephen Hawking, quoted in Cellan-Jones, 'Stephen Hawking Warns'.

11   Sherry Turkle, 'Authenticity in the Age of Digital Companions', *Interaction Studies* 8, no. 3 (2007), 514.

12   Steve Jobs, 'Stanford Commencement Address', Stanford University, Stanford, CA, 14 June 2005.

13   Hawking, quoted in Cellan-Jones, 'Stephen Hawking Warns'.

14   Hugh Herr, 'The New Bionics That Let Us Run, Climb and Dance', TED Talk, March 2014, www.ted.com/talks/hugh_herr_the_new_bionics_that_let_us_run_climb_and_dance?language=en.

15   Elon Musk, quoted in John Markoff, 'Artificial-Intelligence Research Center Is Founded by Silicon Valley Investors', *New York Times*, 11 December 2015, www.nytimes.com/2015/12/12/science/artificial-intelligence-research-center-is-founded-by-silicon-valley-investors.html.

16   Chris Cesare, 'Stanford to Host 100-Year Study on Artificial Intelligence', *Stanford News*, 16 December 2014, http://news.stanford.edu/news/2014/december/ai-century-study-121614.html; John Markoff, 'Study to Examine Effects of Artificial Intelligence', *New York Times*, 16 December 2014, www.nytimes.com/2014/12/16/science/century-long-study-will-examine-effects-of-artificial-intelligence.html.

17   Cesare, 'Stanford to Host 100-Year Study'.

18   Mary Warnock, *A Question of Life: The Warnock Report on Human Fertilisation and Embryology* (London: Her Majesty's Stationery Office, 1984).

19   Fertilisation, Human, and Embryology Act, Chapter 37 (London: Her Majesty's Stationery Office, London, 1990).

Postscript

1   Gavin Newsom, *Citizenville: How to Take the Town Square Digital and Reinvent Government* (New York: Penguin Press, 2013), 113–18.

2   Ibid., 121.

BIBLIOGRAPHY

Abel, Jaison R., Richard Deitz and Yaqin Su. 'Are Recent College Graduates Finding Good Jobs?'. *Current Issues in Economics and Finance* 20, no. 1 (2014).

'About: Secretary of the Treasury Jacob J. Lew'. *US Department of the Treasury*, 5 June 2014. http://www.treasury.gov/about/Pages/ Secretary.aspx.

Ackerman, Diane. *The Human Age: The World Shaped By Us.* New York: W.W. Norton & Company, 2014.

'Advance Care Planning: National Guidelines'. *Concise Guidance to Good Practice* 12. Royal College of Physicians, 2009.

'Agenda Materials: College Board Forum 2014'. *The College Board.* 27–29 October 2013.

'Agenda Materials: College Board Forum 2015'. *The College Board*, 4–6 November 2015.

Ahn, Sun Joo Grace, Jeremy N. Bailenson and Dooyeon Park. 'Short-and Long-term Effects of Embodied Experiences in Immersive Virtual Environments on Environmental Locus of Control and Behavior'. *Computers in Human Behavior* 39 (2014): 235–245.

Aitken, Murray. *Medicines Use and Spending Shifts: A Review of the Use of Medicines in the US in 2013.* IMS Institute for Healthcare Informatics, April 2014.

—— . *Medicines Use and Spending Shifts: A Review of the Use of Medicines in the US in 2014.* IMS Institute for Healthcare Informatics, April 2015.

'Alan Greenspan to Consult for Deutsche Bank Corporate and Investment Bank'. *Deutsche Bank*, 13 August 2007. https://www. db.com/presse/en/content/press_releases_2007_3606.htm.

'Almere, Holland'. *The Self-Build Portal*, 2015. http://www.selfbuildportal.org.uk/homeruskwartier-district-almere.

Ambrosi-Randić, Neala. 'Perception of Current and Ideal Body Size in Preschool Age Children'. *Perceptual and Motor Skills* 90, no. 3 (2000): 885–889.

'America's Elite: An Hereditary Meritocracy'. *The Economist.* 24 January 2015.

'America's New Aristocracy'. *The Economist.* 24 January 2015.

'America's Top Schools 2014'. *Newsweek.* www.newsweek.com/high-schools/americas-top-schools-2014.

Amos, Nicky and Rory Sullivan. 'The Business Benchmark on Farm Animal Welfare: 2014 Report.' *Business Benchmark on Farm Animal Welfare.* 2014.

'Amsterdam Children Fighting Cars in 1972'. *BicycleDutch.* https://bicycledutch.wordpress.com/2013/12/12/amsterdam-children-fighting-cars-in-1972/.

'An Unhealthy Dose of Stress: The Impact of Adverse Childhood Experiences and Toxic Stress on Childhood Health and Development'. Center for Youth Wellness.

'Animal Welfare'. Jeremy Coller Foundation. http://www.jeremycollerfoundation.org/programmes/animal-welfare.

'Antimicrobial Resistance – Why the Irresponsible Use of Antibiotics in Agriculture Must Stop'. *Alliance to Save Our Antibiotics,* June 2014.

APA Task Force on the Sexualization of Girls. *Report of the APA Task Force on the Sexualization of Girls.* Washington, DC: American Psychological Association, 2010.

Appelbaum, Eileen and Ruth Milkman. 'Leaves That Pay: Employer and Worker Experiences with Paid Family Leave in California'. Washington, DC: Center for Economic and Policy Research, 2011.

Archer, Tom and Ian Cole. 'Still Not Plannable? Housing Supply and the Changing Structure of the Housebuilding

Industry in the UK in "Austere" Times'. *People, Place and Policy* 8, no. 2 (2014): 93–108.

Ashworth, Will. 'RiskMetrics Two Years After IPO'. *Investopedia*, 28 February 2010. www.investopedia.com/stock-analysis/2010/riskmetrics-two-years-after-ipo-riskmscimhptrifigacas0304.aspx.

Aubrey, Allison. 'Antibiotic-Free Meat Business Is Booming, Thanks to Chipotle'. *NPR*, 31 May 2012. www.npr.org/sections/thesalt/2012/05/31/154084442/antibiotic-free-meat-business-is-booming-thanks-to-chipotle.

Bagchi, Sutirtha and Jan Svejnar. 'Does Wealth Inequality Matter for Growth? The Effect of Billionaire Wealth, Income Distribution, and Poverty'. *Journal of Comparative Economics* 43, no. 3 (2015): 505–530.

Bailenson, Jeremy. 'Virtual Reality Could Make a Real Difference in Environment'. *San Francisco Chronicle*, 15 August 2014.

Bainbridge, Louis. Louis Bainbridge to James T. Duff, 31 October 1948. In 'The Donora Smog Disaster October 30–31, 1948.' Pennsylvania Historical & Museum Commission. www.portal.state.pa.us/portal/server.pt/community/documents_from_1946__present/20426/donora_smog_disaster/999079.

Ball, David J. 'Policy Issues and Risk–Benefit Trade-offs of "Safer Surfacing" for Children's Playgrounds'. *Accident Analysis & Prevention* 36, no. 4 (2004): 661–670.

'Ballona Wetlands Restoration Project'. 2014. http://ballonarestoration.org.

Banham, John, Kate Faulkner, Roger Graef and Mavis McDonald. *Building the Homes and Communities Britain Needs*. Future Homes Commission, Royal Institute of British Architects, 2012.

Barbier, Edward B. 'Valuing Ecosystem Services As Productive Inputs. *Economic Policy* 22, no. 49 (2007): 178–229.

'Barclays Appoints Hector Sants'. *Barclays*, 12 December 2012. http://www.barclays.com/news/2012/12/barclays-appoints- hector-sants.html.

Barnett, Alina, Sandra Batten, Adrian Chiu, Jeremy Franklin, and Maria Sebastia-Barriel. 'The UK Productivity Puzzle'. *Bank of England Quarterly Bulletin* Q2 (2014): 114–128.

'BBC Poll: One in Five 'Disillusioned' with Westminster'. *BBC News*, 31 October 2014.

Bennett, Drake. 'The Dunbar Number, From the Guru of Social Networks'. *BloombergBusinesseweek*, 10 January 2013.

Bentham, Jeremy. *An Introduction to the Principles of Morals and Legislation.* 1789.

Berman, Rick. 'Commentary: Playing Chicken with Pork'. *PORK Network*, 28 February 2013. http://www.porknetwork. com/pork-news/Commentary-Playing-chicken-with-pork-193903501. html?view=all.

Berrington de González, Amy, Mahadevappa Mahesh, Kwang-Pyo Kim, Mythreyi Bhargavan, Rebecca Lewis, Fred Mettler and Charles Land. 'Projected Cancer Risks from Computed Tomographic Scans Performed in the United States in 2007'. *Archives of Internal Medicine* 169, no. 22 (December 2009): 2017–2077.

'Bevolkingsontwikkeling; regio per maand' (in Dutch). CBS Statline, 26 June 2014.

Bidwell, Allie. 'An African Company Pays People to Learn Computer Science'. *US News & World Report*, 14 May 2015. www.usnews.com/news/stem-solutions/ articles/2015/05/14/andela-an-african-company-paying-people-to-learn-computer-science.

Biehle, Susanne N. and Kristin D. Mickelson. 'Preparing for Parenthood: How Feelings of Responsibility and Efficacy Impact Expectant Parents'. *Journal of Social and Personal Relationships* 28, No. 5, (2011): 668–683.

Blair, Tony. *A Journey: My Political Life.* New York: Vintage Books, 2011.

Blumenthal, Paul and Ryan Grim. 'The Inside Story of How Citizens United Has Changed Washington Lawmaking'. *Huffington Post*, 25 February 2015. www.huffingtonpost. com/2015/02/26/citizens-united-congress_n_6723540. html.

Blundell, Richard, Alan Duncan, Julian McCrae and Costas Meghir. 'The Labour Market Impact of the Working Families' Tax Credit'. *Fiscal Studies* 21, no. 1 (2000): 75–104.

Boesch, Donald F., Leonard Shabman, et al. 'A New Framework for Planning the Future of Coastal Louisiana After the Hurricanes of 2005'. Cambridge, MD: University of Maryland Center for Environmental Science, 2006.

Bond, Allison. 'Blocks, Puzzles Help Kids Prep for School'. *Reuters*, 20 March 2014.

Bornstein, David. 'Out of Poverty, Family-Style'. *New York Times*, 14 July 2011.

Borowtiz, Andy. 'Citigroup to Move Headquarters to US Capitol Building'. *The New Yorker*, 13 December 2013.

Boseley, Sarah. 'Mid Staffordshire NHS Trust Fined for "Avoidable and Tragic Death"'. *Guardian*, 28 April 2014.

Boubekri, Mohamed, Ivy N. Cheung, Kathryn J. Reid, Chia-Hui Wang and Phyllis C. Zee. 'Impact of Windows and Daylight Exposure on Overall Health and Sleep Quality of Office Workers: A Case-Control Pilot Study'. *Journal of Clinical Sleep Medicine: JCSM: Official Publication of the American Academy of Sleep Medicine* 10, no. 6 (2014): 603.

Boushey, Heather. 'Family Policy: The Foundation of a Middle-Out Agenda'. *Democracy* no. 29 (Summer 2013). http://democracyjournal.org/magazine/29/family-policy-the-foundation-of-a-middle-out-agenda.

Boushey, Heather and Sarah Jane Glynn. *The Effects of Paid Family Medical Leave on Employment Stability and Economic Stability*. Washington, DC: Center for American Progress, 2012.

Bowers, Becky. 'Rep. Louise Slaughter Says 80% of Antibiotics Are Fed to Livestock'. *Tampa Bay Times' PolitiFact.com*, 15 October 2013.

Boyland, Emma J., Sarah Nolan, Bridget Kelly, Catrin Tudur-Smith, Andrew Jones, Jason C.G. Halford and Eric Robinson. 'Advertising as a Cue to Consume: A Systematic Review and Meta-analysis of the Effects of Acute Exposure to Unhealthy Food and Nonalcoholic Beverage Advertising on Intake in Children and Adults'. *The American Journal of Clinical Nutrition* (2016): ajcn120022.

Boyland, Emma J., Melissa Kavanagh-Safran, and Jason C.G. Halford. 'Exposure to 'Healthy Fast Food Meal Bundles in Television Advertisements Promotes Liking for Fast Food but Not Healthier Choices in Children'. *British Journal of Nutrition* 113, no. 06 (2015): 1012-1018.

Bradley, Kimberly. 'Model Factories: Fagus-GreCon.' *Monocle*, 69, no. 7 (December 2013–January 2014): 133–4.

Braga, Anthony A. and Brenda J. Bond. 'Policing Crime and Disorder Hot Spots: A Randomized Controlled Trial'. *Criminology* 46, no. 3 (2008): 577–607.

Bramley, Ellie Violet. 'Is Jan Gehl Winning His Battle to Make Our Cities Liveable?'. *Guardian*, 8 December 2014.

Branson, Sir Richard. 'Excerpt from: The Virgin Way: Everything I Know About Leadership'. *Virgin.com*, 23 September 2014. www.virgin.com/richard-branson/why-were-letting-virgin-staff-take-as-much-holiday-as-they-want.

Brat, Illan and Sarah Nassauer. 'Chipotle Suspends Pork Sales at a Third of Its Restaurants'. *Wall Street Journal*, 13 January 2015.

Bredgaard, Thomas and Arthur Daemmrich. 'The Welfare State as an Investment Strategy: Denmark's Flexicurity Policies'. July 2012. http://ilera2012.wharton.upenn.edu/RefereedPapers/BredgaardThomas%20ArthurDaemmrich.pdf.

Brooks, David. 'The Character Factory'. *New York Times*, 1 August 2014.

— . 'Out of Poverty, Family-Style'. *New York Times*, 14 July 2011.

— . 'Stairway to Wisdom'. *New York Times*, 15 May 2014. www.nytimes.com/2014/05/16/opinion/brooks-stairway-to-wisdom.html.

— . 'Support Our Students'. *New York Times*, 19 January 2015. www.nytimes.com/2015/01/20/opinion/david-brooks-support-our-students.html.

Brown, Jane D., and Kelly L. L'Engle. 'X-rated Sexual Attitudes and Behaviors Associated with US Early Adolescents'

Exposure to Sexually Explicit Media'. *Communication Research* 36, no. 1 (2009): 129–151.

British Government. *Number of Individual Income Taxpayers by Marginal Rate, Gender and Age, 1990–91 to 2014–15.* https://www.gov.uk/government/uploads/system/uploads/attachment_data/file/404149/Table_2.1.pdf.

Brown, S. L. 'Family Structure and Child Well-Being: The Significance of Parental Cohabitation'. *Journal of Marriage and Family* 66 (2004): 351–367.

Buchannan, Larry, Josh Keller and Haeyoun Park. 'Your Contribution to the California Drought'. *New York Times*, 21 May 2015. www.nytimes.com/interactive/2015/05/21/us/your-contribution-to-the-california-drought.html?_r=0.

Buck, Amanda. 'Transparency: The Most Dangerous Cities for Walking'. *GOOD Magazine*, 3 September 2010.

'Building Blocks'. *The Economist*, 22 December 2014.

Building in a Small Island? Why We Still Need the Brownfield First Approach. Kemsing, Kent: Green Balance (for the Campaign to Protect Rural England), 2011.

Burden, Amanda. 'How Public Spaces Make Cities Work'. Presentation at TED, April 2014.

Butler, Rhett. 'Brazil'. *Mongabay.com*, 13 July 2014. http://rainforests.mongabay.com/20brazil.htm.

Buzby, Jean C., and Jeffrey Hyman. 'Total and Per Capita Value of Food Loss in the United States'. *Food Policy* 37, no. 5 (2012): 561–570.

Cadwalladr, Carole. 'My Week as an Amazon Insider'. *Observer*, 1 December 2013.

Caldwell, Christopher. 'Revolting High Rises'. *New York Times Magazine*, 27 November 2005.

'Campylobacter". *Food Standards Agency.* https://www.food.gov.uk/science/microbiology/campylobacterevidence-programme.

'Cancel That Violin Class: Helicopter Moms and Dads Will Not Harm Their Kids If They Relax a Bit'. *The Economist*, 26 July 2014.

Card, David and Alan B. Krueger. 'Minimum Wages and Employment: A Case Study of the Fast Food Industry in New Jersey and Pennsylvania'. *National Bureau of Economic Research*, no. w4509, 1993.

Caro, Robert. *The Path to Power, vol. 1 of The Years of Lyndon Johnson*. 1981. Reprint: London: Pimlico, 2003.

Carr, Nicholas. *The Shallows: What the Internet Is Doing to Our Brains*. New York: W. W. Norton & Company, 2010.

Casciani, Dominic. 'Secret Life of the Office Cleaner'. *BBC News*, 19 September 2005.

Casey, Liam. Interview by Piers Fawkes. *PSFK 2015*, 18 May 2015.

Cavendish, Camilla. *The Cavendish Review: An Independent Review Into Healthcare Assistants and Support Workers in the NHS and Social Care Settings*. London: Department of Health, 2013.

Cellan-Jones, Rory. 'Stephen Hawking Warns Artificial Intelligence Could End Mankind'. *BBC News*, 2 December 2014.

Census Bureau (US). *Maternity Leave and Employment Patterns of First-Time Mothers: 1961–2008*. Washington, DC: Department of Commerce, 2011.

Census Bureau (US). *Business Dynamics Statistics: Firm Characteristics Data Tables*. Washington, DC: Department of Commerce, 2015. www.census.gov/ces/dataproducts/bds/data_firm.html.

'Census Shows Rise in Foreign-Born'. *BBC News*, 11 December 2012.

Cesare, Chris. 'Stanford to Host 100–year Study on Artificial Intelligence'. *Stanford Report*, 16 December 2014. http://news. stanford.edu/news/2014/december/ai-century-study-121614. html.

Chandler, Jr., Alfred D. *The Visible Hand: The Managerial Revolution in American Business*. Cambridge, MA: Harvard University Press, 1977.

Chandy, Laurence and Geoffrey Gertz. *Poverty in Numbers: The Changing State of Global Poverty from 2005 to 2015*. Brookings Institution, 2011.

Chang, Chen-Yen and Ping-Kun Chen. 'Human Response to Window Views and Indoor Plants in the Workplace'. *HortScience* 40, no. 5 (2005): 1354–1359.

Chang, Emily. 'China's Famed Pearl River Under Denim Threat'. *CNN*, 27 April 2010.

Cherlin, Andrew J., Elizabeth Talbert and Suzumi Yasutake. 'Changing Fertility Regimes and the Transition to Adulthood: Evidence from a Recent Cohort'. In *Annual Meeting of the Population Association of America, Boston, MA,* May 3, 2014.

Chew, Jesslyn. 'Marriages Benefits When Fathers Share Household Parenting Responsibilities, MU Researchers Say'. *University of Missouri News Bureau,* 8 April 2013. http://munews.missouri. edu/news-releases/2013/0408–marriages-benefit-when-fathers-share-household-parenting-responsibilities-mu-researcher- says/.

Chingos, Matthew M. *Strength in Numbers: State Spending on K-12 Assessment Systems.* Washington, DC: Brown Center for Education at the Brookings Institution, 2012.

Chirnko, Robert S., and Daniel J. Wilson. *Can Lower Tax Rates Be Bought? Business Rent-Seeking and Tax Competition Among US States.* Federal Reserve Bank of San Francisco, Working Paper 2009–29, 2010.

Cho, Illseung, Shingo Yamanishi, Laura Cox, Barbara A. Methé, Jiri Zavadil, Kelvin Li, Zhan Gao et al. 'Antibiotics in Early Life Alter the Murine Colonic Microbiome and Adiposity'. *Nature* 488, no. 7413 (2012): 621–626.

Christensen, Clayton. 'The Capitalist's Dilemma'. Lecture, RSA, London, 23 September 2013.

Chu, Jenny, Jonathan Faasse and P. Raghavendra Rau. 'Do Compensation Consultants Enable Higher CEO Pay?'. *New Evidence from Recent Disclosure Rule Changes,* September 23, 2014.

Churchill, Winston. Hansard HC Deb 28 April 1909, vol. 4, cols. 342–411.

— . Hansard HC Deb 28 October 1943, vol. 393, cols. 403–73.

Cialdini, Robert B., Linda J. Demaine, Brad J. Sagarin, Daniel W. Barrett, Kelton Rhoads and Patricia L. Winter. 'Managing Social Norms for Persuasive Impact', *Social Influence* 1, no. 1 (2006): 3–15.

Citizens UK. 'Living Wage Week 2013'. *YouTube* video, 3:48. 3 November 2013. https://www.youtube.com/watch?v=7Xz0ylCLBgE.

Cloos, Kassondra and Julie Turkewitz. 'Hundreds of Nude Photos Jolt Colorado School'. *New York Times*, 6 November 2015. www.nytimes.com/2015/11/07/us/colorado-students-caught-trading-nude-photos-by-the-hundreds.html.

Cohen, Nick. 'A Tale of Two Cities'. *Observer*, 19 October 2013.

Collins, James C. and Jerry I. Porras. 'Building Your Company's Vision'. *Harvard Business Review*, September 1996.

Collins Atlas of World History. Edited by Geoffrey Barraclough. Ann Arbor, MI: Arbor Press, 2003.

Collinson, Patrick. 'Self-Build: It's Time to Go Dutch'. Guardian, 25 November 2011.

Colvile, Robert. 'Yes, CEOs Are Ludicrously Overpaid. And Yes, It's Getting Worse'. *Telegraph*, 13 October 2014.

Colvin, Geoff. *Humans Are Underrated: What High Achievers Know That Brilliant Machines Never Will.* New York: Portfolio/Penguin, 2015.

'The Common Sense Census: Media Use by Tweens and Teens'. *Common Sense Media Kids Action*, Fall 2015. www.commonsensemedia.org/research/the-common-sense-census-media-use-by-tweens-and-teens.

Competition Commission. *Market Investigation into the Supply of Groceries in the UK.* London: UK Competition Commission, 2008.

Comptroller and Auditor General. *The Criminal Justice System: Landscape Review.* National Audit Office, 2014.

Congdon, Christine, Donna Flynn and Melanie Redman. 'Balancing "We" and "Me": The Best Collaborative Spaces Also Support Solitude'. *Harvard Business Review*, October 2014.

Connor, John M. and Robert H. Lande. 'Cartels as Rational Business Strategy: Crime Pays'. *Cardozo Law Review* 34, no. 427 (2012): 427–489, 430.

Conroy Bass, Brooke. 'Preparing for Parenthood? Gender, Aspirations, and the Reproduction of Labor Market Inequality'. *Gender & Society* 29, no. 3 (2015): 362–385.

'Consumers Face "Lost Decade" as Spending Squeeze Bites'. *BBC News*, 29 September 2014.

'Contrast-Enhanced CT Safe for Most Patients'. Radiological Society of North America. 9 September 2014. www2. rsna.org/timssnet/media/pressreleases/14_pr_target. cfm?ID=757.

'Coordenaçã-Geral de Observção da Terra – OBT: Projecto Prodes: Monitoramenot da Floresta Amazônica Brasileira por Satélite' (in Portuguese). *Ministério da Ciêcia e Technologia e Inovação e Minstério do Melo Ambiente*, 2014. http://www.obt.inpe. br/prodes/index.php.

'Coral Reefs: Facts and Figures'. *IUCN*, 20 March 2013. http:// www.iucn.org/media/facts_and_figures/?12680/ Coral-reefs— Facts-and-figures.

Corlett, Adam and Matthew Whittaker. *Low Pay Britain 2014*.

London: Resolution Foundation, 2014.

Corps of Engineers, US Army Engineer District, New Orleans. *Interim Survey Report, Morgan City, Louisiana and Vicinity*, no. 63. New Orleans, LA: US Army Engineer District, 1963.

'Cost of Outcomes Associated with Low Levels of Adult Numeracy in the UK'. *National Numeracy* and *Pro Bono Economics*. 2014.

'Costco Wholesale Corp.' Marketwatch, 16 January 2016. www.marketwatch.com/investing/stock/cost/financials.

Costanza, Robert, Rudolf de Groot, Paul Sutton, Sander van der Ploeg, Sharolyn J. Anderson, Ida Kubiszewski, Stephen Farber and R. Kerry Turner. 'Changes in the Global Value of Ecosystem Services'. *Global Environmental Change* 26 (2014): 152–158.

Coughlan, Sean. 'Is Five Too Soon to Start School?'. *BBC News*, 8 February 2008.

Council Regulation (EC) 1999/74 of 19 July 1999 laying down minimum standards for the protection of laying hens [1999] OJ L203/53.

Couzigou, Irène. 'France: Territorial Decentralisation in France: Towards Autonomy and Democracy'. In *Local Government in Europe: The 'Fourth Level' in the EU Multi-Layered System of Governance*. Edited by Carlo Panara and Michael R. Varney, 73–96. New York: Routledge, 2013.

Cowen, Tyler. 'Automation Alone Isn't Killing Jobs'. *New York Times*, 6 April 2014.

Coyle, Diane. *GDP: A Brief but Affectionate History*. Princeton, NJ: Princeton University Press, 2014.

——. 'GDP Is A Mirror on the Markets. It Must Not Rule Our Lives'. *Guardian*, 20 November 2014.

Cragg, Gordon M. 'Natural Products as Sources of New Drugs Over the 30 Years from 1981 to 2010'. *Journal of Natural Products* 75, no. 3 (2012): 311–335.

Craigie, Terry-Ann, Jeanne Brooks-Gunn and Jane Waldfogel. 'Family Structure, Family Stability and Early Child Wellbeing', No. 1275 (2010). http://crcw.princeton.edu/workingpapers/ WP10–14–FF.pdf.

Craine, Tim. *Barriers to Housing Delivery: What Are the Market-Perceived Barriers to Residential Development in London?*. London: Greater London Authority and Molior London Ltd, December 2012.

Curtis, Polly. 'French Civil Servant's Confession Strikes a Chord in Drive to Shrink State'. *Guardian*, 23 March 2011.

'Cycling Facts and Figures'. *IAmsterdam*, 2015. http://www.iamsterdam.com/en/media-centre/city-hall/dossier-cycling/ cycling-facts-and-figures.

Dahl, Melissa. 'It's Time to Kill the Performance Review'. *New York Magazine*, 1 June 2015. http://nymag.com/scienceofus/2015/05/time-to-revamp-the-performance-review.html.

Darzi, Ara. *High Quality Care For All: NHS Next Stage Review Final Report (The Darzi Report)*. London: The Stationery Office, 2008.

Daubney, Martin. 'Experiment That Convinced Me Online Porn in the Most Pernicious Threat Facing Children Today: By Ex Lads' Mag Editor Martin Daubney'. *Daily Mail*, 25 September 2013.

Davis, Joshua. 'How a Radical New Teaching Method Could Unleash A Generation of Geniuses'. *Wired*, 15 October 2013.

de Lange, Catherine. 'Sherry Turkle: "We're Losing the Raw, Human Part of Being with Each Other'. *Guardian*, 5 May 2013.

de Ruiter, Jan, Gavin Weston and Stephen M. Lyon. 'Dunbar's Number: Group Size and Brain Physiology in Humans Reexamined'. *American Anthropologist* 113, no. 4 (2011): 557–568.

Dean, Robert G. 'New Orleans and the Wetlands of Southern Louisiana'. *Bridge* 36, no. 1 (2006): 35–42.

DeAngelis, Tori. 'Web Pornography's Effect on Children'. *American Psychological Association Monitor*, 38, no. 10 (November 2007): 50.

Deloitte and Department for Employment and Learning. *Removing the Barriers to Learning: Exploring Adult Perceptions and Attitudes to Participation in Further Education, Part One: Research Report*. 2012.

Department for Business Innovation & Skills. *Motivation and Barriers to Learning for Young People Not in Education, Employment or Training*. BIS Research Paper Number 87, 2013.

Department for Communities and Local Government. *Troubled Families: Progress Information at December 2014 and Families Turned Around at February 2015*. British Government. 10 March 2015.

— . 'PM Praises Troubled Families Programme Success'. 22 June 2015. https://www.gov.uk/government/news/pm-praises-troubled-families-programme-success.

——— . *Tackling Troubled Families* (British Government: 15 December 2011), https://www.gov.uk/government/news/ tackling-troubled- families.

——— . LiveTablesonHousingBuilding.https://www.gov.uk/ government/statistical-data-sets/live-tables-on-house- building#discontinued- tables.

Department for Education. *Barriers to Participation in Education and Training.* By Thomas Spielhofer, Sarah Golden, Kelly Evans, Helen Marshall, Ellie Mundy, Marco Pomati and Ben Styles. National Foundation for Education Research, 2010.

——— . *CANparent Trial Evaluation: Final Report Research.* By Geoff Lindsay, Mairi Ann Cullen, Stephen Cullen, Vaso Totsika, Ioanna Bakopoulou, Susan Goodlad, Richard Brind et al. University of Warwick, 2014.

Department of Energy & Climate Change. *Delivering UK Energy Investment.* London: Department of Energy & Climate Change, 2014.

Department for Environment, Food and Rural Affairs, Department of Agriculture and Rural Development (Northern Ireland), The Scottish Government, Rural and Environment Research and Analysis Directorate, Welsh Assembly Goverment, The Department for Rural Affairs and Heritage. *Agriculture in the United Kingdom, 2012.* National Statistics, 2013.

Department for Environment Food & Rural Affairs. *Food Statistics Pocketbook 2015.* London: National Statistics, 2015.

Department of Health. National Audit Office. The National Programme for IT in the NHS: An Update on the Delivery of Detailed Care Records Systems. London: The Stationery Office, 2011.

Department of Health and Human Services (US). Office of the Inspector General. *Medicare Atypical Antipsychotic Drug Claims for Elderly Nursing Home Residents.* Office of the Inspector General, May 2011.

—— . *The Community Healthy Marriage Initiative Evaluation: Impacts of a Community Approach to Strengthening Families.* Washington, DC: Office of Planning, Research and Evaluation, 2012.

Department of State (US). Department of Commerce (US). *Action Plan for Implementing the Task Force Recommendations.* Presidential Task Force on Combatting IUU Fishing and Seafood Fraud, 2015.

Department for Transport. 'Reported Casualties by Road User Type, Age and Severity, Great Britain, 2011 (TableRAS30002)'. In *Transport Statistics.* 2012. https://www.gov.uk/government/statistics/reported-road-casualties-great-britain-main-results-2011.

Department of Justice (US), Civil Rights Division. 'Investigation of the Ferguson Police Department'. 4 March 2015. www.justice.gov/sites/default/files/opa/press-releases/attachments/2015/03/04/ferguson_police_department_report.pdf.

Devereaux, Jennifer. NewsNation with Tamron Hall, MSNBC, 19 June 2014. Devlin, Kate. 'Marriage Without Children the Key to Bliss'. *Telegraph,* 9 May 2008

Devlin, Stephen, Thomas Dosch, Aniol Esteban and Griffin Carpenter. *Urgent Recall: Our Food System Under Review.* New Economics Foundation, 2014.

Diep, Francie. 'Watch a Spray-On Solar Getting Made'. *Popular Science,* 9 December 2014.

'The Digital Divide: How the Online Behavior of Teens Is Getting Past Parents'. *McAfee,* June 2012. www.mcafee.com/us/resources/misc/digital-divide-study.pdf.

Donaldson, Liam. *150 Years of the Annual Report of the Chief Medical Officer: On the State of Public Health 2008.* London: Department of Health, 2009.

'The Dos and Don'ts of Using Your Phone at a Party'. *Huffington Post,* 26 September 2014.

Drutman, Lee. *The Business of America Is Lobbying: How Corporations Became Politicized and Politics Became More Corporate.* Oxford, UK: Oxford University Press, 2015.

Duckworth, Angela L. and Martin E. P. Seligman. 'Self-Discipline Outdoes IQ in Predicting Academic Performance of Adolescents', *Psychological Science* 16, no. 12 (2005): 939–944.

Dunbar, Robin I. M. 'Neocortex Size as a Constraint on Group Size in Primates'. *Journal of Human Evolution* 22, No. 6 (1992): 469–493.

Dustmann, Christian and Tommaso Frattini. 'The Fiscal Effects of Immigration to the UK'. *The Economic Journal* 124, no. 580 (2014): F593–F643.

'Dye Industry: Fact Sheet'. *Green Cross Switzerland*, 2012. http://www. greencross.ch/nc/en/print/news-info-en/ case-studies/environmental- reports/ten-most-dangerous-sources-of-environmental- toxins-2012/2012/dye-industry. html.

Editorial Board. 'Mr. Bratton Reverses to Go Forward'. *New York Times*, 13 September 2014.

Editors. 'Why Should Taxpayers Give Big Banks $83 Billion a Year?'. *Bloomberg View*, 20 February 2013.

— . 'Small Schools Work in New York'. *New York Times*, 18 October 2014.

'Edward O. Wilson: "The Loss of Biodiversity Is a Tragedy"'. *UNESCO Media Services*, 2 September 2010. http:// www.unesco.org/new/en/media-services/single-view/news/ edward_o_wilson_ the_loss_of_biodiversity_is_a_tragedy/#. U7x4hxZbuuc.

Eisenberg, Staci R., Megan H. Bair-Merritt, Eve R. Colson, Timothy C. Heeren, Nicole L. Geller, and Michael J. Corwin. 'Maternal Report of Advice Received for Infant Care'. *Pediatrics* 136, no. 2 (2015): e315–e322.

'Election 2015 Results'. *BBC News*, http://www.bbc.com/ news/election/2015/results.

Elkin, David. Interview with Neal Conan. 'Can You Make Your Baby Smarter, Sooner?'. *Talk of the Nation*. NPR, 28 October 2009.

Ellicott, Claire. 'NHS Hospital Scandal Which Left 1,200 Dead Could Happen Again, Warn Campaigners'. *Daily Mail*, 9 November 2010.

Ellis, Aleksander P. J., Bradford S. Bell, Robert E. Ployhart, John R. Hollenbeck and D. R. Ilgen. 'An Evaluation of Generic Teamwork Skill Training with Action Teams: Effects on Cognitive and Skill- Based Outcomes', *Personnel Psychology* 58, no. 3 (2005): 641–672.

Ellyatt, Wendy, Al Aynsley-Green, Richard Layrd, et al. 'The Government Should Stop Intervening in Early Education' (signed letter to the editor), *Telegraph*, 11 September 2013.

Engert, Veronica, Franziska Plessow, Robert Miller, Clemens Kirschbaum and Tania Singer. 'Cortisol Increase in Empathic Stress Is Modulated by Emotional Closeness and Observation Modality'. *Psychoneuroendocrinology* 45 (2014): 192–201.

'English Mayoral Elections and Referendums'. *BBC News*, 4 May 2012.

Environmental Protection Agency. Office of Water. *Wetlands: Protection Life and Property from Flooding*, 2006. http://water.epa. gov/type/wetlands/outreach/upload/Flooding.pdf.

Ernst, Caryn. *Protecting the Source: Land Conservation and the Future of America's Drinking Water*. San Francisco, CA: The Trust for Public Land, 2004.

Evans, Stephen. 'Mislabelled Fish Slip Into Europe's Menus'. *BBC News*, 2 April 2013.

EY Item Club. 'EY ITEM Club Special Report on the Outlook for Consumer Spending', September 2014.

Fackler, Martin. 'District in Tokyo Plans to Extend Rights of Gay Couples'. *New York Times*, 13 February 2015.

Farm Assurance Schemes & Animal Welfare: How the Standards Compare: 2012. Edinburgh and Surrey: *OneKind* and *Compassion in World Farming*, 2012.

Feinstein, Leon. 'Very Early'. *CentrePiece*, Summer 2003.

Felitti, Vincent J., Robert F. Anda, Dale Nordenberg, David F. Williamson, Alison M. Spitz, Valerie Edwards, Mary P. Koss, et al. 'The Relationship of Adult Health Status to Childhood Abuse and Household Dysfunction'. *American Journal of Preventive Medicine* 14 (1998): 245–258.

Fernandez, Manny. 'Cheese Whatevers, City Has Them by the Handful'. *New York Times*, 4 August 2010.

Fernández-Armesto, Felipe. *The World: A History*, 2nd ed. London: Prentice Hall, 2010.

Fertilisation, Human, and Embryology Act, 'Chapter 37'. Her Majesty's Stationery Office: London, 1990.

Finkelhor, David, Richard Ormrod and Mark Chaffin. *Juveniles Who Commit Sex Offenses Against Minors*. Washington, DC: US Department of Justice, December 2009. www.ncjrs.gov/pdffiles1/ojjdp/227763.pdf.

Finlay, Stephen, Isabella Pereira, Ella Fryer-Smith, Anne Charlton and Rebecca Roberts-Hughes. *The Way We Live Now: What People Need and Expect From Their Homes*. London: Ipsos MORI and the Royal Institute of British Architects, 2012.

'Fight Cruelty: Chicken FAQ', *ASPCA*, 2015, http://www.aspca. org/fight-cruelty/farm-animal-cruelty/chicken-faq.

Fitzgerald, Alison. 'Koch, Exxon Mobil Among Corporations Helping Write State Laws'. *Bloomberg*, 21 July 2011.

'Flexicurity'. *Denmark: The Official Website of Denmark*. http://denmark.dk/en/society/welfare/flexicurity/.

Flood, Michael. 'The Harms of Pornography Exposure Among Children and Young People'. *Child Abuse Review* 18, no. 6 (2009): 384–400.

Foer, Jonathan Safran. *Eating Animals*. New York: Back Bay Books, 2009.

Ford, Henry and Samuel Crowther. *Great Today and Greater Future*. 1926. Reprint: Kessinger Publishing, LLC, 2003.

Forgacs, Ian, and Aathavan Loganayagam. 'Overprescribing Proton Pump Inhibitors'. *BMJ* 336, no. 7634 (2008): 2–3.

Fractured Families: Why Stability Matters. London: Centre for Social Justice, 2013.

Francis, *Evangelli Gaudium: Apolistic Exhortation on the Proclamation of the Gospel in Today's World*. Vatican City: Libreria Editrice Vaticana, 2013.

Francis, Robert. *The Mid Staffordshire NHS Foundation Trust Inquiry: Independent Inquiry Into Care Provided by Mid*

Staffordshire Foundation Trust, January 2005–March 2009, Vol. 1. London: The Stationery Office, 2010.

Francis, Theo and Ryan Knutson. 'Wave of Megadeals Tests Antitrust Limits in U.S'. *Wall Street Journal*, 18 October 2015. www.wsj.com/articles/wave-of-megadeals-tests-antitrust-limits-in-u-s-1445213306.

Frank, Thomas. 'David Graeber: "Spotlight on the Financial Sector Did Make Apparent Just How Bizarrely Skewed Our Economy Is In Terms of Who Gets Rewards"'. *Salon*, 1 June 2014.

Fredrickson, Barbara L., Tomi-Ann Roberts, Stephanie M. Noll, Diane M. Quinn and Jean M .Twenge. 'That Swimsuit Becomes You: Sex Differences in Self-Objectification, Restrained Eating, and Math Performance. *Journal of Personality and Social Psychology* 75, no. 1, (July 1998): 269–284.

Frey, Carl Benedikt and Michael A. Osborne. 'The Future of Employment: How Susceptible Are Jobs to Computerisation?'. 2013.

Fried, Ben. 'The Origins of Holland's "Stop Murdering Children" Street Safety Movement'. *StreetsBlog Network*, 20 February 2013. http://streetsblog.net/2013/02/20/the-origins-of-hollands-stop-murdering-children-street-safety-movement/.

Frieden, Tom. *Antibiotic Resistance Threats in the United States, 2013*. Centers for Disease Control and Prevention, US Department of Health and Human Services, 2013.

'Full Memo: Jeff Bezos Responds to Brutal NYT Story, Says It Doesn't Represent the Amazon He Leads'. *GeekWire*, 16 August 2015. www.geekwire.com/2015/full-memo-jeff-bezos-responds-to-cutting-nyt-expose-says-tolerance-for-lack-of-empathy-needs-to-be-zero.

Fryer Jr., Ronald G., Steven D. Levitt, John List and Sally Sadoff. 'Enhancing the Efficacy of Teacher Incentives Through Loss Aversion: A Field Experiment'. *National Bureau of Economic Research*, No. w18237 (2012).

'FTSE 100 Directors' Total Earnings Jump By 21% in a Year'. *Thomson Reuters* and *IDS*. 13 October 2014.

Fukuyama, Francis. *Political Order and Political Decay*. New York: Farrar, Straus and Giroux, 2014.

Fuller, Matt. 'Republican Champion of Dodd-Frank Changes Goes After Elizabeth Warren'. *Roll Call*, 28 January 2015.

Fulford, Robet. *Accidental City: The Transformation of Toronto*. Canada: MacFarlane, Walter & Ross, 1995.

'The Fury of the Makers'. *The Economist*, 25 October 2014. www.economist.com/news/united-states/21627659-big-business-angry-small-firms-are-even-angrier-fury-makers.

'The Future of Jobs'. *The Economist*, 18 January 2014.

'Future of Work'. *Courier*, August 2014.

Gamerman, Ellen. 'What Makes Finnish Kids So Smart?'. *Wall Street Journal*, 28 February 2008.

Gapinski, Kathrine D., Kelly D. Brownell and Marianne LaFrance. 'Body Objectification and "Fat Talk": Effects on Emotion, Motivation, and Cognitive Performance'. *Sex Roles* 48, no. 9–10 (2003): 377–388.

Gawande, Atul. 'Overkill'. *New Yorker*, 11 May 2015. www.newyorker.com/magazine/2015/05/11/overkill-atul-gawande.

GeicoInsurance.'FreeRangeChicken:It'sWhatYouDo',0:30.8March2015.https://www.youtube.com/watch?v=3v1wFKKWMCA.

Gentleman, Amelia. 'Do We Need Parenting Classes?'. *Guardian*, 31 March 2012.

'George Osborne: Greater Manchester to Have Elected Mayor'. *BBC News*, 3 November 2014.

Gilbert, Mark. 'British Pubs Cry in Their Beer'. *BloombergView*, 12 December 2014.

Gilens, Martin and Benjamin I. Page. 'Testing Theories of American Politics: Elites, Interest Groups, and Average Citizens'. *Perspectives on Politics* 12, no. 03 (2014).

Gill, Tim. *No Fear: Growing Up in A Risk Averse Society*. London: Calouste Gulbenkian Foundation, 2007.

'Girls and Body Image'. *Girl Scouts and the Dove Self-Esteem Fund*. www.girlscouts.org/content/dam/girlscouts-gsusa/forms-and-documents/about-girl-scouts/research/beauty_redefined_factsheet.pdf.

Global Powers of Retailing 2015: Embracing Innovation. Deloitte, 2015.

'Global Wealth Databook 2014'. *Credit Suisse Research Institute*, 2014. https://publications.credit-suisse.com/tasks/render/file/?fileID=5521F296–D460–2B88–081889DB12817E02.

Glotz, Julia. 'Sainsbury's and Co-op Follow Tesco with Milk Price Cuts'. *The Grocer*, 5 March 2014.

Gomes, Barbara, Natalia Calanzani and Irene J. Higginson. *Local Preferences and Place of Death in Regions within England 2010*. London: Cicely Saunders International, 2011.

Goodin, Samantha M., Alyssa Van Denburg, Sarah K. Murnen and Linda Smolak. '"Putting On" Sexiness: A Content Analysis of the Presence of Sexualizing Characteristics in Girls' Clothing'. *Sex Roles* 65, no. 1–2 (2011): 1–12.

Goodley, Simon and Leila Haddou. 'Revealed: Tesco Hoarding Land That Could Build 15,000 Homes'. *Guardian*, 26 June 2014.

Goodrich, Joanna and Jocelyn Cornwell. *Seeing the Person in the Patient*. London: The King's Fund, 2008.

Government Office for Science. *Foresight: Tackling Obesities: Future Choices, Project Report*. By Bryony Butland, Susan Jebb, Peter Kopelman, K. McPherson, S. Thomas, J. Mardell and V. Parry. Department of Innovation, Universities and Skills, 2007.

Gray, Peter. 'The Decline of Play and the Rise of Psychopathology in Children and Adolescents'. *American Journal of Play* 3, no. 4 (2011): 443–463.

'Great Britain Grocery Market Share (12 weeks ending)'. Kanter World Panel. http://www.kantarworldpanel.com/en/grocery-market-share/great-britain.

'The Great Smog of 1952'. *Met Office*, 10 June 2014. http://www.
metoffice.gov.uk/education/teens/case-studies/great-smog.

Green, Duncan. 'Robert Chambers: Why Don't All
Developments Do Immersions?'. *People, Spaces, Deliberation
(The World Bank)*, 6 September 2012. http://blogs.
worldbank.org/publicsphere/ node/6091.

Griffiths, Jay. *A Country Called Childhood*. Berkeley, CA:
Counterpoint, 2014.

Groceries Code Adjudicator. *Notice of Investigation*.
5 February 2015. https://www.gov.uk/government/
uploads/system/uploads/ attachment_data/file/401349/
Notice_of_Investigation_final. pdf.

Grover, Shawn and John F. Helliwell. *How's Life at Home?
New Evidence on Marriage and the Set Point for Happiness*.
No. w20794. National Bureau of Economic Research,
2014.

'Grunewald'. Visit Berlin. http://www.visitberlin.de/en/
spot/ grunewald.

Guerrera, Francesco. 'Welch Condemns Share Price Focus'.
Financial Times, 12 March 2009.

HM Revenue & Customs. *Child and Working Tax Credits
Statistics: Finalised Annual Awards in 2012–13*. London:
National Statistics, 2014.

HM Revenue & Customs. *National Insurance Fund Account,
For the Year Ended 31 March 2013*. London: The Stationery
Office, 2013. Hakim, Danny. 'Saving an Endangered
British Species: The Pub'. *New York Times*, 17 February
2014.

Halliwell, Emma, Alice Easun and Diana Harcourt. 'Body
Dissatisfaction: Can a Short Media Literacy Message Reduce
Negative Media Exposure Effects Amongst Adolescent
Girls?' *British Journal of Health Psychology* 16, no. 2 (2011):
396–403.

Hamlin, J. Kiley. 'Moral Judgment and Action in Preverbal
Infants and Toddlers Evidence for an Innate Moral Core'.
Current Directions in Psychological Science 22, no. 3 (2013):
186–193.

Hancocks, David. 'Bringing Nature Into the Zoo: Inexpensive Solutions for Zoo Environments'. *International Journal for the Study of Animal Problems* 1, No. 3 (1980): 170–177.

Hand, Larry and Madeline Drexler. 'Public Health Takes Aim at Sugar and Salt'. *Harvard School of Public Health Review*, Fall 2009.

Harlem Children's Zone. HCZ.org, 2015.

Harmon, Katherine. 'How Important Is Physical Contact with Your Infant?'. *Scientific American*, 6 May 2010.

Harris, Nadine Burke. 'The Chronic Stress of Poverty: Toxic Stress to Children'. *Shriver Report*, 12 January 2014.

Harris, William T. 'Elementary Education'. *The North American Review* (1895): 538–546.

Hart, Betty and Todd R. Risley. 'The Early Catastrophe: The 30 Million Word Gap By Age 3'. *American Educator* 27, no. 1 (2003): 4–9.

Hartig, Terry, et al. 'Tracking Restoration in Natural and Urban Field Settings'. *Journal of Environmental Psychology* 23, No. 2 (2003): 109–123.

Hayward, John and Guy Brandon. 'Cohabitation: An Alternative to Marriage?'. *Jubilee Centre*, 2011. http://www.jubilee-centre.org/cohabitation-alternative-marriage-john-haywood-guy-brandon/.

Head, Simon. 'Amazon's Sick Brutality and Secret History of Ruthlessly Intimidating Workers (Excerpt of *Mindless: Why Smarter Machines Are Making Dumber Humans*)'. *Salon*, 23 February 2014.

——. *Mindless: Why Smarter Machines Are Making Dumber Humans*. New York: Basic Books, 2014.

Health and Social Care Information Centre. Prescriptions Dispensed in the Community: England 2004–2014. National Statistics, 2015.

——. Prescription Cost Analysis England 2013. National Statistics, 3 April 2014.

——. Prescriptions Dispensed in the Community: England 2003–13. National Statistics, 2014.

Heckman, James J. 'Skill Formation and the Economics of Investing in Disadvantaged Children'. *Science* 312, no. 5782 (2006): 1900–1902.

Heerwagen, Judith. 'Green Buildings, Organizational Success and Occupant Productivity'. *Building Research & Information* 28, no. 5–6 (2000): 353–367.

'Heinz Tomato Ketchup.' H.J. Heinz Foods UK Limited. http://www.heinz.co.uk/en/Products/Tomato-Ketchup/Products/Heinz-Tomato-Ketchup.

'Helping New Families: Support in the Early Years Through Universal Health Visiting'. *Conservative Research Department.* https://www.conservatives.com/~/media/Files/Downloadable%20 Files/Helping%20new%20families.ashx.

Henley, Jon. 'Why Are Homes in Britain So Small?'. *Guardian,* 16 May 2012.

Hennepin Health. 'Member Spotlight: Ron'. http://content.govdelivery.com/accounts/MNHENNE/bulletins/be91e8.

Herr, Hugh. 'The New Bionics That Let Us Run, Climb, and Dance'. Presentation, TED 2014: The Next Chapter, Vancouver, Canada, March 2014.

Higginbottom, Justin. 'Growing Number of Children with Cellphones Adds Pressure to Purchase'. *Deseret News* (Salt Lake City, UT), 22 April 2012.

Higginson, Irene J., Ilora G. Finlay, Danielle M. Goodwin, Kerry Hood, Adrian G. K. Edwards, Alison Cook, Hannah-Rose Douglas and Charles E. Normand. 'Is There Evidence that Palliative Care Teams Alter End-of-Life Experiences of Patients and Their Caregivers?', *Journal of Pain and Symptom Management* 25, no. 2 (2003): 150–168.

Hill, Peter and Michael Barber. *Preparing for a Renaissance in Assessment.* London: Pearson PLC, 2014.

Hilton, Steve and Giles Gibbons. *Good Business: Your World Needs You.* London: Texere Publishing, 2002.

Hirsch, Donald. *An Estimate of the Cost of Child Poverty in 2013.* Child Poverty Action Group, 5 June, 2013.

Hirschfeld Davis, Julie. 'Adviser Guides Obama into Google Age'. *New York Times*, 4 January 2015. www.nytimes.com/2015/01/04/us/politics/her-task-weaning-the-white-house-off-floppy-disks.html.

Hiss, Tony. 'Can the World Really Set Aside Half of the Planet for Wildlife?'. *Smithsonian Magazine*, September 2014.

Hitt, Michael A., David King, Menna Krishnan, Marianna Makri, Mario Schijven, Katsuhiko Shimizu, and Hong Zhu. 'Creating Value Through Mergers and Acquisitions: Challenges and Opportunities'. In The Handbook of Mergers and Acquisitions. Edited by David Faulkner, Satu Teerikangas and Richard J. Joseph, Oxford, UK: Oxford University Press, 2012.

Holden, Patrick. 'The Price of Milk'. *Sustainable Food Trust*, 16 January 2015. http://sustainablefoodtrust.org/articles/price-milk/.

'Hospitals "Are Medical Factories"'. *BBC News*, 3 December 2008. House of Commons Library. *Supermarkets: Competition Inquiries Into the Groceries Market*. By Antony Seely. SN03653. London: House of Commons Library, 2012.

——. *Directly-Elected Mayors*. By Mark Sandford. SN/PC/5000. London: House of Commons Library, 2014.

Holan, Angei Drobnic and Nai Issa. 'In Context: Hillary Clinton and Don't Let Anybody Tell You That Corporations Create Jobs'. *Tampa Bay Times' Politifact*, 30 October 2014. http://www.politifact.com/truth-o-meter/article/2014/oct/30/context-hillary-clinton-and-dont-let-anybody-tell-/.

Holden, Patrick. 'The Price of Milk.' Sustainable Food Trust, 16 January 2015. http://sustainablefoodtrust.org/articles/price-milk.

Holmes, Anna. 'Untouched Cover Photos Wanted: $10,000 Reward'. *Jezebel*, 21 May 2007.

Home Office. 'Freedom of Information Release: Policing by Consent'. 10 December, 2012. www.gov.uk/government/publications/policing-by-consent.

Hood, Andrew and Paul Johnson. 'What Is Welfare Spending?' Institute for Fiscal Studies, 4 November 2014. http://www. ifs. org.uk/publications/7424.

'Hospitals "Are Medical Factories"'. *BBC News*, 3 December 2008.

Hotez, Peter J. 'Neglected Infections of Poverty in the United States and Their Effects on the Brain'. *JAMA Psychiatry* 71, no. 10 (2014): 1099–1100.

House of Commons Committee of Public Accounts. *Department of Health: The National Programme for IT: – the NHS*. Twentieth Report of Session 2006–07, HC 390. London: The Stationery Office, 2007.

—— . Department of Health. *Review of the Final Benefits Statement for Programmes Previously Managed Under the National Programme for IT: – the NHS*. London: National Audit Office, 2015.

House of Commons. *Directly-Elected Mayors*. By Mark Sandford. SN/PC/5000. London: House of Commons Library, 2014.

Hopkirk, Elizabeth. 'The Netherlands' Almere Leads the Way on Self-Build Communities'. *bdonline*, 6 June 2011. http://www.bdonline.co.uk/the-netherlands-almere-leads-the-way-on-self- build-communities/5019196.article.

'How We Work'. *Andela*, 2015. www.andela.co/how-we-work.

Howard, Kimberly S., Jennifer E. Burke Lefever, John G. Borkowski and Thomas L. Whitman. 'Fathers' Influence in the Lives of Children with Adolescent Mothers'. *Journal of Family Psychology* 20, no. 3 (2006): 468.

Howard, Michael. 'The Movie That Accurately Predicted the Future of Technology'. *Esquire.com*, 23 September 2014.

Hunter, Will, 'The Best Office in the World? Selgas Cano's New Work Space in London', *Architectural Review*, 29 January 2015.

'IBM 2010 Global CEO Study: Creativity Selected as Most Crucial Factor for Future Success', *IBM*, 18 May 2010, https://www-03. ibm.com/press/us/en/pressrelease/31670.wss.

Ilves, Toomas. 'Evolving Into a Genuinely Digital Society'. Speech at Green Library, Stanford University, Stanford, CA, 23 May 2014.

'In Palo Alto's High-Pressure Schools, Suicides Lead to Soul-Searching'. *NPR*, 10 May 2015. www.npr.org/2015/05/10/405694832/in-palo-altos-high-pressure-schools-suicides-lead-to-soul-searching.

'Interview with Jan Gehl'. *American Society for Landscape Architects*. http://www.asla.org/ContentDetail.aspx?id=31346.

'Introducing the Vscan Family'. *GE Healthcare*, 2015. https://vscan.gehealthcare.com/introducing-vscan-family.

Jacobs, Emma. 'Strategies for Calling Time on Long Hours'. *Financial Times*, 18 August 2014. www.ft.com/intl/cms/s/2/510c5bd6-198a-11e4-8730-00144feabdc0.html

Jacobs, Jane. *The Death and Life of Great American Cities*. New York: Vintage Books, 1961.

Jaffe, Ina and Robert Benincasa. 'Nursing Homes Rarely Penalized for Oversedating Patients'. *NPR*, 9 December 2014.

—. 'Old and Over Medicated: The Real Drug Problem in Nursing Homes'. *NPR*, 8 December 2014.

—. 'This Nursing Home Calms Troubling Behavior Without Risky Drugs'. *NPR*, 9 December 2014.

Jambeck, Jenna R., Roland Geyer, Chris Wilcox, Theodore R. Siegler, Miriam Perryman, Anthony Andrady, Ramani Narayan, and Kara Lavender Law. 'Plastic Waste Inputs from Land into the Ocean'. Science 347, no. 6223 (2015): 768–771.

'Jan Gehl: Biography'. *Project for Public Spaces*. http://www.pps.org/ reference/jgehl/.

Jauhar, Sandeep. 'Bring Back House Calls'. *New York Times*, 14 October 2015. www.nytimes.com/2015/10/15/opinion/bring-back-house-calls.html.

Jeffrys, Pete, Toby Lloyd, et al. *Building the Homes We Need: A Programme for the 2015 Government*. KPMG and Shelter, 2014.

Jobs, Steve. 'Stanford Commencement Address'. Speech, Stanford University, Stanford, CA, 14 June 2005.

Joffe-Walt, Chana. 'The Town Where Everyone Talks About Death'. *NPR*, 5 March 2014.

Johnson, James R., Michael A. Kuskowski, Kirk Smith, Timothy T. O'Bryan and Sita Tatini. 'Antimicrobial-Resistant and Extraintestinal Pathogenic Escherichia coli in Retail Foods'. *Journal of Infectious Diseases* 191, no. 7 (2005): 1040–1049.

Johnson, Nathanael J. 'Swine of the Times'. *Harper's Magazine*, May 2006.

Johnson, Sara B., Anne W. Riley, Douglas A. Granger and Jenna Riis. 'The Science of Early Life Toxic Stress for Pediatric Practice and Advocacy'. *Pediatrics* 131, no. 2 (2013): 319–327.

Johnson, Susan R. 'A Developmental Approach Looking at the Relationship of Children's Foundational Neurological Pathways to Their Higher Capacities for Learning'. 7 May 2007.

Johnson, Wesley. 'Children, Some Age Five, Commit Thousands of Child Sex Offenses'. *Telegraph*. 4 March 2013.

Jones, Colin. *Paris: A History*. New York: Penguin Books, 2004.

Jones, Natasha. 'Funding Circle and Santander Announce Partnership to Support Thousands of UK Businesses'. *Funding Circle*, 18 June 2014. www.fundingcircle.com/blog/2014/06/funding-circle-santander-announce-partnership-support-thousands-uk-businesses.

Jones, Nicholas R.V., Annalijn I. Conklin, Marc Suhrcke and Pablo Monsivais. 'The Growing Price Gap between More and Less Healthy Foods: Analysis of a Novel Longitudinal UK Dataset'. *PloS one* 9, no. 10 (2014): e109343.

Kabali, Hilda K., Matilde M. Irigoyen, Rosemary Nunez-Davis, Jennifer G. Budacki, Sweta H. Mohanty, Kristin P. Leister and Robert L. Bonner Jr. 'Exposure and Use of Mobile Media Devices by Young Children'. *Pediatrics* 136, no. 6 (December 2015): 1044–1050.

Kahneman, Daniel and Amos Tversky. 'Choices, Values, and Frames' *American Psychologist* 39, no. 4 (1984): 341.

Kalinauskas, Nadine. 'St. Lawrence Market in Toronto Named World's Best Food Market by National Geographic'. *Shine On*, 5 April 2012. https://ca.shine.yahoo.com/blogs/shine-on/st-lawrence-market-toronto-named-world-best-food-145127435.html.

Kalson, Sally. 'Sexting ... and Other Stupid Teen Tricks'. *Pittsburgh Post-Gazette*, 29 March 2009.

Kang, Yewon. 'Poll Shows Half of Korean Teenagers Have Suicidal Thoughts.' *Wall Street Journal*, 20 March 2014.

Kantor, Jodi and David Streitfeld. 'Amazon's Bruising, Thrilling Workplace'. *New York Times*, 16 August 2014. www.nytimes.com/images/2015/08/16/nytfrontpage/scan.pdf.

Karabarbounis, Loukas and Brent Neiman. 'The Global Decline of the Labor Share'. *Quarterly Journal of Economics* 129, no. 1 (2014): 61–103.

Karabell, Zachary. *The Leading Indicators: A Short History of the Number That Rule Our World*. New York: Simon & Schuster, 2014.

Karoly, Lynn A., M. Rebecca Kilburn and Jill S. Cannon. *Early Childhood Interventions: Proven Results, Future Promise*. Santa Monica, CA: RAND Corporation, 2005.

Keizer, Kees, Siegwart Lindenberg and Linda Steg. 'The Spreading of Disorder'. *Science* 322, no. 5908 (2008): 1681–1685.

Kelly, Bridget, Jason C.G. Halford, Emma J. Boyland, Kathy Chapman, Inmaculada Bautista-Castaño, Christina Berg, Margherita Caroli et al. 'Television Food Advertising to Children: A Global Perspective'. *American Journal of Public Health* 100, no. 9 (2010): 1730-1736.

Kennedy, Jack, Tim Moore and Annabel Fiddes. *Living Wage Research for KPMG: Structural Analysis of Hourly Wages and Current Trends in Household Finances, 2014 Report*. Henley on Thames, England: Markit, 2014.

Kennedy, Robert F. 'Speech at the University of Kansas'. Speech, University of Kansas, Lawrence, KS, 18 March 1968.

Khazan, Olga. 'The Luxury of Waiting for Marriage to Have Kids'. *The Atlantic*, 17 June 2014.

Khimm, Suzy. 'How Paying No Federal Income Tax Helps the Poor Get Off Welfare and Into Work'. *Washington Post*, 18 September 2012.

King, Anthony and Ivor Crewe. *The Blunders of Our Governments*. London: Oneworld Publications, 2013.

'KitKat Collection: 4 Finger Milk Nutritional Information'. Société des Produits Nestlé S.A., 2015. http://www.kitkat.co.uk/content/kitkatcollection/FourFinger.

Kitzman, Harriet J., David L. Olds, Robert E. Cole, Carole A. Hanks, Elizabeth A. Anson, Kimberly J. Arcoleo, Dennis W. Luckey et al. 'Enduring Effects of Prenatal and Infancy Home Visiting by Nurses on Children: Follow-Up of a Randomized Trial Among Children at Age 12 Years'. *Archives of Pediatrics & Adolescent Medicine* 164, no. 5 (2010): 412–418.

Klein, Ezra. 'Big Food: Michael Pollan Thinks Wall Street Has Way Too Much Influence Over What We Eat'. *Vox*, 23 April 2014.

Kleiner, Morris. *Reforming Occupational Licensing Practices*. Washington, DC: Brookings Institute: Hamilton Project, 2015.

Kleinman, Mark. 'Temasek Snaps Up Stake in UK's Funding Circle'. *Sky News*, 2 April 2015. http://news.sky.com/story/1457480/temasek-snaps-up-stake-in-uks-funding-circle.

Koepp, Matthias J., Roger N. Gunn, Andrew D. Lawrence, Vincent J. Cunningham, Alain Dagher, Tasmin Jones, David J. Brooks, C. J. Bench and P. M. Grasby. 'Evidence for Striatal Dopamine Release During a Video Game'. *Nature* 393, no. 6682 (1998): 266–268.

Konnikova, Maria. 'No Money, No Time'. *New York Times*, 15 June 2014.

Koo, Se-Woong. 'An Assault Upon Our Children', *New York Times*, 3 August 2014.

Kramer, Miriam. 'Elon Musk: Artificial Intelligence Is Humanity's Biggest Existential Threat'. *Live Science*, 27 October 2014.

Kristof, Nick. 'Is That Sausage Worth This?,' *New York Times*, 20 February 2014.

——. 'Oklahoma! Where the Kids Learn Early'. *New York Times*. 10 November 2013.

——. 'The Way to Beat Poverty'. *New York Times*, 12 September 2014.

——. 'It's Not Just About Bad Choices'. *New York Times*, 14 June 2015. www.nytimes.com/2015/06/14/opinion/sunday/nicholas-kristof-its-not-just-about-bad-choices.html.

Krommenacker, Thomas and Ben Robinson. *Metro Bank: Breaking the Mould but Breaking the Malaise?* Geneva, Switzerland: Temenos Headquarters SA, 2011.

Krueger, Alan B, Judd Cramer, and David Cho. 'Are the Long- Term Unemployed on the Margins of the Labor Market?'. *Brookings Papers on Economic Activity* (2014): 229–280.

Kruus, Priit, Peeter Ross, Riina Hallik, Reelika Ermel and Ain Aaviksoo. 'Wider Implementation of Telemedicine in Estonia' (English Summary of the Study's Results). Tallinn, Estonia: Praxis / Center for Policy Studies, 2014.

Kuyken, Willem, Katherine Weare, Obioha C. Ukoumunne, Rachael Vicary, Nicola Motton, Richard Burnett, Chris Cullen, Sarah Hennelly and Felicia Huppert. 'Effectiveness of the Mindfulness in Schools Programme: Non-Randomised Controlled Feasibility Study'. *The British Journal of Psychiatry* 203, no. 2 (2013): 126–131.

Lahey, Jessica. *The Gift of Failure: How the Best Parents Learn to Let Go So Their Children Can Succeed.* New York: HarperCollins, 2015.

Lake, Marilyn. 'Minimum Wage Is More Than a Safety Net, It's a Symbol of Australian Values'. *The Age* (Melbourne, Australia), 10 April 2014.

Langer, Emil. 'Ray Anderson, "Greenest CEO in America", Dies at 77'. *Washington Post*, 10 August 2011. www.washingtonpost.com/local/obituaries/ray-anderson-greenest-ceo-in-america-dies-at-77/2011/08/10/gIQAGoTU7I_story.html.

Larsson, Stefan. 'What Doctors Can Learn from Each Other'. Presentation at TED@BCG Singapore, Singapore, October 2013.

Lawrence, Felicity, Andrew Wasley and Radu Ciorniciuc. 'Revealed: The Dirty Secret of the UK's Poultry Industry'. *Guardian*, 23 July 2014.

Lawton, Kayte and Matthew Pennycook. *Beyond the Bottom Line: The Challenges and Opportunities of a Living Wage*. London: IPPR and Resolution Foundation, 2013.

Lazonick, William. 'Profits Without Prosperity'. *Harvard Business Review*, September 2014.

Leadbeater, Charles and Jake Garber. *Dying for Change*. London: Demos, 2010.

'Lean In Collection'. *Getty Images*. http://www.gettyimages.com/ creative/frontdoor/leanin.

LeBlanc, Dave. '35 Years On, St. Lawrence is a Template for Urban Housing'. *Globe and Mail* (Canada), 6 February 2013.

Leicester City Council. 'Council Meat Tests Highlight Labelling Concerns'. 3 November 2014. http://news.leicester.gov.uk/ newsArchiveDetail.aspx?Id=f2792.

Lenger, Friedrich. *European Cities in the Modern Era, 1850–1914*. Translated by Joel Golb. Leiden, Netherlands: Koninklijke Brill NV, 2012.

Lenhart, Amanda. 'Mobile Access Shifts Social Media Use and Other Online Activities'. *Pew Research Center*, 9 April 2015. www.pewinternet.org/2015/04/09/mobile-access-shifts-social-media-use-and-other-online-activities.

Lessig, Lawrence. 'We the People, and the Republic We Must Reclaim'. Presentation, TED 2013, Long Beach, CA, February 2013.

Levine, Marianne. 'LA Becomes Latest, Biggest to Approve $15 Minimum Wage'. *Politico*, 19 May 2015.

Liebenwein, Sylva, Heiner Barz, and Dirk Randoll. 'Zusammenfassung zentraler Befunde: Waldorfschule aus Schülersicht' (in German). In *Bildungserfahrungen an Waldorfschulen*. Edited by Sylva Liebenwein, Heiner Barz and Dirk Randoll, 5–12. Wiesbaden, Germany: VS Verlag für Sozialwissenschaften, 2012.

Liebovich, Mark. *This Town: Two Parties and a Funeral – Plus, Plenty of Valet Parking! – in America's Gilded Capital.* New York: Penguin Random House, 2013.

Lim Miller, Mauricio. 'When Helping Doesn't Help'. *Huffington Post,* 7 May 2012..

Liiten, Marjukka. 'Top Favorite: Teaching Profession' (in Finnish). *Helsingin Sanomat,* 11 February 2004. Cited in Sahlberg, Pasi. *Finnish Lessons: What Can the World Learn from Educational Change in Finland?.* New York: Teachers College Press, 2010.

Light, John. 'Frequently Asked Questions About ALEC'. *Moyers & Company,* 28 September 2012. http://billmoyers. com/content/ frequently-asked-questions-about-alec/.

Lipton, Eric and Ben Protess. 'Banks' Lobbyists Help in Drafting Financial Bills'. *New York Times,* 24 May 2013.

'Living Wage Employers'. *Living Wage Foundation.* March 2015. http://www.livingwage.org.uk/employers.

The Local Goverment Boundary Commission for England. *Counties Pivot Data.* 2014. https://www.lgbce.org.uk/ data/ assets/excel_doc/0006/22839/NEW-Copy-of-Counties-Pivot- Table-2014.xlsx.

'Local Elections'. *France in the United States, Embassy of France in the United States.* 20 December 2013. http://www. ambafrance-us.org/ spip.php?article518.

Locke, Susannah F. 'Robots That Eat Bugs and Plants for Power'. *Popular Science,* 9 October 2009.

Lorber, Janie. 'Former IRS Official Demands Investigation of ALEC'. *Roll Call,* 1 July 2012.

Louy, Richard. *Last Child in the Woods: Saving Our Children From Nature-Deficit Disorder.* Chapel Hill, NC: Algonquin Books, 2005.

Lowe, Simon. 'Plotting A New Course to Improved Governance' in *Corporate Governance Review 2014.* Grant Thornton UK LLP, 2014.

Lowther, Ed and Charlotte Thornton. 'Election 2015: Number of Women in Parliament Rises by a Third'. *BBC News*, 8 May 2015.

Lythcott-Haims, Julie. *How to Raise an Adult: Break Free of the Overparenting Trap and Prepare Your Kid for Success*. New York: Henry Holt and Co., 2015.

MacInnes, Tom, Hannah Aldridge, Sabrina Bushe, Peter Kenway and Adam Tinson. *Monitoring Poverty and Social Exclusion, 2013*. York, England: Joseph Rowntree Foundation, 2013.

Mafi, John N., Ellen P. McCarthy, Roger B. Davis and Bruce E. Landon. 'Worsening Trends in the Management and Treatment of Back Pain', *JAMA Internal Medicine* 173, no. 17 (2013): 1573–1581.

Mackey, Allyson P., Amy S. Finn, Julia A. Leonard, Drew S. Jacoby-Senghor, Martin R. West, Christopher F. O. Gabrieli and John D. E. Gabrieli. 'Neuroanatomical Correlates of the Income-Achievement Gap'. *Psychological Science* 26, no. 6 (June 2015): 925–933.

Magee, Christine. 'Backed by Spark Capital, Andela Will Develop a Continent of Tech Talent'. *Techcrunch*, 25 June 2015. http://techcrunch.com/2015/06/25/backed-by-spark-capital-andela-will-develop-a-continent-of-tech-talent.

Manchin, Stephen. 'Real Wages and Living Standards: The Latest UK Evidence'. LSE Centre for Economic Performance, 6 April 2015. http://blogs.lse.ac.uk/politicsandpolicy/real-wages-and-living-standards-the-latest-uk-evidence/.

Manjoo, Farhad. 'Amazon Not As Unstoppable as It Might Appear'. *New York Times*, 18 December 2014.

Manning, Alan. 'The UK's National Minimum Wage'. *CentrePiece*, Autumn 2009.

Markoff, John. 'Artificial-Intelligence Research Center Is Founded by Silicon Valley Investors'. *New York Times*, 11 December 2015. www.nytimes.com/2015/12/12/science/

artificial-intelligence-research-center-is-founded-by-silicon-valley-investors.html.

Marris, Emma. 'Let Kids Run Wild in the Woods'. *Slate*, 25 May 2014.

Massad, Timothy G . 'Overall $182 Billion Committed to Stabilize AIG During the Financial Crisis Is Now Fully Recovered'. *Treasury Notes (U.S. Department of the Treasury)*, 11 September 2012. http://www.treasury.gov/connect/blog/Pages/aig-182–billion.aspx.

Masters, Jeffrey. 'Storm Surge Reduction by Wetlands'. *Weather Underground*. http://www.wunderground.com/hurricane/surge_ wetlands.asp?MR=1.

Matouschek, Niko and Imran Rasul. 'The Economics of the Marriage Contract Theories and Evidence'. Journal of Law and Economics 51, no. 1 (2008): 59–110.

McColl, Kenneth E. L. 'Effect of Proton Pump Inhibitors on Vitamins and Iron'. *American Journal of Gastroenterology* 104, suppl. 2 (2009): S5–9.

McCullough, Dennis. *My Mother, Your Mother: Embracing 'Slow Medicine", the Compassionate Approach to Caring for Your Aging Loved Ones.* New York: Harper, 2008.

McKenna, Maryn. 'How Your Chicken Dinner Is Creating a Drug- Resistant Superbug'. *The Atlantic*, 11 July 2012.

McVeigh, Tracy McVeigh. 'Scandal of NHS "Death Factories"'. *Observer*, 11 August 2002.

'Measure for Measure'. *The Economist*, 30 November 2013.

'Measuring the Daily Destruction of the World's Rainforests', *Scientific American*, 19 November 2009.

Mekonnen, Mesfin M. and Arjen Y. Hoekstra. 'A Global Assessment of the Water Footprint of Farm Animal Products'. *Ecosystems* 15, no. 3 (2012): 401–415.

Mele, Nicco. *The End of Big: How the Internet Makes David the New Goliath.* New York: St. Martin's Press, 2013.

Meyerson, Harold. 'How Workers Lost the Power Struggle – and Their Pay Raises'. *Washington Post*, 8 October 2014.

'Michigan Becomes 5th US State to Thwart Direct Tesla Car Sales'. *Reuters*, 22 October 2014.

Miller, Claire Cain. 'Study Finds More Reasons to Get and Stay Married'. *New York Times*, 8 January 2015.

Miller, Dana D. and Stefano Mariani. 'Smoke, Mirrors, and Mislabeled Cod: Poor Transparency in the European Seafood Industry'. *Frontiers in Ecology and the Environment* 8, no. 10 (2010): 517–521.

Mirani, Leo. 'The Secret to the Uber Economy: Wealth Inequality'. *Quartz*, 16 December 2014.

Monaghan, Angela. 'UK Housebuilders Counter Ed Miliband's Land-Hoarding Claim'. *Guardian*, 16 December 2013.

Monastersky, Richard. 'Life: A Status Report'. *Nature* 516 (11 December 2014): 159–161.

Monk, Ed. 'The Ultimate DIY Investment'. This Is M*oney.co.uk*, 8 November 2013. http://www.thisismoney.co.uk/money/mortgageshome/article-2491020/The-ultimate-DIY-investment-Novices-urged-self-build-solve-housing-shortage–make-30– cent-profit-bargain.html.

Morgenson, Gretchen. 'The Boss Actually Said This: Pay Me Less'. *New York Times*, 18 December 2005. http://query.nytimes.com/gst/fullpage.html?res=9D01EFDC1630F93BA25751C1A9639C8B63.

Morozov, Evgeny. *To Save Everything, Click Here: The Folly of Technological Solutionism*. New York: Public Affairs, 2013.

Morrison, Todd G., Shannon R. Ellis, Melanie A. Morrison, Anomi Bearden and Rebecca L. Harriman. 'Exposure to Sexually Explicit Material and Variations in Body Esteem, Genital Attitudes, and Sexual Esteem Among a Sample of Canadian Men'. *The Journal of Men's Studies* 14, No. 2 (Spring 2006): 209–222.

Moss, Michael. 'The Extraordinary Science of Addictive Junk Food'. *New York Times Magazine*, 24 February 2013.

Moyer, Virginia A. 'Vitamin, Mineral, and Multivitamin Supplements for the Primary Prevention of Cardiovascular Disease and Cancer: US Preventive Services Task Force Recommendation Statement', *Annals of Internal Medicine* 160, no. 8 (2014): 558–564.

Mufson, Steven and Tom Hamburger. 'Jamie Dion Himself Called to Urge Support for the Derivatives Rule in the Spending Bill'. *Washington Post*, 11 December 2014.

Mullainathan, Sendhil and Eldar Shafir. *Scarcity: Why Having Too Little Means So Much.* New York: Time Books, 2013.

'Müller Corner Fruit Strawberry'. Müller UK & Ireland, 2015. https://www.muller.co.uk/nc/our-brands/mueller-yogurt-desserts-brands/product-details.html.

Mundy, Liza. 'Daddy Track: The Case for Paternity Leave'. *The Atlantic*, January/February 2014.

Musk, Elon. 'All Our Patent Are Belong to You [*sic*]'. *Tesla Motors*, 12 June 2014. www.teslamotors.com/blog/all-our-patent-are-belong-you.

National Audit Office. *End of Life Care.* London: The Stationery Office, 2008.

—— . *The Criminal Justice System: Landscape Review (Report by the Comptroller and Auditor General).* National Audit Office, 7 March 2014. http://www.nao.org.uk/wp-content/uploads/2015/03/The-Criminal-Justicesystem-landscape-review-summary1.pdf.

Neilan, Catherine and Chris Parmenter. 'FTSE 100 CEOs: These Are the Men (and a Few Women) Who Run Britain's Biggest Companies'. *City A.M.*, 20 March 2015.

Nelson, Fraser. 'Milburn: How I Can Help Gordon Brown', *Spectator*, 19 May 2007.

Neumark, David and William Wascher. 'Minimum Wages, the Earned Income Tax Credit, and Employment: Evidence from the Post-Welfare Reform Era'. *IZA Discussion Papers*, No. 26100, 2007. Nicholls, Dana and Peggy Syvertson. 'Sensory Integration'. *New Horizons for Learning, Johns Hopkins School of Education*, 2012.

New Jersey Election Law Enforcement Commission. *Represented Entities, Governmental Affairs Agents and Persons Communicating with the General Public Listed by Expenditures Ranking*, Calendar Year 2013.

Newsom, Gavin. *Citizenville: How to Take the Town Square Digital and Reinvent Government.* New York: Penguin Press, 2013.

'No Quick Fix: Exposing the Depth of Britain's Drug and Alcohol Problem,' part of *Breakdown Britain II*. London: Centre for Social Justice, 2013.

'Nonfarm Business Sector: Labor Share'. *Federal Reserve Bank of St. Louis*, 9 February 2015. https://research.stlouisfed. org/fred2/series/PRS85006173.

Nuikkinen, Kaisa. 'Vision of the Helsinki City School Building Program: Healthy and Safe School Building'. Presentation at the American Institute for Architects' 'Schools in a Flat World' conference, Helsinki, Finland, 11 September 2008.

Nunan, Cólín and Richard Young. 'E.coli Superbugs on Farms and Food'. *The Use and Misuse of Antibiotics in UK Agriculture*, 6. Bristol, England: Soil Association, 2012.

Nutting, Rex. 'Transcript of Holder's Admission on Too-Big-To-Jail Banks'. *Market Watch*, 7 March 2013.

Obama, Barack. 'Remarks by the President in State of the Union Address'. Speech, US Capitol, Washington DC, 20 January 2015.

O'Connell, Ainsley. 'Most Innovative Companies 2015: Revolution Foods'. *Fast Company*, 2015. www.fastcompany. com/3039619/most-innovative-companies-2015/ revolution-foods.

OECD. *Consumer Prices*. OECD, 30 March 2015. https://stats. oecd. org/index.aspx?queryid=221.

—— . *Education At a Glance 2014: OECD Indicators*. OECD Publishing, 2014.

—— . *OECD Income Distribution Database: Gini, Poverty, Income, Methods, and Concept*. OECD, 2014. http://www.oecd.org/ social/ income-distribution-database.htm.

—— . *PISA 2012 Database Tables*. OECD, 2012. http://www. oecd.org/ pisa/keyfindings/PISA-2012–results-snapshot-Volume-I-ENG.pdf

—— . Road Safety Annual Report 2015. Paris: OECD Publishing, 2015.

Ofcom. *Children and Parents: Media Use and Attitudes Report*. 2014.

Office for National Statistics. Annual Survey of Hours and Earnings, 2015 Provisional Results, 2015. http://www.ons.gov.uk/ons/rel/ashe/annual-survey-of-hours-and-earnings/2015-provisional-results/stb-ashe.html.

— . *Divorces in England and Wales, 2012: Number of Divorces, Age at Divorce and Marital Status Before Marriage, Table 3a.* Office of National Statistics, 2012. http://www.ons.gov.uk/ons/rel/vsob1/ divorces-in-england-and-wales/2012/stb-divorces-2012.html.

— . Labour Productivity, Q3 2015, 2015, http://www.ons.gov.uk/ons/rel/productivity/labour-productivity/q3-2015/index.html.

— . Underemployment and Overemployment in the UK, 2014, 2014. http://www.ons.gov.uk/ons/dcp171776_387087.pdf.

— . Labour Market Statistics, December 2015: Unemployment by Age and Duration, 2015. http://www.ons.gov.uk/ons/taxonomy/index.html?nscl=Labour+Market#tab-data-tables.

— . *Marriages in England and Wales (Provisional), 2012.* Office for National Statistics, 2014.

— . *UK National Population Projections – Principals and Variants, 2012–2087.* http://www.ons.gov.uk/ons/interactive/uk-national-population-projections—dvc3/index.html.

— . *2011 Census: Key Statistics for England and Wales, March 2011.* 2012. http://www.ons.gov.uk/ons/rel/census/2011–census/key- statistics-for-local-authorities-in-england-and-wales/stb-2011– census-key-statistics-for-england-and-wales.html#tab—Religion.

— . Live Tables on House Building (Table 209: Permanent Dwellings Completed, by Tenure and Country). London: Office for National Statistics, 19 November 2015. https://www.gov.uk/government/uploads/system/uploads/attachment_data/file/477837/LiveTable209.xlsx .

Ofgem. *The Revenues, Costs and Profits of the Energy Companies in 2013.* 2013.

—— .*Supply Market Indicator for April 2015*. https://www.ofgem. gov.uk/gas/retail-market/monitoring-data-and-statistics/ understanding-energy-prices-great-britain/supply-market-indicator.

Olds, David L., Charles R. Henderson Jr., Robert Cole, John Eckenrode, Harriet Kitzman, Dennis Luckey, Lisa Pettitt et al. 'Long-Term Effects of Nurse Home Visitation on Children's Criminal and Antisocial Behavior: 15-Year Follow-Up of a Randomized Controlled Trial'. *JAMA* 280, no. 14 (1998): 1238–1244.

Olds, David L., Charles R. Henderson and Harriet Kitzman. 'Does Prenatal and Infancy Nurse Home Visitation Have Enduring Effects on Qualities of Parental Caregiving and Child Health at 25 to 50 Months of Life?' *Pediatrics* 93, no. 1 (1994): 89–98.

Olds, David L., Charles R. Henderson, Robert Tatelbaum and Robert Chamberlin. 'Improving the Delivery of Prenatal Care and Outcomes of Pregnancy: A Randomized Trial of Nurse Home Visitation'. *Pediatrics* 77, no. 1 (1986): 16–28.

Olesund, Erik. 'How the Tractor Ruined Farming'. *Green Grid Radio*, 28 June 2014.

Oliver, John. *Last Week Tonight with John Oliver*. Television. HBO, 2014. 'One in Ten British Kids Own A Mobile Phone by the Age of Five'. *uSwtich*, August 2013. http:// www.uswitch.com/mobiles/news/2013/08/one_in_ten_british_kids_own_mobile_phone_by_the_age_of_five/.

'Outdoor Knoxville'. *Legacy Parks Foundation*, 2014. http:// www. outdoorknoxville.com/urban-wilderness.

Overby, Peter. 'Conservative Group's Charity Status Draws Questions'. *NPR*, 19 April 2012.

Panorama. Television. BBC, 2013.

Papadopoulos, Linda. 'Sexualisation of Young People Review.' (2010).

Parliament of the United Kingdom. *Agricultural Incomes and Subsidies* (2012 Data).

Paul, Annie Murphy. 'School of Hard Knocks: "How Children Succeed', by Paul Touch'. *New York Times Sunday Book Review.* 26 August 2012.

Peabody, Francis W. 'The Care of the Patient'. *Journal of the American Medical Association* 88 (1927): 876–82.

People Who Abuse Children (An NSPCC Research Briefing). NSPCC, 2014. http://www.nspcc.org.uk/globalassets/documents/information-service/research-briefing-people-who-abuse-children.pdf.

Perez, Sarah. 'AOL Co-Founder Steve Case Invests $30 Million into School Lunch Company, Revolution Foods'. *TechCrunch,* 5 June 2014. http://techcrunch.com/2014/06/05/aol-co-founder-steve-case-invests-30-million-into-school-lunch-company-revolution-foods.

Perrin, Ellen C., Benjamin S. Siegel, James G. Pawelski, Mary I. Dobbins, Arthur Levin, Gerri Mattson, John Pascoe and Michael Yogman, 'Promoting the Well-Being of Children Whose Parents Are Gay or Lesbian', *Pediatrics 131,* no. 4 (2013); e1374-31383.

'Philip Lymbery: Chief Executive'. *Compassion in World Farming,* 2014. http://www.ciwf.org.uk/about-us/our-staff/philip-lymbery/.

'Physical Activity Guidelines for Children and Young People'. *NHS Choices.* http://www.nhs.uk/Livewell/fitness/Pages/physical- activity-guidelines-for-young-people.aspx.

Pilgrim, Tanya. 'The End of the Supermarket Sweep?'. *Pennington Manches,* 8 October 2012. http://www.penningtons.co.uk/news- publications/archive-news/2012/the-end-of-the-supermarket- sweep/.

Pinkney, David. *Napoleon III and the Rebuilding of Paris.* Princeton, NJ: Princeton University Press, 1972.

'PISA Interactive Data Selection – Variable ST42Q03 ("Math Anxiety – Get Very Tense")'. *OECD,* 2012. http://pisa2012.acer. edu.au/interactive.php.

Pollack, Keshia M., Dan Morhaim and Michael A. Williams. 'The Public's Perspectives on Advance Directives in Maryland: Implications for State Legislative and Regulatory Policy'. *Health Policy* 96, no. 1 (2010): 57–63.

Pollan, Michael. *In Defense of Food: An Eater's Manifesto.* New York: Penguin Press, 2008.

—— . *Cooked: A Natural History of Transformation.* London: Allen Lane, 2013.

Porter, Eduardo. 'A Relentless Widening of Disparity in Wealth'. *New York Times,* 12 March 2014.

Portman, Rob. 'Gay Couples Also Deserve Chance to Get Married'. *Columbus Dispatch,* 15 March 2013.

'Poultry Processors and Retailers Respond to the Campylobacter Claims'. *Guardian.* 23 July 2014.

'Power of Place'. *Steelcase 360°,* No. 68 (2014).

'Press Release'. *Resolution Foundation,* 1 October 2014. http://www. resolutionfoundation.org/media/press-releases/a-record-1–2–million-workers-to-benefit-from-first-real-terms-minimum-wage-rise-for-six-years-today/.

'Press Release: Interface Reports Fourth Quarter and Fiscal Year 2014 Results'. *Interface,* 18 February 2015. http://www.interfaceglobal.com/Investor-Relations/Press-Releases.aspx.

'Preterm Birth (Fact Sheet 363)'. *World Health Organization,* November 2014. http://www.who.int/mediacentre/factsheets/fs363/en/

Price, Catherine. 'Vitamins Hide the Low Quality of Our Food'. *New York Times,* 15 February 2015.

Prime Minister's Office. 'PM: Families Are the Key to Tackling Poverty'. 10 January 2015. https://www.gov.uk/government/news/pm-families-are-the-key-to-ending-poverty.

Priorities USA Action. 'Stage'. *YouTube* video, 1:02. 23 June 2012. https://www.youtube.com/watch?v=oLo0Jwj03JU.

Purvis, Andrew. 'Running on Empty Carbs'. *Guardian,* 22 March 2009.

Quirk, Mary Beth. 'Zappos CSR's Kindness Warms Our Cold Hearts'. *Consumerist,* 17 January 2011. http://consumerist.com/2011/01/17/zappos-customer-service-reps-kindness-warms-our-cold-hearts.

Ramesh, Randeep. 'Give Each NHS Hospital Patient A Single Consultant, Says Jeremy Hunt'. *Guardian,* 23 January 2014.

Randle, Henry W. 'Suntanning: Differences in Perceptions Throughout History'. In Mayo Clinic Proceedings 72, no. 5 (1997): 461–466.

'Ray Anderson, Interface Chairman and Sustainability Leader, Dies at 77'. *Environmental Leader*, 9 August 2011. www.environmentalleader.com/2011/08/09/ray-anderson-interface-chairman-and-sustainability-leader-dies-at-77.

Rayner, Jay. 'Booths: The Honest Supermarket'. *Observer*, 13 November 2011.

Reconnecting Children with Nature: Findings of the Natural Childhood Inquiry. The National Trust, 2012.

'Red Dress Boutique'. *SharkTank Blog*. http://sharktankblog.com/business/red-dress-boutique/.

Redlawsk, David P., Caroline J. Tolbert and Todd Donovan. *Why Iowa?: How Caucuses and Sequential Elections Improve the Presidential Nominating Process*. Chicago: University of Chicago Press, 2011.

Reeves, Richard. 'Bringing Up Baby'. *New Statesman*, 29 January 2009.

Reguly, Eric. 'Time to Put An End to the Cult of Shareholder Value'. *Globe and Mail* (Toronto, Canada). 26 September 2013.

Reich, Robert. 'Big Tech Has Become Way Too Powerful'. *New York Times*, 18 September 2015. www.nytimes.com/2015/09/20/opinion/is-big-tech-too-powerful-ask-google.html.

Reilly, Brendan M. 'Physical Examination in the Care of Medical Inpatients: An Observational Study', *Lancet* 362, no. 9390 (2003): 1,103.

'Rep. Kevin Yoder: Top 20 Industries Contributing to Campaign Committee'. *OpenSecrets.org*, 2 February 2015. https://www.opensecrets.org/politicians/industries.php?cycle=2014&cid=N 00031502&type=I&newmem=N.

Research, Development and Statistics Directorate. *Reducing Homicide: A Review of the Possibilities*. By Fiona Brookman and Mike Maguire. London: Home Office, 2003.

Reuters. 'A.I.G. Pays Its Ex-Chief $47 Million'. *New York Times*, 2 July 2008.

Richter, Brian Kelleher, Krislert Samphantharak and Jeffrey F. Timmons. 'Lobbying and Taxes'. *American Journal of Political Science* 53, no. 4 (2009): 893–909.

Rideout, Victoria. *Advertising to Children and Teens: Current Practices.* San Francisco, CA: Common Sense Media, 2014.

Ridley, Matt. *The Rational Optimist: How Prosperity Evolves.* New York: Harper Perennial, 2010.

—— . 'When Ideas Have Sex'. Presentation at TEDGlobal 2010, Oxford, UK, July 2010.

Rifkin, Jeremy. *The Empathetic Civilization: The Race to Global Consciousness in a World in Crisis.* New York: Jeremy P Tarcher / Penguin, 2009.

Ripley, Amanda. 'How to Graduate from Starbucks'. *Atlantic,* May 2015. www.theatlantic.com/magazine/archive/2015/05/the-upwardly-mobile-barista/389513.

'Robert Rubin'. *Council on Foreign Relations.* http://www.cfr.org/ staff/b292.

Robert-Hughes, Rebecca. *The Case for Space: The Size of England's New Homes.* Edited by Will Fox and Anna Scott-Marshall. Royal Institute of British Architects, 2011.

Robinson, David. *Out of the Ordinary: Learning from the Community Links Approach to Social Regeneration.* London: Community Links, 2010.

Rodrigue, Edward, and Richard V. Reeves. 'Home Visiting Programs: An Early Test for the 114th Congress'. *Brookings,* 5 February 2015. www.brookings.edu/blogs/social-mobility-memos/posts/2015/02/05-home-visiting-funding-reeves.

Rogers, Katie. 'The Vault Apps That Keep Sexts a Secret'. *New York Times,* 6 November 2015. www.nytimes.com/2015/11/07/us/the-vault-apps-that-keep-sexts-a-secret.html?_r=0.

Rogers, Richard. Forward to Jan Gehl, *Cities for People.* Washington, DC: Island Press, 2010.

Roggio, Armando. 'The Zappos Effect: 5 Great Customer Ideas for Smaller Business'. *Practical Ecommerce,* 21 March 2011. www.practicalecommerce.com/articles/2662-The-

Zappos-Effect-5-Great-Customer-Service-Ideas-for-Smaller-Businesses.

Rogowsky, Mark. 'After the New Jersey Ban, Here's Where Tesla Can (And Cannot) Sell Its Cars'. *Forbes*, 15 March 2014

Romito, Patricia and Lucia Beltramini. 'Watching Pornography: Gender Differences, Violence and Victimization: An Exploratory Study in Italy'. *Violence Against Women* (2011): 1077801211424555.

Rosin, Hanna. 'Hey! Parents, Leave Those Kids Alone'. *The Atlantic*, April 2014.

— . 'Why Kids Sext'. *The Atlantic*, November 2014.

Rothstein, Jesse. 'The Unintended Consequences of Encouraging Work: Tax Incidence and the EITC'. *Center for Economic Policy Studies*. Princeton, NJ: Princeton University, 2008.

Rucker, Philip and Joe Stephens. 'White House Economics Aide Summers Discloses Income'. *Washington Post*, April 4, 2009. www.washingtonpost.com/wp-dyn/content/article/2009/04/03/AR2009040303732.html.

Ruddick, Graham. 'Revealed: Housebuilders Sitting on 600,000 Plots of Land'. *Guardian*, 30 December 2015.

Rudegeair, Peter. 'Pay Gap Between Wall Street CEOs and Employees Narrows'. *Wall Street Journal*, 5 April 2015. www.wsj.com/articles/a-pay-gap-narrows-on-wall-street-1428267898.

Rush, Emma and Andrea La Nauze. *Corporate Paedophilia: Sexualisation of Children in Australia*. Australia Institute, 2006.

Russell, Jenni. 'Let's Put Character Above Exam Results'. *The Sunday Times*, 5 June 2011.

Russi, Daniela, Patrick ten Brink, Andrew Farmer, Tomas Badura, David Coates, Johannes Förster, Ritesh Kumar et al. The Economics of Ecosystems and Biodiversity for Water and Wetlands: Executive Summary. Institute for European Environmental Policy & Ramsar Secretariat, 2013.

Ryan, Richard M. and Edward L. Deci. 'Self-Determination Theory and the Facilitation of Intrinsic Motivation, Social Development, and Well-Being'. *American Psychologist* 55, no. 1 (2000): 68.

Sacks, Jonathan. 'The Dignity of Difference: Avoiding the Clash of Civilizations'. *Foreign Policy Research Institute*, July 2002.

Sadik-Khan, Janette. 'New York's Streets? Not So Mean Anymore'. Presentation at TED, New York, NY, September 2013.

Saez, Emmanuel and Gabriel Zucman. 'The Explosion in US Wealth Inequality Has Been Fueled by Stagnant Wages, Increasing Debt, and a Collapse in Asset Values for the Middle Classes'. *LSE*, 29 October 2014. http://blogs.lse.ac.uk/usappblog/2014/10/29/the-explosion-in-u-s-wealth-inequality-has-been-fuelled-by-stagnant-wages-increasing-debt-and-a-collapse-in-asset-values-for-the-middle-classes.

— . *Wealth Inequality in the United States Since 1913: Evidence from Capitalized Income Tax Data*, no. w20625. National Bureau of Economic Research, 2015. http://gabriel-zucman.eu/files/SaezZucman2014.pdf.

Sagi, Abraham and Martin L Hoffman. 'Empathic Distress in the Newborn'. *Developmental Psychology* 12, no. 2 (1976): 175.

Sahlberg, Pasi. *Finnish Lessons: What Can the World Learn from Educational Change in Finland?*. New York: Teachers College Press, 2010.

Said, Carolyn. 'Peers Helps Uber, Lyft Drivers Get Back On Road After Accidents'. *San Francisco Chronicle*, 4 December 2014.

Salazar, Angela. 'BeGood Clothing's New Line – Organic Cotton and Silk Basics'. *SF Gate*, 12 September 2014.

Salam, Reihan. 'The Upper Middle Class is Ruining America'. *Slate*, 30 January 2015.

Sandberg, Shana F., Clese Erikson, Ross Owen, Katherine D. Vickery, Scott T. Shimotsu, Mark Linzer, Nancy A. Garrett et al. 'Hennepin Health: A Safety-Net Accountable Care Organization for the Expanded Medicaid Population'. *Health Affairs* 33, no. 11 (2014).

Sanders, Michael and Elspeth Kirkman. *I've Booked You a Place. Good Luck: A Field Experiment Applying Behavioural Science to Improve Attendance at High-Impact Recruitment Events.*

No. 13/334 Bristol, England: Department of Economics, University of Bristol, 2014.

Sandseter, Ellen B. H. 'Children's Risky Play from an Evolutionary Perspective: The Anti-Phobic Effects of Thrilling Experiences'. *Evolutionary Psychology* 9, no. 2 (2001): 257–84.

Schuck, Peter. *Why Government Fails So Often: And How It Can Do Better*. Princeton, NJ: Princeton Univeristy Press, 2014.

Schumacher, E. F. *Small Is Beautiful: A Study of People As If People Mattered*. New York: Harper Perennial, 2010.

Schroeder, Peter and Kevin Cirilli. 'Warren, Left Fume Over Deal'. *The Hill*, 10 December 2014.

Schwarz, Alan. 'Attention Disorder or Not, Pills to Help in School', *New York Times*, 9 October 2012.

Scientific Report of the 2015 Dietary Guidelines Advisory Committee. Dietary Guidelines Advisory Committee. Washington, DC: USDA and US Department of Health and Human Services, 2015.

'Seafood Fraud'. *Oceana*. http://oceana.org/sites/default/files/euo/ OCEANA_fish_label_english.pdf.

'Sebago Lake'. *Portland Water District*. http://www.pwd.org/environment/sebago/sebago.php.

Sedghi, Ami. 'UK Tops Chart of EU Food Waste'. *Guardian*, 22 May 2015. http://www.theguardian.com/world/2015/may/22/uk-tops-chart-of-eu-food-waste.

Seldon, Anthony. *An End to Factory Schools: An Education Manifesto 2010–2020*. Surrey, England: Centre for Policy Studies, 2010.

Service, Owain, Michael Hallsworth, David Halpern, et al. *EAST: Four Simple Ways to Apply Behavioural Insights*. London: The Behavioural Insights Team, 2014.

Seymour, Philip H. K., Mikko Aro, and Jane M. Erskine. 'Foundation Literacy Acquisition in European Orthographies'. *British Journal of Psychology* 94, no. 2 (2003): 143–174.

Shah, Nigam H., Paea LePendu, Anna Bauer-Mehren, Yohannes T. Ghebremariam, Srinivasan V. Iyer, Jake Marcus, Kevin T. Nead et al. 'Proton Pump Inhibitor Usage and the

Risk of Myocardial Infarction in the General Population'. *PloS One* 10, no. 6 (June 2015): e0124653.

Shapiro, Doug, Afet Dundar, Xin Yuan, Autumn T. Harrell and Phoebe. K. Wakhungu. *Completing College: A National View of Student Attainment Rates – Fall 2008 Cohort* (Signature Report no. 8). Hernon, VA: National Student Clearinghouse Center, 2014.

'She, Robot: A Conversation with Helen Greiner'. *Foreign Affairs* 94, No. 1 (Jan/Feb 2015): 16–22.

Shenk, Joshua Wolf. *Powers of Two: How Relationships Drive Creativity*. Boston, MA: Eamon Dolan, 2014.

Shoda, Yuichi. 'Individual Differences in Social Psychology: Understanding Situations to Understand People, Understanding People to Understand Situations'. In *The Sage Handbook of Methods in Social Psychology*. Edited by Carol Sansone, Carolyn C. Morf and Abigail T. Panter, 119–121. Thousand Oaks, CA: Sage Publications, 2004.

Siegal, James. 'Kids First: What's Good for Kids Is Good for Cities'. *Medium*, 4 March 2015. https://medium.com/@kaboom/kids-first-what-s-good-for-kids-is-good-for-cities-73811301165f.

Singleton, Alex. 'Obituary: Sir John Cowperthwaite'. *Guardian*, 8 February 2006.

'Sir James Crosby Resigns from FSA'. *BBC News*, 11 February 2009. 'Sir Jeremy Heywood, Cabinet Secretary and Head of the Civil Service: Biography'. *British Goverment*. https://www.gov.uk/government/people/jeremy-heywood.

Skenazy, Lenore. 'Free Range Kids: FAQ'. *Free Range Kids*. https:// freerangekids.wordpress.com/faq/.

Slaughter, Anne-Marie. 'Why Women Still Can't Have It All'. *The Atlantic*, 13 June 2012.

Snowdon, Christopher. *Who's Killing the British Pub? Institute for Economic Affairs*. London: The Institute for Economic Affairs, 2014.

'Soil Association 2014 Organic Market Report Reveals Growth in Organic Sales for the First Time in Four Years'. *Soil Association*, 13 March 2014. http://www.

soilassociation.org/news/newsstory/ articleid/6650/soil-association-2014–organic-market-report- reveals-growth-in-organic-sales-for-the-first-time-in-fo.

'Soil: Protect European Soil From Environmental Damage'. *European Environmental Bureau*, 2015. http://www.eeb.org/index. cfm/activities/biodiversity-nature/soil/.

Soper, Spencer. 'Amazon Workers Cool After Company Took Heat for Hot Warehouse'. *Morning Call*, 3 June 2012. www. articles.mcall.com/2012-06-03/business/mc-amazon-warehouse-air-conditioning-20120602_1_warehouse-workers-air-conditioning-breinigsville-warehouse.

'Spare5 – Preview Addition'. *CNET.* http://download.cnet.com/Spare5–Preview-Edition/3000–31709_4–76156057.html.

'Stafford Hospital: Q&A'. *BBC News*, 25 March 2013.

'Stafford Hospital: The Victims of the Hospital Scandal'. *BBC News*, 6 February 2013.

Statistics Netherlands. *Traffic Deaths Down Again.* 18 April 2011. http://www.cbs.nl/en-GB/menu/themas/gezondheid-welzijn/ publicaties/artikelen/archief/2011/2011–029–pb.htm

Steadman, Ian. 'Dutch City Gives Residents a Self-Build Affordable Housing Catalogue'. *Wired*, 18 April 2013.

Steenhuysen, Julie. 'Overuse of Heartburn Drugs is Risky: Study'. *Reuters*, 10 May 2010.

Sternin, Jerry. 'The Viet Nam Story'. http://www. positivedeviance. org/about_pd/Monique%20VIET%20NAM%20CHAPTER%20 Oct%2017.pdf.

Stevens, Heidi. 'Your 11–Year-Old Daughter Wants to Shave. Everywhere'. *Chicago Tribune.* 10 July 2012.

Stevens, Jane Ellen Stevens. 'The Adverse Childhood Experiences Study – The Largest, Most Important Public Health Study You Never Heard of Began in an Obesity Clinic'. *ACES Too High News*, 3 October 2012. http://acestoohigh. com/2012/10/03/the-adverse- childhood-experiences-study-the-largest-most-important-public- health-study-you-never-heard-of-began-in-an-obesity-clinic/.

Stewart, William. 'Is Pisa Fundamentally Flawed?'. *TES Connect*, 27 September 2014. https://www.tes.co.uk/article. aspx?storycode=6344672.

Stone, Brad. 'Costco CEO Craig Jelinek Leads the Cheapest, Happiest Company in the World'. *BloombergBusiness*, 6 June 2013.

Strife, Susan and Liam Downey. 'Childhood Development and Access to Nature: A New Direction for Environmental Research'. *Organ Environment* 22, no. 1 (March 2009): 99–122.

Stuhldreher, Anne and Rourke O'Brien. *The Family Independence Initiative: A New Approach to Help Families Exit Poverty.* Washington, DC: New America Foundation, 2011.

Suggate, Sebastian P., Elizabeth A. Schaughency and Elaine Reese. 'Children Learning to Read Later Catch Up to Children Reading Earlier', *Early Childhood Research Quarterly* 28, no. 1 (2013): 33–48.

Sun, Lena H. 'Johns Hopkins Team Wins US Award for Improved Suit to Fight Ebola'. *Washington Post*, 13 December 2014. www.washingtonpost.com/news/post-nation/wp/2014/12/13/johns-hopkins-team-wins-u-s-award-for-improved-suit-to-fight-ebola

'Survey of Self-Build Intentions.' *Ipsos-Mori*, 12 March 2013. https:// www.ipsos-mori.com/researchpublications/researcharchive/3171/ Survey-of-selfbuild-intentions.aspx.

Sweet, Victoria. *God's Hotel: A Doctor, a Pilgrimage, and a Journey to the Heart of Medicine.* New York: Penguin, 2013.

—— . 'The Efficiency of Inefficiency'. Presentation at TEDxMiddlebury, Middlebury, VT, 9 March 2013.

Tacon, Christine. 'Welcome from the Groceries Code Adjudicator' in *News from the Adjudicator*, 17 November 2015. *https://www.gov.uk/government/uploads/system/uploads/attachment_data/file/477446/News_from_the_Adjudicator_Edition_5_final.pdf.*

Tait, Cameron. *Work That Pays: The Final Report of the Living Wage Commission.* London: Living Wage Commission, 2014.

Taking Stock – Review of 2016 AGM Season. PwC, 7 September 2015.

Talberth, John, Erin Gray, Evan Branosky and Todd Gartner. *Insights from the Field: Forests for Water*. Washington, DC: Water Resources Institute, 2012.

Taleb, Nassim Nicholas. *Antifragile: Things That Gain From Disorder*. New York: Random House Trade Paperbacks, 2014.

—— . *Black Swan: The Impact of the Highly Improbable Fragility*. New York: Random House, 2010.

Tandon, Pooja S., Chuan Zhou, Paula Lozano and Dimitri A. Christakis. 'Preschoolers' Total Daily Screen Time at Home and by Type of Child Care'. *The Journal of Pediatrics* 158, no. 2 (2011): 297–300.

Tanz, Jason. 'The Tech Elite's Quest to Reinvent School in Its Own Image'. *Wired*, 26 October 2015. www.wired.com/2015/10/salman-khan-academy-lab-school-reinventing-classrooms.

Taylor, Henry. 'Who Is the Biggest Employer?' *World Economic Forum*, 17 June 2015. https://agenda.weforum.org/2015/06/worlds-10-biggest-employers.

Teachman, Jay D. 'The Childhood Living Arrangements of Children and the Characteristics of Their Marriages'. *Journal of Family Issues* 25 (January 2004): 86–111.

Temple, Jeff R., Jonathan A. Paul, Patricia van den Berg, Vi Donna Le, Amy McElhany and Brian W. Temple. 'Teen Sexting and Its Association with Sexual Behaviors'. *Archives of Pediatrics & Adolescent Medicine* 166, no. 9 (2012): 828–833.

'Tesco's Travails: Supermarket Sweep'. *The Economist*, 21 April 2012.

Thaler, Richard H. and Cass R. Sunstein. *Nudge: Improving Decisions About Health, Wealth, and Happiness: Revised and Expanded Edition*. New York: Penguin Books, 2009.

—— , and Shlomo Benartzi. *The Behavioral Economics of Retirement Savings Behavior*. Washington DC: AARP Public Policy Institute, 2007.

—— . *Misbehaving: The Making of Behavioral Economics*. New York: W. W. Norton & Company, 2015.

Theodore Roosevelt'. In 'The National Parks: America's Best Idea'. *PBS*, 2009. http://www.pbs.org/nationalparks/people/ historical/roosevelt/.

Thorndike, William. *The Outsiders: Eight Unconventional CEOs and Their Radically Rational Blueprint for Success.* Cambridge, MA: Harvard University Press, 2012.

Timmins, Nicholas. 'NHS Electronic Records Are Two Years Late'. *Financial Times,* 29 May 2006.

'Touch Screens'. *Michael Cohen Group LLC,* 17 February 2014.

Tough, Paul. 'The Poverty Clinic'. *The New Yorker,* March 21, 2008.

Towards a Fine City for People. Copenhagen, Denmark: Gehl Architects, 2004. http://issuu.com/gehlarchitects/docs/ issuu_270_london_pspl_2004/0.

Trasande, L., J. Blustein, M. Liu, E. Corwin, L. M. Cox and M. J. Blaser. 'Infant Antibiotic Exposures and Early-Life Body Mass', *International Journal of Obesity* 37, no. 1 (2013): 16–23.

'Troubled Families'. *Local Government Association,* 29 January 2015. http://www.local.gov.uk/community-budgets/-/ journal_ content/56/10180/3691966/ARTICLE.

Turkle, Sherry. *Alone Together: Why We Expect More from Technology and Less From Each Other.* New York: Basic Books, 2011.

— . 'Authenticity in the Age of Digital Companions'. *Interaction Studies* 8, no. 3 (2007): 501–517.

— .'Connected, But Alone?. Presentation at TED. April 2012.

Turner, Beverley. 'Pubic Hair Is Back Ladies. The Men Don't Care and the Women Can't Be Bothered'. *Telegraph,* 15 November 2013.

Twenge, Jean M., Keith W. Campbell and Craig A. Foster. 'Parenthood and Marital Satisfaction: A Meta-Analytic Review'. *Journal of Marriage and the Family* 65, (2003), 574–583.

Twentyman, Jessica. 'Tesco CIO Sharpens Focus on the Digital Customer Experience'. *I-CIO,* October 2013. http://www.i-cio. com/strategy/big-data/item/tesco-cio-sharpens-focus-on-the- digital-customer-experience.

Ueda, Kenichi and Beatrice Weder di Mauro. 'Quantifying Structural Subsidy Values for Systemically Important

Financial Institutions'. *Journal of Banking & Finance* 37, no. 10 (2013): 3830–3842

Ulrich, Roger S., et al. 'Stress Recovery During Exposure to Natural and Urban Environments'. *Journal of Environmental Psychology* 11, No. 3 (1991): 201–230.

—— . 'View Through a Window May Influence Recovery Surgery'. *Science*, New Series 224, no. 4647 (27 April 1984): 420–421.

Umberson, Debra, and Jennifer Karas Montez. 'Social Relationships and Health a Flashpoint for Health Policy'. *Journal of Health and Social Behavior* 51, no. 1 suppl (2010): S54–S66.

UNICEF. 'Child Poverty in Perspective: An Overview of Child Well-Being in Rich Countries'. *Innocenti Report Card* 7. Florence, Italy: UNICEF Innocenti Research Centre, 2007.

United Nations. Department of Economic and Social Affairs. Population Division. *World Urbanization Prospects: The 2014 Revision, Highlights.* (ST/ESA/SER.A/352).

'"Unplugging' from Technology"', *Action for Children*, 6 January 2016. https://www.actionforchildren.org.uk/news-and-opinion/latest-news/2016/january/unplugging-from-technology/.

Unterman, Rebecca. *Headed to College: The Effects of New York City's Small High Schools of Choice on Postsecondary Enrollment.* New York: MDRC, 2014.

The Use of Medicines in the United States: Review of 2011. Parsippany, NJ: IMS Institute for Healthcare Informatics, 2011.

Vangelova, Luba. 'How the English Language Is Holding Kids Back'. *The Atlantic*, 9 February 2015.

Vardi, Nathan. 'How "The Outsiders" Became One of the Most Important Business Books in America'. *Forbes*, 8 May 2014. www.forbes.com/sites/nathanvardi/2014/05/08/how-the-outsiders-became-one-of-the-most-important-business-books-in-america.

Verdine, Brian N., Roberta M. Golinkoff, Kathryn Hirsh Pasek, Nora S. Newcombe, Andrew T. Filipowicz and Alicia Chang. 'Deconstructing Building Blocks: Preschoolers' Spatial

Assembly Performance Relates to Early Mathematical Skills'. *Child Development* 85, no. 3 (2014): 1062–1076.

Verghese, Abraham. 'A Doctor's Touch'. Presentation at TEDGlobal 2011: The Stuff of Life, Edinburgh, Scotland, September 2011.

Villanova, Peter H., John Bernardin, Sue A. Dahmus and Randi L. Sims. 'Rater Leniency and Performance Appraisal Discomfort'. *Educational and Psychological Measurement* 53, no. 3 (1993): 789–799.

'Vision Zero Initiative: Traffic Safety by Sweden'. *Swedish Government* and *Business Sweden*. http://www.visionzeroinitiative.com/en/.

von Grebmer, Klaus, Amy Saltzman, Ekin Birol, Doris Weismann, et. al. *Global Hunger Index: The Challenge of Hidden Hunger, Synopsis*. Bonn, Germany, Washington, DC, Dublin, Ireland: International Food Policy Research Institute, October 2014.

Wagner, Tony and Ted Dintersmith. *More Likely to Succeed: Preparing Our Kids for the Innovation Era*. New York: Simon and Schuster, 2015.

Wainwright, Oliver. 'Right to Build: Nick Boles Tells Councils to Offer Land for Self-Builds "Or Be Sued"'. *Guardian*, 7 May 2014.

Walker, Tim. 'How Finland Keeps Kids Focused Through Free Play'. *The Atlantic*, 30 June 2014.

Wallop, Harry. 'Food Companies Play Games with Children's TV Advertising Ban'. *Telegraph*, 30 May 2014. http://www.telegraph.co.uk/news/health/children/10865263/Food-companies-play-games-with-childrens-TV-advertising-ban.html.

Walton, Alice G. 'Steve Jobs' Cancer Treatment Regrets'. *Forbes*, 24 October 2011.

Warner, Kimberley, Walker Timme, Beth Lowell and Michael Hirshfield. 'Oceana Study Reveals Seafood Fraud Nationwide'. *Oceana*, 2013.

Warnock, Mary. *A Question of Life: The Warnock Report on Human Fertilisation and Embryology*. London: Her Majesty's Stationery Office, 1984.

Warren, Elizabeth. *Forum.* By Michael Krasny. *Forum,* 88.5 KQED FM, 7 May 2014.

'Water Conservation Tips'. *National Geographic.* http:// environment.nationalgeographic.com/environment/ freshwater/water-conservation-tips.

Watson, Peter. *Ideas: A History of Thought and Invention, From Fire to Freud.* New York: Harper Perennial, 2005.

Watson Robert, Steve Albon, et al. *UK National Ecosystem Assessment: Synthesis of the Key Findings.* Cambridge, England: UNEP-WCMC, 2011.

Welch, H. Gilbert. *Less Medicine, More Health: 7 Assumptions That Drive Too Much Medical Care.* Boston: Beacon Press, 2015.

Weldon, William. Interview, *Knowledge@Wharton,* 25 June 2008. http://knowledge.wharton.upenn.edu/article/ johnson-johnson-ceo-william-weldon-leadership-in-a-decentralized-company.

'Welfare Issues for Meat Chickens'. *Compassion in World Farming,* 2014. http://www.ciwf.org.uk/farm-animals/ chickens/meat-chickens/ welfare-issues/.

Westervelt, Amy. 'Can't Picture a World Devastated By Climate Change? These Games Will Do It for You'. *Smithsonian.com,* 21 July 2014.

Whalen, Jeanne. 'How Glaxo Marketed a Malady to Sell a Drug'. *Wall Street Journal,* 25 October 2006.

'What Have the Immigrants Ever Done for Us?'. *The Economist,* 8 November 2014.

'What Is a Benefit Corporation?' *B Lab,* 2015. http:// benefitcorp.net.

'What Is the Living Wage?'. *BBC News* 2 November 2014.

'Who Are We?'. *Embrace.* 2015. http://embraceglobal.org/ who-we- are/our-story/.

'Who Are the School Truants?'. *PSIA in Focus,* January 2014.

'Who's Up, Who's Down?' *Open Secrets,* 2015. http://www. opensecrets.org/lobby/incdec.php.

'Why Plants in the Office Make Us More Productive'. *ScienceDaily,* 1 September 2014.

'Why Sweden Has So Few Road Deaths'. *The Economist*, 26 February 2014. http://www.economist.com/blogs/economist- explains/2014/02/economist-explains-16.

'Why Waldorf Works: Frequently Asked Questions'. *Association of Waldorf Schools of North America*. http://www.whywaldorfworks. org/02_W_Education/faq_about.asp.

Wildman, Charlotte. 'The "Chicago of Great Britain": Growth and Urban Regeneration in Liverpool'. In *The History Boys: Lessons from Local Government's Past*. Edited by Simon Parker and Joe Manning, 29–38. London: New Local Government Network, 2013.

Wilson, Edward O. *Biophilia: The Human Bond With Other Species*. Cambridge, MA: Harvard University Press, 1984.

— . 'My Wish: Build the Encyclopedia of Life'. Presentation at TED 2007, 2007.

Winkler, Rolf and Douglas MacMillan. 'The Secret Math of Airbnb's $24 Billion Valuation'. *Wall Street Journal*, 17 June 2015. www.wsj.com/articles/the-secret-math-of-airbnbs-24-billion-valuation-1434568517.

Winquist Nord, Christine and Jerry West, *Fathers' and Mothers' Involvement in Their Children's Schools by Family Type and Resident Status*, NCES 2001–032. Washington, DC: US Department of Education, National Center for Education Statistics, 2001. http://nces.ed.gov/pubs2001/2001032.pdf.

Wintour, Patrick. 'Government "Is Starting to Help 120,000 Troubled Families"'. *Guardian*, 29 October 2014.

Witko, Christopher. 'Campaign Contributions, Access, and Government Contracting'. *Journal of Public Administration Research and Theory* 23, no. 2 (2013).

Woloshin, Steven and Lisa M. Schwartz. 'Giving Legs to Restless Legs: A Case Study of How the Media Helps Make People Sick', *PLoS Medicine* 3, no. 4 (2006): e170.

'Woman Dies After Farewell to Horse at Wigan Hospital', *BBC News*, 7 November 2014.

Woodman, Spencer. 'Exclusive: Amazon Makes Even Temporary Warehouse Worker Sign 18-Month Non-

Competes'. *Verge*, 26 March 2015. www.theverge. com/2015/3/26/8280309/amazon-warehouse-jobs-exclusive-noncompete-contracts.

Woods, Lucy. 'Friday Focus: Solar's Future Fantasies'. *PV Tech*, 13 December 2013. http://www.pv-tech.org/friday_focus/friday_ focus_solars_future_fantasies.

'Working Paper: Uprating the UK Living Wage in 2014'. *Centre for Research in Social Policy, Loughborough University*. 2014.

Wuttke, Joachim. 'Uncertainty and Bias in PISA' In *Pisa According to Pisa: Does Pisa Keep What It Promise?*. Edited by Stefan Thomas Hopmann, Gertrude Brinek and Martin Retzl, 241–263. Vienna, Austria: Lit Verlag, 2007.

Yardley, Jim. 'Bangladesh Pollution, Told in Colors and Smells'. *New York Times*, 15 July 2013.

'Young People Sexual Relationships'. *IPPR*. http:// www. ippr.org/assets/media/publications/attachments/youngpeoplesexrelationships.jpg.

World Bank. Long-Term Unemployment (% of Total Unemployment). 2015. http://data.worldbank.org/indicatorSL.UEM.LTRM.2S?order=wbapi-data-value-last&sort-asc.

'Zero to Eight: Children's Media Use in America 2013'. *Common Sense Media*, Fall 2013.

Zhang, Baohui, Alexi A. Wright, Haiden A. Huskamp, Matthew E. Nilsson, Matthew L. Maciejewski, Craig C. Earle, Susan D. Block et al. 'HealthCare Costs in the Last Week of Life: Associations with End-of-Life Conversations'. *Archives of Internal Medicine* 169, no. 5 (2009): 480–488.

'6–inch Low Fat Subs: Nutritional Information'. *Subway*, http:// www.subway.co.uk/assets/pdf/subway-nutritional-values-uk.pdf.

'2011 Minnesota Statutes'. *The Office of the Revisor of Statutes*. www.revisor.mn.gov/statutes/percent20?id=256B.0756&year=2011.

2014 Teen Internet Safety Survey. Atlanta, GA: Cox Communications, 2014. www.cox.com/wcm/en/aboutus/datasheet/takecharge/tween-internet-safety-survey.pdf.

'2015 Year in Review'. *Pornhub Insights*, 6 January 2016. www. pornhub.com/insights/2015-year-in-review.

'475,000 Homes with Planning Permission Still Waiting to Be Built'. *Local Government Association*, 7 January 2016. http:// www.local.gov.uk/web/guest/media-releases/-/journal_ content/56/10180/7632945/NEWS.

List of Interviews and Correspondence:

Bell, Bruce. Interview by authors and e-mail correspondence, October/November 2014.

Bonbright, David. Interview by authors. Palo Alto, CA, 24 October 2014.

Casey, Louise. Interview by authors. 7 November 2014.

— . Interview by authors. 28 November 2014.

Cavendish, Camilla. Interview by authors. 8 September 2014.

—. Interview by authors. London. 25 September 2014. Crombie, David. Interview by authors. 17 September 2014. Dorion, Christiane. Interview by authors. London. 26 September 2014.

Frenald, Anya. Interview by authors. 20 October 2014.

Harris, Nadine Burke. Interview by authors. San Francisco, CA, 6 October 2014.

Heller, Lucy. Interview by authors. 15 October 2014.

Helm, Dieter. Interview by authors. 21 November 2014.

Heywood, James. Interview by authors. 9 October 2014.

Hocker, Paul. Interview by authors. London. 26 September 2014.

Holden, Patrick. Interview by authors. Belvedere, CA. 3 October 2014.

Jacobson, Niclas. Interview by authors. 6 November 2014.

Jameson, Neil. Interview by authors. London. 25 September 2014.

Kelly, Mike. Interview by authors, London. 25 September 2014.

Lymbery, Philip. Email to authors. 29 March 2015.

Lythcott-Haims, Julie. Interview by authors. Palo Alto, CA, August 5, 2015.

Letwin, Oliver. Interview by authors. London. 26 September 2014.

Manzoni, Niccolo and Rosie Wardle. Interview by authors. 5 February 2015.

Mayfield, Charlie. Interview by authors. 22 October 2014.

Melchett, Peter. Interview by authors. 15 October 2014.

Oakeshott, Isabel. Email to authors. 14 March 2015.

Oberfest, Jason. Interview by authors. San Francisco, CA. 27 August 2014.

O'Shaughnessy, James. Interview by authors. 19 November 2014.

Parsa, Ali. Interview by authors. 28 October 2014.

Pittman, Jason. Interview by authors. Mountain View, CA. 5 November 5, 2014.

Ratti, Carlo. Interview by authors. 13 October 2014.

Ricks, Alan. Interview by authors. 8 October 2014.

Robinson, David. Interview by authors. London. 24 September 2014.

Rothe, Matt. Interview by authors. Stanford, CA. 24 October 2014.

Sandefer, Jeff. Email to authors. 3 September 2014

Schwegler, Ben. Interview by authors. 20 August 2014.

Sears, Shawn and Laura. Interview by authors. San Gregorio, CA and e-mail correspondence, October 2014.Seldon, Anthony. Interview by authors. 17 October 2014.

Silva, Rohan. Interview by authors. London. 17 September 2014.

Stein-Greenberg, Sarah. Interview by authors. 23 October 2014.

Stockton, Paul. Interview by authors. 1 October 2014.

Tamkivi, Sten. Interview by authors. Palo Alto, CA. 28 August 2014.

Tatham, Ken. Interview by authors. 16 December 2014.

Thomas, Jeff and Rachael. Interview by authors. 9 October 2014.

Thrun, Sebastian. Interview by authors. Mountain View, CA. 11 November 2014.

Vaarik, Daniel. Interview by authors. Menlo Park, CA. 2 December 2014.

Willis, Paul. Interview by authors. 12 November 2014.

INDEX